BALANCING ACT:
ENVIRONMENTAL ISSUES IN FORESTRY

Hamish Kimmins

Balancing
Act

Environmental
Issues
in Forestry

UBC Press / Vancouver

ISBN 0-7748-0435-1 (hardcover)
ISBN 0-7748-0426-2 (paperback)
Reprinted 1993

Canadian Cataloguing in Publication Data

Kimmins, J.P. 1942-
  Balancing act

  Includes bibliographical references and index.
  ISBN 0-7748-0435-1 (bound)
  ISBN 0-7748-0426-2 (pbk)

  1. Forests and forestry. 2. Forest management
– Environmental aspects. 3. Forest ecology.
I. Title.
SD387.E58K54 1992   634.9   C92-091551-5

Publication of this book was made possible by ongoing
support from The Canada Council, the Province of British
Columbia Cultural Services Branch, and the Department
of Communications of Canada.

UBC Press
University of British Columbia
6344 Memorial Rd
Vancouver, BC V6T 1Z2
(604) 822-3259
Fax: (604) 822-6083

To Ann – my best friend, my love,
and my lifelong companion

CONTENTS

Illustrations and Figures

ACKNOWLEDGMENTS

The ideas and information presented in this book have many origins. I owe my early childhood love of soil, plants, and ecosystems to my first mentor in ecology, Albert Lear – an accomplished and largely self-educated gardener who had great experience-based wisdom about soil and things that grow. My early attempts to integrate knowledge of plants, animals, soil, and climate were encouraged by my high school biology teacher, Eric Regnauld, but the first formalization of my ecosystem view of the world came from my professors: Paul Richards of tropical forest fame; Eric Mobbs, a seasoned tropical forester and educator; John Harper and Buzz Holling who helped me to understand plant and animal populations, respectively; and Evelyn Hutchinson who introduced me to how ecosystems function. The writings of Charles Elton and the powerful personality of Vladimir Krajina both played a formative role in how I came to view forest ecosystems in terms of ecosystem dynamics and diversity, and the critical conservation need for an adequate system of ecological reserves.

Over the past thirty years, I have had the great fortune to visit, work, and study in forests around the world. I have met and discussed both forestry and conservation issues with a variety of ecologists, other scientists, foresters, and members of the general public who are deeply concerned about our environment. From these travels and discussions I have become convinced of our ethical responsibility to pass on our environment and resources in as good or better condition to future generations. I have been persuaded that many, if not most, forest ecosystems are very resilient, and are generally capable of recovery from natural- or human-caused disturbance. However, my experiences also lead me to conclude that each ecosystem has a limit beyond which disturbance will cause the loss of some value for an unacceptable period of time. To all these individuals who have contributed to my practical education, my thanks.

It has been a privilege to have been associated since 1969 with many extremely talented graduate students at the University of British Columbia. Collectively they have contributed enormously to my understanding of ecosystems and to the testing of my ideas. To all of them, I express my appreciation for what they have given to me.

Several individuals were kind enough to review various individual draft chapters in this book: Gordon Weetman and Karel Klinka (silviculture and New Forestry); Tom Sullivan (wildlife and biodiversity) and Michael Feller (fire) of the Department of Forest Sciences, UBC; Jacob Otchere-Boateng, Phil Comean, and others of the BC Ministry of Forests; John Manville (management chemicals) and others of Forestry Canada; and Gordon McBean (climate change) and Phillip Haddock (forestry, silviculture, and forest harvesting) of the Department of Geography and Faculty of Forestry, UBC. Excellent reviews of the entire manuscript were also provided by Roy Sutton and Richard Smith of Forestry Canada, Denis Lavender of the Department of Forest Sciences, UBC, and Ken Lertzman of Natural Resource Management, Simon Fraser University. Significant improvements in the manuscript resulted, but I remain responsible for any remaining errors or misinterpretations. I am grateful for their generosity in giving of their time.

Patsy Quay was her tirelessly cheerful and energetic self throughout the typing of several drafts, and Min Tsze and Wanda Dyck provided support throughout the project without which I would not have devoted as much time to the project. My gratitude goes to these three people. A six-month sabbatical from UBC provided time for the majority of the writing of the first draft, and the BC Ministry of Forests provided a grant to UBC Press to reduce the purchase price of the book. Both organizations are gratefully acknowledged. I am grateful to the staff of UBC Press for their encouragement, helpful suggestions, and general support for this project. It was a pleasure working with them.

To Ann, for being so tolerant of my absences through a second book-writing project, and for being a patient and critical editor, I give my greatest thanks.

BALANCING ACT

Chapter 1

Words,
Pictures,
and
Reality

Words. Their correct usage is important. As we grow up and learn about family, friends, society, and the environment, we accumulate a wealth of knowledge, experience, and mental images. These exist as memories and thoughts in our mind. They are private. We have to externalize them as written or spoken words if we wish to share them with others. The difficulty is that unless we all agree on the meaning of particular words, the images that they create for other people may differ from the images in our mind that the words are supposed to communicate.

The careless use or misuse of language often causes confusion and misunderstanding, and is a factor in many conflicts. Two parties to an argument frequently envisage a different situation from a given set of words, or may describe a particular situation using different words. Many marital difficulties have their origins in such communication problems. Similarly, the inappropriate use of words, or the failure to define the way in which they are being used, has caused problems in the debate over environmental issues in forestry.

The public, often lacking the appropriate technical knowledge, has frequently not understood either side of the arguments about the environmental impact of forest management, and people on both sides of the debate sometimes use words in a way that leaves their intended meaning unclear or ambiguous. In the polarized rhetoric that has characterized exchanges between some environmentalists and some industrialists, adverbs like 'never' and 'forever' have been employed in a way that has created in people's minds images that are often far from the truth.

The old saying that 'a picture is worth a thousand words' has been employed to good advantage by both environmentalists and industrial forest companies. Slide shows given by representatives of concerned citizen groups or by environmentalists frequently present a series of 'environmental horror' pictures, while presentations by forest companies are typically illustrated with depictions of the successful renewal of forests and of fish and wildlife habitats. In many cases, pictures of freshly clearcut or slash-burned forest ecosystems, and of landslides attributed to clearcutting, are an accurate 'snapshot' of the visual condition of the area shown in the picture at the time the photograph was taken. However, the accuracy with which such pictures describe what particular ecosystems will look like in five, ten, fifty, or a hundred years varies greatly. It can range from zero to 100 per cent, according to the type of ecosystem, the degree to which the ecosystem has been disturbed, and the time scale one is talking about. Industrial forestry pictures that seemingly always portray recent clearcuts as vibrant with wildflowers and wildlife and supporting voluptuously green, heavy-foliaged and fast-growing young trees also vary from being completely accurate to being a considerable misrepresentation of reality, depending on circumstances. Pictures presented by both sides in the debate depict only a sample of the ecosystems and management effects they are supposed to illustrate, and not always a representative sample at that.

The misuse of pictures is very similar to the misuse of words. It can create false mental images in the minds of the public. It can lead to the mistrust, misunderstanding, and failure of communication concerning forestry/environmental issues that are contributing to a divorce between a large and moderate segment of the public and the moderate and concerned majority of forest resource managers.

This book is not an attempt to establish a dialogue between the most extreme participants in the environmentalist-industrialist debate, although it would be nice if it contributed positively to such an outcome. Neither is it an attempt to persuade these individuals to take a different point of view. Such people are generally 'true believers.' Their minds are usually already made up. Nor does the book deal with land-use conflicts. It provides no basis for judging whether a particular forest area should be managed for timber production, watershed, and other non-timber values, or simply reserved as unmanaged wilderness. That is a social, not a scientific, issue. The ideas presented here are addressed to the mainstream of the public and foresters: people who are justifiably concerned about the state of both global and local forest environments and the quality of forest management, but are confused by the great discrepancy that often exists between the claims and assertions made by the most extreme proponents of the two sides in forestry/environmental conflicts.

What, then, is the purpose of this treatise? It is to provide the average concerned citizen or forester with an introduction to the ecological aspects of the major environmental issues facing the managers of Canada's great forest resource. Because the production of timber and other wood products is such an important component of this management, and because the growing and harvesting of tree crops generates so many of the conflicts, the major focus of this book is on the environmental consequences of tree-crop production. The objective is to provide a scientific and ecological basis for evaluating the words and pictures that are used in the forestry/environment debate.

Forest science cannot provide all the answers, of course, because many of the issues arise from conflicting social values, not from science. Many of the challenges posed to foresters by the concerned public do not originate as questions about how forest management is affecting ecosystem function and sustainability. They come from disagreements about land use and conflicts about the relative values people place on different aspects of the forest resource. However, there *are* many issues in forestry that are concerned with the actual or potential negative impact of management practices or policies on the long-term productivity and biodiversity of our forest ecosystems. The problem is that the scientific and social aspects of the debate have often become confused. It is time to separate them. If we can agree on the scientific aspects, we will have a much better basis on which to address the more difficult social issues.

It is not the intention of this book to persuade you to join one side or the other of the forestry/environment debate. But it does suggest a way for you to approach the issues, and how you might try to answer questions about their scientific aspects. It raises a variety of questions that must be answered, and summarizes current thinking among forest scientists about the issues that are discussed. The reader should be aware that there continues to be debate among scientists about our current understanding of various aspects of forest ecology, and there will certainly be scientists and academics who may wish to interpret our current understanding of forest ecosystems differently from the views presented here. Further research is undoubtedly needed to resolve these scientific questions, but this book attempts to represent the major body of current thinking on these topics. The text is not referenced the way a scientific treatise would be, but a bibliography presents the type of source materials that the discussion is based on. Individual chapters were reviewed by subject specialists (see Acknowledgments), but the final responsibility for the text remains with the author.

Chapter 2 explores some ideas about why people react so negatively to change, and examines the role that public concern and 'environmentalism' play in the process of conserving resources and the environment. It emphasizes the importance of how we use words, pictures, and 'facts' in our discussion of environmental issues.

Chapter 3 describes the origins and time scales of change in forest ecosystems, and Chapter 4 presents a primer on ecological principles for readers who may lack this background. A basic knowledge of ecological principles is absolutely essential for a realistic evaluation of the ecological impact of forest management and the environmental consequences of other human-induced environmental changes. A second primer is provided in Chapter 5 to describe the strategies and methods of renewable forest management (in contrast to non-renewable, exploitive management or 'timber mining'). This is necessary as background for the subsequent discussions of clearcutting (Chapter 6), slashburning (Chapter 7), and the use of management chemicals (Chapter 8).

The book then proceeds to examine various current forestry issues: old growth (Chapter 9), biological diversity (Chapter 10), 'New Forestry' and the role of 'large organic debris' in maintaining biodiversity and the productivity of forests (Chapter 11), global climate change (Chapter 12), and the impact of acid rain and air pollution on forests (Chapter 13).

Chapter 14 examines the parallel that is often drawn between forestry in Canada (and especially in British Columbia) and deforestation in some parts of the tropics, and Chapter 15 discusses the general failure of forestry in the past to use management planning tools that can account adequately for change.

Finally, Chapter 16 discusses the sustainability of forest values. It examines the major threats to the world's forests, identifies some essential prerequisites for sustainable forestry, and concludes on a note of optimism. Thanks to the wave of public concern about the environment and resources, politicians will have to respond to the urgent need to put all renewable resources on a path to sustainable management, and to strictly regulate the exploitation of non-renewable resources.

CHAPTER 2

The Peter Pan Principle in Renewable-Resource Conflicts

Change

Peter Pan has been a popular bedtime story for children in the English-speaking world since it was written in 1928. It is a delightful make-believe tale of a young boy who lives in 'Never-Never Land,' where nothing ever changes and people do not grow older. Although the book was intended for children, like *Alice in Wonderland, Tom Sawyer,* and other childhood classics, it also holds an abiding appeal for the parents who read it to their young offspring. This popularity is, I believe, a reflection of the human response to change.[1]

To the old adage, 'nothing is certain but death and taxes,' we should add 'and change.' All of us are constantly experiencing change. From birth to death, we pass through different life stages, each of which is marked by different experiences, pleasures, and sorrows. The transition from one stage to the next is full of promise of future experiences, but may also be accompanied by regret over the passing of things familiar and dear.

The changes we experience as we grow up, mature, and age are merely the continuation of changes that have taken place in human society and in the environment throughout recorded history. Lifestyles, clothing fashions, behaviour patterns, family structures, politics, morals, diets, and a myriad of other aspects of our social environment change from century to century, decade to decade. The agricultural land we knew and loved as children is now a housing development. The ugly industrial slum that scarred and polluted the core of a city we knew has been replaced by condominiums, a shopping centre, and a city park. Many areas that were 'brutally' logged less than a century

---

1 Throughout this book you will find the terms 'natural change,' referring to change that is not related to human activities, and 'human-caused change,' the meaning of which is obvious. It can be argued very effectively that humans are as natural an inhabitant of this planet as any other species, and that therefore human-caused change is natural. However, to make the distinction between human-caused change and changes not associated with human activity, the term 'natural' is used to refer to the latter.

ago now carry magnificent forests; some are still not adequately reforested or may show signs of soil damage done at the time of logging. The undeveloped mountain valley we may have visited or read about years ago now has a main highway through it, and the forest is being harvested; the unbroken expanse of old forest is now a patchwork of the brighter green of young forest of various ages, interspersed with the brown of freshly logged areas.

In many parts of the world, people are protesting as forests are stripped by mining, flooded by hydro developments, or removed to free the land for non-traditional agriculture. In other areas, such as parts of Scotland and the English Lake District, people protest the loss of the treeless landscape views that they grew up with as areas that were deforested centuries ago are replanted with trees. In different parts of the world, people chain themselves to bulldozers either to stop forests from being harvested or to prevent new forests from being established. In both cases, the action is to protest change.

The 'quality of the environment' also changes. Calm summer days near cities where we remember clear, sparkling air in our youth are now characterized by the build-up of air pollution. The badly polluted river we were told not to swim in as a child now supports edible fish and is suitable for water-based recreational activities. Many adults at temperate latitudes are 'dreaming of a white Christmas,' the kind they knew as children, which in the future may become only a memory for many people because of global warming.

Change is all around us. It has always been happening, and it will continue to occur.

Many of the recent changes in our social, physical, and biological environments are desirable. Unfortunately, many others are not. But irrespective of whether the past was, on balance, better or worse than the present, most people tend to be nostalgic about the things they experienced earlier in their lives. This may reflect the loss of some happily remembered landscape. It may be due to the increased crowding on the roads, in shops, or at

one's favourite vacation spot, or simply the loss of the conditions, experiences, and emotions one associates with one's childhood. Although change is welcomed by some as a means of escape from previously unhappy, mundane, or uncomfortable circumstances, for many of us a sense of loss accompanies both our journey from one life stage to another and the apparently relentless change in our local, regional, and global environments.

There is in most people just a little bit of J.M. Barrie's Peter Pan. Although we may welcome many of the changes that we experience as we advance in age, there are always some things that we wish would not change. We would all like a private Never-Never Land, where the things that are nearest and dearest to us would remain unchanging forever.

This book is about change, or at least about one aspect of the change that most of us have experienced in the past and will experience in the future: change in the physical, chemical, and biological environments in which we live and on which we, as a society and a species, depend. The focus will be on change in the forested landscapes of the world, but many of the principles are also applicable to other types of ecosystem.

Never-Never Land: 'Second to the Right, and Then Straight on till Morning' [2]

One frequently hears adverbs such as 'never' and 'forever' used with respect to environmental change or the sustainability of renewable resources. On the one hand, environmentalists may talk about ecological conditions being lost 'forever' when humans disturb natural ecosystems or harvest renewable resources (for example, it is often claimed that a certain type of forest can 'never' regrow to its former state if it is clearcut). On the other hand, so-called 'technological optimists' [3] maintain that there

2 The location of Never-Never Land as defined by Peter Pan in J.M. Barrie's story.

3 That is, optimistic technologists – people who believe that the combination of human ingenuity and modern technology can solve any problem: 'After all, we can put a man on the moon.'

will 'never' be an energy or material-resource supply problem, or that productive managed forests will be there 'forever.' One objective of this book is to point out that 'never' and 'forever' are both a very long time, and that reality usually lies somewhere in between. We all use these adverbs in everyday discussions, but when we talk about resource sustainability they have more to do with Peter Pan than with reality.

In a democracy, we have the opportunity to influence change through the political process. But if we are to achieve our long-term objectives with respect to environmental quality and conservation, our choice at the ballot box and our lobbying of elected politicians must be based on informed judgment. Unfortunately, there is a lot of confusion and misunderstanding about the effects of management of renewable resources on the environment. The public is being told by many environmentalists that the environment is being 'destroyed,' that ecosystems will 'never' recover from the environmental changes caused by resource use, and that renewable resources are being exploited in such a way that they can 'never' be renewable again. But this is being countered by many resource managers and senior industrialists with statements that the environment is resilient and will almost always recover from deliberate management-induced disturbance, as well as from natural disturbance. These individuals claim that their management of the forest is benign, but that technology will solve any problem if it turns out that their activities do result in unacceptable environmental effects; that if problems are created, management will be changed and the ecosystems will recover with technical help where necessary.

The Peter Pan principle referred to in the title of this chapter is the seemingly inevitable tendency for discussions about the sustainability of forest resources to become polarized arguments. The issues so often become couched in terms like 'never' and 'forever,' rather than being based on a scientifically sound assessment of the time scales, patterns, and

mechanisms of natural or human-induced change in natural or managed forest resources. Often there seems little hope of finding common ground between the extremes of 'activist environmentalism' and 'industrial conservatism.' However, a careful analysis reveals that if 'never' and 'forever' are considered relative to social and biological time scales, both these words can be either appropriate or inappropriate as descriptors of the consequences of human activities for the environment and natural resources. Both the 'environmentalist' and the 'industrialist' positions with respect to the management of the world's forest ecosystems can be either correct or incorrect, according to the circumstances, context, and time scale being considered.

In the following chapters, the different circumstances in which 'never' and 'forever' can be either right or wrong with respect to resource sustainability are explored. Scientific analysis is presented as an alternative to the frequently unproductive consequence of continued application of the Peter Pan principle: an alternative to continued rhetoric and polarization, and to the focus on conflict rather than resolution. The time has come to leave the rhetoric and polarization behind and to move on to find ways by which we can actually achieve the conservation and sustainable use of forest resources that most people want.

Our environment is too important for us to simply go on arguing about it. Action is needed, but action must be founded on a scientifically based understanding of the problems we face and of the social and environmental consequences of alternative solutions. This book is an attempt to clarify some of the issues that currently preoccupy the media and many members of the public with respect to management-induced or natural disturbance of forest ecosystems. It will try to persuade the reader of the importance of separating these issues into their humanistic and scientific components, so that we can better understand the different points of view of the environmentalist and the industrialist, and learn how to recognize the circumstances in which each point of view is scientifically correct or incorrect.

The Two Phases of Conservation

There are two distinct phases in conservation: the *political phase* and the *implementation phase.* It is important to understand the different roles of these two phases in the achievement of conservation goals. Statements and actions that may be effective, acceptable, and, in some cases, even necessary in one stage may be inappropriate and counterproductive in the other. Attitudes that may help conservation in the earlier political phase may hinder it when attempts are made to actually implement conservation strategies.

In the political phase, an often uninformed and uninterested public must be made aware of the urgency of the many environmental problems that are threatening both their way of life and the future choices of their children and grandchildren. Only when a significant number of people have been awakened to the issues will sufficient political pressure be created to force governments and industry to become more environmentally responsible. Governments must be convinced to pass legislation that will ensure that people receive the necessities of life and that will enable industry to perform its essential role of providing these necessities without threatening the sustainability of different values in both local and global environments. This requires that these environmental issues are placed at the top of the political agenda.

Many decades of warnings about the state of the environment by scientists, academics, naturalists, and resource managers failed to arouse the attention of the general public and most politicians. The logical, scientific, complex, and often cautious arguments on which these urgings were based failed to fire the imaginations of the public and politicians alike, and advances in conservation and improvements in the management of renewable resources were generally slow and infrequent. The way the issues were presented did not constitute 'hot news.'

In contrast, the often verbally violent rhetoric and the tactics of 'activist' environmentalists have been remarkably successful in awakening the public. Skilful orchestration of 'media events,' appeals to the emotions of people who had not previously given much thought to the environment, bold and sometimes scientifically inaccurate and unsupported claims, and doomsday statements that stir the often irrational fears that lurk in all of us have achieved what scientists and a reasoned approach have not: the 'greening' of society. Daily, we witness the virtues of environmentalism being espoused by politicians and right-wing economists who have always been hardline free-enterprisers and who have in the past rejected the 'ecological' point of view. This truly spectacular achievement on the part of a relatively small number of dedicated individuals marks a turning point in the recent relationship between our species and the global environment. Society owes these people a great debt of gratitude.

It appears that major advances in conservation and improvements in resource management rarely occur until there has been a successful completion of this political phase. However, successful long-term conservation and improved resource management are generally not achieved as the *direct* result of the political phase. Real change for the better comes in the form of the new legislation, policy, regulations, economic incentives, institutional structures, and government-sponsored opportunities that are *made possible* by the successful execution of the political phase. These changes are developed and put in place during the implementation phase of conservation. But unless the new policy, regulations, and so on are practical, workable, and scientifically and socially sound, the conservation objectives may not be achieved.

Socially and politically naive solutions to deforestation and the threat of extinction of certain large game species in the tropics provide two examples of the problem.

Recent attempts by several European countries to ban the importation of tropical hardwoods threaten to reduce the economic value of some tropical forests. This might reduce logging in some areas as intended. However, in some Asian tropical countries, logging would undoubtedly be replaced by deforestation if such a ban were successfully instituted. If the tropical timber had no economic value for the local people or the government, and if this loss could not be compensated for by harvesting other resources from the forest, large areas would be cleared and replaced by more economically rewarding agriculture or exotic plantations. Failing to make a living or to generate taxes from the forest, local people or governments would be forced to turn to farming. It appears that this would occur in parts of Malaysia and Indonesia if a tropical timber ban were to become widespread.

Similarly, attempts to save elephants and other large 'trophy' animals in east Africa by banning hunting have not always worked well. In some cases, a simple banning of hunting has led to a black market in animal products fed by active and successful poaching. The regulations achieved little effective conservation because they failed to adequately consider the social and economic aspects of the problem. International bans on the export of ivory and other products have greatly reduced this poaching, but have not solved the problem of rural poverty. Such bans provide no incentive to the local people to conserve wildlife populations.

In contrast, local villagers in Zimbabwe and several other southern African countries have been given licence to take a sustainable harvest of trophy animals. This has created a self-interest in conserving populations of the threatened species on the part of villagers. This is proving to be a successful way of ensuring the maintenance of the animal populations that are now a major source of income for the villagers. For political and social reasons, it is not likely that this approach would work equally well in all African countries, but it does demonstrate the importance of developing socially realistic approaches to conservation issues. Successfully reducing or eliminating the overseas markets for tropical animals and animal products may provide protection for some endangered species, but in many cases active management of the animal resource may work better than prohibition.

There are numerous other examples of conservation efforts that can fail as a result of too narrow a view of the problem. Take, for example, attempts to preserve anadromous fish stocks.[4] The abundance of these fish is affected by overfishing at sea as well as by forest harvesting, which can adversely affect spawning beds and stream habitats. Both issues require attention. The prevention of forest fires in order to protect recreational forests that in fact depend on frequent fire for their desirable condition will in the long run protect neither recreation nor the forest ecosystem; it may increase the risk of a highly destructive wildfire. Public pressure to ban clearcutting from forests in which this method of timber harvesting is not only environmentally sound but also the best way of renewing a particular type of forest may fail to ensure regeneration of that type of forest and the renewal of particular types of wildlife habitat. Inappropriate conservation efforts such as these often fail to achieve their laudable objectives because they are based more on the rhetoric and oversimplification that characterizes the political phase of conservation than on a careful analysis of the ecological and social causes of the problems being addressed, and the ecological and social consequences of various possible solutions.

All concerned citizens should become as involved in the implementation phase of conservation as they have been in the political phase. However, if 'activist' environmentalists wish to contribute as much to this second phase of conservation as they have to the first, they *must* leave behind the rhetoric and scientifically inaccurate assertions that are so often used with good effect in the political phase.

---

4 Anadromous fish are species such as salmon that spawn and spend their first few months or up to a year or two in forest streams before migrating to the ocean. There they spend several years growing and becoming sexually mature before returning to their stream of origin to spawn and die.

Although these statements have their role, and indeed may be necessary, in arousing the interest of the media, the general public, and the politicians, they have no place in the development of practical strategies by which conservation is to be achieved. Individuals who wish to become involved in the implementation phase of conservation must become as knowledgeable as possible about the science and sociology of our urgent environmental issues, and make this knowledge the basis for their action and statements. This appeal is made equally to environmentalists and industrialists. Many foresters and industrial leaders still carry a lot of 'baggage' from the past: old ideas and biases, and resistance to changing the ways in which they conduct their forest business or manage forests. The appeal is also made to the media, who have so often misrepresented forest-resource-conflict situations by oversimplifying them. It is an appeal to return from the Peter Pan world of absolutes and oversimplifications to the scientific and social realities and the real-life complexities of the problems faced by our species. The environment and our future are far too important for the environmental debate to continue to be held in Never-Never Land.

Conservation and Change

The word *conservation* means very different things to different people. The range of meanings that it has for environmentalists and renewable-resource managers is a good example of the problem with words that was described in Chapter 1.

Variously defined in dictionaries and encyclopedias, the meaning of conservation can range from *preservation* (as in the first law of thermodynamics – the conservation of energy), to *the act of preserving, guarding, or protecting* (as in conserving peace), to *the official supervision of a resource* (as in forestry and fisheries), to *the wise use of natural and human resources.*

By conservation, foresters generally mean the sustainable use of forest resources in a manner that does not degrade the collective resource values of a region over the long term (one or several rotations). However, the forestry that is actually practised in the landscape often fails to achieve this objective. Forest management is often not as close to this definition of conservation as it should be. In contrast, many environmentalists believe that conservation means preservation: the setting aside of 'natural,' unmanaged ecosystems as permanent, unchanging 'ecological benchmarks,' wilderness, or wilderness recreation areas. Their use of the word implies a belief that an ecosystem is like a photograph, that it can be framed and 'hung in the landscape,' unchanging like a picture in an art gallery (an 'ecological vignette'), and that simply by placing a reserve on an area of forest, the present values will be available to future generations.

Unfortunately, it is generally not possible to preserve existing forest ecosystem conditions in perpetuity because forests are always changing. In some cases the very act of preservation – the exclusion of forest harvesting or fire, for example – may guarantee that the very values that are to be preserved will be lost. Certainly, some forests will change very little over the next few decades, centuries, or even millennia if we place them in reserves now (unless there is a significant climate change). There is a good chance that such reservation will allow us to die happy in the knowledge that these reserves are relatively unchanged from the time the area was set aside for future generations. But for many of the world's forests, there are no guarantees that they will necessarily be the same when our grandchildren reach old age. On the contrary, there appears to be every likelihood that many forests will have changed by then despite our best efforts to ensure their future availability in their present condition. Because most forests are constantly changing, and because the environment is changing, it seems that we must manage many of the world's forest ecosystems to some extent if we are to conserve particular values.

Having areas of unmanaged forests is important for a variety of reasons. But in addition to having a network of unmanaged forest reserves, we must actively manage other forests to ensure that future generations will be able to enjoy the range of ecosystem values and conditions that we, as a society, feel strongly about. It seems that defining conservation either as *the wise use of natural and human resources* or as *the official supervision of a resource* provides a better basis for developing a successful conservation policy than a definition based on the idea of preservation. The former interpretation of conservation is the one adopted by the United Nations World Commission on Environment and Development in its treatise on sustainable development, *Our Common Future.*

As noted above, there are clearly cases where the rate of change of forest ecosystems is slow enough that the idea of preserving representative examples of past and current conditions for future generations is entirely reasonable. Sufficient examples of old, unmanaged forest should be 'preserved' in this sense to provide a museum of earlier conditions, as well as a variety of other worthwhile values, such as ecological benchmarks, biodiversity reserves, and critical wildlife habitats. But we should not pretend that these preserves are forever. Our strategy of conservation should recognize the inevitability of change and ensure that other, younger forests are set aside as potential future old-growth reserves: areas that in time will become old and provide the values that may have been lost from the original old-forest preserves. In many types of forest, it will make good sense to 'recycle' the old reserves if and when they have lost the values for which they were set aside, replacing them with younger reserves that provide the required values.

Given the magnitude of the present human population (about 5.5 billion in 1992) and its momentum of growth (about 100 million *more* people were added to the world's human population in 1991; a total of 8.5 billion is predicted for 2025), the pressure to use most of the remaining forests of the world to provide forest-based resources will become enormous. This emphasizes the urgency of finding ways to arrest the growth in human numbers and reduce the wasteful use of forest resources, and the equal urgency of completing the global system of ecological reserves, parks, and wilderness areas while we still have choices. It stresses the need to conserve managed forests (to use them wisely) and the harvested products. We must recycle wood fibre and reduce the wasteful and unnecessary use of wood products in order to reduce the rate at which demands for new fibre from forests increase.

Wise use of forests that are dedicated to management and harvesting involves activities that ensure maximum sustainable production of forest products, including timber, wildlife, fish, and clean water, so that the pressure to manage and harvest all forests is reduced. This would increase our ability to create new parks, wilderness areas, and ecological reserves without unacceptable social consequences. Conservation must thus be a balance between short-term preservation of various existing values in some forests, management to ensure the long-term renewal of these values, and management of other forests for a sustainable production of materials and social values needed by society. The greater the production of resources and social values from managed forests, and the more efficient the use by society of the harvested resources, the greater the opportunity to set aside areas to be left in the unmanaged condition, or to be managed for non-material values such as recreation or aesthetics.

Global Conservation versus Local Conservation

Conservation must deal with change, and conservation problems must be considered globally. Some conservationists from tropical latitudes view the wilderness movement in North America as being selfish in the global context. The more forests are locked up as wilderness in North America, the greater the pressure on tropical and subtropical forests to feed the world demand for forest products. Preservation at temperate latitudes may thus have negative implications for conservation at tropical latitudes. However, creation of wilderness and ecological reserves in moderation in any part of the world will contribute to global as well as local conservation.

As we seek the appropriate balance between 'preservation' and 'wise use' in the definition of conservation, we must be sure that the balance we achieve will indeed result in the greatest long-term conservation, both globally and locally, and not simply in a satisfaction of our personal short-term local desires.

CHAPTER 3

Causes and Time Scales of Environmental Change

Introduction

Change occurs continually in both human societies and in the ecosystems on which they depend. It is often changes in the former that drive major changes in the latter.

The complex subject of social and political change is of critical importance in many, if not most, environmental issues. The negative environmental influences that accompany unbridled capitalism have been known for a long time, but the recent political changes in Eastern Europe have confirmed that the answer does not lie in totalitarian communist rule either. The full extent of the environmental degradation under communist governments over the past forty years is now being revealed. Almost all of the discussion in this book is limited to biophysical change in the forest environment, but the importance of the social and political environment in which conservation must be achieved demands at least a passing mention.

The negative consequences of grinding human poverty in the Third World for the remaining tropical rain forests are clearly as bad as, and sometimes worse than, the direct consequences of unregulated logging. In most cases, even exploitive timber harvesting in tropical forests permits rapid reinvasion by so-called primary forest. However, in much of the tropics, the access to forests provided by timber harvesting has led to settlement by poor, landless peasants who strip and burn remaining forest cover and convert the land from sustainable forest to what are frequently non-sustainable agricultural systems. For example, the government-sponsored movement of large numbers of poor, landless people from overcrowded cities in Brazil to areas of the Amazonian rain forest, and from cities such as Jakarta in Indonesia to underpopulated regions of Sumatra, is causing ecosystem change on a scale that most urban dwellers in North America would find hard to imagine, were it not for the coverage of these events in the media.

The extent to which human activity has a negative impact on the environment of a particular country is closely related to the prevailing political system, the level and distribution of wealth, the expenditure of scarce monetary resources on military hardware and warfare, and the effectiveness of the various laws, regulations, and institutions in ensuring sustainable development of the country's resources. Reducing negative impacts on the environment generally requires changes in government policy and regulations as well as a good understanding of the ecology of these impacts, a fact that has been recognized and used effectively by the environmental movement. Conservation and sustainable development clearly have as much to do with politics and social factors as they do with science.

Leaving the important topic of social and political change aside, this chapter discusses change in the major components of forested ecosystems and the extent to which this change is related to human activity.

Biophysical Changes in Forested Landscapes

The Shape of the Landscape

The geological record shows that the shape of the earth's surface has been undergoing continual change. Mountains have been thrust up as tectonic plates moved slowly across the surface of the planet, causing continents to collide and the crust to buckle. The mountains have been eroded again by ice, water, and wind, producing the material from which soil develops. Lakes have formed in valleys following glaciation, volcanic eruption, earthquakes, and other landscape-altering events; they have filled in again as the surrounding landscape eroded. While canoeing in a large river in a broad flat valley, one can often observe evidence of recent changes in the location of the river: old channels that are either dry or still contain ponds or shallow lakes, or active erosion of river banks on the outside of sharp bends in the river.

Large-scale landscape changes such as mountain building and denudation generally occur on a time scale of millions of years. Within the lifetime of a human being, major landscape features can usually

be considered to be permanent. This is not always the case, however. Anyone who has visited the site of a recent explosive volcanic eruption, such as that of Mt. St. Helens in Washington state on 18 May 1980, knows just how much and how quickly the shape of a local landscape can change when volcanism is involved. Earthquakes can also cause dramatic landscape alteration when they trigger major landslides. However, for those who do not live in active volcanic or earthquake areas, there is a reasonable expectation that the physical shape of familiar landscapes will remain essentially unchanged over their lifetime.

Until quite recently, human activities have had relatively little direct effect on the overall shape of the landscape. Human numbers and technology simply could not match the natural processes of uplift and erosion that moulded the surface of the land. Certainly, many areas of the Mediterranean basin show dramatic examples of seriously eroded landscapes where several thousand years of deforestation caused by tree harvesting followed by burning and overgrazing have resulted in the loss of essentially all the soil and the exposure of bedrock over large areas. Similarly, overgrazing in semi-desert latitudes and deforestation in a variety of climates have led to the expansion of deserts, to soil erosion, and to the siltation of valleys and lakes. But human impacts of this type have affected only a small proportion of the earth's surface until very recently. Even now the growth of the human population has affected the plants, animals, microbes, and soils of the earth more than it has affected the actual shape of the landscape. The political map of the world may change with monotonous regularity, but the map of the physical features of the earth has remained essentially constant over many human generations.

Climate and Weather

Although each place on earth is characterized by a distinct climate (the average weather conditions experienced over several decades), the annual pattern of atmospheric conditions that define the average climate are notoriously changeable. Variations in major ocean currents (associated with the climatic phenomena called El Niño and La Niña), in sunspot activity, and in the earth's orbit are all accused of being responsible for year-to-year, decade-to-decade, or longer-term variations in climatic conditions. It seems that it is always either too wet or too dry, too hot or too cold for farmers; rarely are there many years together when atmospheric conditions are just right for the people who produce our food.

The year-to-year variation in climatic patterns is also experienced by urbanites. Many people know the frustration of buying ski equipment at the end of a particularly snowy winter, only to wait impatiently through several succeeding winters of warm, rainy weather for good skiing conditions to return. And many people living in temperate latitudes can remember when it has snowed in the summer (albeit a short-lived 'freak' storm) and been warm enough for sunbathing in midwinter.

Weather (the hour-to-hour and day-to-day atmospheric condition) is also highly variable and often rather unpredictable. We all love to hate the weather forecast. We are acutely aware of how the predicted sunny weekend can so easily turn to rain, and that we should always carry an extra sweater or cover up when hiking in the mountains because of the changeability of mountain weather. Many have experienced the frustration of being caught in the city on a sunny weekend because they cancelled the camping trip on the strength of predicted wet weather.

That the weather changes from day to day and from season to season, and that the annual weather pattern can change from year to year, is not news to most people. However, there are also longer-term changes that most people are less aware of. Many of the landscapes at middle and northern latitudes owe their particular shape, and the type of soils they have, to past periods of glaciation. Cooler world climates in the past led to the accumulation of snow and ice in the high mountains where the remnants of once-mighty glaciers are presently located. Great frozen rivers flowed down into the adjacent valleys and plains, covering them with an enormous thickness of eroded material and ice. The northern forests of Canada, Europe, and the former Soviet Union were pushed many hundreds of kilometres to the south by the last period of glacial advance.

Climate change on this scale is not something that people have experienced within their lifetime, although there are indications that rapid changes in glaciers have occurred over the past few centuries. Take, for example, the 'little ice age' of the fourteenth to nineteenth centuries, when there was a major advance (tens to hundreds of kilometres) and subsequent retreat of glaciers in many mountain areas in the northern hemisphere. Many scientists now believe that an even more dramatic alteration in the world's climate is under way as a result of human activity: the 'greenhouse effect.'

Human activity has had little effect on the periodic changes in world climate in the past, but many scientists now predict that the continuing and accelerating release of so-called 'greenhouse gases' into the atmosphere will cause a major change in world climate over the next half century unless there is an immediate and dramatic reversal of these gaseous releases. Greenhouse gases are released by many mechanisms, including fossil fuel burning (from cars, home heating, airplanes, industrial manufacturing, and so on), deforestation, the manufacture of cement, decomposing urban waste in garbage dumps, and various other domestic and industrial activities. It does not seem very likely that the release of these gases is going to decline rapidly enough to prevent very significant global warming.

If current global warming predictions are correct, we could experience as big a climatic shift in the next fifty years as the one that has occurred over the past ten thousand years: a rate of climate change that is believed to be unprecedented in the past million years. This change is expected to have a bigger impact on global patterns of vegetation than all human activity over the past several thousand years. Human-induced climate change over the next few decades and centuries, and the accompanying changes in vegetation, are certainly going to be much more rapid than changes in the shape of the landscape.

Soils

Soil is the stuff that grows plants. It is the loose material at the earth's surface that holds plants upright so that their leaves can intercept sunlight, and it provides plants with the water and nutrients they need in order to grow. It is an intimate mixture of living organisms (bacteria, fungi, plant roots, and animals), mineral particles of various sizes (from tiny clay particles to large rocks), water, air, and dead organic matter. These constituents are generally arranged in a structure that ensures the drainage of water and an adequate exchange of gases between the soil and the atmosphere.

Soil develops from the inanimate mineral material left behind by glaciers, deposited by wind, water, or gravity, or produced by the physical and chemical weathering of underlying rock. This 'non-soil' material is converted into soil by hardy lichens, mosses, and 'pioneer' plants that are able to invade and survive on the 'non-soil.' These add dead organic matter, which provides a substrate for soil animals and microbes, and the development of soil is underway.

Soil is a 'living,' changing thing. It is not simply the stuff that sticks to your boots and gets tramped into the house. Any successful home gardener knows that even the poorest soil can be improved by adding compost and earthworms. The presence of vegetation, animals, and associated microbes leads to the development of soil over time, and even where soil has been lost because of natural disturbances, such as landslide or erosion, it will gradually be reformed if the exposed area is reoccupied by plants and animals. A good gardener also knows

that soil can be degraded if its organic-matter content is reduced, if the soil animal or microbial activity is adversely affected, or if the 'structure' of the soil is damaged.

Soil damage by erosion, landslide, or physical compaction can occur relatively quickly: in hours or even minutes. Soil deterioration by inappropriate land use (such as loss of soil organic matter and nutrients caused by over-intensive agriculture, or by ecologically insensitive forest harvesting and post-harvest site treatments) may take several decades or several crop rotations. Recovery of soil from severe physical and chemical damage can take many decades or even centuries in very dry, hot, or cold environments. Similarly, it will be very slow in areas with thin soils overlying very hard, erosion-resistant, and nutrient-poor rock: ecosystems in which soil-forming processes are not very rapid. In contrast, soil recovery can be quite rapid (one or a few decades) in climates and landscapes that promote rapid plant growth and active soil animal and microbial populations, and especially where the bedrock is easily weathered and nutrient-rich.

The type of soil that develops in an area depends largely on the climate and on the vegetation, which in turn is largely determined by the climate. As climates have changed in the past, so have vegetation and soils. We do not have much experience of how rapidly soils can change in response to rapid climate change, but if the predicted rate of human-induced climate change does occur, we will soon find out. We do know that rapid alterations in plant cover and soil animals caused by ecosystem disturbance and recovery can result in surprisingly rapid changes in soils – changes that can be either negative or positive.

Much of the change in the world's soils that has occurred over the past two centuries has been the result of human activity, mainly the removal or alteration of the natural vegetation. There are now large and expanding areas of the planet where the condition of the soil reflects past human activity as much as the action of other soil-forming factors.

Vegetation

The major bands of vegetation on earth – tropical and subtropical forests, grasslands and semi-deserts, temperate evergreen and deciduous forests, and northern coniferous forest and tundra – broadly reflect the major climatic zones. As continental drift occurred over hundreds of millions of years, some areas that once had tropical climates were moved towards the poles, and many areas were relocated from more polar latitudes to areas closer to the equator. Over the past million years, successive ice ages have affected the northern hemisphere land masses on a cycle of about 120,000 years. This has caused dramatic latitudinal shifts in the major climatic belts and associated types of vegetation in the northern hemisphere.

The broad vegetation types and the associated animals and microbes migrated over great distances to keep pace with the changes in climate that accompanied continental drift and glacial fluctuations. These ancient climate changes are believed to have occurred relatively slowly. They spanned several or even many generations of long-lived trees. As a consequence, plant and animal communities were able to move slowly across the landscape, keeping up with the slowly changing position of the climatic belts. However, if the rapid climate change that is predicted as a result of the greenhouse effect does occur, some plant species may not be able to shift their geographical location quickly enough to avoid severe climate-related stress. Rather dramatic changes in forest composition and growth are therefore predicted. Some areas presently covered with forest will become grassland. Some grasslands (at present these are often grain-producing farm areas) will become desert. In some cases, climates may become more favourable for plant growth (cold northern areas may become warmer), but it is believed that in most areas there will be negative consequences for the vegetation and the animals that depend on it, including humans, because the rate of climate change will exceed the rate at which living organisms can adapt or migrate.

The combination of plant species that currently occupy an area is the result of one or more of several types of disturbance that may have occurred in the past: landslides, wind storms, fires, insect outbreaks, disease epidemics, human activities such as logging or climate change. After the removal or change in the vegetation that previously occupied an area, a series of plant communities (*seral stages*) successively occupy the disturbed area and are replaced until the original pre-disturbance vegetation is restored. This type of change is called *ecological succession* (see Chapter 4).

The rate of vegetation change due to ecological succession is determined by several factors, but it can be quite rapid in favourable climates on fertile soils. Depending on the severity of the disturbance, the original vegetation may be re-established within a few decades, albeit with younger individuals, as long as the climate remains constant. In the case of severe disturbance, it may take many centuries for the original type of vegetation to redevelop. If the climate changes, complete recovery of the original vegetation may not occur. A new type of vegetation will develop that reflects the new climatic condition. For example, some of the coastal old-growth forests in British Columbia will probably not develop into exactly the same type of forest following natural or human-caused disturbance because today's climate is different from the climate during the 'little ice age'(about AD 1350 to 1870) when many of these forests became established.

Human activity has always had a major effect on vegetation. Clearance of forest for farming and the use of fire to modify vegetation occurred very early in human history – at least ten thousand years ago – and the extent of human impact on vegetation has mirrored the growth in human numbers and the development of technology. Vast areas of the world have been deforested to make way for food production over the past century, a time when human numbers have increased by approximately 360 per cent, from about 1.5 billion to 5.5 billion in 1992. Much of the forest that has not been cleared has been subjected to various forms of exploitation or management, and there are relatively few areas left on earth where the condition of the forest does not reflect to some degree the past activities of humans. This is true of both temperate and tropical forests. Recent studies have suggested that much of our scientific knowledge of the present state of tropical forests has come from studies located in deliberately selected 'best' examples of such forests (i.e., least disturbed). The average tropical forest is often quite a bit different because of past human-caused disturbance.

Human alteration of atmospheric chemistry is believed by many to be altering the global climate. In the long run this could be the greatest single impact that humans will have had on the world's vegetation, exceeding even the clearance of native vegetation for agriculture and the degradation of forests in the past. Without question, humans are now the major factor causing vegetation change on earth.

Animals and Microbes

Animals ultimately depend on plants, which provide them with food, shelter, or a place to live. Because vegetation is constantly undergoing change, one can expect changes in the associated animals. Where the scale of change in the vegetation is small – such as an individual tree dying in a very old forest – there will be little or no measurable change in the animal community. But where the scale of change is large, such as following a large wildfire, a windstorm that blows down large areas of forest, a widespread insect outbreak, or a large clearcut, many animals of the old forest will be replaced by animals of the young forest. Species that require old forest in which to 'make their living' will be partially or completely displaced by animals that are adapted to survive and prosper in disturbed ecosystems and successionally young forests. This is true of both the larger, highly visible animal species that we think of as 'wildlife' and the small and microscopic animals that inhabit the soil and plant components of the ecosystem. The

degree of change in these organisms will reflect the change in their habitat.

Microbial life undergoes a pattern of change over time after an ecosystem disturbance, just as plants and animals do. A profound change in the composition of the soil microbial community occurs after both natural and human-induced disturbance of forest vegetation, and a sequence of microbial changes accompanies the sequence of seral stages back to the original pre-disturbance forest condition. Recent clearcuts, areas affected by wildfire, young forests, and old-growth forests all have a different and characteristic assemblage of soil microbes. This succession in microbial communities in the soil is also seen in individual components of the ecosystem. When a tree dies and falls over, a succession of microbial communities invades and occupies the log. Consequently, the particular micro-organisms that you find in a decomposing log depend on how long the log has been on the ground. They also depend on which types of microbes managed to invade and occupy the log when it first fell.

Because forest animals and microbes are so closely related to the condition of forest vegetation, and because the world's vegetation has been so much affected by human activity over the past two centuries, humans have determined the present status of the world's animals and microbes to a considerable extent. In addition, hunting and trapping have altered the abundance and distribution of many birds and animals. These changes are superimposed on natural changes in animal and microbial life associated with natural disturbance of vegetation and subsequent successional changes. Human-induced changes in animal and microbial communities are becoming increasingly dominant over these natural changes because of the scale and frequency of human disturbance and the alteration of vegetation.

The Role of Human Activity in Causing Environmental Change

Until recently it was thought that of the three major non-living components that determine the biological and functional characteristics of a forest ecosystem – the shape of the landscape (topography), the climate, and the non-living components of the soil – the soil was most subject to human-induced change. Topography and climate were assumed to be relatively constant or beyond the powers of human activity to change them. This assumption must now be re-evaluated. It appears that we may have reached the time in human history when human activity has become a major force in shaping the climate as well as the soils of our planet, and hence the abundance, composition, and productivity of all organisms, including ourselves.

In the chapters that follow, repeated reference will be made to the changes that various natural and management-induced disturbances can cause to global climate and soils. Assuming a continuing supply of sunlight, these are the two fundamental resources on which all terrestrial life depends, and we endanger them at our peril. These changes to the components that determine the biological potential of the forest environment are ultimately of more concern than the important shorter-term changes in plants, animals, and microbes that are caused by natural disturbances or by human activities such as forest management. This is true, of course, only if we conserve the genetic diversity of these life forms.

Time Scales of Change: Social versus Biophysical Time Scales

Much of the forestry/environment debate of the last few years has failed to consider that most important determinant of ecosystem condition: time. So often the argument is about the present condition of a particular forest ecosystem rather than how that ecosystem will change over time.

The 'Snapshot' View of Forest Condition: Instantaneous Analysis of Environmental Impacts

The concerns of environmentalists about forests have frequently been presented in pictures of clearcuts, slashburned sites, or soil erosion taken in the initial weeks or months after the event, with little or no evaluation of how long such conditions will persist. This 'snapshot' evaluation of what are in reality dynamic and ever-changing ecosystem conditions can lead to a serious misrepresentation of the ecological impact of natural or management-induced disturbance. The images of 'ecosystem destruction,' as they are often called, become framed, unchanging, in the back of people's minds, like pictures on a wall. In contrast, the ecological processes of ecosystem recovery in the real world steadily return the disturbed forest through successive seral stages back towards the pre-disturbance condition. 'Snapshot' evaluations are not restricted to environmentalists, however. Many foresters and scientists have made the error of evaluating examples of ecosystem disturbance and recovery over too short a time scale, only to discover later that early evaluations can sometimes be an inaccurate predictor of long-term effects. More will be said on this later.

The Natural Self-Healing Powers of Disturbed Forest Ecosystems

All living systems have natural powers of recovery. A cut finger heals. A broken bone mends. One's immune system fights off infections; most people afflicted with everyday pathogens – colds, flu, stomach upsets, infections – recover. Many tree species are able to grow new leaves when defoliated by insects, while stems of many coniferous trees damaged by fire are able to cover the burn wound, initially with resin and then with woody callous tissue. Similarly, forest ecosystems have an inherent stability resulting from a large number of ecological processes. These processes enable ecosystems to resist changes in their form and function caused by mild disturbance (they are resilient), and recover relatively quickly from more severe disturbance (they are elastic: they 'bounce back') unless the mechanisms of recovery have been damaged. People whose immune systems have become defective, such as AIDS sufferers, may succumb to relatively

Natural disturbance in forest ecosystems

A

A Tropical rain forest in Thailand. Disturbance in this type of forest is usually caused by wind knocking over large individual trees to form gaps that vary in size from a small fraction of a hectare to nearly a hectare.

B Eucalyptus forest in Tasmania, Australia. Eucalyptus forests in this area are killed every few centuries by intense wildfires which can cover hundreds of thousands of hectares. The plants and animals of this forest are adapted to this infrequent but severe disturbance and a new eucalyptus forest is usually established.

C Pine forests in Canada. Much of the northern forest in Canada is killed by wildfire every 60 to 120 years. This produces vast areas of pine forest that are well adapted to this relatively frequent and dramatic natural disturbance.

mild infections; diseases or infections that attack the healing powers of the body can turn relatively mild cuts, abrasions, bone breaks, or infections into killers. Similarly, where a disturbance has destroyed or impaired an ecosystem's processes of recovery, the impact of natural or human-induced disturbance can be very persistent. The individual/ecosystem analogy is imperfect, however. Ecosystems do not die in the sense that an individual organism dies. Ecosystems will always recover either partially or completely from even severe disturbance if the processes of recovery are permitted to operate.

Human Response to Ecosystem Disturbance

Forest managers and forest ecologists are frequently much less alarmed by natural or management-induced disturbance than are the general public or environmentalists. This does not reflect a lack of concern about resources or the environment on the part of people who work with, manage, or study forest ecosystems. Instead, it is based on either experience or scientific knowledge that most disturbed ecosystems will recover within a time period that renders the ecosystem sustainable over the time scales that these people are concerned about.

The media often fan the flames of public concern about ecosystem disturbance. Sometimes this is due to the failure of reporters or their editors to understand the nature of disturbance and recovery in ecosystems. Other times, one gets the strong impression that this may be a business decision. At the time of the 1988 wildfires in Yellowstone National Park in the United States, I was interviewed by a national radio show that was apparently expecting a forest ecologist to respond with a tale of environmental destruction and ecosystem mismanagement, and to point an accusing finger at the resource managers who were to blame for this 'environmental catastrophe.' When I commented that wildfire was a completely natural event in such forests, that much of the Yellowstone Park forest originated from and depended for its character on such fires, and that the forest animals and plants in the area were

adapted to periodic fires, the interview was dropped and never aired. It has sometimes seemed that letters voicing fears about irrevocable and permanent destruction of the environment have received prompt publication in some newspapers, while letters that provide a scientific analysis of disturbance events are sometimes not printed. Clearly, there is the perception by many people that change in forest ecosystems is 'unnatural' or 'bad,' that it must be someone's fault, and that once it has occurred there is little or no prospect of recovering the former ecosystem values. Some environmentalists apparently believe that 'if you clearcut old-growth forests, there can never be another forest like that again,' or that a second-growth forest is in fact not a forest.

The view that a forest ecosystem is like an ancient art treasure that, once destroyed, can never be recreated needs to be analyzed. It lies at the heart of many of the conflicts between environmentalists and the public on one hand and forest resource managers and forest ecologists on the other. The difference in perception goes beyond a simple difference in experience with, and knowledge of, the behaviour of forest ecosystems. It relates also to a different perception of time scales.

Social, Biophysical, and Management Time Scales: A Source of Confusion and Misunderstanding

On the time scale of biological evolution, most forest ecosystems are disturbed very frequently. Wildfire may burn through northern boreal forests every 60 to 100 years, or through some Australian eucalyptus forests every 300 to 500 years. Windstorms blow down many forests in exposed coastal areas or in the path of hurricanes, tornadoes, or typhoons every one or two centuries. Insect outbreaks kill vast areas of eastern Canadian forests (the spruce budworm) and western Canadian forests (the mountain pine beetle or the spruce bark beetle) whenever large areas of forest reach the age at which they become suitable habitat for the insects (every 100 to 200 years). In the

10,000 years since the last major glaciation, and the hundreds of thousands or millions of years over which the species concerned have evolved, this is a very high frequency of catastrophic disturbance. The recovery from disturbance on this time scale is very rapid. However, evolutionary time scales are well beyond the experience of individual humans and beyond the time scale of resource management, so they are not really relevant to the present discussion.

Timber management has a time scale that relates to the life of a tree crop, but should also consider several successive tree-crop rotations in order to address concerns about sustainability. Because so many other forest values (e.g., wildlife, water, recreation) are related to, or influenced by, the age of the forest, management for these other values should be on a similar time scale. However, these resources should also be considered at shorter time scales (such as year-to-year or decade-to-decade variation in wildlife because of hunting pressure or 'natural' predator-prey cycles) that are only a fraction of the tree-crop rotation.

Tree-crop time scales can be as short as five years, as in eucalypts grown in Brazil for charcoal for the steel industry and oil for the manufacture of paint and other chemicals. Poplars and willows grown in Sweden for generating heat and electricity are harvested on three- to five-year cycles. Conversely, tree-crop production periods can be as long as several centuries, as in valuable temperate deciduous hardwood species such as oak and beech, grown for knot-free lumber and veneer for furniture and panelling in our homes. For most conventional timber management at temperate and boreal latitudes, crop rotations range from 50 to 120 years, according to the type of forest. On such time scales, an eight- to twenty-year period of disturbed conditions before the ecosystem is well along the path of successional recovery, and a 40- to 100-year delay before the forest regains a mature condition, may be perfectly reasonable and constitute sustainable landscape management. When considered in terms of our personal life experiences, however, such time spans may seem to be 'forever.'

When you are a young child, your life stretches into the future to a seemingly endless horizon, and every day can seem to be an eternity. For a young child, it is almost impossible to imagine that a harvested forest could ever grow back to its former state. In the frenetic career-development, family-rearing, and mortgage-paying years, time passes rapidly, but the persistence of youthful optimism confers hopes for a long life ahead. It is easier to contemplate the regrowth of a harvested forest and the possibility of enjoying an attractive forest on the site once again before the evening of your life arrives. However, by the mid to late stages of one's life, with the empty-nest syndrome, a possible midlife crisis, and a sobering realization of one's own mortality, time scales tend to contract once again. As we approach retirement, we realize that there are dearly loved values in a particular forest that may be lost to us if it is harvested, and that we will not live to see renewed on the harvested site. Even if the forest is being managed sustainably in an environmentally sound manner, the time scale for the renewal of certain valued conditions of the forest ecosystem may exceed our own longevity. For us as individuals they may be gone forever.

The difference between these social or individual time scales and both the natural time scales of forest ecosystems and the time scales of forest management is a major contributor to the conflict between foresters and some members of the public. Change in forest ecosystems might be accepted by these members of the public if the period of recovery were one or two years: a small fraction of a human life span. Thus, few people grieve the clearcutting of wheat fields, corn crops, or cabbages. These crops will grow again next year. But where the recovery from change takes a significant fraction of a human life span, or several life spans, renewal may be perceived to take forever, and particular values will never be experienced and enjoyed again by individuals for whom disturbance-induced change has created a loss.

The need for disturbance in some types of forest

A

B

C

F

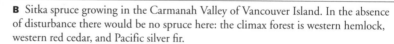

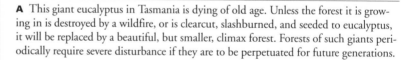

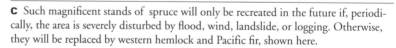

D

E

A This giant eucalyptus in Tasmania is dying of old age. Unless the forest it is growing in is destroyed by a wildfire, or is clearcut, slashburned, and seeded to eucalyptus, it will be replaced by a beautiful, but smaller, climax forest. Forests of such giants periodically require severe disturbance if they are to be perpetuated for future generations.

B Sitka spruce growing in the Carmanah Valley of Vancouver Island. In the absence of disturbance there would be no spruce here: the climax forest is western hemlock, western red cedar, and Pacific silver fir.

C Such magnificent stands of spruce will only be recreated in the future if, periodically, the area is severely disturbed by flood, wind, landslide, or logging. Otherwise, they will be replaced by western hemlock and Pacific fir, shown here.

D This highly productive 80-year-old Pacific silver fir and western hemlock on northern Vancouver Island was established naturally following a major wind storm.

E This western red cedar and western hemlock old-growth forest has very low productivity and some very old trees (many of the cedars are more than 500 years old). It is growing adjacent to the forest shown in D. Apparently the lack of disturbance has led to a stagnation of ecological processes.

F The stands shown in D and E growing side by side on northern Vancouver Island.

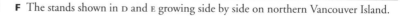

The fundamental difference between human and forest time scales generates the 'never' and 'forever' rhetoric that constitutes the Peter Pan principle of resource use conflict (see Chapter 2). Forest managers may be convinced by experience, knowledge, or precedent elsewhere that they are managing forests in such a way that a wide range of forest values will be renewed and available again in the future. These values may not be available on every hectare every year, but a patchwork of forests of different ages and conditions across the landscape will collectively provide a continuous supply of a wide variety of resources from that landscape. The public, on the other hand, may perceive that the time required for the renewal of certain values is far beyond what they would like or are prepared to accept.

Many of the environmentalists' claims may be defensible from a human time perspective while being incorrect from a management and ecological time scale. Similarly, forest ecosystem recovery times that are perfectly reasonable from a management standpoint may be socially unacceptable. Many forest professionals and scientists are guilty of being insensitive to the human perspective on temporal change, while many environmentalists have seriously oversimplified their view of disturbance and ecosystem recovery by ignoring the natural time scales of ecosystem events. If each side was able to appreciate the other's temporal perspective, it might be easier to design the management-induced disturbance of forests so that it is more acceptable to the public. This is what some of the ideas in Chapter 11 ('New Forestry') are all about.

Summary

Change is one thing we can be certain that we will have to deal with. Some of the changes we experience are natural, while others are largely human-caused. Frequently we try to arrest natural change, such as building costly embankments to restrain a river that has the natural tendency to wander across a floodplain where we have foolishly built cities. Conversely, we face many changes caused by thoughtless human activity: soil deterioration, air and water pollution, and loss of animal species.

There seems to be a general antipathy towards change in modern industrial societies, in contrast to the acceptance of natural events by many more 'primitive' cultures that live closer to nature. Many of the urbanites of industrialized nations have lost touch with nature and have little understanding of the ebb and flow of natural change and its time scales. Some of the natural or human-induced environmental change that is viewed as destructive when considered on a short, urban time scale may be well within natural time scales of ecosystem disturbance and recovery. The challenge is to separate the changes that constitute a real threat to the sustainability of biophysical resources from those that do not. However, biophysical analysis is not enough. In managing forests, a consideration of biophysical patterns and time scales of change must be combined with a sensitivity to social time scales that may be short, and to resource values that may have relatively long renewal times.

CHAPTER 4

A Brief Primer on Ecology and Forest Ecosystems

Introduction

To understand many of the current issues in forestry, one must understand what a forest ecosystem is, how it works, how it tends to change over time in the absence of disturbance, and how well it is able to recover when it is disturbed.

Because so many people do not have such knowledge, it is not surprising that many discussions of the ecological impact of forestry have been based largely on people's emotional responses to snapshot, frozen-in-time images of recently disturbed forest ecosystems. The debate has often lacked any scientific analysis of how the functional processes of ecosystems have been altered by the disturbance, and of how fast and by what mechanisms the ecosystem will recover. The rhetoric that frequently characterizes the political phase of conservation has involved statements that range from being completely accurate, through statements that may be correct in some circumstances but are wrong because they have been made in the wrong context, to statements that are partly or completely wrong under almost any circumstances. While this lack of scientific credibility may not be critical in the political phase, it is inappropriate in the implementation phase of conservation.

It is natural for people to feel emotional if they believe that some aspect of the forest environment that they value or love is going to be lost forever. And it is not surprising that emotional arguments are used to try to prevent such a loss, especially if people do not have a knowledge of the ecological characteristics of forest ecosystems. We are an emotional species. Many of us make major decisions largely on the basis of emotion rather than solely on objective analysis and logic. Falling in love, getting married, having children, buying a house or a car, all involve our hearts as well as our heads, and often our hearts have the final say. Emotion-based decisions can be very good, and decisions based purely on science or 'the cold, hard facts' can be impersonal and fail to satisfy human needs. However, it often helps to combine our emotion-based responses with the best available understanding of the facts of a situation. If we are to be successful in the implementation phase of conservation, it is necessary that policies and regulations designed to achieve conservation are soundly based in science, sociology, and economics, as well as satisfying emotion-based public desires. This is necessary at the very least to ensure that we understand the ecological and social consequences of decisions about resources that are based largely on our emotions.

This chapter provides a brief review of some of the most fundamental aspects of the ecology of forest ecosystems. The ideas presented here, together with a brief review of what forestry is in Chapter 5, should help you understand and evaluate the discussion of various issues in the remaining chapters of the book. Reading these two chapters should also help you make a more informed evaluation of forestry-related issues presented in the media. The treatment of these two important topics is, of necessity, brief, and you are encouraged to consult one or more of the sources in the bibliography if you want more detail.

What Is a Forest?

It is certainly not just trees. The old saying 'you can't see the forest for the trees' has a lot of truth to it. A farm is not a herd of cows, nor the cabbages or corn in the field. It is an area of landscape with a soil, a climate, and appropriate plants, animals, and microbes that make it possible for the farmer to raise a crop of livestock or food plants. Harvest the cabbages or corn, sell the cows, and you still have a farm, because you still have an agricultural *ecosystem*.

It is much the same with forests. A forest is defined as an ecosystem dominated by trees. But the forest is no more the trees than the farm is the cabbages or cows. Ultimately, a forest is a landscape that has the soil, climate, and set of organisms that make up what we think of as a forest. It is a type of landscape in which the redevelopment of a plant, animal, and microbial community dominated by trees will occur naturally, or with management

assistance, following removal of the trees by natural or human-caused disturbance. Of course, if the trees are clearcut, if all the other forest plants are eliminated and their reinvasion is prevented by fire, herbicides, and manual or mechanical methods, if the soil is ploughed to convert it from forest soil to agricultural soil, and if agricultural plants and animals are established and maintained – then you have a farm, not a forest. However, experience from around the world has shown that if a farm in a previously forested area is abandoned, it is only a matter of time before trees 'reclaim their own': a forest eventually returns. Most farms are really forests temporarily masquerading as agricultural land, thanks to the enormous inputs of human and fossil fuel energy that have been invested to roll back the forest and which must be repeatedly invested to keep it away. As we shall see later, most farms are nothing more than early seral stages of a forest. Forest conditions can and will re-establish themselves as soon as we cease to maintain this early seral condition against the ecological forces that are continually trying to re-establish the forest.

Following the death of living trees in a forest, regardless of whether this is caused by fire, wind, insects, disease, or forest harvesting, the natural processes of ecosystem recovery and forest renewal begin to operate. Despite the temporary removal of the very thing that defines a forest – large trees that dominate the landscape – the forest ecosystem continues to exist. Only its condition or seral stage has been changed. The speed and details of recovery will vary considerably according to the type and intensity of the disturbance that removed the trees. Clearcutting is not the same ecological disturbance as a wildfire. A disturbance by windthrow is not the same as a disturbance by disease. Each disturbance has its own particular set of ecological effects. However, all of them return the forest to an earlier seral condition, and the difference in ecosystem condition between the early seral stages created by the different types of disturbance gradually or rapidly decreases with time until eventually the mode of origin of the new forest becomes relatively unimportant. The recovery will also depend on the type of ecosystem where the disturbance has occurred: some ecosystems are fast and others are slow in their rate of recovery.

What Is an Ecosystem?

Twenty years ago, few people had even heard the word 'ecosystem.' Now most people have both heard and used it, but I suspect that relatively few really know what it means. Many people seem to think it is another word for 'environment.' That may not be far from the truth, as long as we can all agree on what 'environment' means. But rather than discuss the similarity of these two words, perhaps it would be better to define ecosystem more rigorously.

Ecosystem means an ecological system; it is the total assemblage of living organisms together with their non-living environment in a particular area. The adjective 'ecological' is derived from the word 'ecology.' Ecology in turn comes from the Greek word *oikos* and the Latin word *logia*. The former means 'house' or 'place to live'; the latter means 'study.' Literally, ecology is the study of the relationships between living organisms and their total environment, that is, their 'house,' or the place where they live or exist. This *total environment* includes the climate, the physical components of the soil, and the topography (the non-living, or abiotic, components of the environment), and all the other organisms (plants, animals, and microbes) that help or hinder them, feed them or feed on them, protect them or are protected by them. These organisms, including the soil-dwelling as well as above-ground organisms, are the living, or biotic, components of the environment. Thus, ecology in its broadest sense is the study of ecosystems: the study of individual organisms or groups of organisms and the total living and non-living environment with which they interact.

If this definition of ecosystem is accepted, it follows that it is much harder to 'destroy' an ecosystem than to change its present condition. Although environmentalists often talk about the destruction of forest ecosystems by forest management, in almost all cases what is really happening is that the condition of the ecosystem has been changed. The original ecosystem condition may be lost or 'destroyed' by forest harvesting, but the forest ecosystem can be said to have been destroyed only if the processes of ecosystem recovery are prevented from operating. If these ecological processes are permitted to operate for long enough, the original condition will often be restored. Only in the most severe and extensive disturbances can one talk about the complete destruction of ecosystems – the Hope Slide in coastal British Columbia, where the entire side of a mountain fell off into the valley below; cases of catastrophic volcanic eruption such as Krakatoa in Indonesia or areas close to Mt. St. Helens in Washington; or the clearing of land for an industrial development.

Ecology versus Environmentalism

Ecology is a science. It makes no value judgments. Ecology on its own cannot tell you if an old-growth forest is better or worse than a young forest or a clearcut. It merely describes and helps us understand the ecological differences. There is no basis in the science of ecology for saying a spotted owl in an old-growth forest is better or worse than a sparrow in a clearcut. They just 'are.' Ecology provides no basis for saying that a 'natural' old-growth forest with many different plant and animal species is better or worse than a 'natural' young forest with a single tree species and low animal diversity, such as a post-wildfire pine forest. It is we humans, either individually, as groups such as environmental organizations, or as a society, that make value judgments, not science.

In contrast to the science of ecology, *environmentalism* is the establishment of a value system concerning the condition of the ecosystems that make up the environment. It is important to make value judgments about our environment and its condition, because we depend on that environment, and some conditions of the environment are better able to satisfy the needs and desires of humans than others. But these judgments are developed on the basis of human desires and needs, not on the basis of ecology. Frequently, terms like 'ecologically sound' and 'ecologically irresponsible' are used that imply an evaluation based on the science of ecology. However, such terms are not based on science, because they imply a value judgment. They should be replaced by 'environmentally sound' and 'environmentally irresponsible.' It is the combination of ecology and society's value judgments about the environment that provides the basis for developing successful conservation policies and strategies.

In the debate over environmental issues and forestry, it is important to separate the science from the value judgments. Both are equally important, but must not be confused, as they so often are, if we are to get to the bottom of our environmental problems and achieve a sustainable relationship between the human species and the global ecosystem.

What Are the Major Characteristics of Ecosystems?

The definition that has just been presented describes the major components of an ecosystem, in much the same way that you would list the wheels, engine, gearbox, axles, seats, radio, and so on in defining the components of a car. However, such a list does not fully describe what a car is, what it does, and how it does it. Similarly, there are other characteristics of ecosystems that we need to describe that transcend the list of physical components. They are the properties of the ecological *system* rather than of the component parts.

Structure. Both the vertical and horizontal structures of the plant community are important as ecosystem characteristics. Vertical structure refers to the vertical layering of different types of plants in the community. Forests can have one or more tree canopy levels, one or more shrub canopy levels, a herb layer, and, sometimes, a moss layer on the

ground. Tree and plant roots sometimes develop a comparable set of strata below ground, the roots of different species occupying different soil layers. The number of plant layers varies with forest age, climate, and soils. Forests can also vary in their horizontal structure: does the vertical structure vary from place to place as you move through the forest? Some are very uniform in vertical structure over large areas, while others are very patchy, with frequent gaps in the canopy that have a different vertical structure than the adjacent closed forest (a forest with a complete, unbroken canopy of branches and leaves). The presence of standing dead trees (snags) and large decomposing logs is an important aspect of the structure of some types of old-growth forest.

Function. Ecosystems are 'natural biomass factories'; they produce plant biomass, animal biomass, and microbial biomass (biomass is simply the weight or mass of living organisms). The forest ecosystem is fuelled by solar radiation (sunlight). This is captured by the leaves of green plants in the process of photosynthesis, and the magnitude of the energy capture is directly related to the quantity of leaves (the 'number of cylinders in the ecosystem's engine'). A forest ecosystem with a small biomass of leaves will generally have less energy capture, less biomass production, and less organic matter than an ecosystem with lots of foliage; there will be correspondingly fewer animals and less microbial life.

Solar energy is stored in ecosystems as chemical energy: the energy of large organic molecules, such as sugars, cellulose, proteins, and lignin, which are the basic chemical building blocks of plants. Consequently, energy capture by photosynthesis will only occur if plants are adequately provided with nutrient chemicals that are the building blocks of these molecules. Plants cannot produce many leaves if they are starved of one or more of the essential plant nutrients, and the efficiency of energy capture is lower in the leaves of malnourished plants than in those of well-nourished plants. People don't grow well if they are malnourished, and plants are no different. If plants are malnourished, so are the animals and microbes that feed on them or on the organic matter they produce. The processes that determine plant nutrition and therefore energy capture and ecosystem productivity are explained later.

Complexity. Ecosystems are complex. They are composed of many individual structural components that interact to determine ecosystem function. The key point about complexity is that most events or conditions in complex systems result from the interaction of many factors. This makes it relatively difficult to predict future events or conditions accurately unless one has a good knowledge of the system. Accurate prediction of future ecosystem conditions and the response of ecosystems to disturbance requires either a good understanding of the ecology of the ecosystem being considered, or practical experience of how such ecosystems have reacted to disturbance in the past, or both. Complexity makes it difficult to make very precise predictions about ecosystems far into the future, but for most ecosystems the overall trends can be predicted on the basis of a sound knowledge of the local ecology. The 'randomness' of ecosystems occurs only within the bounds set by the regional climate, the soil, the topography, and the local biotic community.

Biotic diversity. The number of species of living organisms in a particular ecosystem is one of several measures of the biological diversity of that system. Such a species list is called the *alpha species diversity* of the ecosystem. The way in which these species are arranged vertically within the ecosystem, together with the abundance and arrangement of large decaying logs and standing dead trees, is a measure of that ecosystem's *alpha structural diversity.* But both the vertical and horizontal structure and the number and type of species in the ecosystem vary from place to place on the landscape. This horizontal spatial diversity of ecosystems is called *beta diversity.*

Many lowland tropical rain forests have a very high alpha diversity: they can contain many hundreds, or even thousands, of plant species and many thousands of animal and microbial species in a single hectare, and the plants are often arranged into many different canopy levels, giving high structural diversity. However, some lowland tropical forests vary little over quite large areas; they can have low beta diversity. Unmanaged northern forests – such as the vast boreal forest of northern Canada, Scandinavia, and the former Soviet Union – in flat but well-drained areas tend to have much lower alpha diversity than tropical forests, as well as low beta diversity. Unmanaged old-growth forests in the recently glaciated mountains of western North America tend to have intermediate to low alpha species diversity of plants and animals but higher beta diversity (because of the great local variation in soils and topography). Disturbance of old-growth forests, either naturally or by management, often increases beta diversity of the landscape by creating a mosaic of forests of different ages – a mosaic of different seral stages – and may either increase or decrease alpha diversity. This important topic is discussed in more detail in Chapter 10.

Interdependency or interaction of components. It is well known that both the vegetation and the soils of an area reflect its climate. Deserts have desert climates, desert vegetation, desert soils, and desert animals. Alpine meadows have alpine climates, alpine vegetation, alpine soils, and alpine animals. However, if the soils are significantly different within a particular climatic area, the vegetation will also be different, and so will the animal and microbial community. Similarly, if through management or natural disturbance (such as wildfire) there is a major change in the vegetation on a given type of soil in a particular climatic area, some of the characteristics of the soil and the animal and microbial communities will change. The differences will persist until the vegetation is changed back to its original condition by the processes of ecological succession. As suggested above, the species of animals and microbes in the ecosystem are very much determined by the vegetation, but sometimes it is the animals that determine the type of vegetation. For example, grazing animals that depend on herbaceous plants such as grasses often prevent forests from invading grasslands, thereby perpetuating the ecosystem in the seral stage that is optimum for them.

What this tells us is that there is a high degree of interaction and often a considerable degree of interdependency between many of the different components of the ecosystem.

Tendency to change over time. Virtually all forest ecosystems are periodically disturbed by fire, windstorms, erosion during heavy rain or snowmelt (mostly forests on steep mountain slopes), diseases, insects, or forest management. Ecosystems have processes that are constantly changing their condition back towards a relatively stable, unchanging, and self-replacing condition called the 'climax' after some previous natural or human-induced disturbance. However, even undisturbed climax forests may change slowly over time. For example, in the long-term absence of disturbance, cold northern forests may eventually be replaced by muskeg swamps; forests in such northern climates are not true climax plant communities. Similarly, if they remain undisturbed for many centuries, some cool, humid coastal old-growth forests may lose vigour and 'stagnate.' Forests may also change from one century to the next as a result of climate change. Because this topic of ecosystem change and recovery from disturbance is so important to our understanding of forest ecosystems, it is discussed in more detail later in this chapter.

This brief listing of the major attributes of a forest ecosystem illustrates the fact that ecosystems are very complex. As noted above, this complexity makes it difficult to predict the impact of disturbance on the structure, function, and diversity of forests unless one has extensive and detailed experience of the past response of particular forest ecosystems to disturbance, or one understands the ecological processes that are involved, or both. Because of this complexity and its variation across

the landscape, it is unhelpful to generalize about the ecological consequences of a particular type of disturbance – wildfire, clearcutting, or slashburning – in different types of forest, or about the consequences of different ways of managing a particular type of forest ecosystem. Each type of ecological system and each kind of disturbance has to be considered individually.

Some of the greatest failures in forestry have resulted from the application of a single type of management practice to a wide variety of types of forest ecosystem. Those concerned about improving forest practice risk making a similar error if they try to base new forest management strategies on generalizations about the impact of a particular strategy in different types of forest, or insist on one method of forest harvesting and management being applied everywhere, regardless of the varying characteristics of individual ecosystems or the genetically controlled ecological adaptations of the plant and animal species involved. If, in their attempt to improve forest management, governments were to impose policies and regulations that fail to recognize the structural, functional, spatial, and temporal variability of our forested landscapes, we are unlikely to achieve the conservation and resource sustainability that we seek. It is therefore important that public pressure on politicians with respect to environmental and resource issues be soundly based on a knowledge of ecological principles. This means avoiding generalizations.

As a final note, it has been suggested by some environmentalists that second-growth, and, especially, managed second-growth, forests are not ecosystems, that the only true forest ecosystem is unmanaged old growth. To accept this proposition requires a redefinition of the term ecosystem, and the rejection of a very substantial body of experience and scientific research on the form and function of forest ecosystems, both managed and unmanaged. From the point of view of ecology, this is unacceptable. Managed and unmanaged second-growth forests differ in a number of respects from unmanaged or managed old-growth forest, but they are all forest ecosystems. They all satisfy the basic definition and concept of ecosystem; they all share the same basic attributes.

The Basics of Production Ecology

In order to understand how forest ecosystems change over time and how they recover from disturbance, we have to understand the basic processes of forest growth, something that is called *production ecology.*

Forests capture the energy of sunlight by the biochemical process of photosynthesis, which takes place in their leaves. (A small amount of photosynthesis can also occur in green stems.) This photosynthesis produces sugar by combining the gas carbon dioxide (CO_2) from the air with water (H_2O) that has been taken up from the soil by the roots. The sugar produced by the leaves is called the photosynthate. It provides the energy and basic chemical building blocks that plants need to produce all the other complex organic molecules that make up stems, leaves, roots, seeds, and so on.

The efficiency with which the forest captures sunlight and converts it first to sugars and then into various types of plant *biomass* (literally, the mass or weight of plant tissues, such as stems, branches, leaves, roots) depends on how many leaves it has, the shape of the leaves, and how the leaves are arranged on twigs and branches. Actually, it depends on the total horizontal surface area of the leaves rather than on the number; a few large leaves can do the same job as many smaller leaves that have the same total leaf area. Leaf area determines how much of the available sunlight falling on the forest is captured by the tree crowns. The amount of foliage in a forest (its leaf area) depends on the tree species, how old the forest is, and how much soil moisture and nutrients are available to the trees and other plants.

Both young and old forests generally have less leaf area than intermediate-aged forests, but the variation in total leaf area in ecosystems is much less than the leaf area of the trees. This is because the total leaf area in a forest is made up of tree leaves *and* the leaves of herbs and shrubs. In young forests in which the trees have not yet developed a large leaf area, the herbs and shrubs contribute a significant, or even the major, portion of the total leaf area. As the trees develop a closed canopy, the understorey vegetation (herbs, shrubs, mosses, young trees) is shaded out, and its leaf area is replaced by tree leaf area. Tree leaf area declines as the forest ages, and the growth and leaf area in the understorey increases again because more light filters down to the ground through gaps in the tree canopy.

Forests in a dry climate or on dry sites, such as a rocky ridge top, usually have less foliage than forests in wet climates or on moist soils such as those found in lower-slope or valley-bottom forests. Lack of soil nutrients in infertile soils also limits the amount of foliage that the forest can produce. In humid climates the low leaf area on 'dry,' well-drained sites may be due as much to low nutrient availability as to lack of soil moisture. Nutrients are required for the production of new leaves, as well as to keep them working efficiently. However, forests on moist, infertile mineral soils, such as some tropical forest soils, sometimes do have lots of leaves and appreciable growth rates. This apparent contradiction will be explained later.

Just sitting on a chair reading this book, you are using up energy; your body is constantly using energy just to maintain all its functions and parts. Plants are similar. Some of the sugar created by photosynthesis is used just to keep the plant going before it can do any growing or reproducing (by producing flowers and seeds). Having attended to maintenance and upkeep, and having invested some energy in producing chemicals that help protect themselves against insects and diseases, trees and other plants invest the remaining sugar and energy in producing new biomass. The first demand on this new biomass is the production of new leaves to replace those that the plant lost in the fall or at some other time, and to replace the tiny roots that are found everywhere in the upper soil.

Many or even most of these fine roots die every year, creating a below-ground 'litterfall' (it doesn't actually fall anywhere!). Lost leaves must be replaced if leaf area and photosynthesis are to be maintained, and fine roots must be replaced promptly if the plant is to get the nutrients and moisture it needs for photosynthesis and leaf production. Replacing fine roots can take half or more of all the sugar produced by photosynthesis, and as much as half of what is left may go to replace branches and foliage. Thus, a relatively modest proportion of the annual production of photosynthate actually goes into making tree stems taller and thicker, or to increasing the size of shrubs and herbs.

The amount of yearly photosynthate that goes into tree stems is determined largely by how hard the tree has to work to get its moisture and nutrients, and by how much of its hard-earned photosynthate has to go to pay the 'bill' for maintaining fine roots. This in turn depends on the availability of soil moisture and nutrients. Foresters and farmers are able to harvest much less of the total production (the total photosynthate produced) of their crop plants from infertile or dry sites than from fertile moist sites, because the plants in the poorer sites put so much of their energy into short-lived fine roots as they work hard to find moisture and nutrients. If, through mismanagement, the availability of soil moisture and nutrients is reduced, both farmers and foresters will experience smaller harvests. Soil degradation certainly reduces the area of leaves in a field or forest, and thus affects the total plant growth, but it can have a much bigger effect on the growth of the harvestable parts – corn cobs, potatoes, or tree stems – because it increases the proportion of photosynthate that is put into unharvestable fine roots.

In summary, the art of managing a productive forest ecosystem involves maintaining leaf biomass at a level that captures sunlight efficiently. But this is not enough if the objective is to harvest plant biomass from the forest. The forester must maintain soil fertility and other desirable soil conditions so that as much of the captured solar energy as possible goes into harvestable biomass rather than fine roots. If the goal is to produce trees for timber, most, but not all, of the leaf biomass should be on the crop trees. If the goal is to produce wildlife, enough of the leaf biomass should be on the herbs, shrubs, or other types of plant that the wildlife depend on to ensure that they have an ample supply of nutritious food and habitat. The major details of production ecology are shown in Figure 4.1.

Nutrient Cycling in Forest Ecosystems

You have probably gathered by now that nutrients are pretty important in ecosystems. Solar energy cannot be captured and stored without them. If the stored energy is lost because the forest is logged or consumed by wildfire, there is a more or less constant supply of solar energy just waiting to be captured. But if the soil nutrients that facilitate this energy capture are lost, it often takes quite a long time for them to be replaced. It is not surprising to learn, therefore, that forest ecosystems are pretty stingy with their nutrients. Water in streams flowing through undisturbed forests, especially young to medium-aged forests that are actively building up their biomass and the organic matter in the soil, usually has very low dissolved concentrations of many of the nutrient elements required by plants. Such forests hang on to their nutrients very efficiently: they monopolize the supply. They are able to do this, and to recover from periodic nutrient losses, through the mechanisms of nutrient cycling.

There are three aspects to nutrient cycling (Figure 4.2). All three must be considered if we are to understand the role of nutrients in determining forest ecosystem structure and function, and how forests are able to recover from nutrient loss.

Cycling of Nutrients Into and Out of Ecosystems: The Geochemical Cycle

Forest ecosystems do not have a fixed, unchanging quantity of nutrients because ecosystems continuously receive and lose nutrients.

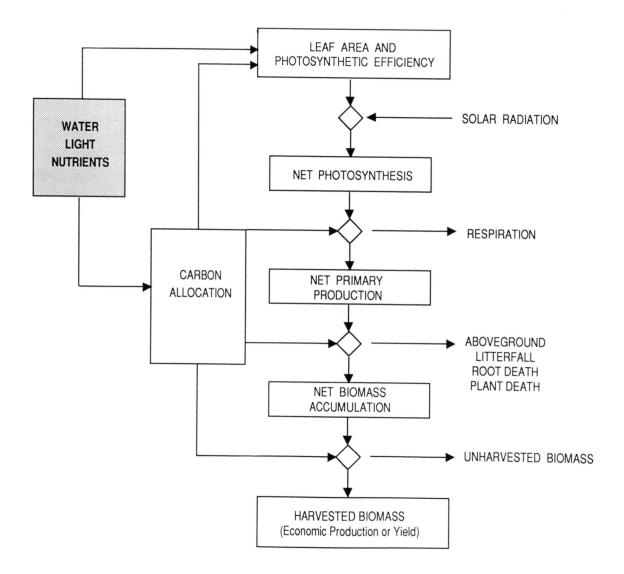

Figure 4.1 The major determinants of economic production (yield) in a forest ecosystem within a particular climatic regime. Clearly, the availability of site resources (water, light, nutrients) are critically important, both directly and indirectly, through their effect on the allocation of net photosynthates (Kimmins 1990, used with permission of the Canadian Institute of Forestry).

Figure 4.2 The three major types of nutrient cycles: geochemical (between ecosystems), biogeochemical (within an ecosystem), and biochemical (within an organism: also referred to as internal cycling) (modified from Kimmins 1987).

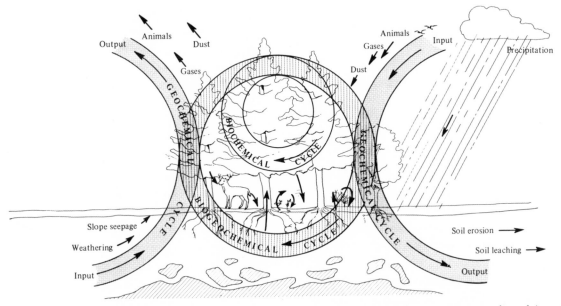

Rain, snow, and dust all provide a steady, if small, annual input of nutrients into ecosystems. The large area of leaves in a forest increases this input: the leaves act like the 'scrubbers' that remove particulate matter from factory chimneys to reduce air pollution. In fact, trees are often planted in and around cities to help remove particles of dust and fog from the urban atmosphere.

Additional nutrients are added by the chemical weathering of rocks. Living plants produce acids, and acids are also produced as dead plant material decomposes. These acids slowly dissolve the pebbles in the soil and underlying rock, just as human-caused acid rain eats away at statues and stone buildings. As the rocks are dissolved, various nutrient elements are released and may be taken up by plants. The action of these acids plays a major role in soil formation. Water seeping down a slope through the soil can also bring nutrients into a downslope ecosystem. Various microbes, on their own or in association with 'nitrogen-fixing plants'[5] such as alders and lupines, capture inert nitrogen

from the air (which plants cannot use directly) and convert it into organic nitrogen that plants can use. Nutrients are also added when the forest is fertilized. These inputs of nutrients to the ecosystem are part of the *geochemical cycle*.

Natural geochemical inputs are extremely important. Although for some nutrients they may amount to only a few kilograms per hectare each year, over centuries this can create a very large store in the ecosystem if the nutrients are successfully captured and retained by the forest. Inputs of that most important nutrient, nitrogen, can occur very rapidly as a result of the activities of nitrogen-fixing organisms. Geochemical inputs also provide a

5 Some plants act as hosts to certain micro-organisms that are uniquely able to capture some of the inert nitrogen gas (N_2) that makes up nearly three-quarters of our atmosphere and turn it into organic nitrogen that can be used by plants. In exchange, the micro-organisms are provided with a place to live – a nodule, either on the plant roots (typical of temperate plants) or the leaves (more typical of tropical plants) – and a supply of energy in the form of sugars and other high-energy organic molecules.

replacement for nutrients that are lost if they are washed (leached) out of the soil by rainwater or snowmelt, nutrients in gases and fly ash lost in smoke during a wildfire or slashburn, nutrients removed in eroded soil, or nutrients in organic matter removed from the site by deer, insects, humans (foresters harvesting trees, peasant farmers collecting leaves and branches), and other animal species.

Geochemical outputs from an actively growing forest are normally less than geochemical inputs; the ecosystem accumulates nutrients over time. When the ecosystem is disturbed by fire, insects, disease, wind, or logging, the situation is reversed. There is a pulse of geochemical output that exceeds input, and the ecosystem nutrient capital is reduced. This period of increased losses usually lasts for only one or two years, because revegetation of the disturbed areas re-establishes the ecosystem's abilities to conserve and reaccumulate nutrients. However, if anything prevents revegetation, the period of nutrient loss and its total magnitude will be increased. If the forest remains undisturbed long enough so that organic matter in live trees, in minor vegetation, and in the soil ceases to accumulate, nutrient accumulation also ceases, and geochemical outputs become equal to geochemical inputs. Very old forests in which there is no net accumulation of organic matter are therefore less biogeochemically conservative than younger, actively growing forests.

The geochemical balance plays a major role in the long-term sustainability of the ecosystem.

Cycling of Nutrients within a Particular Ecosystem: The Biogeochemical Cycle

Trees and other plants take up most of the nutrients they require from the storehouse of nutrients in the soil, although they get most of their carbon and some of their sulphur and nitrogen from gases in the air. The storehouse in the soil is largely associated with decomposing organic matter (dead leaves, branches, animals), but some of the nutrients taken up from solution originated as geochemical inputs. The cycle of nutrient uptake, return to the soil by

various mechanisms, release of nutrients from decomposing organic matter, and the recovery of these nutrients by plant roots is called the *biogeochemical cycle*.

The nutrients taken up by plants are incorporated into plant tissues, but are subsequently lost when leaves and branches fall to the ground and when fine roots and entire plants die. Nutrients are also lost from plants when animals eat leaves or other plant parts, and when rainwater washes nutrients out of the leaves. The nutrients in dead plant parts and those washed out of plants are available for uptake by plants, either immediately or after organic matter has undergone decomposition. Most of the plant nutrients consumed by animals are returned to the ground fairly quickly in urine, feces, or dead animals, but some may become a geochemical output if the animals leave the area permanently. The critically important decomposition of organic matter in the soil is performed by fungi and bacteria, generally in partnership with soil animals of various sizes. These often-microscopic soil organisms are usually as important in the functioning of the forest ecosystem as the much more massive trees.

This plant-soil-plant or plant-animal-soil-plant cycle is very efficient in most forests. The layer of decomposing organic matter at the surface of the soil is usually full of fine roots, fungi, and bacteria. The fungi are often intimately associated with these very small roots in a mutually beneficial relationship called a *mycorrhiza* (literally, a 'fungus-root'; see Chapter 10, footnote 21 for a more detailed definition). These are incredibly efficient at recovering nutrients either directly from decomposing organic matter or from solution in the soil. Both roots and soil microbes secrete acids that attack soil minerals, thus accelerating geochemical nutrient inputs that are promptly taken up by plants as they need them, thereby being built into the biogeochemical cycle.

The biogeochemical cycle ensures that there is a constant circulation of nutrients in the ecosystem, so that there is always a supply of nutrients for uptake by plants. This is essential for their growth. The total amount of nutrients available for uptake will vary somewhat from year to year as annual variations in the weather affect geochemical inputs and decomposition processes, but the large accumulation of nutrients in the organic matter of the forest floor (decomposing leaves, branches, bark, stems, and roots at the surface of the mineral soil) normally ensures that the supply is reasonably constant.

The efficiency of the biogeochemical cycle determines how much of the geochemical inputs are retained in the ecosystem and how much 'leak out.' The characteristics of the cycle also determine the proportion of nutrients that are actively circulating in the ecosystem at any one time. If the circulation is very fast because of rapid decomposition of dead organic matter and efficient uptake by abundant fine roots, rapid plant growth can be supported by a relatively small total ecosystem supply of nutrients, most of which are contained in the living plants. Such forests can have very large leaf areas despite an underlying infertile soil, as long as they are not disturbed too frequently. This is the case in many tropical forests growing on nutrient-poor soils. In contrast, if the circulation is slow because of slow decomposition, nutrient availability may be low and plant growth correspondingly slow despite large quantities of nutrients in the ecosystem, most of which are tied up in a thick, slowly decomposing forest floor. This is the case in mature forests in cold northern areas and in old-growth forests in cool, humid climates, such as parts of the outer British Columbia coast. In the latter, much of the ecosystem's nutrient capital is immobilized in large quantities of slowly decomposing logs. Periodic disturbance may be necessary to stimulate the biogeochemical cycle if the productivity of these ecosystems is to be sustained. This need not be very frequent, however. Once every several centuries may be sufficient to have this effect. The actual frequency required to maintain a given level of ecosystem function depends on the climate, soil, and type of forest.

The speed at which nutrients circulate in the biogeochemical cycle is thus a major determinant of forest productivity. Much of the variation in forest productivity and plant species composition from place to place and from one forest age to another can be explained by differences in this cycle. The efficiency of the cycle also helps determine the sustainability of the ecosystem in the face of periodic disturbance. By determining the proportion of geochemical inputs that are captured and accumulated, the biogeochemical cycle determines the speed of recovery of the site's nutrient capital after disturbance, and thus its long-term productivity.

Internal Cycle: The Recycling Ethic in Plants

People generally appreciate most of the things they have to work hard for. Plants work very hard to get nutrients. They invest a large part, and sometimes the majority, of their annual photosynthetic production in growing fine roots and supplying mycorrhizal fungi with sugars to ensure that their leaves have the necessary nutrients and water. It is not surprising, therefore, that plants tend to 'hang on' to difficult-to-get nutrients if they can. Much of the nitrogen, phosphorus, and potassium (three essential nutrients) in leaves may be transferred by the plant into more permanent plant parts before the leaves are shed, and from stem sapwood (the live part of the stem) before it becomes heartwood (the dead part). Some trees are able to get half or more of some of the nutrients they need for new growth each year by this internal conservation of nutrients. The degree to which nutrients are conserved by internal cycling depends on the difficulty with which plants are able to find nutrients in the soil to provide for the growth that the local climate and other site conditions would permit.

The internal cycle is important as it helps plants to cope with year-to-year variations in nutrient uptake resulting from year-to-year variations in soil nutrient availability. Plants can take up nutrients in excess of their immediate needs during times of plenty, and, by recycling, can retain these for use in future months or years when there may be a shortage in the external supply. Internal cycling is relatively unimportant in a very young forest that is rapidly accumulating foliage biomass and nutrients. However, it can supply more than half the quantity of some nutrient elements needed for new growth in older forests in which the rate of leaf biomass accumulation has slowed down.

The relative importance of these three types of cycle varies for different nutrients, for different plant species, in different kinds of ecosystem, and at different ages of the forest. Clearly, it is difficult to make useful generalizations about forest sustainability, and about the response of ecosystems to, and their recovery from, disturbance unless one has an adequate grasp of the complexities of forest nutrition and ecosystem nutrient cycling.

The Constantly Changing Ecosystem: The Process of Ecological Succession

This book is mostly about change. It is therefore appropriate to spend some time discussing the processes by which unmanaged, undisturbed ecosystems change over time. These processes also account for how and why ecosystems change in the period following some natural or human-caused disturbances. Although the topic of change in vegetation over time was introduced in Chapter 3, it is necessary to examine the topic in more detail here.

Why Do Ecosystems Change?

There are many reasons. Outbreaks of mountain pine beetle (a small black beetle about five millimetres long whose larvae eat the live bark of some coniferous trees) periodically kill mature lodgepole pine trees over vast areas of British Columbia. The caterpillars of the spruce budworm moth regularly alter the forest landscapes in eastern Canada by eating the leaves and killing extensive tracts of mature balsam fir trees. Wind storms levelled about a third of the forests on northern Vancouver Island in 1907, while about 40 per cent of the commercial pine forests in some American southeastern states

were laid flat by wind in 1989. Periodic hurricanes have played a major role in the forested landscapes of the northeastern United States. Trees have been killed by fire over unbelievably large areas in Siberia, northern China, East Kalimantan (an Indonesian province on the island of Borneo), Alaska, and northern Canada.

Throughout human history, people have burned and cleared forests to establish farms, roads, or cities; or have harvested them periodically as part of either forest exploitation or sustainable forest management. There are forests in Japan that have been harvested more or less continuously for nearly a thousand years, and there are forests in Scandinavia and elsewhere in Europe that have been harvested as a part of organized forest management, generally by clearcutting, more than half a dozen times. Two world wars, but especially the First World War, damaged extensive areas of forest in Europe, as wars have done repeatedly over the past thousand years. The First World War completely deforested, devegetated, and severely damaged the soil over large areas in the vicinity of the great battle sites.

All of these types of disturbance remove forest cover and initiate a series of changes in soil condition, microclimate, microbes, animals, and plants. Given enough time before the next disturbance, these changes will return the ecosystem to its predisturbance condition. Even some of the most severely disturbed First World War battle sites now carry productive and often magnificent forests, or have already had one tree crop harvested and are growing a second. This process of recovery, which is largely under the control of the vegetation, is called *ecological succession*. It results in a series of living communities and associated soil and microclimatic conditions that successively occupy and are replaced in a particular area over time following disturbance. Each of these identifiable stages of recovery is called a *seral stage*.

Of course, several other types of ecosystem change are not controlled by the vegetation. Changes in climate (see Chapter 12) result in different patterns of ecosystem recovery from disturbance, and can cause changes in the species of otherwise undisturbed plant communities. The natural invasion of plant diseases or insect pests into areas where they were not found previously, or their accidental introduction by humans, can radically alter the vegetation of a region. Dutch elm disease, spread by bark beetles and the transport of beetle-infested logs from continent to continent, has killed large numbers of elm trees in eastern and central areas of Canada and the United States and in southern England. The introduction of rabbits and the prickly pear cactus into Australia earlier this century led to dramatic alterations in the natural vegetation over much of Australia until these 'pest' species were brought under control. Overpopulation by introduced deer in the Queen Charlotte Islands has resulted in significant changes in the abundance of some plant species. However, these are relatively unusual situations. In most cases, the type of vegetation in an area and its change over time are a consequence of plant processes.

Change Caused by Plants

The major patterns of change in plant communities following a disturbance are caused by the plants themselves. This is called *autogenic change*. It is the major process by which ecosystems recover from disturbance and by which pre-disturbance ecological conditions are re-established. Autogenic successional processes are thus analogous to the way your body mends broken bones or heals itself following a cut. The analogy is imperfect, however, because the ecosystem does not undergo irrevocable death or permanent loss of major components the way an individual dies of disease or accident, or loses a limb because of infection.

By their very presence, plants alter the physical and chemical characteristics of the soil and the temperature, light intensity, humidity, and wind speed beneath their canopy (the microclimate). Plants take up nutrients to create organic matter, which is returned in due course to the soil in the form of dead leaves, roots, stems, and whole plants. The storage of nutrients such as calcium, magnesium, and potassium in the permanent tissues of long-lived plants such as trees, and the creation of acids by tree roots and during the decomposition of organic matter, acidifies the soil. This increases the rate at which rocks and soil minerals are dissolved and at which the nutrients they contain are made available to plants. It also leads to the development of a 'soil' in material that was previously 'non-soil': loose unconsolidated material exposed by erosion or deposited by flooding rivers, for example.

Plant species vary in their ability to tolerate or benefit from the environmental conditions caused by disturbance. The exposed microclimate, the lack of organic matter, and the low availability of nutrients (especially nitrogen) in an area recently exposed by a landslide, by a retreating glacier, or by bulldozers on a construction site severely limits the types of plant that can invade the site. However, there are some hardy 'pioneers' with low nutrient demands that will tolerate drought and high surface-soil temperatures in the summer, and that benefit from the reduction in competition from other plant species. Several such plant pioneers also have the ability to fix atmospheric nitrogen and are thus independent of soil nitrogen, something that most plants cannot do, or do not do very well.

By modifying the microclimate and enriching the soil with organic matter, the pioneers reduce temperature extremes and increase the availability of soil moisture and nutrients. This makes it possible for less hardy plants to become established. However, these plants, once established, usually outgrow the pioneers, shading them out and excluding them from the site. This second wave of invaders further modifies the site, limiting the subsequent invasion of species to those that are able to tolerate the competition for light that they will experience.

This sequence of environmental alteration caused by the plants themselves is only one of several plant-related reasons why one observes a series of different plant communities occupying a site over time after the removal of the previous community. Other reasons include different rates at which plant species arrive at or 'find' such disturbed areas. Many pioneer species produce large quantities of seeds or spores every year, which are rapidly and efficiently distributed by wind, birds, or other animals. These plants are the first arrivals. The second community to occupy a disturbed site may simply be a group of species that are distributed more slowly: they are late arrivals. Later successional species may be those that are dispersed very slowly – it may take decades or even centuries for them to arrive. They may have large, heavy seeds that are not distributed widely, or they may produce seed infrequently, or they may not produce seed in quantity until they are several or even many decades old, unlike the pioneer species, which reproduce annually (herbs) or within their first few years of life (shrubs and some pioneer trees).

Yet another reason for the successional sequence of different plant communities may be differences in rates of growth and in the life span of the different plant species. Many pioneers are short-lived, fast-growing herbaceous species, such as grasses and flowering plants. The second community often consists of somewhat slower-growing shrubs. These may be replaced by fast-growing trees (but slower in the early years than the shrubs), followed in turn by initially slow-growing, shade-tolerant tree species.

The observed pattern of autogenic succession following disturbance – the sequence of seral stages – can be the result of any or all of the above processes, or simply the result of random chance: which species just happen to arrive and become established first. This can depend on which way the wind was blowing at the time of seed dispersal and whether a particular species in an adjacent undisturbed area was producing a lot or a little seed the year after disturbance. It can be influenced by the weather the year after the disturbance, the abundance of animals that eat seeds or seedlings, and various other factors that vary greatly from year to year. The sequence of autogenic successional development

can therefore be rather variable and unpredictable, especially in the first few years or decades. However, the overall pattern on a particular site or the type of soil in a particular climate varies only between fairly well-defined limits because of the limited number of plant species that can live and reproduce there. The more favourable the climate and soil, the greater the number of plant species that can occupy the area and the greater the variability and unpredictability of the successional sequence, and vice versa.

Change Caused by Animals or Disease

In most cases, autogenic processes are responsible for the variation in ecosystem structure and function over time. Other biological processes can sometimes be important, however. Invasions of insect pests that are not native to a region; epidemics of insects or small mammals, such as mice or rabbits, that are native to the area but are often present in low numbers; or the invasion or outbreak of plant disease organisms sometimes take control of the successional process either temporarily or for a prolonged period. This can result in a major alteration of vegetation. The presence of large numbers of rabbits or deer has been shown to affect vegetation dramatically by changing plant species composition or preventing the regeneration of trees. Goats have wreaked havoc with ecosystems in Mediterranean and African countries and elsewhere in the world by stripping the landscape of vegetation and causing serious soil erosion. The depredations by defoliating insects in forests, agricultural crops, or grasslands are legendary, and bark beetles can cause the death of certain types of forest over vast areas.

These *biogenic* successional processes sometimes operate continuously over long periods, such as the browsing by rabbits that has prevented shrubs and trees from invading the grassy 'downlands' of southern England and forests from replacing grasslands (such as the 'Watership Down' in Richard Adams's famous book by that name). More commonly, epidemics of diseases or defoliators are temporary disturbance factors that lead to a new autogenic succession.

Succession Related to Fire, Wind, or Other Non-Living Environmental Factors

Biological factors, such as insects and disease, are not the only reason why plants do not have it all their way as ecosystems change over time. Non-living factors such as fire, wind, or physical soil conditions also play a major, if not *the* major, role in some types of forest.

In climates that have hot, dry summers and frequent thunder and lightning storms, lightning-caused fires may be a characteristic feature of the ecosystem. Although such fires do not normally occur annually, they may occur often enough to interfere with the autogenic processes of succession and prevent the expected development of vegetation over time. Considering that the sequence of vegetation types caused by autogenic processes may span many centuries or even millennia, an average fire frequency of as high as once every fifty years or as low as once every several centuries can be quite sufficient to produce a pattern of succession that is more the result of fire than of plant-driven processes. For thousands of years, native peoples around the world have used fire to clear forests periodically in order to promote the growth in numbers of animals that they hunt and eat, to grow herbaceous or shrubby food crops, or simply to prevent forests from becoming too dense. The present condition of the vegetation in extensive areas of the world, including some of the world's tropical forests, is a result of this historical use of fire by humans.

Periodic wind storms can have much the same effect on autogenic succession. Typhoons, tornadoes, or any other type of strong or turbulent wind can level forest vegetation over extensive areas. Where damaging wind storms occur every one or two centuries, they can result in a substantially different type of forest than would otherwise develop by autogenic succession.

Deposition of soil by flooding rivers in valley floodplains, natural erosion of soil on steep, unstable slopes, and other landscape phenomena, such as boggy soils due to the presence of a spring, are examples of additional factors that can interfere with plant-caused patterns of vegetation change over time.

The actual patterns of ecosystem development after a disturbance can be the result of any one, all, or any combination of these successional mechanisms. As a result, ecosystem development can be quite variable, and the early stages in particular are sometimes rather unpredictable. However, this variation is not unlimited. Each type of forest generally has its own characteristic range of variation in development over time, and in many types of forest this range is quite narrow over ecological time scales of one to several centuries.

Primary and Secondary Succession

The processes of ecological succession can result in different patterns of change according to the type of environment and the intensity of the disturbance that initiates the change.

Succession in dry, hot, cold, wet, or nutrient-poor environments tends to be slow and quite predictable. Relatively few species can survive these physically extreme conditions, and communities of hardy pioneers are required to modify the environment before subsequent communities can successfully invade and occupy the area. Consequently, the sequence of seral stages is monotonously constant. Because these pioneers have to make substantial alterations to physical and chemical conditions before the next seral stage can take over, and because the harsh conditions generally limit the rate at which the pioneers can accomplish this change, the rate of succession tends to be slow.

In marked contrast, succession in more moderate and in favourable environments can be quite rapid, but is much less predictable in terms of seral stages, the species composition of different stages, and the rates of succession. The degree of environmental change between early and late succession is much less than in harsh environments, and the processes of succession often proceed rapidly because of the moderate or favourable conditions. Because many species can be successful in such environments, however, competition between species tends to be more intense, and chance events can determine which species participate in the succession. As a result, there can be significant and relatively unpredictable variation in the species composition and rates of seral change.

The difference in successional pattern and in the recovery from disturbance in dry, moist, and wet environments in coastal BC is illustrated in Figure 4.3.

The differences in patterns of succession that occur in different environments are also seen after different intensities of disturbance. Where disturbance results in the removal of all the environmental modifications caused by the previous succession – such as the soil, the modified microclimate, organic matter, the community of organisms – the recovery process is referred to as *primary succession.* Where disturbance only removes or modifies the existing plant community, leaving the modified soil condition more or less intact, the process is called *secondary succession.*

Landslides, an abandoned road, or a severely burned site undergo primary succession that generally involves an initially predictable series of pioneer and early seral stages and relatively slow rates of succession. Clearcuts, windthrown areas, or insect-killed stands will undergo secondary succession with somewhat less predictable and faster rates of successional change.

In general, primary succession is slower and more predictable in its earlier seral stages than secondary succession. Primary succession in physically favourable environments will obviously be faster and less predictable than in physically unfavourable environments. Similarly, secondary succession will be slower and more predictable in physically unfavourable environments than in moderate and favourable environments. The mid and later stages of primary succession are essentially similar to those

of secondary succession. An example of three seral stages in a forest secondary succession is shown in Figure 4.4.

Climax Forests
If autogenic succession is allowed to proceed uninterrupted for a long period, a seral stage eventually develops that is self-replacing. The species of plants in this stage are not replaced by another set of plant species; they reproduce themselves for many generations. This final, relatively stable, self-perpetuating stage is called the *climax* community.

In the absence of fire, wind, insects, or disease, the character of the climax forest is determined by the regional climate unless features of the soil (excessively wet or excessively well drained, for example) override the influence of climate. In many areas, fire, insects, or disease assert a sufficiently powerful influence to prevent the development of a climatic climax forest; there is a fire climax or a biotic climax forest instead.

Most forests of the world are now disturbed so frequently by fire, harvesting, wind, and biotic agents that true climax forests are increasingly rare. Only in the very humid forests of the world are the speed of autogenic succession and the relative absence of fire sufficient to permit climax forests, or a close approximation thereof, to develop over significant areas. As more and more of these forests are put under timber management, true climatic climax forests will be limited to parks, wilderness, and ecological reserves in areas with a low frequency of fire. If increasing recreational activities in these areas increases the risk of fire, or if there is substantial and rapid climate change (see Chapter 12), we may lose true climatic climax forests from some or all of these reserves.

Other Aspects of Forest Ecology
This chapter has briefly examined the two major processes that determine the functioning of ecosystems: energy capture and the circulation of nutrient elements. It has also briefly considered how ecosys-

Figure 4.3 Change in dry (xerarch), fresh (mesarch), and wet (hydrarch) environments in low elevation coastal British Columbia over time as primary succession proceeds from early seral conditions to climatic climax forest. The solid arrows beneath each of the three diagrams illustrate the degree of successional retrogression accompanying four levels of ecosystem disturbance. The dotted arrows show the degree of successional recovery that might occur over the next hundred years. Clearly, ecosystem recovery is affected by the type of environment and the degree of ecosystem disturbance (modified from Kimmins 1972, used with permission of the Canadian Institute of Forestry).

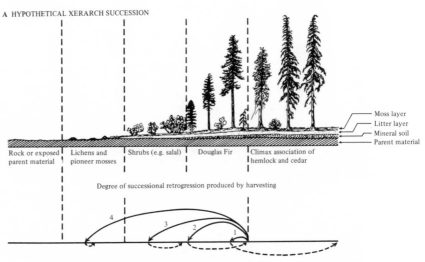

A HYPOTHETICAL XERARCH SUCCESSION

Moss layer
Litter layer
Mineral soil
Parent material

Rock or exposed parent material | Lichens and pioneer mosses | Shrubs (e.g. salal) | Douglas Fir | Climax association of hemlock and cedar

Degree of successional retrogression produced by harvesting

Extent of successional development occurring over (e.g.) 100 years post-harvesting

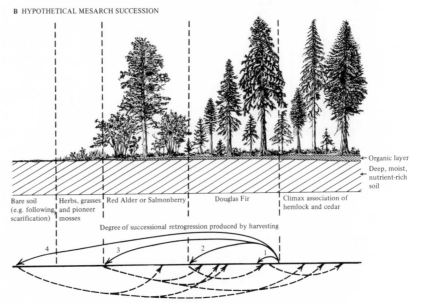

B HYPOTHETICAL MESARCH SUCCESSION

Organic layer
Deep, moist, nutrient-rich soil

Bare soil (e.g. following scarification) | Herbs, grasses and pioneer mosses | Red Alder or Salmonberry | Douglas Fir | Climax association of hemlock and cedar

Degree of successional retrogression produced by harvesting

Extent of successional development occurring over (e.g.) 100 years post-harvesting

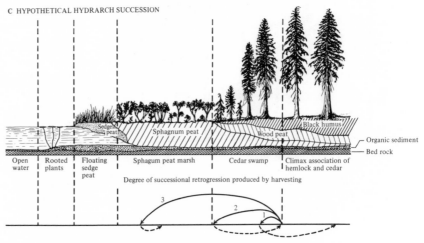

C HYPOTHETICAL HYDRARCH SUCCESSION

Sedge peat
Sphagnum peat
Wood peat
Black humus
Organic sediment
Bed rock

Open water | Rooted plants | Floating sedge peat | Sphagum peat marsh | Cedar swamp | Climax association of hemlock and cedar

Degree of successional retrogression produced by harvesting

Extent of successional development occurring over (e.g.) 100 years post-harvesting

A Young forest stage

B Mature closed canopy stage

C Climax or old-growth stage

Figure 4.4 Three successional stages in a forest following the removal of the previous forest by logging or natural disturbances

tems change over time. There are several other ecological conditions, components, and processes that need to be considered if we are to understand how a forest ecosystem works and how it responds to natural or management-related disturbance. These cannot be discussed in any detail in this book, but some of them are listed here and are referred to again in later chapters.

(a) The characteristics of the non-living environment are very important because they define what organisms can live in the area, the rate of ecosystem recovery from disturbance, and the functional processes (energy capture and storage, nutrient cycling) of the ecosystem that determine its productivity. If the non-living environment is not severely altered, and if there is a source of plant seeds and spores, microbes, and animals that can reinvade the disturbed area, the original ecosystem condition will redevelop in time.

Many aspects of the non-living environment are not greatly altered by most types of ecosystem disturbance. Elevation, aspect, slope, soil depth and texture, soil mineralogy, and regional climate are not altered by forest management or 'normal' types of natural disturbance. Microclimate, soil fertility, and the physical structure or 'architecture' of the soil may be altered, but these normally recover quite rapidly under the influence of autogenic successional processes. Where they recover slowly, the successional development of the ecosystem may be delayed.

(b) The genetic and biological diversity of organisms available for the recolonization of disturbed areas determines the degree to which the ecosystem's potential to recover is achieved. If disturbance removes all living organisms over very large areas, such as hundreds of square kilometres, ecosystem recovery will be much slower than if the living community has been removed over only a small area, such as a few hectares. The initial stages of recovery in very large disturbed areas will be dominated by widely dispersed pioneer plant species or species that survived the disturbance. Many 'late successional' species may require many decades or even centuries before they are able to reinvade the area and become re-established. In smaller areas of disturbance, a wide variety of plant species may be able to invade the area quite quickly, but only those that are able to compete effectively will become established. Where reinvasion of trees is assisted by humans (such as by tree planting in large wildfire areas or large clearcuts), re-establishment of the forest can be quite rapid even in large areas of disturbance.

The size of the disturbed area can thus have a big influence on the pattern and speed of ecosystem recovery. This is seen in nature, where ecosystem recovery after an extensive midsummer wildfire or catastrophic winter wind storm is very different from recovery that follows the death of a single large tree by lightning strike or windthrow. Similarly, succession in a thousand-hectare clearcut will generally be different from that in a ten-hectare clearcut. Size of disturbance alone is not the sole determinant of succession, however. It also depends upon the severity of the disturbance (how many of the original species survive), and the climate and soil in the area. The latter two factors affect the ease with which invading species can become established.

(c) The many and varied processes that are the focus of interest of population and community ecologists play a major role in determining rates of invasion of one seral community by the species of the subsequent community, and in the species composition of any particular seral stage. These processes determine the ability of individual species to compete and survive, and the duration of seral stages. This, in turn, influences the overall rate of ecosystem change and recovery from disturbance.

Understanding population and community ecology involves far more information than can be summarized here. The birth rate of animals and the rate of seed or spore production by plants, the ability of these organisms to disperse and find environments that are not fully occupied by other organisms (or environments in which they can compete and survive), together with their death rate, will help to determine the abundance and distribution of plants and animals across the landscape. A wide variety of beneficial or detrimental interactions between the different species and between different individuals of a single species is also involved in creating and maintaining change in individual communities found in ecosystems.

For further information about the processes that regulate populations and the structure and species composition of communities, you may wish to consult one of the standard textbooks listed in the bibliography.

The Concept of Ecological Rotations

The complexity of factors that in combination determine the rate and pattern of ecosystem recovery from disturbance leads to the concept of *ecological rotations:* the time taken for a particular ecosystem condition to recover to its pre-disturbance condition after a particular type, intensity, and extent of disturbance. This varies greatly according to the type of ecosystem and the particular ecosystem component or condition that one is considering. If one is concerned about thousand-year-old trees (for the few tree species that live this long), clearly the ecological rotation cannot be less than a thousand years, regardless of the type of ecosystem. If one is interested in very tall and large-diameter trees, regrowth of trees to such a size may require only one or two centuries (or even less for some species on some sites) or many centuries for other species on other sites. If, on the other hand, one is concerned with ecosystem function (productivity, nutrient cycling), this can often recover within decades but can take as long as centuries, depending on the type of ecosystem and the character of the disturbance.

Estimation of ecological rotations is clearly something that requires a very site-specific and species-specific evaluation. Generalizations are simply not very helpful. One must consider the type, intensity, extent, and frequency of disturbance in conjunction with evaluations of the non-living and living components of the ecosystem, its functional and successional processes, and how these vary over time if one is to be able to draw useful conclusions about the ecological impacts of a specific disturbance on the sustainability of an ecosystem under a specific disturbance regime. This topic is the subject of most of the rest of this book, and we will return again to the topic of ecological rotations in the final chapter.

Summary

Forest ecosystems are complex functional systems that can be understood, and whose future condition in response to particular types of disturbance can be reasonably well predicted, based on a combination of practical experience of specific local ecosystems and a knowledge of forest ecology. There is no magic here. There is no mystery other than where we have not yet undertaken the necessary ecological research. Failure to understand or accurately predict forest ecosystems reflects a still incomplete knowledge of their ecological processes.

There are a few broad parallels between an individual organism and an ecosystem: they are both highly complex, organized, and integrated systems. However, as noted in Chapter 3, the analogy is limited. Ecosystems do not 'die' the way individual organisms do after severe physical trauma or disease. They recover by the processes of ecological succession, and the recovery pattern is rarely comparable to the developmental stages of an individual organism. An ecosystem is not an individual organism even though there are some characteristics common to these different levels of biological integration.

There has been much adulation by some environmentalists of natural disturbance of forest ecosystems by fire, disease, insects, and wind. These disturbance events and the subsequent successional recovery have been referred to as the 'rebirthing of nature.' Yet at the same time, human-related disturbances have been considered to be 'ecosystem destruction,' and terms like 'environmental rape' and 'the crucifixion of the environment' have been used.

An ecological evaluation reveals that each type of disturbance, whether it is human-caused or the result of non-human events, has its own characteristic effect on a particular ecosystem. A clearcut is not identical to a wildfire, just as a windthrown forest is not identical to a disease-killed forest. However, all these disturbances affect the production ecology of the site. They all affect nutrient cycling. They all cause some degree of change to the microclimate and the soil. All of them change the plant, animal, and microbial life in the area. And all of them initiate a new sequence of successional development.

In the short run, there are significant ecological differences in ecosystems affected by the different types of disturbance, but in the longer term, the key ecological consequence is that a new successional sequence has been initiated. Different disturbances will lead to initial differences in successional patterns, but as time passes the difference in the ecological condition resulting from a specific type of disturbance steadily diminishes as succession returns the forest to its original condition. This phenomenon is called *successional convergence*. Where the frequency of disturbance is low (infrequent fires or forest harvesting on long rotations) the condition of the recovered ecosystem is influenced more by the pattern of ecological succession than by the type of disturbance. Where the disturbance frequency is high (short-rotation forestry or frequent wind storms), the character of the disturbance is reflected in the form and function of the ecosystem.

CHAPTER 5

A Brief Primer on Forestry

Introduction

One reason for the frequent conflict between foresters and environmentally concerned members of the general public has been a lack of understanding by many foresters and non-foresters of what sustained-yield forestry is really all about. A lack of recognition by many foresters of the rapidly changing public attitude towards the environment in general, and forests in particular, has not helped. Similarly, the lack of understanding of each other's objectives that has existed between some environmentalists and some of those who manage the world's forested landscapes has contributed to the polarization of the forestry/environment debate.

Before discussing the various forestry-related issues that are the topic of the following chapters, it is probably useful to have a quick review of the major principles and concepts of sustainable forest management. This should help clarify why, when, where, and how forestry evolved as a human activity; what forestry attempts to achieve; and the major mechanisms that have been developed over the centuries to help foresters attain management goals. An understanding of this topic should help readers evaluate the subsequent discussions of various environmental issues in forestry. It should also help them distinguish between sustainable forestry and forestry that results in 'degradation' of the forest environment: a reduction in productivity and biodiversity, and various other outcomes that society is judging to be unacceptable. As noted in Chapter 4, the science of ecology provides no basis for making such value judgments. They are a product of society's current value system. As a result, what is considered by the public to be good or bad forestry changes over time as society's attitudes towards resources and the environment change.

Before proceeding to a brief primer on the basic concepts of forestry, let us establish in rather general terms what sustained-yield forestry is, and quickly review its development at various times and places in human history. The entire discussion in this chapter represents one vision of what forestry should be. The actual forestry that is practised is frequently quite a bit different, sometimes for good reasons and sometimes not.

A Definition of Forestry

Many people in North America think that forestry is nothing more than logging or timber harvesting. This is not surprising. Compared to Europe, our industrial use of the forest is very recent, and much of the logging in western Canada and in the Pacific Northwest of the United States is still taking place in old-growth and previously unmanaged natural second-growth forests. Relatively few forests that are being harvested in Canada were established as an act of forest management, and tree-tending activities are much less visually obvious than clearcutting or other methods of timber harvesting.

The public's image of a forester is often a person with a hard hat and a chain saw who cuts trees down, rather than a silviculturist who, like a farmer (an agriculturist), harvests, regenerates, tends, and harvests trees again. The public thinks of someone driving a harvesting machine or a logging truck, rather than a professional resource management planner who is concerned with more than just growing and harvesting trees. Even where other aspects of silviculture and non-timber forest management activities are taking place, the most unforgettable impression a non-forester usually gets as he or she drives down an 'active' forest road is a fully loaded logging truck coming the other way!

Harvesting the tree crop is an extremely important part of silviculture in particular and forestry in general, just as the harvest of raspberries, cabbages, corn, and milk is a vital part of agriculture. We could not buy food at the store, or lumber for home repairs at the lumber yard, if it were not for the people who do the harvesting. And, just like agriculture, the bills for planting, protecting, and tending new tree crops cannot be paid until the previous tree crop has been harvested and sold.

But forestry is much more than just harvesting trees, just as farming is much more than just pick-ing fruit and vegetables. Tree crops must be established, managed, and protected. The soil fertility and physical condition must be maintained. And this must be done in a manner that does not cause unacceptable changes in the aesthetic quality of the landscape or damage to water, and which maintains or enhances a variety of other values, such as wildlife habitat. These other values are generally more important in forestry than in farming. They constitute a major difference between these two types of human activity. Silvicultural practices are normally much more constrained by the need to consider non-crop values than are agricultural practices, which take place on land that has generally been dedicated to food crop production with the blessing of society.

Forestry has been defined as the art, science, and practice of managing forested landscapes to provide a sustained production of a variety of goods and services for society. In concept, forestry is definitely people-oriented. If this is not so in practice, one can question whether what is taking place in the landscape is truly forestry. Professional forest management is all about providing one or more of the following from our forested landscapes: jobs, timber products, fish and wildlife habitat, high quality of water and recreational opportunities (including wilderness), hunting, trapping, range values, visually attractive landscapes and views, landscape or community protection (against wind and water erosion, avalanche, and cold air drainage), and, to an increasing extent, a sink for the atmospheric 'greenhouse gas' CO_2 (see Chapter 12). The order of importance of the items in this list will vary from one place and time to another. In many cases only a subset of this list will be managed for in a specific location, according to the local or regional needs of people. Other values that are not on this list may be important in particular forests.

Some people think of forestry only in terms of silviculture: the art and science of establishing, tending, protecting, and harvesting a tree crop. This view tends to dominate where the forest industry is given the mandate to harvest and manage the tree resource only, while other resources are managed by non-forestry agencies. In this situation, which exists in much of Canada, forestry becomes synonymous with timber production. Where industrial foresters are responsible for, and can reap the benefits from, the management of a variety of resource values, the balance between silviculture and management for other values by foresters will reflect more closely what society wants and is prepared to pay for. The balance between management for timber and management for non-timber values thus reflects the political, administrative, and policy framework established by governments.

Growing trees for harvest is certainly a major preoccupation in many of the world's managed forests, but producing timber products is only one, and in some cases even a minor, forest management objective. For example, in some steep, erodible mountain areas of Europe, the forests are managed primarily for protection against landslides, erosion, and avalanche. In many parts of the world, watershed protection is a major value provided by forests. In watersheds with steep erodible slopes and periodic torrential rain such as tropical monsoons or typhoons, tree cutting may be limited to maintaining the health and stability of the trees to ensure watershed protection. Where timber production is an objective within water supply areas, silvicultural activities are (or should be) limited to those that will maintain regulated flows of clear, cool, clean water, or those that will not detrimentally change the natural variation in water quality and flow over time. In dry areas in which much of the annual precipitation falls as winter snow, forest cutting may be done in watershed areas to promote snow accumulation and regulate snow melt. The resulting timber production is a secondary consideration. In heavy snowpack areas, patch harvesting may be done to lengthen the period of spring snowmelt in order to reduce spring flooding and damage to fish habitat.

The provision of hunting, fishing, and forage for domestic livestock, or simply the provision of wildlife habitat, is a very important function of many forests. In fact, the earliest forest regulations in Europe were associated with protecting the hunting rights of wealthy landowners and the nobility. Where these values are important, methods of silviculture and patterns of forest harvesting may be designed specifically to provide or protect these values, and a significant proportion of the potential timber production may be foregone in order to produce these other values. For example, more damage is done to trees in some German forests by managed deer populations than by the acid rain damage that is talked about so much. The animal damage is accepted because the provision of deer hunting is a major management objective in these forests, and deer hunting in some European countries can provide a major portion of the revenue from the forest. The combination of deer management and timber management yields far more social value from the forest than timber management alone. However, this occurs only where the forest company, private land owner, or government agency managing the forest has rights to manage and harvest both the trees and the wildlife for profit. In many cases, such as in Oregon and Washington, where extensive damage is done to planted seedlings by deer, and to larger trees by bears, the rights to manage for timber are separate from the rights to manage wildlife for profit, and timber producers must simply try to protect their trees from wildlife, or tolerate the damage.

As you proceed through this book, the discussion will focus largely on those aspects of silviculture and timber harvesting that have the greatest potential impact on the environment, on non-timber values, and on public opinion. But do not forget that forest management must generally deal with a much broader range of issues than timber management. Wildlife, water, range, recreation, and other social benefits provided by forests must also be managed for. Specific details of how this is, or should be, done will not be covered here.

How Old Is Forestry? When and Where Did It First Develop?

As a human activity to ensure continuing future supplies of various things that people want from forests, forestry has had a long and somewhat checkered history. Most of the earlier attempts either failed or were short-lived. Modern silviculture and forest management as we know them today are only about four centuries old. In most cases, forestry evolved primarily as an activity to ensure continuing supplies of timber products. Although some early European forest reserves were established as hunting preserves or protection forests, the idea of integrated multiple resource management (the management of a forested region to produce sustained supplies of many different resource values) is really quite recent.

It is interesting to note that whenever and wherever societies have tried to develop forestry, it has always been for similar reasons, and there has always been a similar sequence of developmental stages. Hidden in this common historical pattern is an important message about how forestry should be practised.

Stage 1. Unregulated exploitation of local forests for fuel, domestic timber supplies, and military/industrial timber; unregulated clearing of forests for agriculture, wildlife habitat, or domestic stock grazing.

This leads to one or more of: (1) overcutting of local forests, which results in local shortages of fuel, timber, and other forest values, leading to (2) unregulated exploitation of more distant forests, and subsequent overcutting of these forests, and/or (3) colonization of forest resources in other countries by war or commerce, and their subsequent overexploitation.

Stage 2. Institution of legal and political mechanisms or religious taboos to regulate the rate and pattern of forest exploitation to ensure future supplies of forest products and other values. This is the beginning of forestry. It usually involves a centralized, authoritarian, non-ecological, administrative

approach based on legislation and regulation rather than on a knowledge of how forests grow, how they respond to management, and how ecosystems function.

This leads to: (1) failure of the rigid, non-ecological, overgeneralized administrative approach, and (2) a recognition that living, changing, spatially variable forest ecosystems cannot be managed sustainably unless management is based on regulations and techniques that reflect the local ecological characteristics of the resource.

Stage 3. Development of an ecological approach to silviculture and timber management. Although growing and harvesting trees is usually the major focus, where this is done in an environmentally sound manner a sustainable supply of a variety of non-timber resource values is also provided.

This provides sustainable management of many, if not most, of the biological resources of the forest, but does not necessarily satisfy all of a 'developed' society's desires with respect to forested landscapes.

Stage 4. Development of a forest management strategy that is not only environmentally and silviculturally sound but also responsive to an increasingly diverse set of demands by society and to the needs of local communities. This stage is sometimes referred to as 'social forestry.' A much wider range of resource values is managed than in Stage 3, including aesthetics, spiritual values, and wilderness. These values may have little to do with the environmental soundness and sustainability of forestry, but may be of great interest to a society whose wealth and standard of living allows it to be concerned about such values.

Looking at the history of forestry over the past two thousand years, we see that in most cases this evolutionary sequence did not progress past Stage 2, which sometimes occurred directly after the overcutting of local forests or only after history-making wars, colonization of forests in other countries, or both. Political upheavals, social unrest, war, famine, and pestilence, as well as lack of scientific knowledge and a frequent lack of political commitment to good stewardship of forest lands – one or more of these have been involved in the many failures of forestry to proceed from Stage 2 to Stage 3, the stage of modern, ecological forest management.

The Greeks and Romans made a good try, and the recorded writings of Theophratus, the 'grandfather' of botany, show that several aspects of the ecology and silviculture of the major commercial tree species in Greece were well known as far back as 300 BC. For example, he reported on the relationship between the soil and climate where a tree grows and whether it should be used for ships' masts or for fine cabinetry. But the Greeks and Romans failed to get past Stage 2. Their empires and social organization declined before they could apply their accumulated ecological knowledge in reaching Stage 3.

It was left to monks in the monastic settlements of central Europe in the early centuries of the second millennium AD to establish the foundations of modern forestry. With time for silvicultural and agricultural experimentation, they learned about plants and soils and developed methods of forest regeneration and tree culture. Over the years these methods were modified and elaborated into the modern techniques of silviculture. However, in spite of this silvicultural knowledge, the growth of the European population and the arrival of the Industrial Revolution led to overexploitation of their forests for fuel, fodder, industrial wood, and shipbuilding timber. Combined with the heavy demands of frequent wars, this led to local and regional timber shortages. In essence this was a return to Stage 1 from the beginnings of Stage 3. The resulting shortages of forest products led to government-imposed restrictions on harvesting, which is typical of Stage 2. The frequent failure of these regulations to achieve their goals, combined with greater knowledge about how to tend and manage forests, eventually led to the development of the much more ecologically and silviculturally sound forestry that we can see in much of Europe today (at least where it has not been disrupted by

forest decline, which in many cases may be a result of chronic air pollution and acid rain).

The history of forestry in North America is much more recent, but it shows the same general pattern of events. The early European settlers in the United States brought with them a silviculturally sound conservation attitude, but in the face of seemingly unlimited forest resources and a largely unregulated free-enterprise economy, this was soon replaced by profligate forest exploitation. Travellers returning to the United States from timber-short Europe were appalled at the speed, extent, and manner of forest cutting. This led to the development of the modern American conservation ethic and the U.S. federal government forestry administration. Thus, both the national forestry agency and environmentalism in the United States had the same origin: the desire to conserve forests. In contrast to exploitive logging, forestry around the world has always had its origins in some aspect of conservation.

The history of Canadian forestry is even more recent, especially in the west, but again it shows much the same pattern. Unregulated early exploitation near population centres led to colonization and exploitation of more remote forests. The realization that provincial and national shortages would eventually occur in the absence of regulation led to the institution of legalistic and administrative mechanisms. These were intended to ensure sustained future yields of timber while at the same time generating social and economic values from the forest with which to develop the social infrastructure and support services of the country. Well-intentioned, these early Canadian attempts to institute sustained-yield forestry generally lacked a sound ecological foundation, and there was often a lack of political will to enforce the basic mechanisms of forest management and provide the financial support needed to sustain early efforts in silviculture. As a result, modern sustainable forest management for a wide variety of resource values has been slow to become established in Canada. Lack of public pressure to force governments to invest adequately in forestry has allowed this situation to continue, and, consequently, the standards of forest management in Canada still leave much to be desired.

Recognition by forest managers of the frequent ineffectiveness of the non-ecological, administrative approach to achieving sustainable forestry is leading to the adoption of an ecological basis for forest management planning and silviculture (the transition from Stage 2 to Stage 3). As this book was being written, however, rapidly growing public concern about the environment in general and forestry in particular created pressure in Canada for the transition to the final stage of forestry: social forestry. This pressure occurred before the benefits of the ecology-based silvicultural stage of forestry have had time to become apparent. Unfortunately, the public concern that has produced strong demands for additional parks, wilderness, and wildlife protection has not resulted in increased investment in improved forestry that will ultimately be necessary if the public's demand for better forestry on publicly owned forest land is to be satisfied.

The history of forestry thus reveals that this human activity is, and always has been, fundamentally concerned with satisfying the needs of people and the conservation of resources, even though this has not always been obvious from the way forests have been managed (or mismanaged). Initiated to ensure the conservation of forests and a sustained supply of a variety of forest values, forestry passes through several stages during which it fails, more or less, to achieve this goal. Eventually it matures into an ecology-based, environmentally sound, and socially responsive activity that satisfies most of society's demands on its forested landscapes.

The extent to which different countries have passed through this developmental sequence has a lot to do with national wealth and standards of living. As the psychologist Maslow pointed out in his hierarchy of human needs, people's primary concern is ensuring that they and their children have adequate food and water, shelter, and personal security. Only when these basic survival needs have been satisfied will they express concern about issues like environmental quality, resource conservation, and biodiversity. Parents of starving children in a Third World country will cut down the last tree on the hillside, regardless of what that does to the quality of the environment or whether it causes the loss of species, if they perceive this action to be in the interests of themselves and their offspring. Countries that lack these basic human needs will tend to remain in Stage 1 or Stage 2 of the development sequence. It is not surprising, therefore, that the World Commission on Environment and Development (the Brundtland Commission) concluded that the greatest single threat to the global environment and conservation is poverty in the Third World. There is certainly room for much improvement in the way the forests of developed countries are being managed. However, in North America, we have the possibility, because of our wealth and level of education and social support services, of moving through Stage 3 and into Stage 4, a transition characteristic of what has been referred to as a 'post-industrial society.' Many Third World countries do not have this option.

An Outline of Forestry

If the job of a professional forester had to be described in a single word, it would have to be *planning*. Forestry is unique among human activities because of the very long time scales involved in the production of most tree crops. So much can change over a single crop rotation: human population size, technology, climate, economics, land-use demands, politics, and so on. Decisions about forest management made today have implications that span several human generations, during which enormous social, political, economic, technical, and environmental changes will undoubtedly occur. This requires very careful planning.

Wise decisions about how forested landscapes should be managed can result only from careful planning. This involves inventories of current forest resource values, assessments of current social demands for these and other values, predictions of future demands, and predictions about how well each of several alternative site-specific management strategies would satisfy present and future social demands on the forest. This critically important planning function must go on continually to update plans in the light of ever-changing circumstances. The mechanism by which planning is accomplished for a particular forest is the *management plan*.

The Management Plan

In contrast to unregulated exploitation, modern, integrated forest management begins with a statement of the overall land management objectives: What values are to be provided from the forested landscape? Where, in what quantity, and how should the supply of these values vary over time? The overall objectives are defined by the forest owner, subject to prevailing laws governing land use, water, wildlife, and so on. Where the land owner is a timber company, the objectives will almost inevitably be dominated by economic timber production, unless the company also has economic control over non-timber values. Where the public owns the land, forest management objectives are determined by their elected government, and are expressed in the land-use strategy adopted by the government and the laws and regulations developed to achieve the objectives.

In a democracy in which the majority of forest land is publicly owned, people will generally get the forestry they have 'chosen.' The forestry that is practised will reflect the philosophy of the government they have elected. If the majority of people do not like the type of forestry practised by a particular government, and feel strongly enough about it, they will either persuade the government to change its policies or they will change the government. Where a forest is privately owned, or where there are private timber rights in a publicly owned forest, the quality of forestry will reflect both the owner's objectives

and the government's willingness to ensure that any publicly owned values – such as wildlife, fish, water, air, and aesthetics – are protected.

With the land-use strategy and overall objectives of management agreed upon, the next job in preparing a management plan is to describe the ecology of the forested landscape and to make an inventory of its resource values: its climates, soils, topography, vegetation, hydrology, fish and wildlife, and the frequency and intensity of natural disturbance phenomena such as wind, fire, insects, and diseases. Also described are its cultural heritage, range, hunting, mineral, and recreational values; its legal status with respect to land ownership, existing rights, and licences for such things as water use and hunting; and its present state of development: roads, bridges, human settlements, agriculture, mining, and so on – in short, a complete description of everything about its status and all available details about its history: how it got to be that way. All this information is placed in Part 1 of the management plan. This defines the biophysical and social constraints on management, and describes the management opportunities that are defined by the ecology, geography, and sociology of the area to be managed. It identifies the degree to which the initial statement of the overall management objectives can be achieved, and may sometimes result in a modification of this objective. Having defined the resources and their potentials, the plan presents a set of detailed objectives that reflect the intent of the overall management objective. These detailed objectives define a specific objective for each of the resource values identified in Part 1.

Part 2 of the plan explains how the forest manager will achieve the specific objectives of management, given the opportunities and constraints described in Part 1. It is a description of the long-term management strategy over at least one rotation, but it should also consider in the broadest terms the possible future conduct of management over several tree-crop rotations. The plan defines the short-term and medium-term management activities that will be undertaken to implement this strategy. Typically, Part 2 of the plan provides a very detailed account of the coming year's activity, a fairly detailed five-year plan, and the major features of the next twenty years of management or some other intermediate planning period. The plan is updated frequently so that it always provides a view of what will be done in the short term, medium term, and long term; the detail becoming progressively less the further one goes into the future. Successful management planning and implementation of the plan thus requires that foresters know what area of forest they will be managing over the next twenty or more years. Good forestry usually requires that the foresters have long-term tenure of the land they are managing: either they own it or, if it is publicly owned, they have a long-term management contract with the people's representative, the government. Without such tenure arrangements, the long-term planning and economic investment that is the cornerstone of sustainable landscape management cannot or will not be done.

Part 2 of the plan contains separate sections dealing with each of the specific management objectives stated in Part 1. For example, there will be separate chapters on the management of timber (including the planned silviculture), water, wildlife, and recreation in a management plan for a forest in which these four values are important and for which specific management objectives have been stated. A value is not normally managed for unless it is explicitly identified in the management objectives – hence the importance of the accurate statement of these objectives.

Finally, the plan describes how the forester will monitor compliance with it, how the achievement of the objectives of management can be assessed (performance standards), how records of silvicultural and management work will be kept, and how frequently the plan will be updated.

The management plan is the single most important document in forest management. It states the management objectives, determines how they will be achieved, provides a record of work done, and monitors progress. Unfortunately, plans that conform to this description are not always prepared and used. Some of the shortcomings in North American forestry can be attributed to the failure to prepare such plans, and the failure of educational institutions, responsible for producing graduate foresters, to adequately educate and train them in the development of these plans. The failure to have a clear statement of objectives, a plan to achieve them, an adequate system of record keeping, an explicit set of realistic performance standards, and a system for monitoring compliance has resulted in much ad hoc and short-term planning and a frequent failure to achieve the objectives of the landowner.

In British Columbia, the separation of management for water, fish, wildlife, and timber production into different government ministries has weakened the planning process and has often resulted in incomplete management plans. Within the management of the timber resource, too much emphasis in the past was placed on the timber-harvesting phase of planning, to the detriment of future timber values and some non-timber values. The failure of the government to provide the human and financial resources or the financial incentives needed to undertake the necessary planning on public lands has been a major reason for the lack of adequate planning. Lack of appropriate long-term tenures (long-term management contracts between the government and forestry companies) on many publicly owned forest lands has prevented the necessary long-term planning and has limited the ability of foresters to respond to changing weather, fire, insect, and disease conditions that is so necessary in sustained-yield forestry. Lack of long-term planning and tenure may restrict a forester's ability to disperse activities across the landscape in a manner that satisfies aesthetic, wildlife, and water quality considerations, and can lead to the use of newly constructed forest roads before they have become stable ('matured'), thereby increasing the risk of erosion or road collapse on steep slopes.

Successful conservation of the many values of British Columbia's forest will require the commitment of a significantly greater financial expenditure than the public has been willing to make in the past. This commitment to the planning and practice of forestry is essential if our forests are to be managed sustainably.

Management at the Stand Level: The Silvicultural System

In most forests, production of logs for lumber, pulp, or other end uses is an important management goal. The planning and management of this production, which is collectively called timber management, has two major components: (1) silviculture – the growth of tree crops on a particular area from seedling establishment to final harvest, and (2) the organization and dispersion of the silvicultural activities over the entire geographical extent of the forest being managed. The second of these components is described later in the chapter.

A *silvicultural system* is a planned program of activities involved in producing tree crops, from site preparation before or after the previous harvest, through seedling establishment and the tending of the young forest, to intermediate harvests (thinnings), preparations for the regeneration of the next tree crop, and the final harvest. The time period over which this set of activities is conducted is called the *rotation*. Silvicultural systems are generally named according to the method of final harvest, which largely determines the type of silvicultural activities that will have to be undertaken over the subsequent rotation. There are two major categories of silvicultural systems: *even-aged* and *uneven-aged*.

As the name suggests, all the trees in a stand[6]

---

6 A stand is a group of trees that results from a specific final harvest or natural disturbance event, so the term is most applicable to even-aged management. A stand in an uneven-aged forest is simply an area that is defined by the forester for purposes of planning a harvest and the other silvicultural activities that will be applied to that area.

managed under an even-aged system are about the same age. All the crop trees are either cut at the same time, or the stand is harvested in two or three 'passes' several years apart in a manner that results in the establishment of a new population of crop tree seedlings over a relatively short period of time, such as a few years. A forest landscape managed under the even-aged system consists of a mosaic of stands of different ages spanning from the time of the establishment of a new tree crop up to the age at which the final harvest of the tree crop occurs. A significant area of forest is required for all the annual age-classes of this type of forest to be represented: at least several hundred, and normally several thousand, hectares.

In contrast, all ages of trees are found over relatively small areas (a few hectares) in a forest managed under an uneven-aged system. Rather than tree harvests only occurring once (the final harvest) or a few times (final harvest plus intermediate harvests, which are called *thinnings)* over a rotation, as is the case in even-aged stand management, harvests may be taken from a particular uneven-aged stand every five to ten years. These frequent partial harvests may remove only the largest trees, but some of the smaller trees may also be cut in order to maintain a desired age-class structure (a particular mixture of trees of different ages) and size-class structure in the forest.

Silvicultural Activities in Even-Aged Stand Management: The Stand Cycle

The following description of silvicultural activities refers to stands managed under the even-aged system of silviculture. The sequence of stages of stand development in which these activities are applied, from seedling establishment to final harvest, is called the *stand cycle*.

Site Preparation

After the previous forest is harvested, or after natural disturbance, such as fire or windthrow, the site is often not in the ideal condition for seedlings of the desired tree species[7] to be planted or to become established naturally. There may be too much logging debris (logging slash: branches, unused upper sections of the stem, and broken logs) and a variety of unwanted tree species, herbs, and shrubs that may interfere with the establishment and growth of a new crop of the desired trees species. Foresters can make things better for the seedlings of the crop species by burning the smaller components of the slash (the branches and small logs: *slashburning* – see Chapter 7); by moving the slash around with machines to create places where young trees can be planted or seedlings can become established naturally *(mechanical site preparation)*; or by using fire, manual, mechanical, or chemical (herbicide) methods to reduce the 'weed' competition (see Chapter 8). Competing vegetation can sometimes be controlled by using sheep or cattle, benefiting both the seedlings and the farmer or rancher.

Regeneration

When the site is in an appropriate condition for the tree species the forester wishes to grow, it can be planted or the forester can wait for nature to do the job.

Many deciduous broadleaved species resprout from cut stumps (they 'coppice,' like maple) or from buds on the roots (they 'sucker,' like aspen). If these species are to be grown as the next crop, the sprouts or suckers will promptly 'reforest' the area for you. Alternatively, the forester may rely on seeds of desired tree species being blown or carried by animals from the adjacent uncut forest. Both mechanisms, and the germination of seeds of the desired species

that were already present in the upper soil, can result in the establishment of a new crop of trees by *natural regeneration.*

Natural regeneration has the advantage of being 'free,' although harvesting costs may be increased by the use of harvesting methods or silvicultural systems that are needed to promote natural regeneration. In many cases in the past, naturally regenerated seedlings have had better survival and early growth rates than planted seedlings, because of mistakes in one or more of the ways in which the seedlings were grown, the way they were stored while awaiting planting, and the way they were handled and planted. Planted seedlings are often more heavily browsed by wildlife in the first year after planting than their natural counterparts, because they have been fertilized and watered in the nursery, which makes them more palatable and nutritious to herbivores than the natural regeneration. Natural regeneration ensures that the local genetic types are maintained in the forest, although planted seedlings are almost always grown from seed collected locally or under very similar environmental conditions. In fact, planting will often increase the genetic diversity of a forest since most trees in a natural stand are closely related and may even have come from only one or two parent trees (e.g., a Douglas-fir forest after a wildfire). Seedlings grown from seed collected from many ecologically similar but spatially separate sites will generally have a broader genetic diversity than natural regeneration. Consequently, there is somewhat less concern about the genetic aspects of regeneration than in the past. Natural regeneration usually, but not always, requires the use of much smaller clearcuts than can successfully be regenerated by planting because of the need for microclimatic modification and for the input of seed from the adjacent mature forest. For many species, especially late seral and climax shade-tolerant or shade-demanding species, use of final harvest methods other than clearcutting will often promote natural regeneration (see the descriptions of the *seed tree, shelterwood,* and other harvest methods that follow).

---

7 The desired tree species or species mixture is determined by matching the ecology of the tree species to the ecology of the particular site (ecology-based tree species selection); or by a prediction of society's needs for, and the potential economic value of, the fibre, timber, or other biomass components of different tree species when they will be ready for harvest; or by consideration of other values, such as biodiversity, insect and disease resistance, windfirmness, wildlife habitat, slope stability, streambank stabilization, or aesthetics. Normally, some combination of these considerations is used to select tree species for forest renewal.

Against the advantages of natural regeneration must be set the fact that in many forest ecosystems it is unreliable, especially where clearcutting is the harvest method. Regardless of the harvest method, trees may produce adequate quantities of seed only every five to twenty years. The *seedbed* condition in the harvested area may be unsuitable for germination and seedling establishment, whereas planted seedlings may flourish. Where appropriate seedbed conditions are created by the forester, these may be difficult or impossible to maintain until a good seed crop is produced by the trees. Small mammals *love* tree seeds, especially large seeds, and their voracious appetites may ensure that very few seeds remain uneaten. Weed competition, even from diminutive herbs or mosses, may prevent tree seeds from germinating and the resulting tiny germinant seedlings from becoming established. Where natural regeneration is unreliable, where the forester wishes to change tree species (because of fungal diseases in the soil, for example) or the relative abundance of individual species in a mixture of species, or where 'genetically improved' seedlings are to be used, the forester must establish the next crop by planting or artificially seeding the area.

Planting has several advantages over natural regeneration. Two- or three-year-old trees can be planted, which can give them a head start over the competing weeds and reduce the need to control weeds by herbicides or other means. In cases of extreme weed competition, even older and larger trees can be planted in order to overcome weed problems that cannot easily be controlled, or different tree species can be planted – species that are tolerant of the weeds. One can control the number, the species mixture, the spatial distribution across the area, and the genetic type of the trees (foresters sometimes use seedlings grown from seed collected from trees specially selected for particular genetically controlled characteristics).

Because of a lack of understanding of seedling physiology and ecology, a failure to apply this understanding to the production of seedlings in forest nurseries, or the inappropriate storage and careless handling and planting of seedlings, tree planting in the past has not always been very successful. Many planted seedlings have died, and the root systems of some that have survived have developed very poorly, leading to the risk of tree instability problems as the trees get older and taller. Now that these problems have been widely recognized, improvements are being made in all phases of the production, handling, and planting of seedlings, and the past few years have seen a substantial improvement in the success of planting and the subsequent plantation performance in British Columbia and elsewhere in Canada. Further improvements are needed, however, and some of these improvements must await a better understanding of the ecology and physiology of seedling growth that research may provide.

There is a long list of advantages and disadvantages for both natural regeneration and planting. The debate as to their relative merits has raged for many decades and will doubtless continue for a long time. The logical resolution to the argument is that the choice of method should depend on the ecological characteristics of the species being regenerated, the site (the climate and soils), the biological factors that determine the relative success of naturally regenerated and planted seedlings, and a variety of management considerations, including economics. It is very difficult to make useful prejudgments about this in an area that is as ecologically diverse as British Columbia. The decision should always be made locally and should be site-, species-, and situation-specific. In most cases, reforestation involves both approaches. Natural regeneration nearly always adds additional seedlings and species to a planted site, and planting is often used to fill in areas that natural regeneration has failed to reforest or to ensure a desirable mixture of species.

Stand Tending and Protection

If you plant carrots in your garden in the spring and then ignore the garden totally until the fall, you will probably not harvest many carrots. Most gardens require weeding, and you may have to control slugs if you wish to put food from your garden on your table. You can be fairly certain that most of the farmers who grew the food you buy in the store had to control weed competition and a variety of animals that would have liked to consume the food plants you will be eating.

It is much the same in forestry. Young tree seedlings can be killed or severely suppressed by competition from other plant species, and may need to be protected from various animals that would like to eat them. The majority of seeds produced by trees in unmanaged forests never make it to germination, and the majority of young seedlings that are successful in becoming established do not survive for more than a few years or decades because of these biological and other types of hazards. Successful forest renewal often requires protection of the desired crop trees from various risks, and regulation of competition between the crop trees. This is referred to as *stand tending*.

Protection of tree seedlings from animals is generally difficult because of restrictions on the use of insecticides, because it is expensive to enclose plantations with high fences to keep out large animals such as deer, and because of the difficulty of protecting seedlings from small mammals. However, repellents have been developed from natural animal products (e.g., the urine or scent glands of large predators) that will deter deer and other browsing animals, and a certain amount of damage is simply accepted. In many cases, damage can be controlled to some extent by manipulating the slash and non-crop vegetation. For some types of animal damage, removal of these helps to reduce damage; in other cases these ecosystem components should be retained to afford the seedlings protection. Sometimes problems can be reduced by ensuring that there are mixtures of tree species that vary in their susceptibility to animal damage. Each problem situation should be evaluated individually. Weeds and non-crop trees can be controlled

successfully by manual cutting, the use of herbicides, or some other weed control method (see Chapter 8).

In addition to controlling animal and plant 'pests' or the damage they do, stand tending includes controlling the number of trees and the tree species composition in the stand. Far more seedlings become established by natural regeneration or are planted than are needed for the final crop. In the case of planting, this is to shorten the time it takes for the individual tree crowns to meet as their branches get longer *(canopy closure)*. Once canopy closure occurs, much of the competing vegetation is shaded out, giving the crop trees control of the site. This improves the availability of light, water and nutrients to the crop trees and, therefore, their rate of growth. Canopy closure also leads to the death-by-shading of the lower tree branches. Such *self-pruning* causes the live crown (the live canopy or crown is the section of the tree carrying live branches with foliage) to rise up as the trees get taller. Self-pruning is desirable in timber management because the quality of the wood in the section of the stem with live branches *(crown wood* or *juvenile wood)* is not as good for many purposes as that in the section of the stem that lacks live branches *(bole wood* or *mature wood)*. The lumber made from crown stem sections will have many knots in it and has a tendency to warp.

If the stand remains at the same density (number of trees per hectare) for many years, the growth in diameter of the trees will slow down. As they grow, the trees will become tall and skinny. This reduces their economic value, marketability, and resistance to damage from wind and snow, in comparison to trees grown in stands at lower density. Consequently, the forester generally removes some of the trees in an activity called *spacing* (or *pre-commercial thinning),* either before or shortly after canopy closure. Spacing increases the rate at which the remaining trees get 'fatter' (that is, it increases their diameter growth), or at least prevents a reduction in diameter growth. It also delays the shading out of the herbs and shrubs in the understorey, and this may benefit wildlife.

However, increased diameter growth is achieved at the price of increased juvenile wood and reduced mature wood production until the canopy once again closes. This problem can be overcome by pruning the remaining trees: some of the lower live branches are cut off. Pruning is quite expensive, so it is done only when it increases the future value of the tree enough to justify this silvicultural investment. If spacing reduces stand density too much, herbs, shrubs, and non-crop trees may invade the site and cause an undesirable increase in competition for soil, water, and nutrients. Although a well-developed understorey may benefit some wildlife species and will often help maintain soil fertility, increased competition for moisture can sometimes result in reduced tree growth. If spacing delays canopy closure for too long, it can result in reduced total timber production, and may reduce total value per hectare even though it increases the size and value of the individual trees that remain.

Besides tending a young stand and protecting it from wildlife browsing, weeds, and insect pests, foresters must protect the forest from both un-planned human-caused fire and wildfire. Considerable resources are committed to this end, including slashburning to reduce the risk and difficulty of controlling fire in recently logged areas, steps to promote fire prevention, and improvements in fire detection and fire fighting.

Commercial Thinnings

As the trees in a young forest grow and get taller, some do better than others. The losers in the upward race for sunlight eventually fall behind in height so badly that they are entirely shaded by the larger trees and die. The dead trees fall to the ground after a number of years and decompose, to enter once again the various nutrient cycles on the site: 'ashes to ashes, dust to dust.' Over the life of the tree crop, a significant proportion of the wood produced by the growing forest is transferred to the forest floor in the form of trees killed by lack of adequate light, unless the forester harvests these trees before they die. This is called *commercial thinning*.

Commercial thinning has not been used as widely in western North America as in Europe. This is generally because of the high costs and the lack of a market in this part of the world for the small-diameter harvested stems, other than for pulp. Logs from commercial thinning are much smaller, and therefore less valuable, than the logs from a final harvest, and it costs more to harvest a cubic metre of wood in several small logs than in a single large log. The lack of commercial thinning has also been due to the large areas of mature forest available for harvest; there has been no need to take intermediate harvests to satisfy the public's demand for wood. In contrast, commercial thinning is a regular feature of silvicultural systems in Scandinavia, central Europe, Japan, and many other forested countries that do not have large areas of mature and old-growth forest. In Sweden, at least two commercial thinnings are required by law, and such thinnings provide 25 to 30 per cent of the total volume of tree logs harvested from the forest. Undoubtedly, commercial thinning will become more important in North America in the future, with a variety of consequences for the thinned forest ecosystem. Significant areas of second growth stands in Oregon and Washington are now being commercially thinned, and current research in wood utilization and harvesting techniques will lead to an increase in this practice in western North America.

Thinned stands are often visually more attractive than unthinned stands because of the larger trees with longer green crowns, the greater amount of light reaching the ground, and the better development of the understorey vegetation. This more diverse and abundant herb and shrub layer improves the forest for several species of wildlife, but the loss of standing dead trees and the reduced input of dead trees to the ground may have adverse effects on some other wildlife species, such as cavity nesting birds. The reduction in the addition of dead trees to the forest floor (the layer of organic matter at the surface of the soil) alters its depth, chemical nature, and speed of decomposition. Forest floors in stands that have been regularly thinned are generally quite shallow, have much less rotting wood, decompose more rapidly, and generally have a higher proportion of their nutrient content in an available form than forest floors from unthinned stands.

Final Harvest

This is often the most important stage of the silvicultural cycle in terms of its impacts on the visual, wildlife, and other non-timber values of the forest ecosystem. It is also the stage of timber management that creates most of the economic value generated by forestry. The final harvest can be done in different ways, resulting in several different silvicultural systems (Figure 5.1).

Clearcutting. Defined as the harvesting of all trees in a single cut from an area of forest large enough so that the 'forest influence' is removed from the majority of the harvested area, clearcutting is discussed in more detail in Chapter 6. This harvest method is often followed by some form of site preparation before planting or natural regeneration, or the clearcut area may simply be left to regenerate naturally. Sometimes, sufficient seedlings and/or saplings that were present in the forest understorey before clearcutting survive the harvest; such trees are called *advance regeneration.* This is common when areas that get lots of snow are logged in the winter, because the snow pack protects the small trees. If they are seedlings of desirable species, in good physical condition, free of diseases and parasites, and physiologically capable of responding to the new conditions in the clearcut, this advance regeneration may be accepted as the next crop.

Where this is not the case, the advance regeneration may be deliberately removed mechanically or by fire, and the area either planted or allowed to regenerate naturally. Advance regeneration can consist of either a single species or a mixture of species.

A Single tree selection

B Group selection

C Patchcut

D Shelterwood

E Seed tree

F Clearcutting

Figure 5.1 Diagrammatic representation of six different silvicultural systems. Single-tree and group selection systems are appropriate for uneven-aged forests. Patchcut, shelterwood, seed tree, and clearcutting are all appropriate for even-aged forests. The degree of above-ground microclimatic forest influence is shown by the cross-hatching.

Sometimes there is a combination of advance regeneration and planting, the planted trees being used to fill areas that have failed to regenerate naturally. Normally, additional tree seedlings will become established over time by natural regeneration in areas that have been planted or in which advance regeneration has been retained.

The stand that results from clearcutting is usually more or less even-aged, and is relatively uniform in height even if it is not even-aged (advance regeneration may vary greatly in age). This creates the need for spacing and renders some level of commercial thinning desirable to reduce between-tree competition to acceptable levels later in the stand cycle. Stands of uniform height that are not spaced or thinned may undergo periods of growth stagnation as competition builds up, followed by accelerated growth as stand self-thinning occurs. Self-induced mortality in such natural or managed stands may be quite periodic and this can result in wide variations in tree diameter growth (the width of annual growth) at different times in the life of the stand. This is undesirable if the tree is to be made into lumber for house construction or various other uses. The lumber will be prone to warping and will not make good houses.

Contrary to the belief of some environmentalists, clearcutting does not automatically result in single-species forests *(monocultures)*. Natural regeneration in clearcuts made in mixed-species forests often results in mixed-species second-growth stands of very similar composition to the original stand. Mixtures of species are often planted (increasingly so in recent years), and even when a single species is planted, natural regeneration of the other species present in the adjacent forest generally ensures a multi-species crop. Subsequent spacing or thinning operations can turn mixed-species stands into single-species stands if this is the management objective, but this is true for any harvest system, not just clearcutting.

Similarly, post-harvest site treatments such as slashburning may favour a particular species, such as Douglas-fir on many sites at low elevation in coastal western North America, but this is a result of the site treatment, not the clearcutting. Where the original forest contained other species of trees, the initial advantage conferred on the Douglas-fir by the slashburning will decline after a few years, and natural regeneration of the other species will enrich the species composition of the stand. This will often result in a mixed-species stand of trees with fairly uniform height, unless this natural regeneration is cut out in a subsequent spacing or thinning. Where natural or managed monoculture forests are clearcut, the new crop generally consists of a single species, whether it be from natural regeneration or planting. If the management objective is to convert from monoculture to mixed-species stands, mixed species planting should be done.

Shelterwood. This is essentially a clearcut in which the final harvest is done in two or sometimes more stages. In essence, it is one very heavy thinning or a series of increasingly heavy thinnings at short intervals near the end of the rotation. However, the objective of these partial harvests (referred to as *regeneration cuts)* is not just to make an intermediate timber harvest. It is to gradually increase the windfirmness of the trees that are to be retained, improve their capacity to produce seed, improve the forest floor as a seedbed for natural regeneration or planting, and finally to establish a new crop of naturally regenerated or planted seedlings beneath the remaining mature crop trees.

By removing the overstorey trees gradually, the seedlings are established in a modified microclimate; this is generally the main purpose of this system. In areas that are subject to frosts during the growing season, regeneration of frost-sensitive tree species will often be much more successful with the shelterwood method than with the clearcutting system. Some of the most aggressive, shade-intolerant competitor weed species may be reduced somewhat in vigour in a shelterwood in comparison to a clearcut, and this may facilitate regeneration. However, shelterwood systems on moist, fertile sites with partially shade-tolerant understorey species can experience such severe weed problems as to cause natural regeneration or plantations to fail entirely unless this competition is controlled. Weed control may be more difficult in a shelterwood than a clearcut, but not necessarily so. It will depend on the weed control strategy used.

Shelterwood is a very suitable silvicultural system for a hot, dry climate or dry site. On such sites, successful natural regeneration may require scattered shade, and planted trees may benefit greatly from it. In a humid climate or on a moist site, weed control problems may make it a very difficult system to operate. In areas with frequent high winds, or where the residual trees have poor natural stability because of shallow or small root systems, many of the overstorey trees left after a shelterwood cut may be blown over unless supported by cables, disrupting the regeneration. There are many examples of such regeneration problems in western Oregon and Washington where shelterwood or other partial harvest systems were used in old-growth Douglas-fir from 1930 to 1955. It is therefore not a suitable system where tree stability is a problem.

In the past, shelterwood harvesting has generally required the use of ground-based harvesting equipment such as skidders and tractors rather than aerial cable systems. This can help to prepare an improved seedbed for natural regeneration by disturbing the organic forest floor, but it can also cause increased soil damage on wet sites or other sensitive soils, and may require an extensive network of temporary roads if shelterwood harvesting is done in very steep, mountainous country. Often such temporary roads are what cause much of the damage to soils, slopes, and streams attributable to timber harvesting. Recent developments in harvesting methods and technology offer the possibility of less site-disturbing systems of log removal for shelterwood harvests.

The shelterwood system is gaining popularity among advocates of 'New Forestry' (see Chapter 11) because it can provide continuing and future habitats for cavity nesting birds and other wildlife that depend on, or benefit from, the presence of large live or dead trees in a stand. In the normal shelterwood system, the residual trees are removed as soon as the area is satisfactorily regenerated. In 'New Forestry,' some or even most of these trees would be left as 'wildlife trees.'

Other systems. There are several variants of the above even-aged systems, including seedtree, strip-cut, and patchcut harvests. Each of these has a role to play in resolving some particular silvicultural or management problem on a particular type of site. In most cases, the major difference between even-aged systems and uneven-aged systems (described in the next section) is the degree of ecological change that is caused. Single-tree selection grades into group selection, which grades into small patch-cutting. This in turn grades into shelterwood, which grades into clearcutting. The terms are often used as though there were some fundamental difference between them. In reality, however, they are all members of the same continuum of harvest-related disturbance – from the removal of single trees (mimicking natural tree death) to the removal of large patches of forest (mimicking large fires or windthrows, albeit with some differences in ecological impact because of the removal of some portion of the tree stems and/or the lack of standing dead trees). The major difference between the silvicultural systems is the degree to which the 'forest influence' is removed at the time of harvest. This is explored in more detail in Chapter 6.

Uneven-Aged Stand Management: The Selection System

Each stand in an even-aged forest develops through a complete stand cycle over a time period equal to the length of the tree crop rotation. There will be a sequence of management activities over the rotation, many of which, like the final harvest of trees, will only occur once each rotation. In contrast, activities in the stands of an uneven-aged forest managed under the selection system occur more continuously. There is no clear series of stages making up a stand cycle like that of an even-aged forest.

In this system, individual large trees (single-tree selection) or small groups of large trees (group selection) are cut periodically throughout the rotation (perhaps every five to ten years), natural regeneration usually being relied upon to reforest the gaps so created. Intermediate-sized trees may also be cut to control competition, promote regeneration, and regulate stand structure and age distribution. The result is a forest that has trees of all ages, or at least several age-classes covering the full age range of the forest in every stand. Obviously, the system is applicable only to an uneven-aged forest. In humid climates, single-tree selection is suitable only for very shade-tolerant tree species. Group selection is more suitable for species that are somewhat less tolerant of shade.

Well managed by experienced foresters and under the right conditions, this can be a very productive silvicultural system. It is excellent where environmental conditions, protection considerations, or aesthetics require that forest cover remain continuously on the landscape. In many cases, group selection will be more practical and may be more successful than single-tree selection.

Forest renewal in uneven-aged stands managed under the selection system is usually accomplished by natural regeneration. This will occur as site resources of light, moisture, and nutrients are made available by the removal of individual trees or small groups of intermediate and larger-sized trees. The availability of seed, seed predation, competition from non-crop understorey species, and seedbed conditions can all act to limit the success of natural regeneration in selection forests, and selection harvesting would not normally be done where these factors constitute a significant impediment to the establishment of new crop trees. Sometimes a light disturbance of the forest floor improves the regeneration, and sufficient disturbance is often achieved during the extraction of the harvested trees. In many cases, no additional treatment is needed.

Weeding is usually not necessary in uneven-aged stands, as this system is normally practised only with shade-tolerant tree species or in climates where the desired trees are shade-tolerant or even shade-demanding – like Douglas-fir in hot, dry climates – and where weed competition does not preclude regeneration.

Spacing of dense patches of young regeneration is done as needed to maintain relatively even growth of intermediate-sized trees, and to maintain a target number of trees of various different sizes.

Thinning (the removal of some intermediate-sized trees) is done to maintain the desired mixture of tree sizes and to salvage harvestable trees that would otherwise die, unless they are to be retained as snags for wildlife habitat.

There is no final harvest, as the removal of the largest trees is essentially a stand-thinning operation. Large old trees are harvested as they reach the maximum desired size, or to maintain a desired stand structure.

Selection cutting is an excellent harvesting method for hot and dry forests, and may be the most appropriate system for some snow-dominated subalpine forests where regeneration in clearcuts is difficult and advance regeneration is the appropriate system of forest renewal. Selection harvesting works best where trees are not too large and the forest already has an appropriate range of tree sizes and ages. It may also require a lot of temporary roads (skid trails) by which to remove the cut trees. This can be a problem in steep mountain country or on sensitive soils. It is not generally a problem on flat or gently sloping land with well-drained soils that are not subject to compaction.

Some even-aged forests can be converted to uneven-aged selection forests if this is a management objective. The potential to do this successfully will depend on the ecology of the trees and the minor vegetation species involved and the overall ecology of the forest in question. The transition takes at least one full rotation to complete. In some types of forest, significant problems of windthrow and damage to the roots and stems of the remaining large trees are encountered throughout the conversion period. In some cases, this root damage permits the entry of decay organisms into the remaining trees, leading to increased risk of windthrow, death, or reduced timber value.

European forests in which the uneven-aged selection system is practised successfully have mostly been managed that way for centuries. They have the right stand structure and age distribution, a system of timber extraction roads is in place, the system is applied only to shade-tolerant species, and the forests are generally quite healthy, except in areas of acid rain damage, because diseased or insect-attacked trees are removed regularly. Group selection is more common in Europe than individual tree selection.

Successful application of the selection method in unmanaged west coast North American old-growth 'rain forests' may be very difficult because of one or more of the following: topography, wind, damage to the roots of residual trees, large rotting logs and standing dead snags that limit the movement of harvesting equipment, damage to smaller trees caused by the felling of very large old trees, the presence of parasites or diseases, and worker safety considerations. Selection logging of unroaded areas in steep, mountainous terrain may require more extensive road construction than clearcutting, and this can increase the risk of damage to the site and to streams and fish habitat, although not necessarily so. Selection logging in forests where some of the trees are infected by fungal 'root rots' may hasten the spread of the disease and result in many of the remaining trees dying from the infection before they are harvested. In such situations, small patch logging or small clearcuts may be necessary to reduce the problems of root disease in the next tree crop.

The selection system requires experienced silviculturists who can supervise the selection of trees for harvest, and harvesters who can accomplish the tree felling and removal of logs without damaging the remaining trees. 'Selective logging,' where

harvesters have simply been permitted to go in and take the valuable timber without regard to the structure, age, and condition of the remaining stand (as in 'diameter-limit' cutting), has been shown to have negative effects on the long-term productivity of many of the forests where it has been applied. Such exploitive selective logging early in this century in northern Sweden led to the passing of laws that such forests must be harvested by clearcutting.

Management of the Whole Forest: Annual Allowable Cuts

There are many stands in a managed forest, each of which will be in one stage of the stand cycle described above (even-aged stands) or in one stage of stand management (uneven-aged stands). Part 2 of the management plan should describe how the silvicultural activities in all these different stands will result in a fairly steady employment of forest workers, a reasonably constant supply of logs to a particular mill or market, the ability to respond to changing economic and market conditions, and a continuous supply over the whole managed area of a variety of wildlife habitats and the various other values that are described in Part 1 of the plan.

Spatial Distribution of Harvesting across the Whole Forest

Achievement of a fairly constant level of employment, yield of logs, and various other resource values within a given region is a common objective of sustained-yield forestry. Where this is the case, it is the responsibility of the forester to ensure that the total area harvested and the size and geographic distribution of individual harvested areas are consistent with the achievement of these goals.

Where an even-aged forest that is managed under a single management plan covers a very large area, where the harvest in any one year is concentrated in a few large clearcuts, and where the harvesting over a period of years is all located in a relatively small portion of the entire area, employment and log supply in that local area may be sustained for only a portion of the rotation. There will be a high level of harvest-related employment for that period, followed by a period equal to the length of the rotation in which silviculture, protection, road maintenance, and management of other resource values will be the sources of continuing employment in the woods.

Where not much silviculture or other resource management is practised, this can result in a 'boom-and-bust' effect on local communities. It can also result in large fluctuations over time in the abundance and species composition of the wildlife in the local area, and in the provision of various other resource values. Where this contravenes the objectives of management, the problem can be solved by dividing the forest into a series of smaller regional cutting cycles within which harvesting and other silvicultural activities will be conducted throughout the rotation (Figure 5.2).

The impacts of timber harvesting on future log supply, employment, wildlife, fish and streams, landscape aesthetics, and recreation are all very much affected by how the annual harvest is divided between different areas. This 'landscape' level of forest management is every bit as important as the stand level, but has generally not received as much attention until quite recently.

Annual Allowable Cuts

Another very important aspect of forest management at the whole-forest level is the calculation of the permissible rate of harvest: the annual allowable cut (AAC). This can be calculated in various ways, but basically there are two major inputs to the calculation.

Volume or area of mature forest or old-growth. The volume of economically harvestable timber in mature or old-growth forests is divided by the number of years that you wish the supply of this type of forest to last:

$$\frac{\text{volume of mature and old-growth timber}}{\text{desired duration of the supply of old growth}}$$

If there is a high risk of losing these forests to fire, insects, or disease, foresters may wish to harvest them relatively quickly. Similarly, if the forests have reached the age at which they are no longer accumulating timber volume or value, or if the rate at which these are being accumulated has declined, it may be desirable to harvest such forests fairly quickly. In contrast, where it will be many years before the young forests resulting from earlier logging and forest renewal are ready for harvest, foresters may harvest the mature and old growth more slowly to sustain an even flow of logs and employment in the future. In many cases, the desired duration of the older forests will be a compromise between these two conflicting considerations.

Another consideration is the desire to produce a 'normal forest' in terms of areas of different age classes. If the goal is to produce a managed second-growth forest that has equal areas of forest of all ages, up to the length of the tree-crop rotation, on each type of forest site (a 'normal' forest), the rate at which the mature and old-growth forest is harvested will be influenced by this management objective. Frequently, the desire to change a mature or old-growth forest to a forest with a 'normal' age class distribution within one rotation results in an uneven flow of logs from that forest during the period of conversion. In contrast, if the objective is to ensure a fairly constant flow of logs in the subsequent rotation, foresters may plan for a varying rate of logging during the conversion from unmanaged forest to managed forest.

Annual increase in the harvestable timber volume in an immature forest. If an even-aged forest has its land area or its timber volume divided equally among all age classes of forest up to rotation age (that is, it has a normal age class distribution), the volume of timber that can be harvested annually is equal to the growth (the 'increment') over the whole area, less the volume that has been lost to fire, insects, diseases, and wind damage, and the volume in the area assigned to parks or other non-timber production land uses. This is somewhat like having $100

Stand age (years)

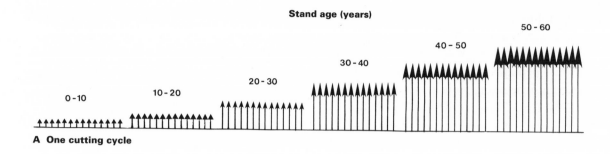

A One cutting cycle

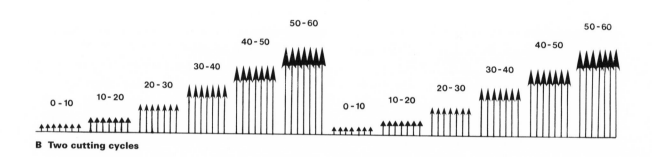

B Two cutting cycles

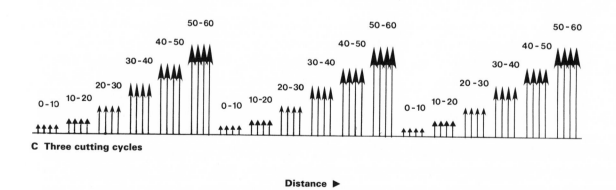

C Three cutting cycles

Distance ▶

Figure 5.2 The concept of 'cutting cycles.' **A** shows a forest composed of six age classes, all forests of one age class being grouped together in a single even-aged block. This forest has a single cutting cycle. **B** shows a forest with two cutting cycles. Each age class can be found in two different areas. **C** shows a forest with three cutting cycles (from Kimmins and Duffy 1991).

invested in a bank at 10 per cent interest, where the $100 represents the total volume of all tree age classes at the start of a year, and the $10 of interest represents the growth of the trees that year. If the $10 interest is taken out of the bank each year (less if some of it is used to pay certain 'bills' – the losses just mentioned), always leaving the $100 to earn interest over the next year, the 'capital' will never be depleted (Figure 5.3).

The manner in which the AAC is calculated is much more complicated than this, of course. For one thing, it depends on the rate at which young stands become economically harvestable, as well as how fast they are growing. Where a particular forest has lots of young stands but few that are old enough for harvesting, it is clearly not possible to annually harvest a volume equal to the increment on the young stands. The harvest rate will depend on whether the landowner wishes to change the age-class structure of the forest, and if so, how quickly. It also depends on whether an even flow of logs and sustained employment are overriding considerations, or whether maximizing economic value to the landowner is the major objective. Once calculated, by whatever method, the AAC is usually modified to ensure that non-timber values are protected, and to account for the risk of losses to fire, insects, and disease. The calculated AAC is reduced to allow for the expected loss of forest land base to non-timber production land uses, and of timber to natural tree-mortality processes.

The AAC is calculated only on the 'harvestable' volume of economically important trees. Consequently, it can be increased considerably without increasing the area of forest harvested if tree species not previously harvested become usable, and if a greater proportion of each tree is harvested (for example, harvesting logs as small as ten centimetres in diameter rather than only logs twenty centimetres or larger in diameter). In a managed forest, the AAC depends upon how fast the trees are growing. Consequently, it can be raised if silvicultural treatments accelerate tree growth, again without

increasing the area being logged.

Some foresters and economists have argued for a raising of the AAC in anticipation of the increase in future timber harvests that will result from increased tree growth caused by fertilization, thinnings, or other practices. This is called the *allowable cut effect* (ACE). However, there is considerable controversy among foresters about the ACE. Many feel that there are too many untested assumptions and too many unpredictable future risks (insects, wind, fire) to be certain that the increased volume resulting from silvicultural treatments will still be there when the stand is harvested. Consequently most foresters do not accept any acceleration of the AAC caused by this 'annual allowable cut effect.' It is argued that the AAC should not be increased until the faster tree growth and greater volumes achieved by more intensive forest practices are actually available for harvest. Current forest management policies on public forest lands in British Columbia do not provide incentives to the forest industry to practise such intensive silviculture.

The manner in which AACs are calculated varies from country to country and province to province, but it is always controversial and always of major importance in evaluating the sustainability of forestry. The rate and distribution of harvest has a major influence on a wide variety of forest and social values. Establishing a rate of harvest that will satisfy the management objectives of the forest owner and society in general must be considered one of the major responsibilities of a forester.

Sustained Yield

Most people, including most foresters, assume that it is the fundamental responsibility of professional foresters to practise 'sustained yield,' whatever that is. This is not necessarily a correct assumption. Landowners may deliberately liquidate the forests on their land over a short period of time with no thought of reforestation. They may replace the forests with golf courses, agriculture, hobby farms, playing fields, cities or housing developments,

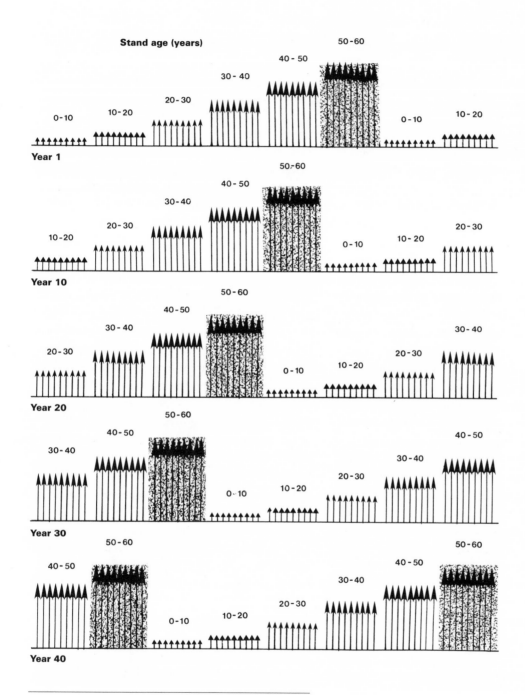

Figure 5.3 This diagram shows the oldest age class of a forest being harvested (the 50–60 year old stand). The volume of timber in this age class stand is equal to the increase in volume on all the younger age class stands over the ten years that this age class is being harvested. If the forest has a 'normal' age class structure, as shown in this diagram, this rate of harvest can be maintained in perpetuity: sustained timber yield (from Kimmins and Duffy 1991).

roads, reservoirs, or some other land use. Or they may harvest the trees on all of their land and leave nature to reforest the land. It all depends on whether or not sustained yield is the stated objective of management for the forested area. For most public forests, sustained yield is the objective, and the forestry practised there should reflect this.

Most managed forests, public or private, do in fact have as their primary objective some interpretation of the term sustained yield. Unfortunately, there is a lot of confusion and disagreement about what this means. For timber-management foresters using the even-aged management system, it may mean that the long-term goal is to achieve a 'normal' forest age class distribution over one or more rotations, and a long-term sustained production of log volume (the AAC), log value, employment, and other resource values once the 'normal' condition is achieved. It is assumed that there will be some irregularities in the supply of these resource values in the short run as a previously unmanaged forest that lacks the age class structure of a managed forest is modified to achieve the sustained-yield goal: 'short-term pain for long-term gain.' If the objectives of management are to force an even flow of log volume during the transition period, it may take much longer to achieve a 'normal' forest, and there may be a lower total social value produced.

There is some confusion between the terms 'sustained yield' and 'even flow.' The former refers more to the average long-term flow of values from the forest. The latter describes the degree of variation around this long-term average. Most foresters subscribe to the goal of sustained yield, but this is generally not interpreted to imply an actual even flow. AACs are not expected to be met exactly every year. Fire, insects, or windthrow may require a period of accelerated logging to harvest the killed timber. Significant increases in prices paid for wood may suggest accelerated harvesting to take advantage of the increased social value that can be created by selling logs at high prices. Periods of bad weather, strikes, or lack of log markets (no one will

buy the timber, or the price paid for harvested products is very low) may result in the annual harvest falling significantly below the AAC for one or more years. Consequently, foresters may only be required to achieve the AAC averaged over a five- or ten-year period. In British Columbia, a forest company can log 50 per cent above or below its AAC in any one year, as long as it is within 10 per cent of its quota over a five-year period. Where there is a major fire or insect outbreak, accelerated harvest levels may be allowed that exceed these guidelines until the killed trees have been salvaged, but the AAC will then be reduced for a period of time to compensate.

A further and perhaps more fundamental confusion about sustained yield arises with respect to the spatial distribution of resource values in forests under sustained-yield management. Under even-aged management, it is assumed that sustained supplies of various resource values will be provided by a mosaic of stands of different ages scattered across the landscape. In any one stand there will be a change over time in various resource values as the area proceeds through the stand cycle. Thus, even where there is regional sustained yield of different values, these values cannot be found all the time in any one place. In contrast, the resource values of a given uneven-aged stand do not vary much over time. A fundamental difference between these two management systems is thus the provision of sustained yield at the individual stand level versus the whole-forest level. Both offer sustained yield, but at a different spatial scale.

Where an even-aged forest is managed on a single cutting cycle over a regionally extensive forest area, large areas of forest will fall into a single age class. For local communities, either human or non-human, there will be little sense of sustained yield, especially if all the annual harvesting is concentrated in one area. In contrast, if there is a separate cutting cycle in every major watershed in the forest (such as a third- or fourth-order watershed: see Chapter 6 for a discussion of watershed order), there will be more or less continuous harvesting and silvicultural activities in every watershed of this size throughout the rotation. If there is a change from the former to the latter forest management strategy, what may have appeared to be exploitive, non-sustainable forestry from a local perspective may now appear to be sustainable management, even though, over the whole forest, the rate of harvest has not changed. Within a major watershed, however, there are many minor watersheds (such as first- or second-order watersheds). Each of these smaller watersheds may be harvested in a single year: there will be no sense of sustained yield in such a small subunit of the larger watershed. To gain sustained yield at the first-order watershed scale, it is necessary to practise uneven-aged management.

Forestry and Economics

Forests can be managed for a wide variety of values. Where forests are publicly owned and the management objective is to sustain non-commodity values, the costs of management must be paid by the public through their taxes, or by the forest users who benefit from these values. Where forests are managed for commodities such as wildlife, water, or timber, the costs of management are normally recovered from the sale of these commodities.

Where timber production is a major management objective, the economics of stand and forest management is normally of prime concern. This is true whether the forest is owned privately by a timber company, a small woodlot owner, or by the government on behalf of the public. Governments generally consider timber-production forests an important source of revenue with which to pay for social programs, just as public timber companies are concerned about the economic return to their shareholders.

Decisions in Canadian forestry in the past have too often been based predominantly on economic criteria. Negative impacts on the environment or on communities were often ignored or given little attention. With the changing public attitude towards both the environmental and the social consequences of forest management decisions, the role of economics has been reduced. However, some members of the public apparently expect that timber companies and governments can, and should, pay little or no attention to 'the bottom line,' and that environmental and social concerns, not economic ones, should drive decisions. This is unrealistic. Forest management can be very expensive, and unless there are reasonable expectations of a financial return, neither industry nor government may choose to invest in it. There are other, more rewarding ways of investing available capital or taxpayers' dollars. Because of economic considerations, there generally has to be a compromise between the quality of forest management that a forester would like to practise and what he or she is actually able to practise. There will often be a conflict between the level of environmental protection the public would like to have and the level that is possible, given prevailing resource economics and government budgets.

This book is not the place to explore the tools of economic analysis that can be used to evaluate the trade-offs between economic returns from timber management and the costs of better forest management and environmental protection. Nor is it intended to elaborate on the arguments between those who believe that forest companies are basically greedy institutions whose main goal in life is to exploit public resources, and who maintain that the escalating costs associated with 'environmental protection' are reaching the point at which some companies may choose to leave the forestry business. This brief section on economics does have a point, however. Among other things, good timber management requires careful planning, the matching of harvesting equipment to the site, and access to specialists for advice on how to limit potential negative impacts on non-timber values. A company or government must make sufficient profit from timber production to pay for these services and to conduct all management activities to high standards. Negative environmental consequences often arise from corner-cutting; inadequate planning, staffing, supervision and monitoring; and lack of appropriate harvesting and road building equipment. On average, these negative consequences are more likely to occur if the profit margin is low.

Thus, sustainable development of forests is more likely to occur under favourable economic conditions than conditions of public or corporate poverty. This was a basic conclusion of the Brundtland Commission. As our society searches for methods of sustainable resource management, the economics of the alternative choices must be considered if the social values provided by forestry are to be sustained and if the profit margins needed to pay for high-quality forest management are to be achieved.

Summary

The reality of forestry has often deviated from what has just been described. That is because society has used the word 'forestry' to apply equally to all four stages in the development of this human endeavour: unregulated exploitation, administrative and largely timber-oriented forestry, ecology-based and silviculturally sound forestry, and social forestry. The term 'forestry' has been applied equally to logging and to the entire process of managing forests for a sustainable supply of a variety of values. It is therefore not surprising that a public that has experienced little more than the consequences of the first two stages of forestry, or has seen only logging and not all aspects of forest management, should have so little faith in foresters. As forestry in Canada evolves through Stage 3 to Stage 4, the true nature of forest land management will be revealed to the Canadian people.

Forestry is what a professional forester does. The major activity is planning the management of the forest to achieve the objectives pertaining to forest land as defined by the resource owner and prevailing legislation. This includes the development of management plans; the selection of appropriate silvicultural systems; and the regulation of harvests of timber, wildlife, and other products to ensure sustainability of yields; the designation of lands for non-consumptive uses; and the protection of the forests from fire, insects, and diseases. Foresters also have a responsibility to the landowner and to society in general to ensure that the planned management is carried out and the desired values are supplied and conserved.

One of the key responsibilities of a forester is the calculation of the annual allowable cut of timber, the choice of how this cut will be distributed across the landscape, and the selection of the harvesting method to be used. Most of the environmental issues that are discussed in the subsequent chapters pertain to this calculation and these choices.

The origins of forestry are the same as the origins of conservation and many aspects of the environmental movement: the desire to sustain the supply of a variety of values that a society wants from its forests. The job of a forester is to manage forest ecosystems in a manner that achieves this objective. There is therefore no *fundamental* conflict between forestry and the environmental movement. Disagreements stem from different interpretations about what the objectives of management and the balance of resource values should be. Conflict arises when exploitative forestry masquerades under the title of sustained-yield forestry, or where poor management practices result in damage to the resource. Disagreements can also be caused by a confusion between the scientific and social dimensions of these issues (see Chapters 1 and 2).

CHAPTER 6

Clearcutting: Ecosystem Destruction or Environmentally Sound Timber Harvesting?

Introduction

Of all the things that foresters do, clearcutting probably causes the most outrage and anger in the public. Literally a case of 'trees: now you see them, now you don't,' clearcutting is the silvicultural practice[8] that creates the greatest and most persistent change in how a forested landscape looks. Of all the timber harvesting methods, it has the potential to create the greatest degree of ecological change in the harvested ecosystem. This change may be either desirable or undesirable, acceptable or unacceptable, according to the type of forest and the management objectives for the forest. Contrary to popular belief, clearcutting is not all bad, just as it is not always the appropriate way to harvest the timber crop in a managed forest.

This chapter opens with a discussion of several commonly asked questions about clearcutting, and examines the claim that environmentalists sometimes make: 'If you clearcut an old-growth forest, there can never be another forest like it on the site again.' Similarly, it will examine the claim of the forest industry that we can have 'forests forever' with clearcut harvesting. It will then examine the variety of ecological impacts that clearcut harvesting can have, and how clearcutting affects various ecosystem attributes.

The chapter will continue with a discussion of whether the environmental problems often attributed to clearcutting are an inevitable consequence of this type of harvesting, or whether they reflect how, when, and where clearcutting is done or are largely the result of post-clearcutting site treatments. The discussion will close with some comments about the types of ecosystem in which clearcutting should and should not be done, and

---

8 Yes, clearcutting is a silvicultural practice as well as a harvesting method. It is the best way to establish a new forest consisting of certain types of trees. The word 'silvicultural' is like 'agricultural.' It is an adjective that describes activities associated with the establishment, tending, and harvesting of tree crops, while 'agricultural' pertains to similar activities associated with food crops.

the types of tree species for which it is appropriate.

There are few forest practices to which the adverbs 'never' and 'forever' have been applied more than they have been to clearcutting. It is a good example of the action of the Peter Pan principle (see Chapter 2). By the end of the chapter you should have a better understanding of the ecology of clearcutting and its environmental impact, and a better basis on which to judge when the claims of 'never' and 'forever' may be true or false.

Some Commonly Asked Questions about Clearcutting

There is a lot of confusion about what clearcutting is and what its effects on the environment are. Before talking about the environmental impact of clearcutting, let us examine a number of commonly asked questions about it.

What Is a Clearcut?

As the name implies, a clearcut is an area of forest that has been completely cleared of all trees other than seedlings and occasional saplings. When a forest is clearcut, all the trees are cut at about the same time, and all the young trees that regrow in the area will be similar in age and size. Clearcutting is the harvesting practice most commonly used in the conversion from unmanaged to managed forests. It is also the most common method of harvesting in managed timber-production forests around the world.

In managed even-aged forests grown for timber, clearcut harvesting is usually done when most of the trees are large enough to produce a specific type of product, such as sawlogs or logs for making plywood. If the intention is to produce large pieces of timber for building construction, the forest may be grown and clearcut on quite long rotations (60 to 120 years in British Columbia, depending on the climate and soil type). If the tree crop is to be made into book paper, tissue paper, newsprint, cardboard for packaging, or charcoal for energy, the forest may be clearcut when it is much younger and the trees much smaller.

The above definition of clearcutting should be easy to understand and apply. Unfortunately, things in real life are a little more complicated. If you cut all the trees in an area measuring 50 metres by 50 metres (a quarter of a hectare or roughly half an acre) in a forest that is, let us say, 50 metres tall, you would have created a clearcut according to this definition. However, life for a deer, a small tree seedling, a moss, or an earthworm in the middle of this 50-by-50-metre clearcut would be very different from that in the middle of a 500-by-500-metre clearcut area (25 hectares or about 62 acres). Their experiences in a 25-hectare square clearcut would also be very different from their experiences in a 25-hectare clearcut that was 100 metres wide and 2,500 metres (2.5 kilometres) long.

The reason for this apparent conundrum is that, ecologically speaking, a clearcut is not defined by the removal of just the trees, but by the loss of the forest conditions that are created by the trees. These conditions include the shade and, in summer, the cooler daytime and warmer nighttime air temperatures, lower soil temperatures, and increased humidity of the air. These conditions are collectively referred to as the *forest microclimate* (the climate near the ground). As one walks from a forest out into the middle of a large clearcut, one passes through an area called the *edge* or *ecotone,* in which the microclimate is intermediate between that of the forest and that of the clearcut. This is sometimes reflected in much better early growth of planted or naturally regenerated trees near the edge of a clearcut than in the middle, except where deer browsing is a problem. Deer also like the ecotone!

In the 50-by-50-metre harvested area mentioned above, all of the area from which the trees have been removed will still have a modified microclimate; the entire cut area will be ecotone. Similarly, a long, narrow harvested area can also be mainly ecotone with a modified microclimate, even when it has a large total area. Such long, narrow areas are much less ecologically altered than square or round clearcuts of similar total area, because the majority of the land area in the latter will have a completely unmodified microclimate. Long, narrow harvested areas from which all the trees are removed in a single harvest would more accurately be called 'strip cuts.' This concept is shown in Figure 6.1.

So far, 'clearcut' has been defined mainly in terms of the removal of all the large trees and the resulting loss of forest microclimate over most of the area. But clearcutting changes more than the microclimate. As explained in Chapter 4, a forest ecosystem is a very complex interacting system of living plants, animals, and microbes, with a soil, an atmosphere, a forest microclimate, and various types of dead organic matter in various stages of decay. Trees capture solar energy by photosynthesis and pass this energy to soil organisms when their leaves, branches, and other parts die and fall to the ground. They also excrete carbohydrates and other organic molecules from their fine roots into the soil, where these high-energy chemicals are used by soil microbes. As a result, there are high densities of these microbes in the *rhizosphere,* the volume of soil immediately surrounding these fine roots. This input of dead organic matter (the *litterfall)* and organic molecules fuels the below-ground ecosystem; it provides the food – the energy and nutrients – needed by soil organisms, which in turn maintain a fertile and productive soil for the roots of plants by ensuring a continuing supply of nutrients for uptake by plants and a well-structured and aerated soil.

In a clearcut, this supply of dead organic matter and organic molecules to the soil is temporarily reduced or eliminated. For a time, the soil organisms can use the reserves of organic matter built up at the soil surface by past litterfall, and also the logging debris, or *slash,* which consists of the leaves, branches, upper stem sections, and any other tree parts left behind by the logging. Soil biological activity can therefore continue unabated, or may be increased, for some time after clearcutting. However, if for some reason the clearcut were to remain unvegetated for many years and no more organic 'fuel' was added to the soil, the below-

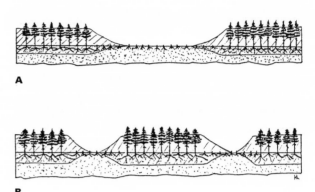

A

B

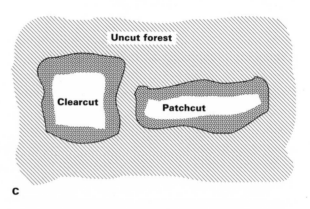

C

Figure 6.1 A shows a clearcut, an area in which the above- and below-ground influence of the trees has been removed in more than half the area. **B** shows two patchcuts, which do not qualify as clearcuts because the microclimatic and soil influence of the adjacent trees affects more than half the area from which trees have been removed. **C** shows that whether an area is a clearcut or not depends as much on the shape of the harvested area as the size. Large areas that are long and narrow may not be clearcuts because the adjacent forest still modifies the soil and microclimate in the ecotone (the shaded area). The two harvested areas are the same total size but have a different area without forest influence.

ground ecosystem would eventually run down, with adverse consequences for the plants that eventually reinvade the area. There would be a temporary loss of critically important microbial species in the clearcut area. The input of litterfall is very important as a renewable supply of energy for soil organisms and nutrients for plants, and in many forests the maintenance of soil fertility depends on annual litter inputs. Any home vegetable gardener knows that the soil will become 'tired' after several years of cropping if compost is not added.

Over most of the area of a small clearcut or a large clearcut that is long and narrow, and in the ecotone area of an extensive clearcut area, there is an annual input of dead organic matter and organic chemicals to the soil. Leaves blown by wind from the trees in the adjacent forest, together with the organic excretions and annual death of the fine roots of these trees (these roots can grow out for great distances into the harvested area), ensure a continuing, if somewhat reduced, input of organic matter and nutrients to the soil in the ecotone. Thus, in addition to the modified microclimate, the soil processes in the ecotone area of a clearcut, and in the shelterwood, patchcut, and the other harvesting systems shown in Figure 5.1, remain much more similar to the processes of a forest soil than in a truly clearcut situation. This belowground ecotone effect is thought to be another reason why regeneration of some species often takes place better in the ecotone than in the middle of a large clearcut.

How Long Does a Clearcut Last?

A harvested area is not a clearcut if the major ecological conditions and processes characteristic of a forested environment remain more or less intact. A patchcut or a shelterwood are not clearcuts in the ecological sense because there is still some degree of *forest influence* over the entire harvested area or the majority thereof. Similarly, a clearcut loses its status as soon as a significant degree of forest influence has been re-established by natural or management-

assisted processes. As a clearcut is reforested, or as it is revegetated by herbs and shrubs, the microclimate beneath the vegetation becomes modified, litterfall is restored, and the soil is once again fully occupied by living roots. Full restoration of the forested condition does not occur until the branches of the new community of trees touch, reducing the light to the understorey vegetation and re-establishing what is called 'closed forest' conditions both above ground and in the soil. This *canopy closure* stage marks the termination of the clearcut condition, but there is obviously a progressive loss of the ecological conditions that characterize true clearcuts from the time the clearcut is reinvaded by minor vegetation, to the time of tree canopy closure and full occupancy of the soil by the fine roots of trees and their associated microbes.

If we wish to make an ecological impact analysis of clearcutting, a clearcut should be defined in terms of its ecological characteristics. An environmental and social impact analysis, on the other hand, requires a broader perspective, including aesthetics and any visual differences between the clearcut and surrounding older forest. Following canopy closure, which can occur when the trees are still quite small (anything from less than one metre to ten metres tall, according to how close the trees are growing to each other), the young new forest will still look very different from the surrounding areas of older forest. The young forest is often a lighter green, its canopy has a smoother surface texture (more velvety) than the rougher surface of a mature or old-growth forest, and, in the case of a planted forest, the lines in which the seedlings were planted may remain visible for several years. Some people will still call such a young forest a clearcut because of this visual difference, but from an ecological perspective this is incorrect after canopy closure has occurred and forest conditions have been re-established over the whole area.

The new forest will be in a different seral condition from the pre-harvest forest, but it will be a young forest, not a clearcut. This does not deny the importance of aesthetics or the visual and structural differences between a young second-growth forest created by clearcutting and the unmanaged forest it replaces. Nor does it imply that the ecological conditions of the new forest are the same as those that prevailed in the mature forest before the timber harvest. It simply says that in ecological terms the clearcut condition – an early or pioneer seral stage – lasts only until succession has restored a forest seral stage.

Why Do Foresters Feel They Have to Clearcut Forests?

There are many reasons why clearcutting is the most widely used timber harvesting method around the world. Sometimes it is because clearcutting satisfies most closely the ecological requirements of the young seedlings of the tree species to be grown as the next timber crop. This may be the same species or a mixture of species as in the forest that has been harvested, or a different species or species mixture. Often there is strong pressure to use clearcutting because of the economics of harvesting: certain types of harvesting equipment operate more efficiently with clearcutting than with non-clearcutting methods, and the use of such equipment may be dictated by tree size, slope, soil, or other considerations. The risk of wind damage (windthrow) and diseases may limit partial harvests in some forests. Clearcutting is the method normally used where forests have been killed by fire, insects, or disease. Clearcutting may make it much easier to get a new forest established because site preparation (the control of weeds, the removal of excessive logging slash, the disturbance of an undesirably thick forest floor) may be much easier in a clearcut than a partially cut area. Worker safety is another consideration. In some types of old forest it may be more dangerous to do partial felling than clearfelling. In some cases in the past, clearcutting has been used simply because of a lack of knowledge or experience of any other method: 'that's the way it has always been done.'

When done with a sensitivity to the ecology of the ecosystem being harvested and to the ecological requirements and tolerances of the local species, clearcutting is an environmentally sound timber harvest method in many kinds of forests. In other types of forest, reforestation and the re-establishment of forest conditions following clearcutting may be so difficult and take so long as to render this method of harvesting quite inappropriate and unacceptable. In some forests, clearcutting is inappropriate because of aesthetic and recreational considerations, even though it may be environmentally sound and silviculturally successful. In yet others, it may be unsuitable because of slope and snow instability problems, water supply considerations, or a desire to satisfy the habitat requirements of those wildlife species that depend exclusively on large old trees or on the structure of an old or uneven-aged forest.

The wide variation in suitability of the clearcut method is reflected in the range of legal requirements regarding clearcutting around the world. On the one hand, laws were passed centuries ago banning clearcutting in steep mountainous parts of Europe, where avalanche, soil erosion, and land slides were a problem following clearcutting. There are still strict laws on the size of area from which all trees may be removed in the steep areas of the European Alps, where the risk of avalanche and slope instability make clearcutting inappropriate. Similarly, legal restrictions were recently placed on harvesting tropical forest in steep, erodible hill and mountain areas in Thailand, where the combination of torrential monsoon rains, illegal logging, and deforestation by local farmers following the logging led to landslides, flooding, and the destruction of villages (these laws have not been successful since the majority of logging in Thailand continues to be unauthorized and illegal). On the other hand, the present law in Sweden requires that most forests be harvested by clearcutting. The use of uneven-aged silvicultural systems in northern Sweden in the earlier part of this century led to the forest in that area becoming degraded after successive partial cuts.

This resulted in the requirement that clearcutting be done to keep the forests 'healthy' for tree production, recreation, and wildlife (mainly for game animals). Similarly, bad experiences with partial cutting in some forests in Oregon and Washington in the first half of this century led to a return to clearcutting in these forests. More recently, the positive role of clearcutting in modern forest practice has been reaffirmed in legislation in Oregon.

In cold northern climates, or in cool and very wet climates, forests can stagnate[9] if the ecosystem is not disturbed periodically by fire, insects, disease, windthrow, or logging. Many northern muskegs (sphagnum bog forests) in Scandinavia, the former Soviet Union, Alaska, and Canada were once productive forests, and would have remained so had they been subjected periodically to fire, logging, or other disturbance processes. In the prolonged absence of such disturbance, the forest was replaced naturally by bogs because of soil temperature problems. In some parts of the cool temperate rain forests of northern coastal British Columbia and the Alaskan coast, even forests on steep slopes may move   progressively towards a boglike state or a very slow-growing, shrub-dominated open forest if undisturbed for very long periods. This is because of the excessive accumulation of humic substances in the mineral soil and the very deep acidic forest floors dominated by decaying logs that can occur in such climatic areas. Soil chemical changes that can occur in nutrient-poor forest soils in areas of high

rainfall can also lead to forest deterioration unless the soil is disturbed periodically.

The tendency towards forest 'deterioration' can be observed in parts of northern and west coast Vancouver Island, where the climate is cool and very humid. Old-growth forests in these areas that have remained undisturbed for many centuries have very low rates of growth; even the young trees grow very slowly. In contrast, some of these Vancouver Island forests have been blown over regularly in windstorms (once a century, for example), or the soil has been disturbed by flooding or landslides. These recently disturbed areas support highly productive closed forests. It is thought by some that if done in a manner appropriate to the particular site and its ecological condition, clearcutting can reinvigorate the ecological processes of such stagnating forest sites, speeding up decomposition and resulting in a young forest with much higher rates of energy capture and nutrient cycling than in the undisturbed forest.

Success in duplicating the desirable effects of natural disturbance in such cool and humid forests requires a good knowledge of how both old-growth and second-growth forests function in these climates. Traditional timber harvesting methods may not duplicate exactly the natural mechanisms of disturbance, and the forests that develop after harvesting may not be the same as the forests that develop after natural disturbance, at least initially. Further ecological research is required before we can design optimum management-caused disturbance regimes that will emulate the desirable effects of natural disturbance. For many northern forests, existing data suggest that the optimum disturbance is provided by clearcutting, while in others, partial cuts produce the appropriate levels of disturbance.

More southerly forests in warmer, drier climates generally do not appear to have the same disturbance requirements as humid and cool or cold northern forests. They already have faster organic-matter decomposition and nutrient cycling. However, few of these forests have remained undisturbed for long

---

9 Environmentalists generally dislike terms such as 'decadent old-growth' and 'stagnating forest' because these terms have often been used by foresters in the past to justify the harvesting of old-growth forests. In terms of aesthetics, forest recreation, wilderness values, and so on, there is no question that these terms deny the considerable value of such forests to a certain segment of society (including the author). In terms of timber production objectives, these terms are both reasonable and accurate. In terms of the ecological functioning of the forest at the primary production level, they may or may not be correct. For a variety of ecological reasons, some forests that have not been disturbed for a long time 'slow down'; their functional processes stagnate. In other forests, there may be no such requirement for periodic disturbance to maintain productivity.

so there is little evidence whether or not their processes would slow down if they did remain undisturbed for long periods. Most have been subjected
periodically to fire, insects, or logging. In very
hot, dry forests, severe disturbance of the forest
community is usually undesirable if continued
forest growth is the objective.

Now let us look in more detail at some of the
arguments for and against clearcutting.

Silvicultural Reasons for Clearcutting
The major silvicultural reason for clearcutting has
to do with the ecological requirements for successful reforestation and subsequent stand growth of
particular tree species. Regeneration of tree species
whose seedlings are badly affected by shade is
generally much more successful in clearcuts than in
partial-cut systems. The seedlings of many tree
species that we use to build houses and furniture or
make paper require high light intensities or grow
much better under such conditions. They regenerate and grow much better in a well-designed and
managed clearcut than in the partial shade of a
forest managed under an uneven-aged partial-cut
system. Some tree species in some types of forest
will regenerate only in full sunlight.

Certainly, there are many important pulp and
timber species whose seedlings will tolerate remarkably low light conditions, and in a hot, dry climate,
shade may be an absolute requirement for successful tree seedling establishment, even for species that
may be intolerant of shade in a wetter climate.
Once established, however, most shade-tolerant tree
species in humid forests grow best in full sunlight,
and in hot, dry forests shade-requiring young trees,
once established, grow best without competition
for soil moisture from larger overstorey trees.
Consequently, a shelterwood harvest in such dry
forests may be superior in terms of rotation-length
tree growth to an uneven-aged silvicultural system,
such as individual-tree or group selection. In shelterwood systems, sufficient trees are left standing at
the time of the main harvest to provide shade and

other aspects of forest influence to the young
seedlings, but are removed to give the seedlings full
sunlight once they are well established. However,
shelterwood may not provide habitat for certain
animal species as well as some uneven-aged silvicultural systems do.

Table 6.1 shows how we can use our knowledge of
the ecology of different tree species and ecosystems
to select harvesting methods that ensure good forest
regeneration.

Other silvicultural reasons for clearcutting
include easier weed control, easier site preparation
to promote forest regeneration (either natural
seedlings or planted seedlings), the greater possibility of changing tree species or of using genetically
improved seedlings, and a lower requirement for
skill and experience. Successful selection silviculture
in uneven-aged forests generally requires greater
knowledge, experience, and supervision than does
even-aged silviculture. If there is a lack of such
expertise, clearcutting may be a more reliable silvicultural system for achieving forest renewal than
many alternatives that require high levels of technical skill and knowledge.

These silvicultural reasons may or may not result
in clearcutting being used as the harvest method,
because a silvicultural system that is optimum for
tree crop production may not necessarily sustain
other forest values that are being managed for.

Economic Reasons for Clearcutting
In most cases it is less expensive and more profitable
to clearcut than to use an alternative harvest system.
Economics has undoubtedly been, and continues to
be, a major reason for clearcutting, and this has
sometimes led to the misapplication of the system.

The international lumber and pulp market is
highly competitive, and where jobs depend on the
production of logs at low cost, clearcutting will often
be the method of choice. Given the current price of
timber and the current government tax and royalty
system, there are some areas in British Columbia
where timber harvesting is economical if clearcutting

is used and not economical under alternative harvesting systems. The higher volume of trees removed per hectare in clearcut harvests, and the greater ease of felling and removing the logs, generally makes the cost per cubic metre of wood harvested lower in clearcutting than in alternative systems. A major cost in logging is the building of roads and bridges to provide access to the harvesting area. Where only a portion of the trees are harvested, their sale value may not cover the cost of the road. A clearcut on the same site may yield a sufficient volume of logs to cover the costs of roading, yarding, and transportation to the mill, and provide enough profit for the logging company or mill to stay in business and practise silviculture.

Against this argument, however, must be set the lower regeneration costs and site-preparation costs that alternatives to clearcutting may provide. With some types of harvesting equipment, the cost of moving logs from the stump to the road may not vary greatly between different silvicultural systems. In forests where such equipment can be used, and if overall silvicultural costs are considered, there may not be a great difference in the combined cost of logging and reforestation between clearcutting and some alternative harvesting methods.

The fact that clearcutting may be more profitable cannot be accepted as a rationale for clearcutting if the practice leads to a failure of forest regeneration or to some unacceptable environmental impacts. Conversely, the aesthetic appeal of partial harvest systems should not lead to their use if this causes unacceptable soil disturbance, increased disease and insect problems, or failure to adequately regenerate the forest. Clearly, there has to be a balance between economic, silvicultural, and environmental considerations.

Table 6.1 Suitability of different silvicultural systems for the regeneration of tree species according to the tolerance of the species to different microclimate conditions and the sensitivity of the site to disturbance

		Tree species that are:		
		Intolerant of exposure to open microclimates; tolerant of shade	**Tolerant of exposure to open microclimates**		**Require exposure to open microclimates; intolerant of shade**
			More tolerant of shade	**Less tolerant of shade**	
Ecosystem sensitivity to disturbance	**Low**		Clearcutting[2]	Clearcutting	Clearcutting
			Seed-tree[2]	Seed-tree	Seed-tree
			Small-patch harvesting	Small-patch harvesting	
	Medium	Shelterwood[1]	Shelterwood[1,2]	Shelterwood	
		Group selection[1]	Group selection[1]		
		Single-tree selection[1]	Single-tree selection[1]		
	High	Protection Forests. No timber harvesting except where necessary to maintain the health of the forest and its protection functions			

Notes: This type of analysis must be done for each different climatic area. There are several variants of the shelterwood method not shown here that vary in their suitability under different site and climatic conditions.

[1] Suitable only where competition between tree seedlings and competing vegetation is not a problem
[2] Suitable only in favourable climatic conditions
Source: Modified from Klinka et al. 1990

Worker Safety Considerations

Alternatives to clearcutting are much easier and safer to apply in managed forest than in the first harvest of wild, unmanaged forest, especially very humid west coast old-growth forest in mountainous terrain. The large old trees in such forests, many of which have dead tops and huge dead branches, are not called 'widow-makers' without reason. It is considered to be safer for forest workers to harvest such forests by the clearcut method than by alternative systems. Salvaging logs from forests that have been windthrown is often more dangerous than from forests that have been felled in an orderly manner. Thus, silvicultural methods that increase the area of windthrown forest that must be salvaged may increase the risks to forest workers.

Both the government agencies responsible for forest worker safety and insurance and the workers and their families take a pretty dim view of silvicultural and harvesting systems that increase the risk of death or injury. Consequently, clearcutting has been the most commonly used method in the conversion from unmanaged to managed forests, especially in harvesting west coast old growth and forests that have a high risk of windthrow. Appropriate management of second-growth forest may make it possible to harvest trees safely and successfully by non-clearcut methods in forests where clearcutting is the appropriate method of harvesting unmanaged old-growth forest. Development of new harvesting equipment that reduces danger to tree-fellers, and payment schedules for fellers that permit enough time to reduce work hazards, may alter the role of safety considerations in the future choice of harvest method. Such developments would obviously have economic implications.

Environmental Reasons

Except when helicopters or balloons are used to remove logs from a harvesting area, roads are an indispensable part of the harvesting system. Unfortunately, many of timber harvesting's negative effects on the environment are caused by roads: siltation of rivers, slope instability and subsequent landslides, and loss of productive land.

Some cable logging systems, such as skyline or long-reach grapple yarders, require a lower length of main haul roads than ground-based log extraction systems such as skidders and tractors. Other cable systems, such as conventional grapple yarders, may require more haul roads, but cable systems usually result in far fewer skid roads than ground-based systems. Thus, cable systems such as the skyline system can significantly reduce the environmental impact of harvesting because of this reduction in roading, especially in steep terrain. However, these cable systems operate most efficiently in clearcuts and may be uneconomic or impractical in uneven-aged forests or small patchcuts. Tractors and skidders are often the only practical way to remove logs from partially harvested uneven-aged stands, unless one can use horses, helicopters, or balloons. New cable systems are being designed that may make it possible in the future to use these more environmentally-friendly log-removal systems economically in non-clearcut harvesting.

The high risk of soil damage accompanying the skidder harvesting of steep slopes can be an environmentally sound reason for clearcutting with cable yarding in such areas, albeit with small clearcuts. Where, for reasons of slope instability, neither complete removal of tree cover nor the high road density of tractor or skidder logging is acceptable, partial logging using helicopter, balloon, or horse systems should be used, or the area should remain unlogged.

Clearcutting has sometimes been misapplied. It has sometimes been done badly. It has often been done in a way that causes a dramatic alteration in the visual quality of a landscape. In western North America, clearcuts have often been larger than they need to be and perhaps should be. This has been compounded by locating successive clearcuts next to previous ones. When correctly applied in the right place and at the right time, however, clearcutting is not the ecological disaster that some people have been led to believe. Often the environmental problems caused by clearcutting are associated with the roads, not with the clearcutting itself. This requires better road building and/or the use of harvesting equipment that requires less roading, and not necessarily a switch to another harvesting system. In some cases, alternatives to clearcutting may require a greater density of roads, with increased risk of environmental damage. Alternative harvesting systems can and should be used to replace clearcutting in some areas, but where this is done solely for aesthetic reasons, there may be a high price to pay in terms of logging costs, soil damage, and increased threats to streams. There are ways to avoid this risk, but they are not always used.

The high costs of putting in roads for the first time, the safety of workers when harvesting in forests that have very large dead or partially decayed trees, and the damage that would be done to the roots of residual trees by non-clearcut harvesting are some of the factors used to justify clearcutting as the appropriate harvest system in 'first rotation' harvesting of many west coast old-growth forests. In subsequent harvests, alternative harvesting techniques and silvicultural systems may be much safer and more feasible than in the first cut.

Do Clearcuts Have to Be So Large?

Economies of scale and simple convenience have often led to clearcuts being much larger than desirable from the point of view of aesthetics, wildlife, soil stability, watershed, and other considerations. Excessive clearcut size is probably the single greatest mistake that has been made in the application of clearcutting. Of course, as more and more of a valley is converted from mature to young forest, adjacent clearcut-harvested areas become contiguous. In this way, a series of smaller clearcut areas may be linked over several decades, giving the appearance of a single large clearcut. Thus, the problems that arise from clearcut harvesting may result more from the spatial distribution of clearcut patches across the landscape than from the use of the clearcut method and the size of individual clearcuts.

Visually, small clearcuts may help for a while. However, unless the logging of a particular valley is spread out over a long period, such as half or more of the entire rotation, the visual, and wildlife, impacts of a few large clearcuts will eventually be rather similar to those of many smaller clearcuts.

There is still much discussion as to whether it is better to disperse many small clearcuts or patchcuts throughout the forest, resulting eventually in an intimate mosaic of small patches of forest of many different ages, or to have larger clearcuts resulting in large areas of forest of similar age. Wildlife concerns in the late 1960s and early 1970s pushed logging towards the former conclusion. However, as the amount of remaining old growth declined, small clearcuts linked up over large areas, leaving scattered small patches of older forests that are believed to be too small to satisfy the requirements of certain old-growth-dependent wildlife species. Consequently, arguments in favour of a mosaic of large, medium, and small clearcuts, and large, medium, and small reserves of mature timber have recently been advanced by wildlife managers and forest ecologists who have been studying old growth and biodiversity. This topic is discussed further in the chapter on old growth (Chapter 9).

Why Do Foresters Clearcut When It Looks So Ugly?

Much of the public antagonism about clearcutting in North America, especially in the west, has arisen because of the distasteful appearance of many clearcuts in the immediate post-harvest period, and the clearcutting of large areas over a relatively short period. Unfortunately, these concerns have become confused with the more persistent and ultimately more important issue of environmental degradation. Although the public concern over aesthetics is now being balanced by concerns over 'ecosystem integrity' and biodiversity, there is still a lot of confusion between the visual and ecological impacts of forestry practices. Many industrial forest companies, even those that have been practising environmentally

Undesirable clearcutting practices

A

B

A Excessive roads on a steep clearcut and skidder-logged mountain slope in the Canadian Rockies. This level of soil disturbance is unacceptable. Such areas should be cable-harvested. The problem here was the wrong choice of harvesting equipment, not the fact that the area was clearcut. Adjacent areas that had been partially cut had a similar density of roads.

B Severe soil erosion following poor logging practices on Vancouver Island. This is usually caused by poor road construction and maintenance. It is absolutely unacceptable, even though the ecosystem will eventually recover.

sound management, have in the past been very insensitive to the issue of aesthetics and the rapidly changing public perceptions of, and attitudes towards, the visual aspects of forest harvesting. Much of the conflict between forestry and the public in the past could probably have been avoided had these companies been more aware of and responsive to the public's concerns about what clearcuts look like and the aesthetic consequences of having too few cutting cycles (i.e., concentrating their timber harvesting in a few areas rather than dispersing it throughout the forest).

In comparison to a growing or mature crop of corn or cabbages, a freshly harvested corn or cabbage field can look pretty desolate and unattractive. However, the ugly stage of agriculture does not usually persist for very long: a few weeks or months. It is soon forgotten in the annual cycle of ploughing, planting, tending, and crop harvest. Silviculture, the growing of tree crops, has a much longer cropping cycle than agriculture. As a result, the visually unattractive post-harvest phase lasts much longer even though it usually occupies a smaller proportion of the overall crop cycle. With the difference in crop production time scales, the 'ugly duckling' stage of silviculture seems to dominate the public's perception of forestry much more than their perception of the less visually attractive stages of agriculture.

The aesthetic or visual quality of the landscape can have a great influence on the pleasures of outdoor recreation, and ugly clearcuts can devalue many types of forest-based recreation until the area is again clothed in green trees of significant stature. However, the ugly stage of the tree-crop rotation cycle is not forever. In many cases it is short-lived relative to the tree-crop cycle, but this is not necessarily short-lived with respect to the public's desires: five to fifteen years in humid coastal forests, and fifteen to thirty years in very cold northern or subalpine forests. In areas of high recreational value and visual quality, visual damage over such periods may be unacceptable, and harvesting systems may be required that are more compatible with aesthetics and recreation. In other areas, the loss of visual values over such a period may be accepted because of other benefits from using the clearcutting system.

To many people, the very young stages of biological and ecological systems are less attractive than the intermediate and mature stages. But visual appearances should not be confused with function. A small patchcut with no untidy logging debris and no ugly soil disturbance may not be any more ecologically intact, nor the ecosystem any more sustainable, than a less attractive larger clearcut with lots of rotting logs and patches of soil disturbance. Similarly, leaving lots of standing dead, broken, and misformed trees in a clearcut may look awful, but it can provide future habitat for cavity-nesting birds and other animals, and thus maintain biodiversity. Leaving broken stems and older, partly decomposed logs on the ground in a clearcut site may look wasteful to some people but will contribute to the long-term maintenance of soil organic matter and may serve a number of other important ecological functions (see Chapters 10 and 11). Rotting logs may be 'packed lunches' for soil organisms for decades to come. On sites on which the soil becomes very dry in midsummer, large rotting logs may provide moist microsites that never dry out and in which animals and microbes that are important to long-term site productivity can survive the summer drought. A very 'clean' and tidy clearcut in which there is no apparent 'waste' and no untidy debris has lost a lot more of its wildlife habitat and its stock of nutrients and organic matter than a site with a lot of logging debris left on it, unsightly though that debris might be until the site is revegetated. 'Small, tidy, neat, attractive, and no waste' does not necessarily equal 'low environmental impact.'

In some cases, the land management that would have resulted from a more positive reaction to public pressure over aesthetic issues would have created less environmental disturbance and better forest management; sometimes things that look ugly are indeed more ecologically altered and less

environmentally desirable than things that look more pleasing. In other cases, however, the outcome would have been more aesthetically pleasing than environmentally friendly. The results would have done more for short-term recreational values than for the long-term sustainability and biotic diversity of the forest. In some cases, response to public concern, such as for 'cleaner' logging and less 'waste,' can result in greater damage to important soil resources on the site.

Does Clearcutting 'Destroy' the Forest Ecosystem?
From the frequency of statements in the media about how clearcutting is 'destroying the environment,' it is clear that many people have become convinced that forests may soon be gone from the face of the planet, and that the major cause is clearcutting. Questions such as 'Are the results of clearcutting *forever?*' or 'Is clearcutting destroying the world's forests?' or 'Will there be *any* forests left in ten years?' are clearly at the heart of the current public concerns about clearcutting, even though the genesis of these concerns may have been the appearance of harvested forest landscapes rather than any actual assessment of environmental degradation.

Understanding the answer to this question requires some knowledge of how forest ecosystems work, of how they recover from disturbance, and of the goals of forest management. Consequently, if you chose to skip Chapters 4 and 5 and do not have this knowledge, you might want to read them before proceeding. Equipped with this knowledge, you will be in a better position to judge between 'good' and 'bad' clearcutting. It will be easier to distinguish between those forest ecosystems and management objectives for which clearcutting is both environmentally sound and socially acceptable, and will result in the sustained renewal of our forests, and those situations in which clearcutting, or the way it has been applied in the past, is clearly unacceptable.

Without any question, clearcutting changes a forest ecosystem. And it would be correct to say that it temporarily 'destroys' certain conditions and values of a forest. For example, clearcutting destroys the shade cast by trees. It destroys the forest microclimate. It destroys those aspects of wildlife habitat that were provided by the clearcut trees. All these things are created by the vegetation, however, and are not an inherent characteristic of the landscape itself, the way soil is to a considerable extent. As the trees, herbs, and shrubs of the forest regrow, these conditions are recreated. Thus, in ecological terms, the change caused by clearcutting is only 'destruction' if the mechanisms of ecosystem recovery, especially vegetation recovery, have been significantly damaged. Where this is the case, regrowth of the forest and recovery of all the many related conditions may be unacceptably delayed, and the adjective 'destroyed' is much more relevant.

What are the mechanisms or conditions that ensure forest renewal? There are several, but the following are the most important.

Reinvasion of the area by the organisms that will make up the new forest. In a well-managed forest, either clearcutting will facilitate natural regeneration of trees or seedlings grown from seed collected in the area before harvesting will be planted. If no natural reinvasion of the harvested area by trees occurs because all seeds and seedlings on the site before harvesting have been killed and because there are no adjacent forests from which seeds can come, or if no seedlings are available for planting, one can say that the forest has been 'destroyed' until such seeds or seedlings become available. The forest will have been converted into a meadow or a shrub community.

Once well established, herb and shrub communities may be able to resist invasion by trees for many decades. Consequently, if for some reason reforestation is delayed for a decade or more, reforestation by natural or human-assisted mechanisms may be difficult and slow. Generally, this is not the case. In the absence of prompt natural regeneration, trees are normally planted within a few years. Even if planting is not done, trees normally reinvade clearcut areas within a few years or decades, and

most animals and microbes of the forest either remain in the clearcut area or return to the clearcut area from adjacent forested areas once the redeveloping vegetation provides the habitat values that they require.

The fertility and physical properties of the soil. If clearcutting has resulted in massive soil erosion or a substantial reduction in soil fertility, regrowth of the forest and recovery of the ecosystem to its pre-harvest condition may be significantly delayed. Loss of some or all of the surface layers of soil will require the development of a new soil or soil layers in the badly disturbed areas. This development will occur if the area is occupied by a pioneer plant community that is adapted to the altered soil and microclimatic conditions. In hot and dry or very cold climates, on nutrient-poor sandy or gravelly soils, or on erosion-resistant exposed bedrock, this can be a slow process, requiring many decades or centuries. In areas with a mild, humid climate or deep deposits of soil 'parent material,' or on geologically young bedrock materials that weather easily, it may take only a few years or decades. Most forest ecosystems have intermediate environmental conditions, and redevelopment of soil where it has been lost or badly degraded may require periods of time ranging from several decades to several centuries. Where ecological succession involves nitrogen-fixing plants such as red alder or lupines, the recovery of nutritionally or physically damaged soil can sometimes be surprisingly rapid. Massive soil erosion caused solely by clearcutting is rare in western North America. In contrast, erosion caused by poorly constructed roads is far too common and is a frequent and legitimate cause of protest by environmental groups.

The microclimate. In hot, dry, or very windy climates, or on sites where frost is a problem, young seedlings may require microclimatic protection for establishment and early growth. This may be provided by shrubs or trees, large rocks, logs, or simply a very 'hummocky' ground surface. The 'nurse' function of the forest canopy in providing a sheltered microclimate is very important in severe climates, and clearcutting in such areas may create such harsh microclimates that redevelopment of the forest is difficult and slow. For example, clearcuts in hot, dry savannah forests, in subalpine forests close to the alpine treeline, or in northern forests close to the arctic treeline, may take many decades or even centuries for adequate reforestation.

The answer, then, is yes, clearcutting may 'destroy' a variety of forest conditions for some period following the harvest, and no, these conditions are not lost forever. The time taken for their recovery will depend on whether the ecological mechanisms of recovery have been damaged. Just because a clearcut looks ugly says absolutely nothing about whether these mechanisms have been impaired. Judging the ecological impact of clearcutting, therefore, requires an analysis of ecological processes and not just temporary, though highly visible, changes in the structure and visual appearance of the ecosystem.

If a Mature Forest or an Old-Growth Forest Is Clearcut, Will There Ever Be Another Forest Just Like It Again?

Not surprisingly, the answer is, 'it depends.' It depends on how long you mean by 'ever,' and what you mean by 'another forest just like it.' The answer will vary according to whether the clearcutting has damaged the ecosystem's mechanisms of recovery (as discussed above), whether it is the forester's goal to recreate the original conditions, and whether global climate change will permit any of the forests of the world to maintain their present condition or to return to it if disturbed naturally or by humans.

How Long Is 'Ever'?

If 'ever' means within the lifetime of the person asking the question, the answer in most cases will be 'no.'

Because most native forests, even in the tropics, take half a century, a century, or even longer to regrow to the height, average tree diameter, and

general appearance of a mature forest, most of us will not live to see the renewal of the pre-logging forest condition on a particular clearcut site. Unless we were to discover the elixir of life and live for centuries, none of us would personally witness the regrowth from seedling to mature specimen of the giant trees of cool temperate rain forests, such as the tall eucalyptus forests of Tasmania or the coastal forests of hemlock, western red cedar and Douglas-fir of the Pacific coast of North America. Trees can grow remarkably fast in some environments. For example, eucalyptus forests planted in southern Brazil can reach more than thirty metres in height in five years. Visually impressive forests can regrow in that area well within the lifetime of most people. For most of the world's temperate and northern forests, however, it takes at least one or two centuries for forests on very productive sites to develop the cathedral-like atmosphere that people often associate with the term 'old-growth,' and even longer on medium- and low-productivity sites.

Having said this, it should be noted that many of the forest giants of cool temperate rain forests are much younger than many people think. Trees can grow remarkably fast on the moist, fertile sites in the mild, humid climates where such forest giants are typically found. Giant trees are generally not found where trees do not grow rapidly, unless they are of a species that can live for a thousand years or more. The majority of the forests in Oregon were less than 400 years old when Europeans first came to the area. The giant eucalypts in Tasmania (can be more than three metres in diameter and a hundred metres tall) can be less than 300 to 400 years old, and the giant Sitka spruce of the Pacific coast of Canada, about which there has been so much controversy (in the Carmanah Valley, for example) are often in the 250- to 400-year age class, not the thousand years or more that many people assume them to be. It should be possible to grow such forest giants on a moist, fertile site in a managed forest on a 200- to 250-year rotation.

Judging the impact of clearcutting in terms of

human life spans is perfectly reasonable if one of the stated objectives of forest management (see the discussion in Chapter 5) is to maintain or to renew within a human life span a particular ecological condition or visual appearance of the forest. However, it is an unreasonable basis on which to evaluate clearcutting if foresters are deliberately maintaining second-growth forest conditions that are different from those of the original old-growth forest, or where trees are being grown on a 50- to 100-year cropping cycle to provide materials desired by society. As long as the *renewability* of all desired ecosystem values is sustained, and as long as a mosaic of forests of different ages is maintained across the landscape, there will be a sustained supply of these resource values from the region, even though at any one location within that landscape the supply of particular resource values may be intermittent.

Will the Future Forest Be 'Just Like' the One that Has Been Cut?

Chapter 4 pointed out that a forest is a very complex ecological system. It has many components and processes. It is a landscape with a soil and a climate capable of supporting tree growth. It has trees, smaller plants, birds, other animals, and microbes. It is a living system fuelled by solar energy that produces plant biomass that feeds the herbivores and decomposer organisms, which in turn feed other animals and microbes. The 'conveyor belts' within this natural 'factory' are chemical nutrients and water. The complex forest system can be described in terms of its species composition and genetic make-up, its vertical and horizontal structure, its content of organic matter and nutrients, its rate of energy capture and transfer between organisms, and its rate and patterns of nutrient cycling and organic matter decomposition (carbon cycling).

Because of the complexity of a forest, no two forests are *ever* exactly the same, and no single forest remains the same for very long because of the natural processes of change. Forests are not like pictures – you cannot frame them and hang them on

the wall so that they are always there, unchanging. So, the question of whether the forest that regrows in a clearcut is 'just like' the forest that has been clearcut should not be based on the expectation of an exact duplicate. That never happens in nature anyway. There is always change over time in species composition, production, rates of growth, and various aspects of biodiversity.

Asking whether a second-growth forest will be the same as the previous forest is similar to asking about the biological characteristics of generations of people who live in a particular house. The couple who own the house will not live there forever. They will either move away or grow old and eventually die. If their birth children remain in the house, the biological characteristics of the occupants of the house will change; the children may be similar to the parents (they are of the same species and share the same genetic material), but they will certainly not be identical. They will have different fingerprints, and may have many other physical differences, but they are more similar to their parents than to the members of another family that might move into the house. The house would still be much the same, however, since the new family is still of the same species. If completely different species moved into the house, such as mice and spiders, it would be a very different sort of place. Thus, we might rate the house occupied by the children as being very similar to when it was occupied by the parents, still quite similar when occupied by another family with the same general social, cultural, and ethnic background, less similar if occupied by people from a completely different social, cultural, and ethnic background, and quite dissimilar if the house is abandoned by humans and occupied by spiders and mice.

If a clearcut landscape (the 'house') is reoccupied by the seeds, spores, and young (the offspring or 'children') of the plants and other organisms that previously occupied the area (the 'parents'), and if the resources of the landscape (the nutrients, organic matter, and so on, which are analogous to the contents of the house and the family's bank account) are still intact, the forest that regrows will essentially be the same as the original forest, though never 100 per cent identical. It will develop through its 'baby,' 'teenage,' and 'midlife' condition, and may in due course come to resemble its 'parent' forest rather closely. If, on the other hand, the landscape is occupied by a different 'family' of the same set of species, the future forest will still be similar, but less so. If a completely different set of tree and animal species with significantly different ecological characteristics occupies the landscape, you still have a forest that will function in much the same way as the original forest, but it will certainly be ecologically different. If the trees are completely and permanently replaced by herbs and shrubs, then the ecosystem will have become very different indeed.

Where a clearcut is allowed to regenerate naturally, or where it is replanted with seedlings of the same species grown from seeds collected in the original forest or nearby, and if the biological and non-living resources of the landscape are intact, then it is difficult to argue that the new forest is any more different from the original forest than parents and children successively occupying the same house are different from each other. In both cases, the difference is largely a function of age. Given time and a reasonably constant climate, essentially the same forest type will generally redevelop.

Where a clearcut is regenerated, naturally or by planting, with an earlier seral species, the forest will be more different than if regenerated directly from the 'parent' trees. However, if the species is the natural seral species for the area, using seed gathered in the same general area, there is nothing unnatural about the new forest. Indeed, nature often replaces late seral or climax species with early seral species following a natural disturbance. If this seral forest is left unmanaged and if there is a source of seeds of the later seral and climax species, these will in due course invade the early seral forest. Eventually the original forest would be re-established, unless we humans have in the meantime changed the climate,

or the area is disturbed again. We cannot compare the latter situation with the family in the house analogy, because there is no such natural succession of species involved in human communities. The discussion of this question has been focussed on the forest's stand level response to clearcutting. Depending on the pattern and rate of harvesting a large area of forested landscape, the future landscape may differ significantly from the pre-logging landscape even if the differences at the stand level are small. Thus, this question as well as many other questions need to be evaluated at both the stand and the landscape scale.

Does Clearcutting Damage the Ecosystem's Mechanisms of Recovery?

The simple answer is 'no' if the harvesting is done in a silviculturally and environmentally sound manner, and in some cases 'yes,' if the harvesting is mismanaged. Delays in the recovery of the ecosystem can occur if clearcutting results in undesirable changes in microclimate (a problem in harsh climates), the loss of nutrients if 'whole-tree' harvesting is done (a problem on infertile sites; this is described later in this chapter), the erosion or compaction of soil during removal of the logs, or the full occupation of the clearcut by herbs or shrubs that prevent or slow the establishment and growth of trees. If these species form a dense cover over the area, they may slow the 'normal' process of succession by many decades, which is why it is not uncommon for foresters to control the growth of these non-crop plant species with fire, manual or mechanical means, grazing of domestic animals such as sheep, or herbicides. However, such 'weed' problems are not specific to clearcutting, and they may be much worse following other types of harvesting systems because it may be more difficult to control the weeds where an area has not been clearcut. In some cases, such as in the management of very shade-tolerant European beech forests in France, a form of group-selection harvesting is sometimes done because it reduces weed problems –

the trees in this case are more shade tolerant than the weeds – but this is a rather uncommon example.

Ecosystem recovery can be damaged by inappropriate post-harvest slashburning treatment. This is a problem of post-harvest site treatment, not clearcutting, although there are situations where using non-clearcut harvest methods may eliminate the need for slashburning because less logging slash is produced at any one harvest.

If Climate Change Occurs or Acid Rain Intensifies, Can the Original Forest Regrow after Clearcutting?

The most probable answer is 'no.' However, if the climate were to change enough or air pollution were to become bad enough to have a significant effect on the regrowth of a forest in a clearcut, the regeneration and regrowth of forests managed under non-clearcut systems would also be affected. Unmanaged forest reserves would probably change as well, though more slowly; mature trees may be less sensitive to these changes than young trees. Certainly, if the climate were to become hotter and drier, it might become appropriate in some forests to switch from clearcutting to a system such as shelterwood, or even to an uneven-aged forest with selection harvesting. Alternatively, clearcutting could be combined with the planting of species or ecotypes that are adapted to the altered climatic conditions.

The idea that one can preserve a living system, unchanging forever, in the face of changing environmental conditions is not supported by the available facts. One can preserve a landscape view in a photograph or painting (until it fades), but, as noted in Chapter 3, the single most fundamental characteristic of ecosystems is that they change over time.

Evaluation of the Ecological Impacts of Clearcutting

Clearcut harvesting of timber has the potential to affect every component, every process, and every attribute of the forest ecosystem. No single 'ecological impact' can be discussed. Long-winded though it may seem, there is no alternative to going one by one through a list of potential impacts. Each topic in the following discussion could be the subject of a lengthy textbook. Obviously the treatment here is greatly simplified.

Let us start by examining the effects of clearcutting on ecosystem components, and continue by discussing its effects on ecosystem attributes and resource values.

Effects on the Components of the Ecosystem

Climate and Microclimate

The overall character of a forest is determined by the regional climate. It is believed that total and irreversible deforestation over many thousands of square kilometres in some parts of the world would result in a significantly altered regional climate because of the role of forests in the hydrological cycle (cloud formation, atmospheric humidity) and radiant energy balance (affecting air temperatures). In some humid tropical areas, significantly smaller areas of deforestation may result in local changes in humidity and precipitation. For example, conversion of large areas of Brazilian rain forest to grassland for cattle ranching, or simply deforestation and soil degradation due to inappropriate agriculture (sometimes this follows exploitive forest harvesting), raises the risk of regional climate alteration that could pose a major threat to the character of the downwind forests. This is not clearcut forest harvesting, however. It is massive change in land use. Clearcut timber harvesting as part of sustainable forest management has little effect on regional climate.

In contrast, clearcutting has a dramatic effect on microclimate. Light intensity, air temperature and humidity, wind speed, and the daily fluctuation of temperature inside a closed forest differ greatly from those conditions in the middle of a clearcut. Clearcutting removes the microclimatic forest influence, although logging slash may significantly modify the microclimate in the ten to twenty centimetres above the soil surface. A modified summer microclimate is re-established as soon as herbs and shrubs develop continuous cover across the harvested area, and the forest microclimate is restored as soon as trees regrow and form a closed canopy. This forest microclimate is not constant over time. It will vary somewhat with the stand density (number of trees per hectare), the tree height, and the degree of canopy closure as the stand matures.

Soil

Unlike microclimate, which is inevitably changed by clearcutting, many aspects of the soil may remain essentially unaltered by clearcutting. Soil depth and texture; the abundance of coarse fragments such as pebbles, stones, and boulders; and the mineralogy and origin of the soil mineral material generally do not change. Other aspects, such as soil temperature and moisture, may be changed a little, while yet others – soil microbes, soil organic matter, and, on some sites, soil temperature and moisture – may be significantly altered. It depends on the type of ecosystem (slope, aspect, elevation, soil type, vegetation type and condition before harvest, and climate), the type of harvesting equipment used, the equipment operator's skill and concern for the soil, the time of year of the harvest (how wet the soil is; winter logging over snow versus summer logging), and several other factors.

Helicopter and skyline logging may limit soil changes to temporary changes in soil temperature and moisture, and resultant changes in soil animals, microbes, and chemistry; there may be little or no physical impact on the soil. Skidder and tractor logging, in contrast, can cause soil compaction, reduced aeration and drainage, loss or burial of the nutritionally important surface layers of the soil, and loss of slope stability because of altered slope hydrology over some portion of the harvested area. However, the negative impact of this type of logging equipment can be kept to a minimum by winter logging over snow or by logging only when the soil is dry, by minimizing the number of skid trails, by ensuring only one or two passes with the equipment over each patch of ground, and by ensuring that the skid trails are 'put to bed' – that is, will not cause erosion and will support satisfactory future tree growth – right after the harvest is completed. As noted earlier, these effects are not unique to clearcutting. They are more of a consequence of the harvesting equipment used.

Some physical impact from logging may be desirable. It may improve the soil for natural regeneration or planted seedlings, and may help control weed growth. Sometimes clearcutting creates so little soil disturbance that foresters have to burn or mechanically disturb the site to put it in the appropriate ecological condition for the new forest to get established either by planting or by natural regeneration.

Soil fertility is often increased for several years after clearcutting because of reduced uptake of nutrients by plants and the increased release of nutrients from decomposing slash and the forest floor. Where this 'assart flush'[10] of nutrients is excessive, it may lead to the loss of some nutrients by soil leaching, and can sometimes lead to a loss of gaseous nitrogen by 'denitrification.' The flush of nutrient availability can make the growth of nutrient-demanding herbs and shrubs very prolific for up to a decade after clearcutting, which can pose problems for natural regeneration of trees and for the survival and early growth of planted tree seedlings. However, it also fosters the early growth of the trees, which often grow faster in the first ten to twenty years than would be expected based on long-term site quality considerations. This nutrient flush is not 'unnatural.' It occurs after any natural disturbance that kills or removes the trees.

The nutrient losses into streams by leaching are

---

10 The assart effect is the period of increased nutrient availability in the soil following ecosystem disturbance. This results from one or more of the following: reduced nutrient uptake, increased rate of decomposition of soil organic matter, and increased quantity of material to be decomposed (slash, in the case of logging, or trees and other plants killed by a natural disturbance).

usually relatively minor compared with the losses in harvested material, especially if whole-tree harvesting (WTH) is done. Where only large logs are removed, losses of the most critical nutrients are generally much less. The difference in nutrient removal between WTH and removal of just the larger logs varies between different types of forest (greatest for evergreens with lots of foliage), between forests of different ages (greater for short-rotation crops than long-rotation crops), between different times of year (mainly for deciduous species), and between different nutrients (generally greatest for nitrogen and phosphorus). The risk of nutritional problems caused by WTH is generally much greater with short-rotation (15 to 30 years) than long-rotation (60 to 120 years) crops.

The effects of clearcutting on soil fertility are thus highly variable, as are the ability of the site to withstand the loss of nutrients without a reduction in tree growth and the rate at which the nutrient capital of the site recovers over time.

Clearcutting on very steep, inherently unstable slopes can significantly increase the risk of landslides ('slope failures'). The stability of such slopes may depend considerably on the strength of the tree roots. As the roots decay and lose strength after logging, they may no longer be able to hold the soil mantle during unusually heavy rainfall or excessively rapid snowmelt 'events,' such as heavy rain falling on an early winter snowpack, as commonly occurs in late November in coastal British Columbia, Washington, and Oregon. As the new forest regrows, the declining strength of the old roots is replaced by new roots of trees, herbs, and shrubs, but there is often a period of minimum total root strength in the ten- to twenty-year period following clearcutting, sometimes as early as five years. Post-clearcutting slope failures often occur in this period. The significance of root strength for slope stability varies in different climates, on different soils, and with different tree species, but it is certainly an important consideration in many mountain forests. However, most slope failures attributed to timber

harvesting have been shown to be related to poorly built or poorly maintained roads rather than to the loss of root strength.

Forests on steep, unstable slopes should *not* be clearcut. Enough live trees should be left to ensure the maintenance of sufficient live-root biomass for slope stability. This is usually not a problem in deciduous broadleaf forests, in which the cut stumps or roots resprout or sucker, respectively. It is also less of a problem for the few conifer species that can stump-sprout. Such problems of slope instability can also be caused by wildfire, insect and disease outbreaks, or windthrow events that temporarily remove or reduce root strength on a steep slope.

Vegetation

Like microclimate, vegetation is inevitably altered by clearcutting: the large, dominant trees on the site are all removed. This alters the vertical structure of the plant community. It also changes the species composition. Some canopy epiphytes (plants that live non-parasitically on other plants, such as mosses or ferns growing on large tree branches or on tree stems) that depend on mature tree canopies will be lost until the trees in the subsequent stand reach a size and condition suitable for them. Many plants that cannot survive in a closed forest invade the clearcut, while species that grow in the cooler, more humid, and shady forest often exhibit stress symptoms when exposed to the open clearcut microclimate. Some die. Others resprout from underground organs, producing leaves and stems that are adapted to the new microclimate. Some plants that barely survive in mature forests benefit greatly from the new conditions.

Plant species diversity increases in many if not most cool temperate and northern forests following clearcutting. In many tropical forests the reverse occurs. Species diversity is reduced, although this is generally more the result of deforestation and altered land use rather than clearcutting followed by the managed re-establishment of native forest. Where tropical forest is replaced by tropical pine, oil palm, or eucalyptus plantations, there is usually a dramatic reduction in plant and animal species diversity.

Site treatments following clearcutting, such as slashburning, mechanical site preparation, or herbicides, may favour certain plants over others, and result in reduced plant species diversity. This is not a direct consequence of clearcutting, however. Such changes in species composition are generally fairly short-lived unless they lead to dominance of the site by a single species, such as fireweed, bracken fern, or some shrub species. Where such treatments are specifically meant to prevent or break up dense populations of these competing plant species, they will increase plant diversity.

As ecological succession proceeds, the frequently diverse early plant community is shaded out as a tree population or tree community closes canopy. This early successional forest may comprise a single or a small number of species and is often dense. Such young forests have low plant species diversity, structural diversity, and animal species diversity. However, as these stands self-thin by competition for light, water, and nutrients, understorey species and seedlings of shade-tolerant tree species may become established. As the stand matures and the canopy develops gaps, plant and animal diversity increase. Promotion of more open stand conditions by silvicultural activities such as thinning can help to increase and maintain this diversity. Where silviculture promotes mixed-species stands with less than complete canopy closure, managed forests may be considerably more diverse than unmanaged forests that develop after a natural disturbance. In many cases, site variation within a clearcut area and variable levels of site disturbance – undisturbed areas, scarified areas, skidroads, and clumps of advance regeneration – ensure that young forests in clearcut areas do have some diversity in tree species and canopy structure.

Microbial Life

The species composition of microbes in the forest (mostly in the soil but also in dead and dying trees and freshly fallen logs) depends on the regional climate; the microclimate; the type, size, age, and condition of decaying organic matter; the past history of disturbance on the site, such as whether the forest has just been burned; and chance. Many microbes are very territorial. If a particular species of fungus invades a freshly fallen tree, it may be able to exclude other species of fungi. Thus, the microbial community in a decaying log will often depend on which species finds the log first. This in turn may depend on which type of insect attacked the log first and inoculated it with microbes.

Because clearcutting alters the soil microclimate and the quantity, size, and chemistry of decomposing organic matter, there is a marked change in soil microbial populations. The death of live tree roots that previously supported populations of fungi generally results in an increase in bacterial populations and the animals that feed on them, a decline in the abundance of fungi and fungi-feeding soil animals, and a change in the types of fungi. These microbial changes will persist until regrowth of the forest re-establishes a forest microclimate, a characteristic quantity and quality of organic forest floor, and a soil full of tree roots.

Relatively little is known of the changes that clearcutting causes in the diversity of soil microorganisms. This is partly because of lack of research and partly because the concept of species diversity that works fairly well for plants and animals is much harder to apply in the subterranean microbial world. Although many species of fungi can be identified with specific tree diseases or have identifiable above-ground fruiting bodies, the majority of soil microbes apparently exist in a genetically less repeatable and distinct form; there are thousands of 'genetic isolates' of what might be considered a 'species' of microbe, each of which is genetically unique. The detailed effects of clearcutting or any natural or management-induced disturbance on this microbial 'genetic soup' is simply not known, and may be beyond the powers of science to find out for the foreseeable future. Perhaps all we can say is that there is constant change in the genetic constitution of this complex community, that the present diversity is the outcome of millions of years of repeated disturbances, and that it will inevitably change again because of natural and human-induced disturbance.

Deforestation and the replacement of trees and shrubs by grasses or other herbs for several decades can result in the loss of certain species of fungi that tree seedlings may require for growth. Such semi-permanent loss of tree cover is highly unusual in forestry. It can occur following extensive wildfires that eliminate all trees and tree seeds over large areas, and can also result from exploitive logging followed by burning and agricultural land use. It is not something that occurs commonly in sustained-yield forest management. In tropical forests, the heating of soil that occurs after clearcutting and burning can similarly eliminate fungi that are required for forest re-establishment. However, this is not a major problem if clearcut sites are not burned.

As more is learned about the forest soil microbial community and its interactions with plants, management practices may be developed to achieve specific goals with respect to the composition of this important soil community.

Wildlife and Soil Animals

'Wildlife' is defined here as the vertebrate (mammals, birds, and reptiles) and invertebrate (mostly insects) life of the forest: not only the familiar and common large game mammals and birds, but also the smaller vertebrates and invertebrates that spend at least some, if not most or all, of their time above ground. The term 'soil animals' refers to vertebrates and invertebrates that live exclusively in the soil.

As with soil microbes, wildlife and soil animals are habitat-specific; they depend on access to appropriate shelter, food, and breeding habitat. Forest harvesting changes all of these, and among the various types of forest harvesting, clearcutting has the most dramatic effects. It has very important im-

plications for all species of wildlife and soil animals.

'Nature abhors a vacuum' is an oft-heard expression based on the fact that evolution has produced plant and animal species that are able to live in almost any terrestrial environment on earth. Almost irrespective of how an ecosystem is disturbed and changed, there will be a group of animals that will gain an advantage and another group that will be disadvantaged. A few species of wildlife are relatively insensitive to change in the forest. They are the gypsies of the non-human animal world; they can make a living almost anywhere.

As clearcutting alters plant species composition, plant community structure, microclimate, and soil, there will be a change in animal species that are dependent on specific vegetation and soil conditions. Those that are adapted to and depend on early successional conditions may be favoured, and those that are adapted to and depend on later successional conditions will be adversely affected. As ecological succession results in the regrowth of the forest, the early-successional animal species will be lost, and the later-successional species will once again occupy the area.

The effects of clearcutting on wildlife and soil animals varies with the size, shape, and orientation of the clearcut; with the age of the adjacent forest; and with the ecological characteristics of the ecosystem (climate as determined by latitude, longitude, aspect, elevation, windward/leeward, and so on; topography; geology and soils; and vegetation prior to disturbance). It also depends very much on the post-harvesting site treatment, such as mechanical site scarification, slashburning, and weed control. There are many cases in which changes caused by these treatments have been wrongly ascribed to clearcutting. There are also examples in which changes in animal populations that *appear* to be caused by clearcutting are really caused by something else.

In the central interior of British Columbia there has been a dramatic decline in the abundance of woodland caribou, one of the very few animal species known to require old-growth, interior, high-elevation forest for its survival. In winter caribou feed on lichens that grow on the trees in these subalpine forests. It has been suggested that this decline is being caused by high-elevation clearcutting. However, the decline has been shown to be the result of increased wolf predation, not a shortage of winter habitat although this may be a problem in the future if current rates of logging in the interior subalpine forest continue at the present rate. Increased wolf numbers are the result of more abundant moose in lower-elevation forests. Because moose populations are generally favoured by clearcutting, it could be argued that clearcutting is still to blame, but research has shown that the increase of moose in the area of caribou decline is a result of the expansion of the geographic range of moose. Before the 1920-30 period, moose were not found in central BC, but they have since invaded the area from northeastern BC. This spread predated commercial forest harvesting in most of the area, but may have been influenced by a history of vegetation and land-use changes: vast areas of forest were burned off during the gold rush in the latter part of the last century, and significant areas in valleys were cleared for agriculture. Thus, it would seem that the decline of the caribou is not caused by the recent onset of clearcutting in their critical winter habitat. Human alteration of forest vegetation in the region has undoubtedly contributed to the problem, however.

A major recent concern about clearcutting has been the loss of snags and, subsequently, the loss of the bird and other species that feed on wood-boring insects or that live in cavities in the snags. Because of worker safety, and in some climatic regions because of the hazard of lightning strikes, it has been traditional to cut down all snags. This eliminates the habitat and food source for snag-dependent animal species, and may constitute the most significant potential negative impact of clearcutting on wildlife. The topic is discussed further in the chapters on biodiversity and old growth (Chapters 9 and 10).

Fish and Water

Clearcutting can have significant impact on the quality, quantity, and timing of water flows in forest streams and rivers (streamflow). The quantity and quality of streamflow are primarily a function of climate, topography, soils, and watershed size and order,[11] but these characteristics can be altered by forest harvesting. The extent of the alteration depends on the proportion of the watershed occupied by harvested areas (clearcuts or partially harvested areas) on which forest regrowth has not yet re-established the original water balance and hydrological control. Small, low-order watersheds are often contained within a single clearcut, and the characteristics of the small streams in such watersheds can be significantly altered for several years or even decades. Where the clearcut occupies only a portion of the watershed (as in the case of many second-, and most third-, fourth-, and higher-order watersheds), the effect on the stream will be proportional to the percentage of the watershed in recent clearcuts or partial cuts. Thus, the question 'what is the effect of clearcutting on a watershed?' cannot be answered until one has defined the watershed order, the proportion of the area that has been harvested and has not yet recovered hydrologically, and a number of other factors.

Like other animals, fish depend on appropriate habitat and food supply. If clearcutting alters the stream habitat and aquatic organisms, fish abundance and productivity will be altered. Stream warming, reduction of input of leaf litterfall and insects from streambank vegetation, loss of streambank stability, loss of 'security cover' for fish, and sedimentation of streams can occur as a result of forest harvesting that goes right to the streambank.

---

11   A small stream that has no tributaries is a first-order stream; it drains a first-order watershed. Two or more first-order streams combine to form a second-order stream draining a second-order watershed (the aggregate of all the first-order watersheds contributing to the stream). Two or more second-order streams combine to form a third-order stream draining a third-order watershed, and so on.

With the exception of sedimentation, all of these can be avoided through the retention of buffer strips ('riparian leave strips') of either understorey or undisturbed forest. However, buffer strips have to be carefully designed to avoid subsequent stream damage caused by the windthrow of larger trees in these strips. Many of the larger trees will not be windfirm unless very wide riparian forest reserves are created. If only narrow riparian strips of forest are left, it may be better for the stream if large trees were carefully removed, leaving smaller trees and lesser vegetation to take over their role in stabilizing the streambank and providing stream cover. Most stream sedimentation is caused by the roads and bridges that accompany any type of timber harvesting. The fact that clearcutting may require fewer roads, and may result in less soil disturbance than some alternative harvest systems, results in there being no simple relationship between the method of timber harvest and stream sedimentation.

Clearcutting can result in one or two years of increased nutrient input to streams (the assart period). This generally improves the productivity of fish, but can result in short-term, one- or two-year increases in nutrient concentrations to undesirable levels in some small first-order or ephemeral streams (streams that flow only during the rainy season). For example, in dry areas the nutrient enrichment of streams entering lakes already polluted, or 'enriched,' by urban and agricultural discharges can be undesirable. Increased levels of nitrate in streams that provide drinking water may be similarly unacceptable, although there have been very few reports of clearcutting causing such levels to exceed drinking water standards, even in the smallest streams. The most famous case of elevated streamwater nitrate levels, the Hubbard Brook experiment, resulted from the *deforestation* of a small, first-order watershed (simply cutting the trees down, not logging) followed by repeated annual devegetation using broad-spectrum herbicides. It was not a study of clearcutting, although a follow-up study did show some short-term elevation of

nitrate in a commercially clearcut first-order watershed of similar character. The experiment took place in a northern temperate hardwood forest in the northeastern U.S. In contrast, studies of the effects of clearcutting on the loss of nutrients in streamwater in western Oregon, Washington, and British Columbia have shown very small and very short-lived alternatives in the chemistry of streamwater.

While the loss of nutrients to streams is undesirable for land resources, such losses from clearcut areas are generally short-lived, relatively small, and compensated for by natural nutrient inputs early in the subsequent rotation. The extent of these losses reflects the logged area's speed of revegetation. Where such nutrient losses to streams are unacceptable, either the area must be revegetated rapidly, which in most cases occurs naturally, or forest harvesting must be conducted in a manner that leaves a cover of plants over the harvested area to reduce leaching losses.

Both fish habitat and streamwater characteristics will return to pre-harvest conditions as the forest regrows. However, if excessive quantities of logging debris are permitted to accumulate in gullies or in ephemeral or permanent streams, 'debris torrents' can be caused during major rainstorms or 'rain-on-snow' events. These torrents can inflict severe and very persistent damage to streams. The removal of large old logs from the stream habitat by a debris torrent is particularly damaging to stream diversity and fish habitat. Removing all large streamside trees and snags reduces future inputs of such logs, and can reduce the rate at which a stream recovers from this type of damage. It can also have long-term detrimental effects on fish and streams even in the absence of debris torrents. There is some concern that although natural debris torrents can sometimes be damaging to streams, they also constitute an important long-term contribution to stream diversity. Forest management that successfully eliminates all natural debris torrents in the future may therefore have a negative long-term impact on some stream values unless there is an adequate input of snags and streamside trees into the stream.

Effects on Ecosystem Attributes and Resource Values

Ecosystem Function

Ecosystem function refers to the capture and storage of solar energy as plant biomass, the transfer of this energy to the biomass of herbivores and carnivores, and the dynamics of dead organic matter as it is decomposed by soil animals and microbes. It also refers to the dynamics – the cycling – of the nutrient chemicals that are combined with solar energy in the complex molecules of living matter. Without an adequate supply of these chemicals, energy capture, storage, transfer, and release cannot occur at rates that would otherwise be expected.

Clearcutting has a major, albeit temporary, impact on ecosystem function. The sudden elimination of most of the living leaves in the clearcut area virtually terminates the capture of solar energy and its storage in new organic matter. Substantial quantities of organic matter and the nutrients they contain are removed in harvested materials, and most of the unharvested plant biomass is transferred to the forest floor, where it begins to decay. Many decaying logs are broken into smaller pieces and scattered over the harvested area. Unless the harvested area revegetates, all the soil organic matter will eventually be lost by microbial decomposition. This occurs rarely because revegetation and reforestation normally occur quite rapidly, long before all the organic matter has decomposed.

Nutrient uptake is greatly reduced or terminated by clearcutting, leading to an increase in nutrient availability. The release of nutrients from dead organic matter is accelerated because of the microclimatic and microbial changes that accompany clearcutting, and because of the increased quantity of material available for decomposition. Some of the nutrients released will be lost by soil leaching; some of the nitrogen released may be lost to the atmosphere as gas through the processes of denitrification or ammonification. This assart period continues only as long as the supply of easily decomposable organic matter is maintained. If reforestation is delayed until after the assart period, the new forest may experience significant nutrient deficiencies.

Losses of organic matter and nutrients normally last for only one to a few years; they are terminated as the area revegetates and is subsequently reforested.

The extent of the loss in harvested materials is determined more by the proportion of the tree biomass that is harvested – only the larger logs, called a 'stem-only' harvest, versus the entire stem plus leaves and branches, called 'whole-tree' or 'full-tree' harvesting – than whether or not the harvest is a clearcut. Whole-tree harvesting in a shelterwood or selection forest will ultimately cause as large a harvest-related nutrient removal as a clearcut, although the latter will probably have the greatest leaching loss.

Biodiversity

There are many different aspects of the diversity of forests (see Chapter 10). There is the diversity of physical environment as defined by climate, slope, elevation, aspect, and type and depth of soil. These collectively determine the type of vegetation, and hence the animal and microbial life, that will occupy an area after a disturbance, and also the speed of ecosystem recovery following the disturbance. The landscape-level diversity of physical environments is not affected by clearcutting or by any other timber-harvest system. Consequently, the landscape-level diversity of ecosystems is not affected either. However, logging disturbance can increase the diversity of microsites, resulting in an increase in biodiversity at a very local spatial scale in the subsequent forest.

Alpha species diversity is the number of species in a given ecosystem type; it is a measure of local species diversity. *Beta species diversity* is a measure of species diversity across the landscape; it is the difference in species composition between the different ecosystems found in a particular landscape, such as a major valley. *Geographical species diversity* is the variation in the species list across large regional geographical units, such as a province. Each of these measures of species diversity can also be applied to the structural diversity of the different units. *Temporal diversity* refers to the change in the species list and vegetation structure of a particular ecosystem over time, from the time of a disturbance until the ecosystem has returned to its original condition. *Genetic diversity* refers to the amount of genetic variation within a particular species in a particular ecosystem and across its geographical range.

Because there are so many different types of diversity in both the non-living environment and the biological community, the effects of clearcutting on biodiversity are inevitably complex. Generally speaking, clearcutting does not alter landscape diversity. It can cause either an increase or a decrease in alpha species diversity for a few years after harvest. Depending on the original beta diversity and the size and spatial distribution of the clearcuts, it can result in either an increase or a decrease in beta diversity, especially structural beta diversity, that will persist for a long time. Clearcutting usually causes a reduction in alpha structural diversity until the regenerating forest begins to self-thin or is thinned by foresters. The subsequent increase in structural diversity often continues as the forest matures towards an old-growth condition. Like a large natural wildfire, clearcutting could potentially cause some change in genetic diversity, but this does not usually occur in managed forests where there is a program of local seed collection and gene conservation. In fact, for some tree species a planted clearcut may have greater genetic diversity than a forest naturally regenerated after a wildfire from a very small number of surviving parent trees.

The major effect of clearcutting on local (alpha) plant species biodiversity is usually the initiation of the normal temporal pattern of change in diversity characteristic of that ecosystem after natural disturbance. Subsequent site treatments, such as slashburning, may alter this temporal pattern from that which occurs naturally, or simply change it from the pattern that accompanies one type of natural disturbance to the pattern that accompanies another type. The major effect at the regional level is usually an increase in beta diversity in previously unmanaged forests, and little effect on beta diversity in previously managed forests.

Biodiversity and its loss from managed forests is considered in greater detail in Chapter 10.

Carbon Storage and the Greenhouse Effect
Considerable concern has been expressed of late about the release of carbon to the atmosphere when old-growth forests are clearcut and replaced by second-growth forests. Old-growth forests in humid temperate and northern climates are normally characterized by large quantities of carbon in a thick forest floor (especially in cool, humid forests) and by an abundance of decaying logs, which are often large in humid coastal old growth. In humid climates, there is also a lot of humus in the mineral soil. Substantial quantities of this carbon are lost following clearcutting, regardless of whether or not the site is slashburned. Carbon released in a few minutes from forest floor material and logs that are consumed in a slashburn would normally be released by decomposition over the following five to ten years anyway.

Clearcutting in humid forests certainly causes a substantial release of carbon. Dry forests normally have much less forest floor and decomposing logs from which loss could occur. Frequent fires in the past or rapid decomposition in such dry forests have already released the carbon in dead trees and litterfall back to the atmosphere. In almost every case, however, the carbon dioxide released by clearcutting will be recaptured in the new tree crops before the end of the next tree-crop rotation, and often this will happen in the first few decades. But this is not the whole story. If the harvested materials are made into structural wood that is built into long-lived buildings, a well-managed forest produces a net removal of carbon from the atmosphere in spite of the initial release of carbon when the old-growth forest is harvested. In contrast, if the harvested materials are turned into short-lived products such as newspaper, harvesting humid old-growth forests will make a one-time net contribution to the greenhouse problem. However, this contribution is more a function of the end use of the harvest products than whether or not they are harvested by clearcutting.

The topic of carbon storage and release in forests is discussed further in Chapter 12.

Aesthetics and Recreation
Clearcutting affects non-material as well as material resource values of the forest. Humans place great value on how things look, as evidenced by society's enormous investment in such things as architecture, art, cosmetics, clothing fashions, and gardening. People care very much about how forested environments look, regardless of the environment's ecological condition.

As noted earlier, clearcutting causes a dramatic change in the visual appearance of the forest and can therefore have a major, if temporary, impact on the aesthetic qualities of the forest and on recreational values. Hiking across a freshly harvested cabbage field, corn field, or clearcut forest is not a particularly aesthetic experience, but this ugly stage of crop production is a relatively small proportion of the crop production cycle. Unfortunately, while that portion amounts to only a few months in agriculture, it can extend from several years to several decades in forests, depending on the climate, type of forest, utilization level (how much of the cut trees is harvested), and speed of revegetation and reforestation.

The negative aesthetic impact of clearcutting can be greatly reduced by applying modern techniques of landscape architecture and visual resource management. Small, elongate or irregularly shaped clearcuts, retention of unlogged patches within larger clearcuts, and locating cuts with respect for visual corridors and visually sensitive landscapes can greatly reduce conflicts over the aesthetics of clearcutting. In some recreationally important areas, however, acceptable amelioration of these impacts may not be possible. In such areas, different harvesting systems should be used, or the forest should not be harvested.

Clearcutting: The Method versus How It Is Done and Subsequent Site Treatments
Both the ecological and the visual impacts of clearcutting can be affected as much by how clearcutting is done as by the fact that it is the harvest method. Tractor skidding in selection or shelterwood systems on steep slopes can have a much more negative impact on soils, water, and fish than a well-designed clearcut with logs removed by a skyline or helicopter. Poorly built roads in a selection forest will cause more problems than a well-designed road in a clearcut.

The size, shape, location, timing of the removal of adjacent mature forests, and various other aspects of clearcut layout and regional forest management can have as much effect on the regional impact of timber harvesting as the fact that clearcutting is the harvest method.

Sometimes the environmental impacts attributed to clearcut harvesting result from subsequent site treatments such as slashburning or mechanical site preparation. While it can legitimately be argued that such treatments, may sometimes be necessitated by using clearcutting as the harvest method, this is often not the case. If logging slash is heavy enough to inhibit reforestation in a clearcut, this may also happen in a shelterwood cut. Where mechanical site preparation is indicated in a clearcut, there may be a similar requirement in a shelterwood. An advantage of selection harvesting is that slash problems are generally reduced. However, it may be difficult to get the desired natural regeneration in some types of forest managed under the selection system if the soil is not disturbed in some way. It may be difficult to disturb the soil mechanically in such forests without damaging the remaining crop trees.

Nutrient removal in harvested materials is a

Clearcutting

A

B

C

A The traditional 'progressive clearcutting' of unmanaged forests on southern Vancouver Island. Silviculturally successful plantations can be seen in the background. Where logging in the past was 'exploitive' and 'wasteful,' the forests that have developed naturally are generally quite diverse in structure and species composition. More intensive harvesting and silviculture in the past two to three decades ('good forestry' by Scandinavian or central European standards) has generally resulted in more uniform forests of lower species diversity. Recent changes in regeneration and stand-tending practices are attempting to produce plantations with a more diverse structure and composition.

B More recently there has been a move to leave small patches of uncut timber to break up large areas of clearcuts. Small patches may be subject to windthrow, and the 'fragmentation' of the remaining mature forest may reduce the value of these reserves for some species of wildlife.

C Where forest fragmentation is a problem, wildlife managers may recommend a diversity of harvesting patterns, sizes, and shapes of clearcuts and reserves, and, where appropriate, a mixture of clearcutting and alternative silvicultural systems.

concern in nutritionally poor forest sites. Clearcutting with whole-tree harvesting should not be done on such sites if productivity is to be maintained without fertilization or the use of nutritional nurse crops such as alder, a nitrogen-fixer. However, whole-tree harvesting can be just as serious a problem with shelterwood or selection harvesting, except that the losses occur more slowly over time. Forests in which whole trees are removed at the time of thinning (a mid-rotation harvest) as well as at the final harvest will suffer nutritionally even more than forests that have only a final harvest.

Are the Ecological and Other Impacts of Clearcutting 'Forever'?

The answer depends on which time scale you use to define 'forever.' Evolutionary time scales for long-lived trees in forests cover thousands to millions of years. Ecological time scales covering natural cycles of ecosystem disturbance and recovery cover large fractions of a century up to thousands of years. Forest management time scales of tree crop production in northern forests generally span half a century up to one and a half centuries, but eucalyptus plantations in Brazil managed for charcoal and oil products are managed on a four- to five-year rotation. In contrast, 'social' time scales range from a few years (the four- to seven-year political cycles) to the one or more decades that adults in midlife or beyond can hope to survive or continue to enjoy walking in the forest.

According to the time scale used to measure ecosystem recovery from clearcutting, the recovery can occur almost instantly (evolutionary time scale), very rapidly (ecological time scale), acceptably rapidly (forest management time scale), or unacceptably slowly (the visual alteration caused by clearcutting as perceived by a senior citizen, for example). Recovery can appear to be 'never,' or the forest can appear to be sustainable 'forever.' It is important that foresters be sensitive to public opinion. If important social values that are lost temporarily by clearcutting cannot be renewed acceptably within some social time scale, the harvesting method should be modified if this can be done in an environmentally sound, safe, and practical way. Where there are no pressing social issues, a level of clearcutting disturbance that permits ecosystem recovery to some desired condition within the prevailing management time scale should be acceptable.

Where Is Clearcutting an Appropriate Practice?: An Environmental Triage

Considering the ecological requirements of desired plant and animal species, the ecological characteristics of particular ecosystems, and the variety of ecological effects of clearcutting, it is possible to classify timber-production forest ecosystems into those that should not be clearcut, those that should be clearcut, and those where there is a choice if we want to sustain a particular set of resource values.

Ecosystems That Should Not Be Clearcut

Forests growing in very hot, dry climates often require a modified forest microclimate for successful natural regeneration. Because planted seedlings in such forests may have very poor survival and growth rates in an unmodified clearcut microclimate, clearcutting is inappropriate. Areas subject to severe radiation frosts (frost caused by the cooling of the soil surface and plants on a very clear night) may also regenerate much better if there is a sheltering overstorey, or shelterwood.

Forests growing on steep, unstable slopes or on slopes where there is an unacceptable risk of snow avalanche or cold air drainage should not be clearcut, or clearcuts should be sufficiently small and dispersed to protect against these hazards. Continuous tree cover over either the entire area or all but small harvested patches is required on such slopes to maintain soil and snowpack stability, and to protect the valley below from cold mountain air.

Very-high-elevation subalpine forests with deep winter snowpacks may require the presence of tree stems to create a modified thermal environment for successful natural regeneration. Tree stems warmed by spring sunshine reradiate heat. This melts the snowpack surrounding the stem, thereby increasing the number of weeks a seedling growing close to the stem receives sunlight. A seedling in this modified environment can grow two or three times faster than a seedling at some distance from the tree stems. It is important to retain trees to create 'thermal islands' in such subalpine environments, or to leave very tall stumps that can create the same effect. Tree stems or tall stumps may also be needed to protect seedlings on steep slopes in heavy snow-pack environments from being bent over and crushed as the snowpack creeps (as opposed to avalanches) down the slope during the winter.

Where the visual quality of a landscape has very high recreational significance and must be pro-tected, it may be desirable to retain continuous forest cover. The visual impact of clearcutting can be greatly ameliorated by having small, scattered cuts that are carefully shaped and located to blend in with natural variations in the shape, colour, and texture of the landscape. However, in cases where this is not sufficient, uneven-aged management or non-clearcut, even-aged silvicultural systems should be used.

Where many small streams with significant fish-eries or water supply values meander throughout a floodplain, it is sometimes not possible to clearcut without adversely affecting these other resources. Such areas should be either reserved as riparian strips or selection-logged, with individual large trees being carefully removed at well-spaced time intervals. The importance to streams of the peri-odic input of large logs for the long-term character of the stream environment suggests that not all trees in such environments should be harvested.

Clearcutting watersheds in sloping topography generally has little adverse effect on streams as long as (1) the proportion of the watershed that is hydro-logically altered is below the level that increases peak streamflow during storms or rain-on-snow events; (2) adequate riparian leave strips are retained;

(3) logging slash is not allowed to accumulate in gullies and over-ephemeral streams; (4) roads and skid trails do not cause water quality problems; and (5) there are no slope stability problems. Where these conditions cannot be satisfied, alternative har-vesting systems should be employed.

Clearcutting may be restricted in forests where there are endangered species of plants or animals that have an absolute requirement for continuous mature forest cover. In some cases the requirement may be for old-growth forest and no harvesting at all. In other cases a switch from clearcutting to an alternative system may perpetuate the species and permit some level of timber harvesting to continue (see discussion in Chapter 11).

Ecosystems That Should Be Clearcut

The growth of many cold northern forests is lim-ited much more by low soil temperature during the summer than by the long, cold winters. If this type of forest is not disturbed periodically, a thick layer of acidic organic matter and mosses can develop at the soil surface. This insulates the soil, promoting the development of permafrost, or at least very low summer soil temperatures. In nature, fire normally performs soil warming and ecosystem rejuvenation in these northern forests, but we are increasingly controlling wildfires because we think of them as being destructive. Partial logging may maintain low soil temperatures and in such forests lead to stag-nating nutrient cycles and forest deterioration, whereas clearcutting can reinvigorate soil processes and ecosystem productivity. However, clearcutting in boreal and sub-boreal forests in Canada has a history of regeneration problems. Although this is often as much a problem of the misapplication of clearcutting as it is of clearcutting, itself, there is clearly much room for improvement in regenera-tion practices in Canada's boreal forests. We must understand more clearly the differences between natural disturbance by fire, insects, and wind and the disturbance caused by timber harvesters. In some cases, the problems are apparently related to excessively large clearcuts or to the coalescence of many clearcuts over the years. In other cases, problems can be caused by one or more of the following: soil compaction, invasion by grass, wrong choice of tree species, poor planting, unhealthy seedlings, or excessive wetness. Our regeneration strategy may also be wrong. It may be inappropriate to manage some boreal forests for repeated crops of one tree species (e.g., spruce). Alternative tree crops (e.g., pine, spruce, pine or deciduous, conifer, deciduous) may be required, or the forests may need to be managed on a longer rotation.

Clearcutting is the harvesting method of choice where the desired new forest is of light-demanding species whose light requirements are not satisfied by alternative harvesting systems. In humid climates and on wet, fertile sites, competition for light from herbs and shrubs may present the growth of light-requiring conifer seedlings. The greater ease of applying some methods of weed control in a clearcut than in non-clearcut areas (because of the danger of damage to the residual trees) may also suggest clearcutting on brushy sites. On the other hand, if seedlings of the desired tree species are more shade-tolerant than the weeds, clearcutting may not be the best harvesting strategy.

In forests where there is a major problem of wind damage, clearcutting may be a safer and more effective way of harvesting and regenerating previously unmanaged forests. Once a forest is in a managed uneven-aged condition, windthrow may not be such a problem, but the use of seed tree, shelterwood, or small-group selection systems in previously unmanaged forests can lead to serious wind damage problems, with associated worker safety problems in some types of windthrown forests.

Forests that have been killed by insects over large areas (hundreds or thousands of hectares) are normally salvage-logged by clearcutting unless they are in a park or ecological reserve. Even in a park, they may be logged if there is a safety problem, such as in a public campground. In a managed forest, such areas are logged to gain the social value of jobs and capital creation that would otherwise be lost, and to reduce the risk of serious summer wildfire in the dead forest. Naturally windthrown trees can lead to significant outbreaks of insects, such as bark beetles, that can attack and kill large areas of adjacent mature forest unless the windthrown stems are promptly removed. The infamous Bowron River clearcut in central BC that is so often quoted by environmentalists and the media as an example of the clearcutting policy in the province had its origins in extensive windthrow in and adjacent to the Wells Gray Provincial Park. Spruce bark beetles breeding in this windthrown material then killed large areas of spruce forest in the Bowron Valley outside the park. It was the harvest of this largely beetle-killed forest that resulted in the huge clearcut. Clearcutting has often been used to try to limit the extent of such insect outbreaks, or at least to salvage the dead trees.

Forests where there is extensive root disease or dwarf mistletoe (a parasitic plant) that would be spread to the remaining live trees or new regeneration by non-clearcut harvest methods will normally be clearcut. In some cases, the area may be replanted to a species that is less susceptible to the disease.

Ecosystems Where There Is a Choice

In many forest ecosystems, either clearcutting or an alternative harvest system may be equally good from an environmental or silvicultural point of view. Whether or not clearcutting is applied should depend on a careful evaluation of social and economic considerations and the objectives of forest management. In some cases, clearcutting, modified or unrestricted, may be the system of choice after such an analysis. In other cases, alternatives will be chosen.

Concluding Statement

The issue of clearcutting has become so confused with a variety of other environmental issues that it has become increasingly difficult to have a scientifically based discussion of the practice. By accident or design, the environmental debate has entwined this timber harvesting practice with the issues of tropical deforestation, biodiversity, climate change, soil degradation, resource exploitation, flooding, landslides, and overlogging. Students in both primary and secondary schools are learning from the media and certain segments of the environmental movement that clearcutting is an inherently evil, environmentally destructive practice that threatens to destroy life on earth as we know it. It is virtually impossible to browse through any environmentally concerned book without seeing a west coast clearcut compared with a deforested area in the tropics. The word 'clearcutting' is increasingly being used as a synonym for words like exploitation and terms like resource depletion.

There is little doubt that clearcutting has sometimes been applied where it was environmentally inappropriate, and that it has often been applied in a way that has adversely affected wildlife, fish, water, or recreational resources, albeit temporarily. Clearcutting practices that were not a concern, or that were acceptable, a couple of decades ago are being challenged today. It is also clear that many areas that were clearcut in the past are now supporting productive, biodiverse, sustainable, and attractive second-growth forests. In many cases where clearcutting did have negative effects, these could have been avoided by better planning and implementation. In some cases, these negative effects could probably not have been avoided, and an alternative to clearcutting should have been used.

The purpose of this chapter is not to defend clearcutting or to lobby for this practice. Rather, it is to point out that no one harvest system is appropriate everywhere: not clearcutting, not shelterwood, and not selection harvesting. It also demonstrates the wide range of questions that must be addressed in reaching a logical conclusion as to which harvest method should be used. So many of the problems with forestry in the past have arisen because a single management method was applied everywhere in the incredibly ecologically diverse landscapes of British

Columbia. Inevitably, this resulted in unacceptable environmental and other impacts in some areas. My only endorsement with respect to the choice of harvest method is that the decision be made after careful consideration of the local site and landscape ecology, the local species ecology, and the appropriate social and broader environmental considerations. It would indeed be an irony if in its concern over clearcutting the public required politicians to legislate a single harvest method everywhere. We know that this would not work. It would not ensure the sustainable resource management, community stability, and conservation of biodiversity that we seek.

CHAPTER 7

Slashburning: Responsible Land Management or Playing with Fire?

Introduction

When forests are harvested, some tree parts are not used and are left lying on and in the ground. This material is called *logging slash,* or simply *slash.* It generally consists of branches, foliage, and the small-diameter top section of the tree stem (collectively referred to as 'tops' or crowns). Sometimes it also includes a lot of larger woody material that is decayed, broken, misshapen, or otherwise unusable or unsaleable. Besides the debris created by harvesting, there may already be a lot of logs lying on the ground from trees that died naturally in the decades before the forest was harvested.

Many of the trees in some old, unmanaged forests, and sometimes in younger, managed forest as well, have extensive fungal decay inside their stems. As these trees are felled, the stems may shatter, and it may be physically impossible, or very expensive, to pick up and remove the broken pieces. Even when a stem containing decay does not shatter, it may have no economic value because no one will buy the product it might be made into or pay a price that will cover the costs of harvesting it. Who wants to build a house using wood that is half rotten? And very rotten stems are not much good for making wood chips or paper either. Undecayed stems may also be left. They may be very crooked. They may come from a species of tree for whose wood there is no market or no available method of manufacturing it into a saleable product. Sometimes stems of large trees that are not decayed break into unusable pieces when they are felled. This type of loss can be reduced by careful felling and by 'banding' the base of trees such as large old western red cedars before they are felled to prevent shattering or splitting of the lower stems.

The amount of slash left on a logged site varies greatly. It depends on a number of factors, including the age, species composition, and condition of the forest before the harvest; the type of harvesting equipment used; and the proportion of tree biomass that is harvested. Enormous quantities of slash (many hundreds of tons per hectare) are often left after harvesting old-growth forest in areas with a wet climate, such as the west coast forests of British Columbia or the wet eucalyptus forests of western Tasmania. Many of the trees in these forests have broken, deformed, or decayed stems and large quantities of big branches. Much less slash is created when younger forests are harvested because there are fewer unusable tree stems and less branch material. Where forests are *whole-tree harvested* (removal from the site of the entire above-ground tree, including stems, branches, and foliage), the amount of slash is minimal. With the increasing trend towards whole-tree harvesting, logged areas will have less and less slash in the future. This is a cause for concern; it is discussed in Chapters 6 and 11. Even where whole-tree harvesting is not used, less slash is left today than in the past because much smaller logs can now be recovered, processed into lumber, and sold economically.

Logging slash can create several problems. By providing lots of fuel, it may increase the risk of a fire starting in a young plantation. It will increase the intensity, rate of spread, difficulty of control, and environmental impact of any such fires. It will often make regeneration more difficult and less uniformly distributed across the site. It can limit access to the site by some large game animals, but provide cover for small mammals that may damage young tree seedlings. Heavy logging slash generally makes subsequent silvicultural operations more difficult, more dangerous for workers, and more expensive.

Because of the increased availability of both light and nutrients, understorey plants often become much more abundant after harvesting. Dense communities of herbs and shrubs can develop. If these become well established before planted or natural tree seedlings begin to put on significant height growth, the tree crop may become suppressed and even die. The severity and duration of these early plantation weed problems depend on the soil moisture and nutrient status, which vary greatly from site to site, and on the regional climate. Whether or not there is a problem also depends upon how sensitive to

competition seedlings of the desired tree species are. Seedlings of shade-tolerant tree species may be able to cope with heavy competition for light; herbs and shrubs may not be a major problem and the shelter they provide may even be beneficial on some sites and in some climates. The development of post-harvest weed problems may also be determined by the amount of soil disturbance caused by logging. Such disturbance can make weed competition problems better or worse, depending on the effect of the disturbance on the processes that determine post-harvest vegetation development.

The presence of large quantities of logging slash or a dense herb and shrub community can make it very difficult or even impossible to reforest a harvested area rapidly and effectively. Thick, dense layers of slash or dense shrub growth may make it almost impossible for tree planters to do their job, and can inhibit or greatly retard natural regeneration for many years. In coastal old-growth forest, the slash can be two to three metres deep. Where such delays in reforestation are unacceptable, foresters may use mechanical equipment to push the slash into piles or windrows, or simply to expose *plantable spots*. These are small areas, one or two metres in diameter, where the forest floor or the mineral soil is exposed. A tree can be planted, or seeds falling naturally on the area can germinate and seedlings become established. To control herbs and shrubs, foresters may use herbicides (see Chapter 8), but this will not solve the problem that planters and some wildlife species have in moving through a deep accumulation of slash or through the standing dead stems of shrubs. Heavy slash will also prevent the use of sheep or other domestic livestock as a weed control method. Alternatively, foresters may use fire to clear the site of slash and competing vegetation, thereby rendering planting easier, natural regeneration more successful, access by large species of wildlife (such as deer or elk) better, and the risk of fire lower.

Fire that is used to solve problems in forest management or to improve wildlife habitat is called *prescribed fire.* The use of prescribed fire to deal specifically with slash-related problems is called *slashburning.*

This chapter is about the use of fire to prepare a harvested site for reforestation. It will focus mainly on the burning of logging slash. Slashburning has been the subject of considerable disagreement between different foresters, different forest scientists, and foresters and environmentalists. Some maintain that slashburning is environmentally damaging and irresponsible. Others maintain that its effects are benign or beneficial, or that long-term benefits outweigh the short-term costs.

Like the application of the practice itself, the argument over slashburning has been characterized by too many generalizations. There has not been enough understanding on the part of both the public and many foresters about the short- and long-term ecological impacts of slashburning on particular forest sites. If this chapter achieves nothing else, I hope it will provide a glimpse of the complexity of the issue. Slashburning is neither all good nor all bad. It depends on where, when, and how it is done, and whether or not it achieves the forest manager's objectives, assuming that these are appropriate for the site and the location. If you examine the extensive scientific literature on slashburning, you can find studies that support almost any point of view on almost any slashburning-related issue, according to where, when, why, and how the burning was done.

Do Foresters Have to Slashburn Sites After Harvesting?

No, they don't. But they do have to solve the problems created by logging slash and by competing vegetation. In most cases, there are several different ways in which foresters can deal with these problems: whole-tree harvesting to avoid creating slash; mechanical piling, crushing, or rearrangement of slash; mechanical, manual, biological, or chemical control of weeds; or the use of fire. Each of these alternatives has its advantages and disadvantages.

Sometimes slashburning is the best and most environmentally friendly way to solve slash and weed problems and ensure rapid reforestation and good growth of a new forest. Prescribed fire may sometimes be an effective way of dealing with weeds in the absence of slash problems.

Whole-tree harvesting removes most of the fresh logging slash, and dragging the tree tops off the site may literally 'sweep' the area clean of the above-ground parts of shrubs and herbs. Most of these plants will resprout from roots or underground stems, but there will be a few years in which competition for light is reduced, and this may be all that is needed to get the new tree crop growing. On the other hand, logging slash can smother or suppress competing vegetation, and as long as seedlings can be planted or natural regeneration can be established, some slash may have the beneficial effect of reducing weed growth. Consequently, while whole-tree harvesting may give an initial advantage, such areas can sometimes have worse weed problems in the long run than areas on which slash is left.

Whole-tree harvesting removes a lot of nutrients and organic matter that would otherwise stay on the site and contribute to soil fertility, nutrient cycling, and site productivity in the future. Logging slash can be considered as 'packed lunches' for earthworms and other important soil animals both in the short term (leaves and twigs) and later in the life of the stand (stems that become rotting logs). Unused biomass, such as logs left on a harvested site, may appear to be a waste of resources to some people, but not to the ecosystem, of which it is simply a part of nature's cycle of growth, decay, and nutrient recovery. In most cases, much of the larger woody debris that remains on site after a slashburn would have been removed by whole-tree harvesting. Many of the nutrients in the ash also remain on site, whereas they would have been removed in whole-tree harvesting.

Mechanical site treatment leaves all unharvested material on site unless the piles or windrows of slash are burned. By putting all the slash, organic matter, and nutrients in a few small areas, however, most of the site is 'robbed' of this material. The area covered by slash piles is certainly enriched in organic matter and nutrients, but it may be impossible for trees to grow on the slash until the piles or windrows have decayed considerably and physically 'settled down.' Consequently, many of the nutrients released as the slash decomposes may be leached away or lost by gaseous release, as in the case of nitrogen. Even where growth on the piles does occur, the plants on top and the soil beneath the piles may simply not be able to hold on to all the nutrients being released. Also, in piling up the slash, much of the forest floor and even some of the upper mineral soil may be removed from the area between the piles, further impoverishing the site. In addition, soil compaction may occur. Mechanical slash treatment can be a good option where soils are not sensitive to compaction or erosion and if there is minimum redistribution of slash and forest floor, but in many cases it poses much greater environmental risks than carefully executed slashburning. Mechanical treatment can also lead to more serious future weed problems because it creates soil surface conditions that favour the invasion of the site by rapidly growing herb, shrub, and pioneer tree species.

Herbicides can be a very effective and environmentally friendly way of reducing competition between tree seedlings and herbs and shrubs (see discussion in Chapter 8), but they do not help much where there is a combined problem of heavy slash and heavy herbaceous or shrubby growth. The use of herbicides may be restricted because of public concern over water quality and other issues, so they may not be available for use even though they may have lower impacts on the soil than fire or mechanical methods.

In comparison with these alternative methods of solving slash, weed, and other site-preparation problems, slashburning may be either better or worse in terms of environmental impact, cost, and effectiveness. It depends on the factors discussed below.

How Is Slashburning Done?

Slashburning is normally done only after clearcutting. In partial cutting systems, such as selection or shelterwood, there may not be sufficient slash following a harvest to require slash disposal. Where these harvest systems create slash problems, the risk of damage to the remaining trees from slashburning may be unacceptably high, or the cost of doing it without damaging these trees may be prohibitive. Slashburning is sometimes done in shelterwood systems where the remaining trees have a thick, fire-resistant bark, as in Douglas-fir or western larch in BC, and where there is little danger of damage to the trees' fine feeding roots, such as in dry climates or on dry sites where the forest floor is not thick and most of the roots are protected in the mineral soil. Most slashburning is associated with clearcutting, however.

After an area has been clearcut, a bulldozer is used to put a 'fire guard' around the area to be burned. This is simply a strip of ground two to five metres wide from which all the slash and forest floor is cleared to prevent the spread of fire. The slash is then ignited. The pattern of ignition is important. Ideally, a hot fire is established in the middle of the burn, causing a rapidly ascending column of heated air and smoke. This draws in air from the surrounding area, resulting in strong winds blowing from the edge of the clearcut towards the central fire. The edge of the clearcut is then ignited; and this peripheral fire is drawn into the centre by the winds created by the rising central smoke column. Variations on this basic ignition pattern can result in different types of fire behaviour that are appropriate for different situations. For example, on very steep slopes with large amounts of slash, the area is burned in long, narrow strips along the contour starting at the top of the slope and progressing downslope. This removes the risk of fire running upslope through unburned slash and escaping into adjacent forests or harvested areas.

In the past, slash was ignited by hand with a *drip torch:* a canister containing a mixture of gasoline and diesel fuel that is ignited as it drips out of a spout onto the slash. Nowadays ignition is usually done using a drip torch slung underneath a helicopter, or by dropping from a helicopter small incendiary devices that look like golf balls. Helicopter ignition is faster and safer than manual ignition, and generally results in a more predictable burn and better fire control.

Traditionally, slashburning has been done after the first rain in the fall, when the larger woody material is still dry but the fire danger in the surrounding forest has been reduced somewhat. Fall burning can result in two problems that have led to widespread criticism of the practice. First, fall slashburns can be very hot because the forest floor is often still fairly dry and because of the large amounts of dry woody material. Very hot fall fires have often resulted in damage to the soil and the possibility of long-term reduction in site productivity. Second, because of the calm weather during Indian summer when most fall burning has been done, slashburning can create smoke problems that the public is increasingly intolerant of. Smoke from slashburns at this time of year may get trapped in stagnant air in valleys and the lower atmosphere (because of temperature inversion) instead of moving to higher altitudes, where it can be dispersed by winds.

As a result of these concerns, there has been a move away from fall burning to burning in the spring or early summer. Soil and fuel moisture conditions at this time generally result in relatively cool fires, a low risk of undesirable consumption of the forest floor and damage to the mineral soil, and a relatively low danger of the slashburn escaping and becoming a wildfire. Spring and early summer atmospheric conditions usually promote the rapid dispersal of smoke. However, some forest areas can experience very warm dry weather in late spring and early summer, accompanied by unpredictable and strong winds. This can greatly increase the danger that spring burns will escape and become damaging wildfires. Spring burning is not very popular among the foresters of such areas.

A major difficulty with slashburning is that there are relatively few days in a year when the combination of atmospheric conditions, soil conditions, and the *fire danger rating* – a measure of the risk of a prescribed fire escaping and becoming a serious wildfire – reduces the risk of site damage, smoke accumulation, and slashburn escape to acceptable levels and yet permits an effective slashburn treatment to be applied. This means that a lot of slashburns may be ignited over the few days that satisfy the increasingly restrictive burning criteria, and this can contribute to smoke accumulation problems in spite of good air mixing. It also increases the risk that there may not be enough people and equipment to manage all the burns properly.

How Do the Ecological Impacts of Slashburning Compare with Those of Wildfire?

Fire as a Natural Component of Forest Ecosystems

Fire is a natural component of most forest ecosystems, which, almost by definition, constitute a fire hazard: they are largely made of wood or other combustible materials. The natural incidence and ecological role of wildfire varies from frequent and necessary for the maintenance of the unmanaged forest in a productive condition – such as in the cold northern forests of Alaska, the Yukon, and the Northwest Territories – to infrequent and damaging to ecosystem productivity. Some ecosystems have evolved with frequent fire, and require fire or some similar disturbance to maintain their natural condition. In other ecosystems, the natural condition reflects very long periods in which fire has not been an important ecological force. All variations in between can be found.

Northern boreal forests owe their character, and in some cases their existence, to frequent wildfire (once every sixty to a hundred years). In the absence of fire, some cold northern forests will develop into muskeg, and their abundance of wildlife has historically been very dependent on the periodic disturbance created by fire. At the other end of the latitudinal spectrum, tropical rain forests are not normally thought of as fire-affected ecosystems. However, much of the world's remaining tropical forest has been affected at some time by shifting cultivation, which generally involves slashburning, and much damage is done to individual large trees by lightning strikes, which can lead to destructive fires in the dry season. Consequently, even these humid forests have not been entirely fire-free. Many subtropical forests have been greatly affected by fire.

Tropical forests are currently being burned on a much larger scale than in the past. Extensive deforestation by cutting and burning followed by agricultural activities is taking place in the forests of Brazil, Indonesia, and various other tropical countries. Sometimes this is an officially sanctioned activity; often it is caused by illegal logging and shifting cultivation. Huge areas of tropical forests in Kalimantan (Borneo) and Sumatra have been burned by human-caused forest fires over the past decade. Some people would argue that this recent use of fire in the tropics is 'unnatural,' whereas the traditional 'slash-and-burn' shifting cultivation that has been practised by primitive forest tribes for a very long time is 'natural.' However, the major differences in scale, frequency, and environmental impact between the historical and current burning of these forests simply represent two points along a continuum of forest disturbance and burning that has been increasing steadily as a result of population increase and the invasion of tropical areas by Europeans. No attempt will be made here to resolve the argument about the relative 'naturalness' of these two scales of fire impact in the tropics, but the evidence suggests that it is more a question of scale and frequency than 'natural' or 'unnatural.'[12]

12 Clearly, the total impact of large-scale deforestation, whether caused by exploitive logging or clearance for agriculture, is very different from the traditional disturbance caused by shifting cultivators. The discussion here is limited to the effects of fire.

In spite of the relative infrequency of most wildfire events other than in boreal or savannah forest, many forests owe their character to fire. The giant 'wet sclerophyll' eucalyptus forests growing in high-rainfall areas of Tasmania and other states in southeastern Australia are replaced by southern beech (*Nothofagus*) and other cool temperate rain forest species unless the forest is burned by catastrophic fire every 250 to 350 years. California redwood forests (*Sequoia*) also benefit from, and may even require, periodic fires for their continued existence. If fire is excluded from such forests for a long time, the sequoias may eventually be replaced by more shade-tolerant coniferous species. This is such a concern in some of the National Parks in the Sierra Nevada mountains of California that the Parks Service has had to resort to periodic burning of some stands in order to maintain their structure and species composition.

Many of the unmanaged pine forests of the world depend upon periodic fires to prevent their replacement by other species, or to prevent catastrophic wildfires. Some pine forests that experience low-intensity fires in the understorey every few years become almost 'fireproof.' Except in the case of a raging wildfire driven by hot, dry summer winds, these frequently burned forests are rarely killed by fire, whereas pine forests from which fire has been excluded for many decades may experience explosive wildfire events. The growth of a dense understorey of herbs, shrubs, and young pines provides a 'fire ladder' that can lead a low-intensity and environmentally benign surface fire up into the tree canopy, where it becomes a destructive crown fire.

Clearly, fire is an important ecological factor that has helped to create and maintain the diversity and characteristics of forests around the world.

Ecological Impacts: Wildfire versus Slashburning
The ecological impacts of wildfire can vary from benign, as in the low-intensity fire in the grassy understorey of a pine forest in northern Florida, to catastrophic, as in the wholesale killing of boreal

forest overstorey trees or of Australian eucalyptus forest over large areas. In the larger scheme of things, however, what appears catastrophic to the human eye may be nature's way of perpetuating a particular ecosystem. The wildfires that burned much of Yellowstone National Park in the summer of 1988 were merely repeating a cycle that has undoubtedly occurred hundreds, if not thousands, of times since the glaciers retreated. Old lodgepole pine forests, soon to be replaced by Engelmann spruce and other shade-tolerant species or killed by bark beetles, were removed by fire, stimulating the release of seed from cones that are specially adapted to release the protected seeds only after a fire (*serotinous* cones). The short-term 'destruction' is nature's way of sustaining the area's pine forests.

Very hot summer wildfires can remove much of the organic matter and cause the loss of a lot of nutrients from the affected ecosystems. They can also cause significant physical soil damage and can have a long-term negative effect on site productivity. By removing all live trees over large areas, extensive wildfires can remove the seed source by which an area will reforest, and areas burned in large, hot wildfires may take many centuries to reforest. However, because most of the trees in many wildfire-killed forests remain standing, and because in most cases not all of the forest floor is consumed, the ecosystem may not be as badly damaged, or set back as far in its successional condition, as first appears. Scattered trees or patches of trees, or trees in moist gullies or streambank areas, often survive to provide a seed source for natural reforestation. Alternatively, the damaged trees may resprout, although most coniferous trees do not have this ability. In such cases, the recovery of the ecosystem can be quite rapid, and forests in fire-prone areas are generally well adapted to surviving this perfectly normal ecological event. Many of Australia's eucalyptus forests depend on periodic hot fires to reduce disease problems or to prevent the eucalypts from being replaced by climax temperate rain forest or other forest species.

There are several ways in which the ecological impacts of slashburning may differ from those of a wildfire. First, because slashburning normally follows clearcutting, slashburned sites have already lost most of the tree stems that would have remained standing for some time after a wildfire. These dead trees provide some shade and some reduction in wind, and contribute a supply of slowly decomposing organic matter to the soil when they fall over. For those species with serotinous cones, the dead standing trees also provide a seed source for the renewal of the forest.

Second, much of the heat generated in a wildfire may be released high above the ground as the fire races through the forest canopy, while the accompanying fire on the ground often has a relatively low severity and consumes relatively little of the forest floor. Most of the combustible fuel is in the standing live and dead trees. In contrast, all of the fuel and the heat energy release in a slashburn are on or near the ground. Thus, in a hot slash fire that consumes much of this fuel (quite common in fall slashburns), much or even all of the forest floor may be consumed. In the worst cases, significant heat damage may also be done to the upper mineral soil. Damage to soil can also happen in a wildfire, of course, because such fires often occur under conditions of extreme summer fire danger, but the risk may be greater in a hot fall burn than in many summer wildfires. As slashburning is increasingly restricted to spring and early summer when damage to the forest floor and mineral soil is minimal, the impact of slashburning on the soil will become less relative to the ecological impact of wildfires. Piling slash in the summer and burning the piles in the fall or winter can cause the most severe soil damage. This practice became common in the northwestern U.S. in the past two decades in response to public pressure against the smoke and blackened hillsides caused by summer or fall broadcast burning. The concentration of energy release in the piles and the long duration of high temperatures under the piles caused much more soil damage than a fast-moving broadcast burn through scattered slash.

Catastrophic wildfires are often thought to be a very infrequent event, whereas people think that slashburning is done every rotation. In some unmanaged boreal forests, however, fire frequency has been greater in the past – every 60 to 80 years – than the anticipated frequency of harvesting these forests – every 100 to 110 years. In addition, slashburning will probably be used much less often in the future than in the past. In fact, it may well go down in history as a management tool almost exclusively restricted to the conversion from unmanaged to managed forests. The large quantities of slash that are created when unmanaged or old-growth forests are harvested will not occur in the managed forests of the future. The increasing use of whole-tree harvesting will further reduce the need to burn slash, although the impacts of these two practices need to be carefully compared. In many cases, appropriate use of slashburning may be deemed to be the more environmentally friendly method of dealing with problems caused by logging slash. If applied in an ecologically sensitive manner, slashburning can cause less loss of nutrients and organic matter than whole-tree harvesting, leave more coarse woody debris on the site (see Chapter 11), and cause less soil compaction.

Now that we have seen some key differences between slashburning and wildfire, it is time to consider some similarities. The most important one is that the ecological effects of both wildfire and slashburning are incredibly variable. They vary according to the character of the fire: its heat emission and its duration. This in turn depends on weather conditions before and during the fire, and the amount and distribution of organic matter that can burn, namely, the fuel. The ecological impacts vary greatly between dry, nutrient-poor sites and moist, fertile sites. They also vary tremendously within a wildfire or a slashburned area, which usually has a mosaic of unburned, slightly burned, and heavily burned areas, and may have some patches that have been 'burned to a crisp.' Recovery from wildfire or slashburning will be slow where revegetation is slow, and rapid where successional recovery is rapid. The presence or absence of nitrogen-fixing plants following the fire will have an important effect on the long-term consequences of the fire on site productivity. Because of this variability, useful generalizations about either slashburning or wildfire are scarce, and many qualifiers are necessary whenever you make such generalizations. That is why there are so many 'ifs,' 'ands,' and 'buts' in the above discussion. Developing useful statements about the ecological effects of fire requires a careful site-specific and case-specific analysis.

Ecological Effects of Fire: A Detailed Analysis

The major ecological effects of fire, whether wildfire or slashburn, can be divided into effects on soils, including soil animals and microbes; on the plant community; on animals; and on the atmosphere. In aggregate, these determine the effects on the ecosystem.

Effects on Soils

The major effect is the loss of organic matter and some nutrients. Most of the nitrogen and sulphur and some of the phosphorus, potassium, and calcium contained in the organic matter consumed in a fire may be lost. Some are converted to gases, and some are simply carried away as particles in the rising smoke (fly ash and particulate losses). The ash that is not lost from the site reduces the acidity of the remaining forest floor and soil (raising the soil's pH). This generally increases the availability of the remaining nutrients if the soil was originally quite acidic, which is normal in coniferous forests. Thus, although fire may sometimes cause the loss of a significant proportion of the ecosystem's nutrient capital, it may actually increase nutrient *availability* for several years. Initial tree growth may be improved on a site that has actually been nutritionally degraded and on which production over the whole rotation may have been reduced (but see the discussion of nutrient cycling in Chapter 4).

Problems caused by slashburning

Severe soil damage caused by slashburning on sites that should not have been burned. **A** Fifty centimetres of organic matter over limestone rock on Vancouver Island were lost when the area was slashburned. In a dry climate, recovery from such damage would require centuries or millennia. In the humid climate of western Vancouver Island, recovery of the ecosystem from this disturbance on this nutrient-rich rock will require one or two centuries. **B** On nutrient-poor granite rock it would probably take two or three times as long.

Very hot fires can damage soil structure at the surface of the mineral soil, and this can lead to surface soil erosion. Where a hot fire kills the understorey vegetation on steep slopes, the stability of the slope may be reduced, increasing the risk of soil erosion and landslides.

In cold northern climates, the removal or reduction of the insulating layer of living and dead organic matter at the soil surface by fire allows the heat energy of sunlight to reach the mineral soil, warming it up and improving both fertility and ecosystem productivity, even if some or many of the nutrients in the forest floor have been lost during the burn.

Fire can have a significant effect on the soil animals and microbes that play such an important role in organic matter decomposition, nutrient cycling, and maintenance of the architecture, drainage, aeration, and other important characteristics of soils. Excessive loss of organic matter and extreme heating of the soil will negatively affect soil organisms. Moderate heating and ashing of organic matter may increase microbial activity, improve decomposition and nutrient availability, and stimulate more soil animal activity.

Effects on the Plant Community

Only the above-ground parts of perennial plants are killed in most wildfires and slashburns. Most perennial herbs and shrubs resprout within weeks or even days of the fire, from buds on roots or other underground organs (ecologists call this the *bud bank*). Where there is a well developed bud bank, the minor vegetation may be fully recovered within a year or two. Most broadleaved tree species can also resprout from bud banks on the stump or the roots. For example, when fire kills aspen trees, the roots are stimulated to produce thousands of sprouts (called *root suckers*) per hectare. Fire thus perpetuates aspen forest, and this species could be lost from boreal forests if it was not periodically disturbed by fire or by other mechanisms. Most coniferous trees, on the other hand, do not have this resprouting ability.

When the foliage and branches are burned off and the stem dies, the stump and roots are no longer supplied with carbohydrate and they die also. Fire thus favours species that are able to resprout from bud banks. Among conifers that can sprout after the killing of branches or the stem by fire are the redwoods of California, which are clearly adapted to fire. Some conifers compensate for their inability to produce sprouts by having a thick dead bark that insulates the temperature-sensitive living tissue from fire. Thick-barked species, such as Douglas-fir, Ponderosa pine, and larch, are able to survive quite hot surface fires, therefore, fire generally favours these species over thin-barked species.

In addition to resprouting from protected below-ground buds, the plant community may recover from fire as a result of seeds stored in the soil. Most forest floors contain lots of ungerminated but viable seeds in what ecologists call the *seed bank.* Seeds of some species in the seed bank require heating by fire before they will germinate, and fire will stimulate the growth of dense communities of such species. Seeds of other species in the seed bank are killed by fire. Because the seed banks of different fire-sensitive species may occur at different depths in the forest floor, fires that burn deeply can cause the germination (or simply the survival) of seeds belonging to different species from those whose seeds would germinate (or survive) after a fire that scarcely warms the soil. The same is true for species resprouting from bud banks. Different species have their bud banks at different depths in the soil, and fires of different severity will kill the bud banks of different species, resulting in different post-fire plant communities.

The seeds of different species carried by wind or animals into a burned area from adjacent unburned areas have different germination requirements. The humid climate of coastal British Columbia favours the establishment of fire-adapted species, such as fireweed or bracken fern, and also certain species of moss. One particular moss, the little hair-cap moss, can become so densely established within a year of the fire that it prevents seeds and spores of other plant species from reaching the ground. The moss acts like a 'fitted plush carpet,' denying the wind-blown seeds access to the soil. Where this occurs, plants such as salal, fireweed, and bracken fern, which spread by rapidly elongating underground stems called *rhizomes,* are favoured over species that spread by seed. Where these rhizomatous species were already present or became established before the mosses, they may occupy the entire area within a few years, leading to a very different pattern of plant community development than if the little hair-cap moss had not been present. By favouring the moss, a fire can cause a very different pattern of early plant succession.

As you can see, the response of the plant community to fire can be highly variable. It is often controlled by chance events. For example, the direction the wind is blowing at the time seed is being released from certain species may determine whether or not those species participate in the plant community of an area recovering from fire-caused disturbance. The arrival of herb, shrub, and tree seeds either before or after the establishment of a thick moss layer can result in greatly different patterns of community development.

Effects on Animals

In spite of what you may have learned from Walt Disney films and Smokey-the-Bear anti-fire campaigns, most animals are not burned alive by wildfire or by slashburns. In runaway catastrophic wildfires that may occasionally travel at more than a hundred kilometres an hour for short periods, humans and other animal species may be overtaken and killed. Most mobile animals, however, either move out of the fire's way, seek refuge in lakes or large rivers, or burrow underground until the fire has passed. They are not killed. Slow-moving soil animals may be consumed if the forest floor is burned, but even they can often escape by moving to lower, cooler layers in the soil. The young of many vertebrate species may be killed, as well as many insects. However, the greatest effect on most animal species is loss of habitat.

Where a fire removes plant food species; shelter from wind, rain, cold, and heat; and the security cover (called *escape cover* as it provides somewhere to hide) required by an animal species or its prey, the suitability of the area for that species will be reduced. Its habitat will have been lost. The loss is not permanent, however. The area will become suitable for the species again as soon as the plant community regrows and re-establishes the necessary habitat features. Small mammals such as mice either remain in a burned area or return to it even before the smoke has cleared. Larger animals may not use the area until it has 'greened-up' – a process that may take from a few weeks to a few years.

If animals that have been displaced by fire move into unburned areas, they will have to compete with the residents already there. They may perish if they are not able to move to such areas and essential habitat requirements do not develop rapidly.

Because slashburns generally do not affect a large area, and because there are usually adjacent areas of uncut forest and areas in various stages of forest regrowth following logging and slashburning, the effect of slashburning on the regional animal community is usually very minor. There is a negligible risk that slashburning alone will lead to loss of species in well-managed forests, although there may be a temporary reduction in local populations. Sometimes that is an objective of the slashburn: to reduce seed predation or browsing damage to seedlings.

Effects on the Atmosphere

One of the major complaints from the public about slashburning is the smoke: the smell, the fly ash, the effects on people with chronic respiratory problems, the reduction of atmospheric clarity, and the loss of views and of visibility for flying.

The saying 'no smoke without a fire' works the other way as well: 'no slashburning without smoke.' Smoke management has become one of the major factors determining slashburning policy. In earlier years, foresters burned slash whenever the conditions were right to achieve a desired severity of burn. This is no longer true. In many areas the major consideration today is, 'Will there be an unacceptable accumulation and persistence of smoke?' Smoke management areas have been established within which slashburning is limited to weather conditions in which smoke disperses rapidly.

Another atmospheric consideration is the rapid release of carbon dioxide (CO_2) into the atmosphere during the burn. Carbon dioxide is a so-called 'greenhouse gas' (see Chapter 12), and its release into the atmosphere has been implicated as the major contributor to the risk of significant global climate change. It is therefore reasonable to ask whether slashburning and wildfire are significant net contributors to the observed increase in atmospheric CO_2 levels. Nitrogen oxides are also greenhouse gases, and are also produced by forest fires.

It has been estimated that slashburning in British Columbia released about 2 million tons of carbon in the five years from 1981 to 1986. In comparison, wildfires released about 24 million tons of carbon in the four-year period from 1982 to 1986. These losses compare with an estimated increase of about 192 million tons of carbon stored in the province's 45 million hectares of forest over this period.

These figures are approximations only, and are subject to a variety of estimation errors. However, they are thought to indicate order-of-magnitude relationships. If the numbers are correct, slashburning contributed less than 10 per cent of the release of carbon from wildfires, while the combined fire releases were only about 12 per cent of the estimated uptake by the forest. This large estimated net uptake of CO_2 by the forest is thought to reflect regrowth on areas denuded by fire, insects, and logging over the past century and a reduction in losses to wildfire because of improved fire control.

Perhaps of even greater significance to this discussion is the fact that most of the slash and forest floor materials burned in a slashburn would have decomposed naturally over the subsequent five to ten years anyway, releasing much of the carbon it contained as CO_2 or methane. Slashburning simply accelerates an inevitable release of CO_2. Thus, on a regional basis over a five- to ten-year period, slashburning will not make a significant contribution to the greenhouse problem unless it reduces future forest growth by damaging soil fertility. Where this occurs, slashburning will probably have a negative effect on the atmosphere by reducing CO_2 removal by the regrowing forest. Where slashburning improves site fertility and/or speeds the return of forest cover (by helping to control herbs and shrubs that could delay reforestation, for example), it will have a positive effect on the atmosphere in the future. Thus, it is the effect of slashburning on long-term site productivity and forest growth that is important in the debate over the contribution of forestry to the greenhouse problem, not the short-term release of CO_2.

So, Is Slashburning Responsible Management or Playing with Fire?

As with so many questions about the ecological impacts of forest management, the answer must be, 'it depends.'

Fire is a natural component of many forests, so there is nothing inherently unnatural about slashburning. This does not suggest that the ecological effects of slashburning are the same as those of a wildfire. Because the location of the major fuels differs between a slashburn and a wildfire (on the ground versus in standing trees), the character of these two types of fire can vary greatly, and slashburning can potentially cause more damage to the soil. However, slashburning can be done under soil and climatic conditions that minimize negative effects on the soil (such as in the spring), whereas wildfires generally occur in the heat of the summer, when they can have a very great impact on the soil. In a wildfire, many of the killed trees are left standing, providing a partially modified microclimate, a habitat for cavity-nesting birds and animals, a food source for animals that feed on insects in standing

dead trees, and a supply of organic matter and nutrients to the soil as the dead trees fall over and decompose. Also, much of the ash from burned material remains on the site. On slashburned sites, a lot of woody material and nutrients have already been removed in harvested materials that would have remained on the site after many wildfires, and the intense convection column in a 'hot' slashburn may remove more fly ash than in some wildfires.

Slashburning is an important and, if used correctly, environmentally sound tool in the forest manager's toolbox. It can achieve site preparation for planting and regeneration with fewer negative impacts on heavy, wet, compactible soils than mechanical site preparation. It can provide effective short-term reduction of weed problems without the use of herbicides where the latter are considered unacceptable, or reduce the quantity of herbicides needed (as in 'brown and burn,' in which a very light application of herbicide is used to desiccate rather than kill herbs and shrubs, which are then removed by a quick, low-severity burn that has minimal site impact). It can remove the need to do whole-tree harvesting, which in some cases can result in the loss of significantly more nutrient and organic matter than a spring slashburn. Slashburning can improve the nutritional quality and availability of browse for herbivorous wildlife, although this will depend on its effect on plant succession, and make a clearcut more accessible to large browsing animals.

The history of slashburning policy and practice in British Columbia has run the gamut from 'burn everything, as hot as possible,' to 'don't burn anything.' The former has resulted in everything from very severe and long-lasting damage to forests with thin rocky soils or organic soil right over bedrock, to good site preparation and the establishment of very productive new forests on moist, fertile, weedy sites. The latter has resulted in everything from well regenerated, naturally or artificially established forests with their original organic matter and nutrient capital intact, to prolonged regeneration delays, incomplete regeneration, unregenerated brushfields, or areas that have suffered soil damage when the unabated slash hazard resulted in wild or human-caused fires in the harvested area, or sometimes when mechanical alternatives to slashburning were used.

Recognition of the environmental damage that accompanied the scorched-earth approach of the early days of BC forestry led to a 'don't burn any-thing' policy. This resulted in large areas of heavy slash accumulation in some types of forest, which contributed to poor restocking of the new forest, or which subsequently burned in a wildfire, some-times doing more soil damage than a well-con-trolled slashburn. This caused a return to a widespread and often uncritical application of slashburning. Over the past eighty years, this alter-nating between two approaches has gone through several cycles. It is clearly time to stop the 'pendu-lum swing' in slashburning policy.

The current strategy in British Columbia is to limit slashburning on the basis of risk of soil dam-age and problems of smoke accumulation. The slashburning that is done is justified mainly in terms of silvicultural objectives, although some burning is done to improve range and wildlife habi-tat conditions. The high cost of slashburning small areas may restrict the use of this practice where there are strict limitations on clearcut size. The pre-sent policy has encouraged whole-tree harvesting as a way to avoid the problems of slash accumulation. As already noted, however, this method has its own set of problems.

A final but very important consideration is the risk of slashburning 'escapes.' Anyone who has investigated slashburning knows that far too many slashburns escape into and damage adjacent mature forest or young plantations. Slashburning is nor-mally done only in calm weather, but winds are notoriously unpredictable. Strong winds sometimes arise before a fire is out, causing it to leap fire guards and start a fire in the adjacent uncut forest. Sometimes winds that occur weeks or even months after the slashburn can fan smouldering embers

that have survived under a tree stump and cause a new and damaging fire. And sometimes fires simply do not behave the way the forester expects, and get out of control.

The majority of slashburns are well controlled and do not escape. However, escaped slashburns have sometimes been responsible for killing large areas of mature forest and young plantations. The dead trees in the former case can sometimes be har-vested but often are not, causing economic and social loss. On the other hand, such escaped burns create areas of dead snags that, if they are left stand-ing, may be good for some wildlife species, such as cavity-nesting and snag-feeding birds. Damage to young plantations is simply a loss.

Improved techniques for planning, predicting, and controlling slashburns, and for detecting and extinguishing post-burn 'hot spots,' should reduce the risk of slashburn escapes, but they will probably still occur for a variety of reasons. In some areas, escapes are very rare. In others, they are unaccept-ably common. Where they are common, slashburn-ing should probably be used less if the escapes are caused by unpredictable winds and fire behaviour. If they are caused by poor fire planning and man-agement, slashburning should be suspended until improved planning and management systems are put in place.

Conclusions

The available evidence suggests that slashburning should continue to be a site-preparation option for foresters. While there are clearly some sites for which the risk of damage to soil and long-term site productivity and of smoke accumulation are unac-ceptable, many sites will be unharmed or benefited by a low-severity burn. Some sites will be benefited by even a high-severity slashburn. As with all aspects of forest management, the decision whether or not to burn should be soundly based on an understanding of ecosystem-level forest ecology, a careful ecological classification of the site, and a consideration of social and management issues. It also requires a good knowledge of fire science and the techniques of fire management, and considerable skill in the implementation of this practice.

The effect of slashburning on atmospheric quality should not be dismissed. Smoke accumulation may be unacceptable in some local areas. In many cases, however, smoke accumulations are very transitory, and the longer-term net benefits of slashburning should be weighed against short-term smoke problems.

There is a general lack of understanding by the public of why slashburning is done, of the environmental consequences of alternatives, and of the ecological effects of burning. As a result, most people have little basis for evaluating slashburning other than the nuisance of the smoke and the ugly blackened scene of a recently burned area. Foresters will have to do much more to help the public understand the slashburning issues if they expect the public to allow them to go on using this management technique.

It is expected that slashburning will, and always should, be part of forestry in BC and the northwestern U.S., but its use may decline greatly as we move from harvesting old-growth to managing second-growth forest. Considering the damage to the site that slashburning has sometimes caused in the past, strict controls on this very useful but very powerful tool are certainly warranted. In designing these controls, the environmental impacts of the alternative solutions to problems created by logging slash must be carefully evaluated. Decisions must not be made based solely on short-term aesthetic impacts. The piling and burning or whole-tree harvesting that has sometimes resulted from concerns about the aesthetics of broadcast slashburning is often a greater threat to the sustainability of the forest resource than broadcast slashburning if the latter is conducted with a sensitivity to soils and other ecosystem components and processes.

CHAPTER 8

Chemicals in Forest Management: Responsible Use or Environmental Abuse?

Introduction

Many people who live in today's urban environment have either forgotten or never experienced the joys and tribulations of growing their own food. For many young city-dwellers living in condominiums, high-rise apartments, or housing co-operatives, the idea of a vegetable patch at the bottom of the garden has become little more than folklore from the past.

The physical separation of people from the primary source of the material things they need and want is a major problem for our society. Many urban children think that milk and vegetables come from the supermarket, that cars come from the auto showroom, and that woollen sweaters come from the department store. There is a failure to understand that metal products originate as ore bodies in the ground that must be mined, that in 'developed' countries, most of the food we eat comes from farms where it must be grown, and that almost all of the plant and animal fibre for the clothes we wear are a product of the management of plants and animals by farmers. This lack of understanding leads to a failure to recognize that someone, somewhere, must manage and harvest a portion of nature's abundance if we are to be fed, clothed, and housed, and that in some cases the form and function of unmanaged ecosystems have to be altered in order to provide the materials people want and expect. The public has every reason to be angry about oil spills, but people often fail to realize that their insistence on driving cars and using plastics provides a major reason for the transport of oil. Rarely do people relate the flooding of valleys for hydroelectric schemes and the building of power stations to their expectation and demand that lights will go on at night and that the oven will heat up to cook their food.

A vegetable patch in your garden can provide some important lessons. If you merely plant seeds in the spring and do nothing again until midsummer or fall, you will be very disappointed. Slugs, snails, and a legion of insects will gratefully accept your contributions to their food supply. They, rather than you, will harvest your crop. Similarly, a variety of garden weeds will make life very tough for your planted vegetables unless you tend your patch fairly regularly. Weeds can be defined as plants that grow well in spite of your best efforts to stop them, or as plants that grow where you don't want them. They compete with your frequently less robust ornamental flower and food plants for light, soil moisture, and soil nutrients. Unless they are controlled, weeds will ensure that you harvest little or nothing from what you plant.

A similar hard-earned experience of both farmers and backyard gardeners is that if you take crops from the land year after year without putting back organic matter and nutrients, the soil will eventually become exhausted. To be successful, farmers, whether professionals or backyard amateurs, must return organic compost, manure, and/or inorganic fertilizers to their soil if they wish to continue to provide food for their table year after year.

Because of a lack of sufficient organic compost and the economics of applying organic fertilizers, or both, inorganic fertilizers are generally used to maintain or increase the growth of many of our food and tree crops. Inorganic or synthetic organic fertilizers dominate food and fibre production, even though 'organic farming' and the use of compost by backyard farmers are definitely on the increase. Too much inorganic fertilizer without adequate additions of organic matter can accelerate the loss of the original organic matter from agricultural or backyard soils by stimulating microbial activity. Although initially beneficial, too much microbial activity for too long in the absence of organic matter additions can exhaust the fertility of the soil, reduce the soil's resistance to erosion, and lower the water and nutrient-holding capacity and productivity of the soil. This is usually not a problem in forestry because fertilizers are applied only at long intervals and because most forests have an organic forest floor and a substantial annual input of organic matter in the form of leaf fall and fine root death.

Nevertheless, there is increasing interest in using society's organic waste – sewage sludge, pulp mill sludge, dead fish from fish farms, and so on – as a source of slow-release forest fertilizer.

This chapter is about the use of chemicals in forest management to maintain the fertility of the soil and to control the weeds, insects, and other organisms that can frustrate the best efforts of foresters to produce tree crops. It is not intended to be a comprehensive evaluation; the topic is immensely broad and complex. Rather, it addresses the broader question of whether the use of chemicals in forestry is a responsible thing or simply a 'cop-out,' a way of patching up mistakes made as a result of inappropriate or careless management. I will deal with three categories of forest chemicals in increasing order of their potential to have an adverse environmental impact: fertilizers, herbicides, and insecticides.

The Use of Fertilizers in Forestry

Ten thousand years ago, forests covered much of the earth's land surface. Only in very cold, very hot, very dry, or fire-dominated landscapes and some very wet sites were trees absent. Without question, trees have been the most successful form of terrestrial vegetation. However, as the human population grew and farming became a major means of obtaining food, trees were stripped from more and more areas. Because food production is normally greatest and most economically rewarding on the most fertile soils, much of the world's more productive forest soils were taken over by agriculture and dedicated to food production. Consequently, the remaining forests in many countries are restricted to sites with poorer soils.

The inherently low nutrient status of the mineral soil underlying many of the world's forests is not a major problem for unmanaged forests that have not been disturbed frequently. Trees are very efficient at accumulating nutrients from small annual inputs released from rain, rock weathering, and biological fixation of nitrogen, and at building these into soil organic matter and a very 'tight' biogeochemical cycle (see Chapter 4). If left undisturbed long enough, forests will improve the fertility of even the poorest soil as long as the climate or some other factor does not limit plant growth. This is why tropical rain forests were able to develop in the Amazon basin of South America on soils that from a nutritional standpoint are among the poorest in the world. Not all the soils in the Amazon basin are nutrient-poor, but large areas of very ancient and very infertile soils in that area are. Managed on long rotations with the removal of only the larger logs, which contain relatively small amounts of the more critical nutrients, forests on medium- and low-fertility soils can be completely sustainable. Things change, however, when we start to treat forests growing on nutrient-poor sites more like farms.

As trees are harvested from the forest, both organic matter and nutrients that would otherwise have been returned to the soil are removed. These would have contributed to the maintenance of soil fertility and site productivity in the future had they remained. The extent of this harvest removal depends on whether we take just the large logs, the entire stem, or the entire tree, and how frequently the forest is harvested – how old the trees are at harvest time. When we harvest trees, there may also be a temporary leakage of nutrients out of the ecosystem by soil leaching. The extent of this leakage can vary from negligible, such as in many clearcut northern forests, to the loss of a major portion of the ecosystem's nutrient capital. This can happen when tropical rain forest is stripped from very poor soils, as in parts of the Amazonian rain forest, and reinvasion of the forest is delayed by shifting cultivation or attempts at permanent agriculture. The potential for this type of loss is generally greater with clearcutting than with non-clearcut harvesting methods, unless clearcuts revegetate rapidly. Because rapid revegetation is the rule in most managed forests, especially at temperate and northern latitudes, significant nutrient loss by soil leaching following forest harvesting or natural ecosystem disturbance is believed to be rare in these

forests. Only in cases of complete and sustained devegetation have major and sustained leaching losses been reported (e.g., the Hubbard Brook study in New Hampshire in the northwestern United States).

Whether soil fertility problems occur as a result of timber harvesting ultimately depends on whether the combined nutrient losses in harvested materials, by soil leaching and by other mechanisms such as gaseous losses of nitrogen, are greater than the quantity of nutrients that are added to the ecosystem by natural processes and by forest managers over the period between successive harvests. More immediately, it depends on whether or not these losses reduce the supply of nutrients for uptake by the trees so much that their growth is impaired.

Harvesting forests infrequently, such as every 80 to 100 years, poses much less threat to long-term soil fertility than harvesting crops on short rotations, such as every 20 to 30 years, because most or all of the harvest-induced nutrient losses will be replaced naturally over the longer period. Thus, traditional shifting cultivation even on infertile soils in the tropical rain forest was sustainable when the area was left under forest cover for 80 to 100 years before the next period of one or two years of farming, a frequency that occurred when human populations were very low. However, it is often not sustainable if the fallow period is reduced to between 20 and 30 years or less as the population increases. The input of litterfall and the capture of nutrients from rainfall and weathering soil minerals can re-establish soil nutrient reserves over the longer period, but not when the forest is disturbed too frequently or on too large a scale.

The threat to the fertility of forest soil is greater when branches and foliage are removed together with the stem than when only the stem is harvested. The foliage of many tree species is rich in several important nutrients and should be left to decompose in the forest, just as the home gardener should compost vegetable scraps and garden waste and return the resulting compost to the vegetable patch to maintain the fertility of the soil. Harvesting the whole tree on short rotations can significantly damage forest soil fertility and reduce the growth of future tree crops unless the soil is naturally rich in nutrients and organic matter, or the lost nutrients are replaced either by natural processes or by the land manager in the form of fertilizers.

Foresters may choose to apply fertilizers where forest soil is initially poor in nutrients or has low nutrient availability, or where the frequency and intensity of forest harvesting poses a threat to soil fertility. Unlike farmers, they do not have to apply fertilizers every year. In fact, they may only use them once or twice in a hundred-year tree-crop rotation. This low frequency reflects the efficiency with which many forests respond to nutrient additions, the efficiency with which added nutrients are held by the forest, the duration of the trees' growth response, and also the economics of tree-crop production. The forester who harvests only once every 50 to 100 years simply cannot afford to apply fertilizer every year the way a farmer does when producing the nutrient-demanding annual food crops that we like to eat.

Forest fertilizers are sometimes applied in a 'spot' treatment close to the roots of tree seedlings at the time they are planted in order to get them started. This is particularly important for phosphorus fertilizer on clay soils that rapidly immobilize phosphorus. However, most forest fertilization is done when the forest is a bit 'hungrier' for nutrients. Human babies need small amounts of food. If you have teenagers in the house, you will never be able to keep the fridge full of food. The appetite of people in midlife is usually more modest, and elderly people often eat relatively little; their nutrient and energy needs are much smaller. Forests are similar. Small trees place modest demands on soil nutrients; they need a small but continuous supply. Rapidly growing 'teenage' plantations literally mine the soil for nutrients. Their fine roots fill all fertile areas, and tree growth at this stage is often limited by the lack of nutrients. As the stand gets older, the trees

are able to satisfy more of their needs by recycling nutrients that are already stored internally, and every year their need to take up additional nutrients from the soil declines somewhat (Figure 8.1). Very old forests have a relatively low nutrient uptake demand. Foresters generally apply fertilizers when trees have the greatest uptake requirement because adding nutrients at this time is likely to have the greatest beneficial effect on growth and produce the greatest economic return on the investment in fertilization.

The forest's ability to respond to fertilization can be stimulated by thinning, a partial harvest in which one of every three trees may be removed, for example. Normally, forests are fertilized only after such a thinning.

Forest fertilizers are usually applied as small pellets distributed over the forest using helicopters or small fixed-wing aircraft. The most commonly used fertilizer in northern forests has been nitrogen, applied either in a readily soluble form such as ammonium nitrate, or in a synthetic organic form such as urea (a natural organic substance that is produced synthetically as a fertilizer) that requires chemical alteration once it reaches the soil before it is available for uptake by the trees. In some parts of the world, such as parts of Brazil and Australia, phosphorus has proven to be the most effective fertilizer, while specific nutritional problems that

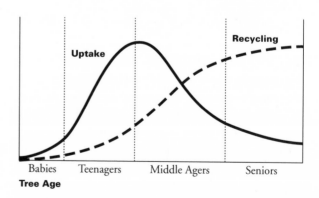

Figure 8.1 Variation in the uptake demands of trees as they age, and of the contribution made to the trees' nutrient economy by internal cycling of nutrients

require potassium, sulphur, iron, boron, zinc, or some other nutrient element require a site-specific fertilizer treatment.

Traditionally, nitrogen fertilizers used in forestry have been synthetic, that is, manufactured, inorganic or organic chemicals. There is, however, a slowly growing interest in using organic wastes as a source of nitrogen fertilizer – urban sewage sludge, animal waste, and compostable urban garbage where these materials are available. Other organic materials, such as pulp mill sludge, have also been shown to improve tree growth in forest soils poor in nutrients and organic matter. Wood ash from wood-fired energy-generation facilities, an ancient form of agricultural and forest fertilizer, is attracting increasing interest as concern over the economic and environmental costs of fossil fuel energy has led to increasing use of wood and wood waste as a 'bioenergy' fuel. At the same time, there is an increasing problem of how to dispose of all the wood ash being produced.

Although forest fertilization is generally accepted as an environmentally friendly thing to do, some people occasionally express the concerns that are addressed in the following questions.

Can the Use of Forest Fertilizers Damage the Forest Ecosystem?

All life depends on access to nutrient chemicals (including carbon) because organic matter, including our own bodies, is made up of inorganic chemicals from the soil and air in combination with energy that was derived ultimately from sunlight. Consequently, it is very unlikely that fertilization will damage a forest. Addition of excessive amounts of nutrients, addition of nutrients too frequently, and addition of an inappropriate balance of nutrient elements certainly has the potential to cause short-term disruptions of ecosystem function, damage the small feeding roots of some tree species, and temporarily disturb plant physiology or soil microbial populations. However, unlike agriculture, where the economics of annual food crop production

promotes the frequent use of fertilizers as long as fossil fuels are cheap, the economics of forest crop production greatly restricts the use of fertilizers even where it is environmentally sound and biologically effective. Also, because modern forest fertilization programs are normally based on a pretreatment assessment of the tree crop's nutritional needs, it is unlikely that problems of nutrient imbalance will occur. It is very unlikely that forest fertilization will result in damage to forest ecosystems.

Because many forests grow on nutrient-poor soils or under conditions of low nutrient availability, the addition of fertilizers generally increases the capture of sunlight by the forest, thereby increasing tree growth. More nutrients enable the trees to develop a greater quantity of leaves, which intercept more light, and better nutrition increases the efficiency with which the intercepted light energy is used to produce new biomass. Fertilizers also make many understorey plants more nutritious as food for wildlife, as long as they are not shaded out by the increased growth of tree leaves. This is not likely to happen immediately because foresters generally fertilize a forest only after it has been thinned, with some trees being removed to make more room for the others to develop more leaves and therefore grow faster. Sufficient light reaches the understorey plants in thinned and fertilized stands so that the herbs and shrubs can take advantage of the increased nutrient availability for several years. Thus, fertilization normally improves both the quality and the quantity of food for wildlife species that eat the understorey.

The experience of agriculture has taught us about the dangers of overuse of fertilizers, such as the accelerated loss of soil organic matter and pollution of groundwater. Because of the low frequency of fertilizer application in forestry (once every twenty to thirty years rather than annually or several times a year as in agriculture), the relatively low application rates (such as 200 to 300 kilograms of nitrogen per hectare), the high levels of soil organic matter, the low nutrient status of most forests, and the high nutrient uptake demand of most forests, these concerns are normally not applicable to forest fertilization. However, the use of fertilizers in both agriculture and forestry can mask management-induced reductions in inherent soil fertility and long-term site productivity. Fertilizers should be used only to increase production, not as a way to justify the continued use of management practices that damage soil fertility and site productivity.

Does the Use of Forest Fertilizers Cause Water Pollution?

In the 1970s, there was concern about the risk that forest fertilization might pollute forest streams, that is, cause undesirable nutrient enrichment. Many studies were done, and they confirmed that, in spite of the nutrient-retention efficiency of forests, there is sometimes a short-term increase in the concentration of nutrients in forest streams following a forest fertilization. Yet this concentration is not as great as one that can result from the growth of nitrogen-fixing species like red alder which commonly invade and grow on moist sites in coastal BC following timber harvesting or natural disturbances in the forest.

If the availability of nutrients after fertilization exceeds the plants' ability to take them up or the capacity of the soil to absorb them, some of the nutrients may be washed out of the soil by rainwater. Applying a large quantity of readily available nutrients to a nutrient-starved forest growing on soil that is low in organic matter may result in leakage of some of the nutrients from the ecosystem. The trees may simply not be physiologically able to respond fast enough to take up all the available nutrients, and the soil's nutrient-retention capacity may simply be too low. The use of slow-release fertilizers or several small applications of soluble fertilizers will usually eliminate or minimize leaching losses in such situations, although the latter option may be limited by the increased cost of application. On average, leaching losses will be greater in areas with high rainfall than in somewhat drier areas.

Loss of fertilizer nutrients into groundwater and streams can be a problem on both nutrient-rich and nutrient-poor sites. In the unfertilized condition, very fertile forests often 'leak' much larger quantities of nutrients into the groundwater and streams than nutrient-poor forests, which generally retain their nutrients tenaciously. Nutrients added as fertilizer may suffer the same degree of leakage. However, fertilizers are usually not used on forest soils that are so fertile that the risk of leaching is high, because the probability of increasing tree growth by fertilization on such sites is low.

The pulse of increased nutrient concentration in streamwater that sometimes occurs after fertilization is normally found only for a short distance downstream from the point at which the nutrients reached the stream. Forest streams are ecosystems that have nutrient uptake and cycling processes just as the forest does. Nutrients leached into streams are usually taken out of solution quite rapidly both by organisms that are short of nutrients and by various chemical and exchange processes. As a result, most undisturbed forest streams have very low concentrations of dissolved nutrients. In fact, fish production in many lakes and forest streams in coastal British Columbia is believed to be limited by a lack of such nutrients. The undisturbed forests in these areas are so efficient at retaining nutrients that not enough of them reach streams and lakes to support the rates of fish growth that most fishermen would like to see.

Before heavy commercial fishing began off the coast of British Columbia, the millions of salmon that returned from the ocean to spawn and die each year added huge amounts of nutrients to lakes and streams in the form of their carcasses. As a result of overfishing, fish habitat damage, water pollution, altered stream temperature, or changed streamflow rates, salmon runs are reported to have declined in some rivers. Where this has occurred, the magnitude of this nutrient addition has been reduced. Undoubtedly, this has affected the aquatic productivity of some lakes and streams. In recognition of the limitation of fish production posed by a shortage of nutrients, a program of adding fertilizer directly to some aquatic ecosystems has been undertaken by fisheries authorities. It would therefore seem that in this part of the world the addition of some nutrients to lakes and streams as a result of forest fertilization may often be a good thing, as long as the added nutrients are in the appropriate balance. Nitrogen is the most commonly used fertilizer nutrient in forests, whereas streams and lakes are often most limited by phosphorus. Adding too much of any one nutrient to any living system can have counterproductive effects.

Before leaving the topic of fertilization and water quality, a few words of caution are needed. In Scandinavia and some other parts of Europe, acid rain is adding large quantities of nitrogen to the soil annually, and there is concern about nitrogen pollution of groundwater. Regulations restrict the use of nitrogen fertilizers in ecosystems affected by nitrogen-rich acid rain. Similarly, many streams and lakes in drier climates or in areas of intensive agricultural production or urbanization have become polluted because of the addition of nutrients in runoff or soil leachate from agricultural land, or the dumping of inadequately treated sewage effluent. In such situations, even minor additions of nutrients to groundwater, streams, or lakes by forest fertilization programs could cause the further enrichment of lakes and exacerbate undesirable growth of aquatic plants. Generalizations about the effects of forest fertilization on nearby water bodies are thus inappropriate because so many factors are involved in determining whether there will be any biological or ecological impact. Each situation must be evaluated in terms of the local ecology and the behaviour of nutrients in the local ecosystem.

Does Forest Fertilization Contribute to the Greenhouse Effect?

The manufacture and use of fertilizers generally involves the use of energy derived from fossil fuels, and therefore has the potential to contribute to the greenhouse effect by releasing CO_2 into the atmosphere (see Chapter 14). If the fertilizer stimulates tree growth, however, many times more carbon may be taken out of the air and stored by the forest than was released in the manufacture, distribution, and application of the fertilizer. Forest fertilization certainly has a much more favourable carbon balance (CO_2 taken out of the air minus CO_2 released to the air) than fertilizers in agriculture. However, the carbon stored in this increased tree growth will be released back to the atmosphere eventually, and one is left with the net release of the fossil fuel carbon used in the fertilizer activity. Thus, although forest fertilization almost always increases the growth of forests and thus the removal of CO_2 from the atmosphere, there may be a long-term environmental price to pay in the form of global warming. Where fertilizers are manufactured using 'waste' natural gases that would otherwise have been released to the atmosphere or 'flared-off' (burned), the net effect on the atmosphere appears to be positive.

Although the use of synthetic forest fertilizers appears to be a positive thing with respect to the greenhouse effect, it would seem to be even better to use natural biological fixation of nitrogen (by growing lupines, alder, or other nitrogen-fixing plants, for example), or 'natural' organic fertilizers such as sewage sludge, animal manure, pulp mill sludge, fish farm and fish factory waste, and other such materials where available. The careful use of these materials as forest fertilizers appears both environmentally and economically attractive because alternative disposal methods for these wastes are often expensive; they normally require the use of fossil fuel energy (and thus release CO_2); and such disposal methods may cause environmental damage in the form of air pollution or groundwater contamination. Forest fertilization in the future will probably use both strategies depending on their availability and economic efficiency.

Is It All Right to Use Forest Fertilizers to Maintain Forest Productivity?

One of the fundamental objectives of forest management should be conservation of soil organic matter and nutrients. These 'environmental legacy' values should be passed on to future generations either unimpaired or at acceptable levels. This does not mean that there should never be any changes in soil organic matter and nutrients. Fluctuations occur naturally during a tree-crop rotation or following natural disturbance, and this variation is not a matter for concern as long as the long-term average condition is maintained. Similarly, as humid temperate old-growth forest is converted to managed second growth, some decline in site organic matter levels is expected and unavoidable, but soil organic matter should not decline between managed rotations.

The basic principle of organic-matter conservation does not imply that there should never be a reduction in organic matter in a forest. Some forests have accumulated so much undecomposed organic material that there is a slowing down of nutrient cycling, acidification or other undesirable changes in the mineral soil, and stagnation of forest growth. In such forests, some reduction in organic matter and a change in the composition of the forest floor may be very desirable if one's objective is to promote tree growth. However, this fundamental management objective does mean that there should be no significant and sustained rotation-to-rotation decline in these values that would decrease ecosystem productivity and resilience.

Fertilizers may be used to help sustain soil organic matter and nutrient levels, improve the productivity of naturally infertile sites, and help naturally disturbed or management-disturbed ecosystems recover faster than they otherwise would, but they are no substitute for conservation of the natural site fertility. Where possible, effective and economical natural means of maintaining site fertility, such as use of nitrogen-fixing species or fertilizers derived from organic waste materials, should be used

instead of fossil fuel-based synthetic fertilizers. If a mineral nutrient, such as potassium, phosphorus, or magnesium, is in short supply and cannot be supplied any other way, the conventional use of inorganic mineral fertilizers is appropriate.

In conclusion, although there have been environmental concerns about the use of fertilizers in agriculture, these concerns are not generally applicable to forests. This is because the frequency and rate of application of fertilizers in forestry has been much less than in agriculture. There are great potential benefits in using them to raise the level of forest growth. There appear to be few environmental reasons to limit fertilizer use in forests within a program of site organic matter and nutrient conservation, and with appropriate concern for water quality. An exception would be the use of nitrogen fertilizers that can cause soil acidification in forest areas that already receive abundant acid rain.

The Use of Organic Wastes as Slow-Release Forest Fertilizers

The use of materials such as urban sewage sludge, pulp mill waste, dead fish produced by fish farms, and compostable urban garbage as forest fertilizers has already been mentioned. Many types of waste produced by urban societies can be reduced by the three R's: reduction in use, reuse, and recycling. Reduction and reuse do not work for human bodily wastes and wastes produced by food production systems. The larger the human population, the greater the production of these materials, which most developed industrial societies tend to shun. Recycling of these wastes in forests offers many advantages over alternative disposal methods.

Dumping of organic wastes into lakes, rivers, or the ocean was one of the most commonly used disposal methods in the past. This is no longer socially acceptable, and in many places such dumping has been made illegal. In some cases it may cause undesirable changes in these aquatic and marine ecosystems. In others it may pose a human health hazard. Even where there are no significant risks, the public may simply think that it is bad. Putting these materials in landfills is no longer socially acceptable either: the 'NIMBY' ('not in my backyard') syndrome is increasingly limiting this disposal option.

Incineration of organic wastes can result in air pollution problems (it can be a major source of dioxins), it is expensive, and it requires the use of fossil fuels, which adds to the greenhouse effect. The resulting ash may contain undesirable inorganic chemicals in highly concentrated form, such as toxic heavy metals. Disposal of this toxic ash is expensive and may pose a threat to the environment, whereas the same material applied over large areas of forest in unconcentrated form (i.e., the original organic waste material) is not known to constitute an environmental hazard.

Application of organic wastes to agricultural land can be both a socially and an environmentally sound disposal method. There is a history going back centuries or even millennia in Japan, China, and other ancient cultures of using 'night soil' (human feces and urine produced at night) as agricultural fertilizer, and this is still done in many developing countries. However, this disposal method cannot be used everywhere and is not suitable for all types of organic waste. Traditional recycling of human waste involved material uncontaminated by all the other chemicals that are flushed down toilets or tipped into sewers by urban populations, especially in developed countries. These other chemicals can limit the use of urban sewage sludge in food production systems. For example, if there are significant amounts of heavy metals such as cadmium in organic matter that is added annually to agricultural soils, there is a risk that these toxic materials will be concentrated into plant or animals tissues that are harvested for human food.

Although the disposal of organic waste materials on agricultural lands is often the most logical solution where heavy metals are not a problem, in some areas there may be a risk of contaminating groundwater bodies (aquifers) with nitrogen in the form of nitrate. Agricultural soils often do not store nitro-

gen as efficiently as forest soils. Where water quality considerations are paramount, or where there is insufficient land for disposing all the organic waste produced, the agricultural alternative may not solve the disposal problem.

Given the social, environmental, and economic problems associated with most traditional methods for disposing of or recycling organic wastes, the 'forest alternative' appears very attractive. Organic waste materials generally release their nutrient content more slowly than inorganic or synthetic fertilizers, they contain a wide spectrum of plant nutrients, and the addition of organic matter improves several aspects of the soil in addition to its nutrient status. Increasing the productivity of managed forest lands near mills and markets using waste organic materials reduces the pressure to log more remote areas that society might wish to designate as park or wilderness. This could help reduce land-use conflicts. Increasing production close to mills or manufacturing plants also reduces the use of fossil fuels to transport logs from remote logging sites.

There are environmental concerns about using organic wastes in forests, of course, and research must be done to ensure that they are used in a manner that does not pose unacceptable environmental or health risks. Concerns have been expressed about heavy metals and pathogenic organisms. However, after nearly two decades of research in various parts of the United States, the risks appear to be negligible and the benefits to society and the environment enormous where applications of organic wastes as forest fertilizers are based on scientifically sound and ecologically sensitive guidelines. A large proportion of the sewage sludge from the city of Seattle and surrounding municipalities in Washington is currently disposed of in this way.

Use of Herbicides in Forestry

If a home gardener or farmer does not control weed growth, food and flower production may be greatly reduced or completely prevented. Weeds will simply

Site preparation

Excessive site preparation on steep hill slopes in the Golden Downs Forest, South Island, New Zealand. Restrictions on the use of herbicides and fire, and the ineffectiveness and cost of manual control of the very thorny shrub gorse (introduced from Europe) led to the use of mechanical clearing. If not controlled, this shrub will take over the site and completely prevent tree growth. However, the soils on this site have been severely disturbed and site productivity badly damaged by the removal of much of the top soil. Mechanical site treatment was an 'environmentally unfriendly' solution to the problem.

take over the field, vegetable patch, or flower bed. It is the same for planted or naturally regenerated tree seedlings. Most of them will die as a result of competition from other plant species unless this competition is controlled.

A 1937 study found that after four months a single rye plant (a type of grass) growing in a large pot had produced 623 kilometres of fine roots with a total surface area of 639 square metres. It is not surprising, therefore, that a small conifer seedling with a much smaller root system planted in a weedy site will have a very difficult time competing with grasses and other non-crop plants for soil moisture and nutrients. Weeds also greatly reduce the growth of crop trees by competing for light, but even when young trees are not shaded, non-crop vegetation can have a very negative effect on their growth for many years by competing for below-ground soil resources.

There is presently a great concern among the public and most foresters about Canadian forestry's long history of failure to regenerate harvested forests adequately. This concern is justified. In the past, investment in forest renewal in Canada has been inadequate, and there has been a lack of government policy to ensure prompt reforestation. In fact, there has been relatively little of what the average European forester would think of as forest management until the relatively recent past (see the discussion of the history of forestry, Chapter 4). However, in our rush to plant trees to make amends for the failures of the past, we sometimes lose sight of the fact that planting baby trees is not enough: they also have to be cared for. Most natural seedlings in most unmanaged forests die. They are eaten by herbivores, killed by diseases, or outcompeted by other plants. The same fate awaits many of the seedlings that we plant unless we take some action to free them from these agents of seedling death.

Weed control can be conducted in a wide variety of ways. Burning a site and then planting it immediately can give the seedlings three to five years of reduced competition, which may be enough time for them to gain a competitive edge over the weeds. However, burning that is hot enough to significantly reduce weed problems can result in nutritional damage to the soil. Manual weeding of herbs and shrubs can reduce above ground competition in the growing season when the weeding is done but must normally be repeated every year, or even several times during one growing season, for several years because many of the cut plants will promptly resprout. Manual weeding, however, does relatively little to reduce below-ground competition. Similarly, hand cutting of deciduous trees that are competing with young conifers can sometimes give long-lasting relief from competition, but will normally require several repeated weedings before the crop trees are 'up, up, and away.' Sprouts from cut stumps of deciduous trees can grow one or even two metres high per year, compared with only a fraction of a metre of annual height growth by young planted seedlings. These sprouts can rapidly catch up and overtake the slower-growing crop trees even when these are several metres tall. Also, several or even many sprouts will take the place of every deciduous stem that is hand cut. Mechanical site treatment can effectively control weed competition for several years, but in some cases the treatment may make competition worse in the long run. It can create an ideal soil surface for the establishment of new weeds, especially fast-growing, competitive woody species. Incorrectly applied, mechanical site preparation can also do significant physical and/or nutritional damage to the site by compacting or scraping off the top soil.

Using plant-eating animals such as sheep can eliminate many of the problems of burning, hand weeding, and mechanical methods, and it creates marketable animal biomass at the same time. There is renewed interest in this technique of site preparation and plantation weeding, which has a long recorded history in Europe, dating back to at least the 1600s. There are sometimes impediments to using this option, however. There are often not enough suitable animals and skilled herders to do all the weeding that needs to be done; the animals can damage crop trees if they are not managed carefully. Damage to soil structure may be caused on wet, fine-textured soils. If care is not taken, domestic livestock may introduce diseases to wildlife populations and compete with them for food. The livestock may attract predators such as wolves, coyotes, or bears, and they may pollute streams with urine and feces, temporarily rendering them unsuitable for drinking water. Grazing animals such as sheep may be useful for controlling herbs, but may not tackle shrubs such as those in the raspberry or blueberry families. Pigs and goats will consume a much wider range of species, but will also eat crop trees and pose a much higher risk of soil damage. They are more appropriate for site preparation than plantation maintenance. Domestic livestock will generally not control competing vegetation effectively where a lot of logging slash limits their mobility. Biological weed control using domestic livestock clearly has its place, but not everywhere. Many of these potential problems can be solved, and more research is warranted into making this user-friendly weed control method viable.

Alternatives to weed control that may be useful in some situations include the use of tree species that are tolerant of the weed competition, such as shade-tolerant species; the use of fast-growing species that can outgrow the weeds; the use of very large seedlings to give them a head start; or the use of very dense plantations that will rapidly shade out the weeds.

Any of these methods may be appropriate under particular circumstances. Manual weeding may be feasible near communities where the cost of labour is low and its availability is high, such as during periods of high unemployment. Mechanical methods may work well on soils not subject to compaction and erosion, and where nutrient loss caused by soil disturbance is not a problem. Grazing can be an excellent method where farmers and grazing animals are available nearby and potential conflicts with wildlife can be overcome. Fire can be effective where it can be used safely, economically, and without risk of long-term soil change. However, there will always be situations in which these and other methods either are not available, are too expensive, cause too much risk to the environment, or are technically not feasible. In such cases, the judicious use of herbicides may be the most environmentally friendly, practical, or economical alternative.

Herbicides are chemicals that are toxic to plants. Most chemicals in high enough doses will kill plants (table salt or nitrogen fertilizer, for example). However, when we talk about herbicides, we normally refer to chemicals characterized by their ability to kill plants, or certain types of plants, in low dosages. The earliest herbicides used by humans were mostly inorganic chemicals, such as copper sulphate, arsenic compounds, or sulphuric and other acids. The development of organic chemicals similar to natural plant growth hormones (2,4-D and 2,4,5-T) during the Second World War led to the development over the past four decades of a wide range of plant-killing chemicals. Some of the more recent synthetic herbicides have their origins in *allelochemicals:* substances produced by plants to inhibit or eliminate competing plant species. Allelochemicals are members of a broader class of 'secondary chemicals' that includes natural insecticides, repellents, and fungicides that evolved in plants to control their animal and fungal enemies.

The massive use of herbicides as a chemical weapon during the Vietnam War earned for them the public anger, distrust, and condemnation that had previously been reserved for insecticides such as DDT. In the early 1960s, Rachel Carson led the crusade against the overuse of DDT, which had been lionized by the public in the 1940s and 1950s as the saviour of millions of lives, and for its part in dramatically increasing world food production. Because it was so effective, insecticides were inevitably used to excess, just as antibiotics have been overused by the medical profession. Birds in particular suffered from the bioaccumulation[13] that occurs with many organochlorine insecticides, and this was the impetus for Rachel Carson's book *Silent Spring.* The increasing use of herbicides and their indiscriminate use in the 1960s in the U.S. led to growing concern among some ecologists,[14] but it was not until Agent Orange was used as a defoliant in Vietnam that public opinion turned against herbicides.

The extensive devegetation of mangrove and other forests during the Vietnam War by American forces using repeated applications of herbicides was accompanied by allegations that a toxic impurity (a type of dioxin) in the herbicide Agent Orange, or simply repeated exposure to high concentrations of the herbicide, was causing illness and birth defects in rural Vietnamese communities and sickness in returning soldiers. Together with the general public's antipathy towards the war, this resulted in a drastic decline in public acceptance of herbicides in the late 1960s and early 1970s. This class of management chemical has never recovered its reputation.

While herbicides are still widely used in agriculture to produce the food we eat and by homeowners to maintain their lawns and yards, the public is

---

13 The term bioaccumulation refers to the tendency for certain chemicals, such as fat-soluble DDT, to become progressively concentrated as the organic matter they are contained in passes through a food chain: plants > herbivores > carnivores. Innocuously low levels of such chemicals in plants can lead, through the process of bioaccumulation, to concentrations in carnivores high enough to impair reproduction, behaviour, health, or survival.

---

14 The early warnings of Frank Egler should be acknowledged.

increasingly restricting their use in forests. It seems that regardless of the type of chemical, its level of toxicity, its carcinogenicity (cancer-causing potential), or its teratogenicity (potential for causing birth defects), if you call something a herbicide, the public will try to stop its use in forests. People have become convinced that using any type of herbicide in forestry poses an unacceptable threat to the environment and to public health, whether or not scientific evidence supports their conviction and regardless of whether similar chemicals are used to grow the food plants they eat.

Let's take a look at various questions that are commonly asked about the potential environmental impact of using herbicides in forestry.

Do Herbicides Destroy the Soil?

Soil is a living system made up of animals, microbes, live plant roots, dead organic matter, mineral particles, air, and water. It has a physical structure and a variety of processes that are critically important in ecosystem function. To damage the soil, herbicides would have to damage one or more of these components or characteristics in a manner that affected the functioning of the soil system.

Available scientific evidence suggests that the rates at which herbicides permitted for forestry use in Canada are applied are not toxic to soil organisms other than the roots of the target plants, do not bioaccumulate in forest soils, do not damage soil structure, and do not directly cause the loss of soil organic matter. If herbicides kill or damage a significant proportion of the plant community, there may be some leakage of nutrients out of the ecosystem into groundwater or streams, and a short-term increase followed by a temporary reduction in the input of organic matter into the soil in the form of above-ground litterfall and dead roots. But these effects result from a change in the vegetation, not from the use of herbicides to cause the change. They also occur with manual, mechanical, or fire-based methods of weed control that control the target vegetation to the same extent, except that

in the case of some mechanical or fire-based methods, nutrient losses are normally higher. In the case of mechanical control, there is sometimes the additional danger of damage to soil structure. Manual weed control in forestry has a temporary and minor impact on most forest weeds because they promptly resprout. Thus, manual control probably causes the least nutrient leakage.

Annual applications of herbicides in agriculture have not been shown to have a direct adverse affect on soil organisms and soil structure, although the maintenance of a weed-free condition may increase soil nutrient leakage and lead to reduced soil organic matter levels and increased erosion. It is therefore highly unlikely that very infrequent use in forests, which temporarily reduces the vigour and coverage of weeds instead of eliminating them, would have any direct adverse effects on soils. One of the few potentially negative effects is the killing of nitrogen-fixing plants such as alder, thereby depriving the ecosystem of future nitrogen input by biological fixation. However, this loss results from killing the alder, not from using herbicides. It occurs whether the plants are killed manually, mechanically, chemically, or by fire.

The removal of all minor forest vegetation might also have a potentially negative effect on soil stability and susceptibility to erosion on steep slopes. Broadcast applications of herbicides to steep unstable or erodible slopes that would result in devegetation should not be permitted. Herbicides currently licensed for forest use in Canada are not sufficiently broad-spectrum to achieve such devegetation, so this point is academic.

Do Herbicides Kill Wildlife?

Wildlife ecologists have conducted tests in which foliage from forest areas sprayed with currently registered forest herbicides was fed to wildlife. These have not revealed any negative effects. This is not surprising since herbicides registered for use in Canadian forests have extremely low mammalian toxicity. They have been specifically selected to interfere with plant biochemical processes that do not occur in animal biochemical systems. Because most herbicides in current use are rapidly absorbed by vegetation, or adsorbed and/or deactivated by dust on foliage or soil particles, wildlife are exposed to contaminated foliage only briefly.

The lack of demonstrated negative effect of herbicides on wildlife is reflected in the fact that herbicides are sometimes used by wildlife managers to improve the habitat of large mammalian herbivores such as deer and elk. Woody plant species that have grown too large to be of value to the herbivores as food are sprayed to kill the above-ground parts and cause the plants to resprout from undamaged below-ground organs. These sprouts are palatable and nutritious, and are favoured by wildlife. The major negative effect of herbicides on animals is the change of habitat, such as the temporary loss of food species or escape cover in larger clearcuts. There are also examples in which control of all non-crop vegetation has led to plant seedlings being damaged by wildlife and insect herbivores with nothing else to eat. For most wildlife species, spraying clearcuts with herbicides will have at most a short-term negative impact on habitat, and may significantly increase the availability of some desired plant food species. Injecting the chemicals directly into individual hardwood trees or spot-spraying them around planted seedlings would greatly reduce their effects on wildlife compared to broadcast applications. Perhaps the most negative aspect of herbicide use as far as some wildlife species are concerned is that, if successful, it hastens the replacement of herbs, shrubs, and deciduous trees by coniferous forest. This reduces the available food and habitat for some species, but speeds the development of habitat for others.

Do Forest Herbicides Contaminate Streams and Kill Fish?

Research has shown that where adequate buffer strips are left, either complete protection is afforded or only minute quantities of herbicides ever reach streams.[15] Where herbicides have entered streams, usually where there was no buffer strip, measurable quantities (a few parts per million dropping rapidly to parts per billion or the detection limit) have been found in the streamwater for a few hours or a few days after the application. This most commonly occurs immediately after the first post-spray rainfall, when any chemical on foliage overhanging a stream can be washed into the water. The amount of herbicide becomes unmeasurable within a few hundred metres downstream of the application site. It is adsorbed by the sediments and decomposed by microorganisms in the stream. Even where herbicides have been deliberately sprayed right across small stream channels during research trials, the concentration of herbicide in streamwater has been minute and short-lived, and has declined rapidly with distance downstream. Where 'pesticide-free zones' have been established around water courses, measurable levels in streamwater have not been detected.

Studies with fish have shown no measurable effects of short-term exposure to extremely small quantities of the herbicides that are presently registered for use in Canadian forests. These are the types of exposures and concentrations that have been observed where forest herbicides have been shown to reach streams. Similarly, there have been no demonstrated human health effects of the herbicides at concentrations to which the public would be exposed.

There is obviously a greater risk of a herbicide being leached into a stream if heavy rain immediately follows the application than if the application is followed by a dry spell. Most of the forest herbicides used in Canada (glyphosate, for example) are

---

15 These comments refer to herbicides that are currently licensed for use in Canadian forests. Herbicides that move readily through the soil with soil water have a greater probability of reaching streams. The extent of such movement is highly dependent on rainfall, slope, soil depth, soil organic matter content, and soil physical and chemical properties. The risk of herbicides reaching streams varies greatly with the types of herbicide and the time of year they are applied. Some herbicides are virtually immobile in forest soils while others are more susceptible to being leached.

applied in mid to late summer, traditionally a dry period, but hexazinone and 2,4-D may be applied in the spring. Hexazinone requires moisture to become active in the soil. Streamflows are often low in mid to late summer, so even minute quantities of herbicides entering streams at this time may produce measurable concentrations using very sensitive detection instruments. The greatest risk of herbicides entering streams occurs when they are applied to sites where the soil is saturated or partly flooded at the time of the application, where the soil is very coarse or where there is little soil organic matter. Accidents or equipment malfunctioning are other reasons why herbicides may sometimes reach water courses.

It has been shown that a major cause of herbicide problems in agriculture is the inadequate education and training of applicators. At one time this was true in forestry also, but the problem has been reduced by much stricter licensing and training requirements. People who handle and apply herbicides in forestry are now required to hold a current pesticide applicator's licence.

There may be significant environmental and human-health concerns about the contamination of groundwater and streams by the annual application of herbicides to agricultural land. However, differences between forestry and agriculture in the type of herbicide used, the frequency of use, and the dosage, as well as differences in the behaviour of herbicides in forest and agricultural ecosystems, make comparisons difficult and generally invalid. Care must always be taken to prevent the over-spraying of streams and to prevent spray equipment from being flushed out close to a stream, two events that would significantly increase the risk of herbicides reaching bodies of water. Of course, there is always a small risk of such accidents, but with current regulations, their enforcement, and generally increased environmental awareness on the part of foresters and herbicide applicators, examples of such problems have become rare.

All the evidence suggests that the major ecological impact of herbicide use in forestry occurs when plants are killed. In most forest herbicide applications, some of the target species are only partially killed and some species are not affected. This differs little from the impact of manual cutting, and the overall environmental impact of herbicides is generally less than that of fire. In many cases it is also much less than the impact of some methods of mechanical weed control. However, people are not concerned only about the environmental impacts of herbicides; they are equally concerned about the implications for human health.

Does the Use of Forest Herbicides Pose a Human Health Risk?

The human health risks of herbicides used in forestry are a function of both their inherent toxicity or other potential negative effects on the human body (such as the potential to cause cancer or birth defects) and the risk of human exposure to the chemicals at concentrations and for periods necessary to cause these health effects. Herbicides legally registered for use in Canadian forests have a very low level of human toxicity. Furthermore, their behaviour in the forest environment reduces the risk of human exposure to almost zero.

In British Columbia, roads leading to the sprayed area are closed during the application of the herbicide, and warning notices must be posted around the treated area for the next six months. Vegetation that has been exposed to a herbicide dies rapidly, reducing the likelihood that people could be exposed by eating sprayed plants. Wildlife species and fungi are not known to bioaccumulate the herbicides used in forestry, so people would not be exposed by eating animals or mushrooms in the vicinity of a sprayed area. The risk of exposure through drinking water is also extremely low. As noted above, research has shown that in most herbicide applications, no measurable quantities of herbicide reach water courses. In the few cases where this has occurred, extremely short-lived pulses of very low herbicide concentrations have been restricted to sections of the stream close to the sprayed area. These concentrations are so far below any known toxicity range for the herbicides currently used in Canadian forests that there is essentially no human health risk via drinking water. As an additional precaution, herbicide usage is generally restricted in public water supply watersheds or around streams that have water-use licences.

There is a lot of public concern about health risks associated with using herbicides, but there are also health risks associated with alternative methods of weed control. Accidents involving workers during manual weeding operations are not uncommon and pose a much greater threat to human health than the careful application of herbicides. This is reflected in the high insurance premiums for workers doing manual weeding. The public has a great antipathy towards aerial spraying, yet forest workers have a much greater risk of exposure in manual application or ground application by machine than when aerial application is used. Application by helicopter under appropriate weather conditions poses very little risk of herbicide drift away from the application site. There are few human health hazards associated with fire-based or mechanical means of weed control.

The public has come to hate herbicides. An ecologist's suggestion that the careful and limited use of specific herbicides in forestry is environmentally acceptable and poses no significant public health risks or risks to the integrity of the ecosystem is usually greeted with scorn and rejected outright by concerned environmentalists. The fear engendered by the use of Agent Orange in Vietnam and the dramatization of herbicide issues in the media have combined to generate an understandable level of concern. However, research by independent scientists, many of whom (including this author) conducted the research because of concern over the potential negative environmental effects of herbicides, simply do not support the public's current attitude towards the use of herbicides in forestry.

The need for weed control in forestry today frequently represents a failure to practise regeneration silviculture effectively in the past: delays in the replanting of harvested areas, poor planting, poor-quality seedlings, or the planting of the wrong species or size and type of seedling. If regeneration silviculture becomes more successful in the future, the need for all forms of weed control should decline. Seedlings of the right species (based on its ecology and the ecology of the site), of the right age, in the right condition, handled and planted correctly, will overcome many of the regeneration problems of the past. However, there will always be situations where weed control is needed in forests. Herbicides are frequently not the first choice to control weeds because often there are alternatives that are as good or better. Even when herbicides appear to be the best choice, most foresters now avoid using them whenever they can because of negative public reaction and the enormous commitment of time and effort that is often needed to secure a permit for a herbicide treatment and to hold public meetings on its proposed use. However, in some situations there may be no effective alternatives, and the responsible and environmentally-sensitive use of herbicides in forestry is often much less environmentally damaging than other available methods. Where herbicide use is environmentally sound and both environmentally and economically the best option, it should be available to foresters, albeit under the current strict controls.

Concentrations of Synthetic Chemicals in the Environment

Advances in analytical instrumentation have made possible the detection of vanishingly small quantities of some chemicals. Not very long ago concentrations of parts per million (ppm) were beyond our analytical detection abilities for many substances. Concentrations below this level gave zero values, which was not surprising since one part per million (1 in 10^6) is like one centimetre in ten kilometres. Imagine looking for a penny one centimetre in diameter along ten kilometres of road!

As instruments became more sensitive, however,

detection limits of parts per billion (ppb; 1 in 10^9) were achieved. Concentrations below this level gave zero values. One part per billion is like one centimetre in 10,000 kilometres, or one centimetre in a distance roughly equal to the length of the air route from Montreal to Tokyo, or from London to Cape Town, South Africa. Imagine looking for a penny between eastern Canada and Japan. Recent analytical advances now make it possible to measure in the parts per trillion (ppt; 1 in 10^{12}) range for some chemicals. This is equivalent to one centimetre in a distance equal to twenty-six times the average distance from the earth to the moon.

Another way of thinking about these vanishingly small concentrations is that one part per billion is equivalent to one teaspoonful (5 millilitres) in 80 swimming pools, 50 metres long, 25 metres wide, and 5 metres deep. One part per trillion would be one teaspoonful in 80,000 such pools. One part per quadrillion (ppq; 1 in 10^{15}) would involve 800 million such pools. In the U.S., Environmental Protection Agency (EPA) standards for dioxin levels in pulp mill effluent were set a few years ago at thirteen parts per quadrillion! This is about one teaspoon in 6 million Olympic-sized swimming pools. These standards are being revised based on a re-assessment of the dangers to human health posed by these chemicals and the risks posed to humans by these vanishingly small concentrations. It is now suggested that earlier assessments overstated the risks to humans from dioxin, but the fact remains that some of the dioxins (there are more than 200 different types) are exceedingly toxic to some organisms.

As these gigantic strides in analytical chemistry have occurred, there has been no comparable advance in our understanding of what these very low concentrations of various chemicals mean for living organisms or for ecosystems. Are they toxic (poisonous), carcinogenic (cancer forming), teratogenic (birth-defect causing), or behaviour-altering at these concentrations? In most cases the answer is that we do not know, but for many chemicals, observed negative biological effects have ceased at the parts per million level or above. (For many chemicals damaging levels are closer to parts per hundred.) There is very little scientific data about negative effects in the parts per billion range. For most chemicals, we know nothing about effects in the parts per trillion range, primarily because at these concentrations there have been no observable effects.

This does not suggest that we should be unconcerned about low levels of potentially noxious chemicals. Even extremely low concentrations of very toxic, carcinogenic, or teratogenic chemicals are cause for concern. However, the risks of exposure need to be critically evaluated. Natural foods and our environment are full of chemicals that are potentially harmful to our health. Our body's digestive and chemical defence mechanisms and our eating habits generally enable us to avoid their negative effects. The problem comes when we are exposed to them in high enough concentrations and for sufficient periods that our bodies are not able to repair or prevent damage. Also, when a chemical undergoes bioaccumulation, even very low initial levels may eventually become concentrated enough to have adverse biological or ecological effects. If herbivores eat lots of contaminated plants, and if the chemicals are stored in their bodies rather than being excreted or detoxified, the chemicals may be concentrated to many times the levels in the plants. If herbivores accumulate noxious chemicals such as DDT and other fat-soluble chemicals the carnivores that eat them may further concentrate these substances. Concentrations of the chemicals in carnivore tissues can be high enough to affect their behaviour, growth, survival, or reproduction. When humans eat predators such as salmon or scavengers such as crabs, health concerns may arise if the noxious chemicals are concentrated in the animal parts that are eaten. Bioaccumulation can also occur if soil animals that accumulate chemicals are then eaten by birds.

Bioaccumulation occurs only for certain types of chemical, such as those that are soluble in fat. Many of the substances that the public is concerned about are rapidly degraded into harmless inorganic chemical components by microbes. Bioaccumulation of fat-soluble insecticides such as DDT was the major problem with the use of this chemical. The herbicides currently registered for use in Canadian forestry are not known to bioaccumulate. Dioxins, however, are reported to bioaccumulate.

In a world where chemical analysis abilities are increasing far more rapidly than the evidence concerning the biological or ecological effects of the chemical being analysed, the media have contributed to the development of unsubstantiated fears in the public mind. They have frequently quoted environmental concentrations of chemicals in the parts per billion, trillion, or even quadrillion range as though they were per cent or parts per million data. Generally this has been done without any comment on the potential for bioaccumulation, the mobility of the chemical in the environment, how long the chemical lasts before being decomposed, and the risk of human exposure to levels that could pose health problems. Although analytical capabilities have become a thousand, a million, and a billion times more sensitive, there has been little change in the way the media have discussed concentration data.

Everyone must be concerned about pollution of the environment. We must clean up environments where our waste products and synthetic chemicals are either impairing ecosystem function or threatening the health and survival of species we are concerned about, including humans. But cleaning up pollution and preventing environmental contamination costs money, and when money is scarce we want to spend the available dollars in dealing with the most serious problems first. Making wise decisions about pollution therefore requires an understanding of the ecological behaviour and effects of each potentially noxious chemical in each type of environment where it may occur. Considering the many environmental pollution problems society faces, the use of herbicides in forests scarcely even deserves a mention. Compared with the environ-

mental damage we all cause by driving our cars to work, the damage to people's health caused by smoking, drinking, and unhealthy diets, and the frequently indiscriminate use of toxic chemicals by many urban dwellers, the responsible use of those herbicides that are registered and allowed to be used in Canadian forestry is a non-issue, despite all the publicity it is given in the media. This statement in no way contradicts legitimate public concern about irresponsible and cavalier uses of herbicides which should not be tolerated whether this is in agriculture, forestry, or peoples' backyards.

In many cases, it is not necessary to use herbicides in forestry. Many weed problems can be prevented by better silviculture, and other solutions can be found to many existing weed problems. In some cases, however, the alternative to not using herbicides may be a long delay in reforestation with commercially valuable tree species, or an increase in the negative environmental impact of weed control. Regeneration delay may be good for some species of wildlife, but may delay the development of tree cover required by other animal species. Delay will result in a reduction in the allowable rate of forest harvesting, which means reduced employment and capital creation – things most people with a family and a mortgage are concerned about. The public has been highly critical, and rightly so, of past failure to reforest harvested areas promptly. However, the same public often wishes to restrict some of the useful methods – including herbicides – by which prompt reforestation can be achieved on very weed-prone sites. If there were significant environmental and human health concerns associated with current chemical methods of weed control in Canadian forestry, this restriction would be both reasonable and necessary. In the absence of scientific evidence to support such concerns, they are not justified. There seems to be little logic in eliminating the responsible use of herbicides, or any other appropriate method, where careful analysis reveals that such use is silviculturally and environmentally the best weed control option.

Use of Insecticides in Forestry

Insecticides (chemicals that kill insects) have been both a bane and a blessing in the post-war period. Chemicals such as DDT were responsible for saving millions of lives in the past half century by controlling disease-bearing insects, such as malaria-carrying mosquitoes, and making possible enormous increases in food production. Combined with improved education, sanitation, and health care, this contributed to a rapid increase in population in developing countries where disease and starvation had previously limited the number of people. The resulting world population increase is one of the fundamental causes of the environmental problems we now face: tropical deforestation, overgrazing, the spread of deserts, excessive use of fossil fuels (a problem caused mainly by the developed nations), water pollution, and the greenhouse effect. It seems that there really is no 'free lunch.' The price for the early benefits of using insecticides has been the much larger problems now. Because of the relationship between the development of effective insecticides and growth in population, and between population increase and global environmental degradation, this class of chemical, by its very success, has to be considered as one of the causes of our current environmental predicament.

In addition to the immediate short-term benefits and long-term problems caused by the early profligate use of insecticides, there were short-term problems. The tendency to use insecticides as 'chemical bulldozers' resulted in the poisoning of non-target animals (mostly due to bioaccumulation where birds fed on insecticide-contaminated insects and soil animals), the killing of natural enemies of insect pest species, and rapidly growing immunity in the pests that were supposed to have been controlled. Excessive use of insecticides in agriculture in an attempt to eradicate rather than merely control insect pests led to the development of resistance to these poisons. This in turn led to 'insecticide addictions,' in which more and more insecticides had to be used just to keep damage down to an

acceptable level instead of eliminating it. Farmers who stopped using these chemicals ran the risk of being put out of business, because excessive use of insecticides had eliminated the natural mechanisms of pest control. Sometimes they indulged in 'insurance' applications, applying insecticides even when there was no problem – the 'just in case' and 'if a little is good, more is better' philosophy.

Looking back on the 1930s to 1960s, we see a history of frequently excessive, indiscriminate, and environmentally unsound uses of insecticides, mainly in agriculture and public health, but also sometimes in forestry. What have we learned from this, and how are insecticides currently used in forestry?

Because of misuse or overuse of insecticides in the 1950s, 1960s, and to some extent in the 1970s, scientific concerns and public pressure have greatly reduced their use in forestry. The major trends in insect control over the past decade have been towards the use of: (1) insect disease organisms such as the bacterium *Bacillus thuringiensis* var. *kurstaki* (BTK), a micro-organism that produces a substance toxic to caterpillars); (2) biological controls, including breeding and releasing natural parasites and predators; and (3) the use of silvicultural methods to reduce insect abundance and damage, including mixtures of different tree species rather than single-species tree crops, and the use of non-susceptible tree species. Insect sex attractants, or *pheromones* (chemicals released by an insect to attract members of the opposite sex), have been identified, synthesized in the laboratory, and used to bait insect traps or to concentrate insects in a small area where they can be killed. This has been particularly useful with various types of beetles that attack trees. And in the last resort, where control is not possible, the insects are left pretty much to their own devices, and the dead and damaged trees are simply salvaged and used.

The use of chemical insecticides in Canadian forestry has declined over the past two decades. In most cases, they have been replaced by BTK. This sometimes works very well, but it is subject to the vagaries of weather and other factors that can cause considerable variation in effectiveness. The major continuing use of insecticides is in New Brunswick, and to a lesser extent in Newfoundland. In these parts of eastern Canada, balsam fir forests are regularly attacked by an insect called the eastern spruce budworm, whose caterpillar stage eats the foliage of balsam fir and white spruce (and other trees when it is really hungry). As far as we know, balsam fir and spruce forests in Newfoundland, Atlantic Canada, Quebec, and Ontario have always been killed periodically by the spruce budworm. Vast areas of forest of similar age become suitable habitat for this insect at much the same time. Triggered by a variety of factors including climate, the insect numbers explode and large tracts of forest are killed. The budworm then declines until the forest has regrown, at which time the cycle is repeated. This is nature's way in such forests, but it puts the insect in direct competition with humans. The forests become ready for harvest by humans at the same time that the budworm starts to kill them.

In the 1950s a political decision was made in New Brunswick to maintain the forest industry. This decision required the protection of mature budworm-susceptible forests by spraying with insecticides. In recent years, large areas have been sprayed with fenitrothion, an organophosphate insecticide closely related to malathion and diazinon, insecticides that are commonly used in agriculture and gardening. Fenitrothion is not thought to pose unacceptable health risks when applied correctly, but it undoubtedly disrupts the predator-prey systems of New Brunswick and may have other ecological and social effects. In evaluating the social and environmental acceptability of this budworm-control policy, the social and environmental effects of the insecticide program must be compared with those caused by the killing of large areas of forest by the budworm. Although such forest death is natural, as a society we must judge which is the least unacceptable disturbance to the ecosystem. BTK is also used against the budworm in New Brunswick, on a scale similar to the use of fenitrothion. It may

replace the chemical insecticide in the future.

From an environmental standpoint, biological control is almost always preferable to a chemical insecticide. Sometimes, however, a combination of a very small application of insecticide in conjunction with biological control has produced the best results. This so-called 'integrated control' requires considerable sophistication and a very accurate monitoring of the pest. It is therefore generally more applicable in highly controlled agricultural situations than in forestry.

Experience with defoliating insects in British Columbia has been that outbreaks are generally shorter-lived and less destructive to forests than the spruce budworm/balsam fir situation of eastern Canada. Outbreaks have often collapsed by the time the situation was detected and plans for a control action were developed. The recent response to such outbreaks has been to let nature take its course, accept some growth loss where it occurs, and salvage-log areas of killed forest where the extent of such areas warrants the cost of road building. This strategy may be reasonable in even-aged forests with clearcutting, but it will not work as public pressure begins to require foresters to use uneven-aged stand management with selection harvesting. The defoliators kill smaller trees and seedlings as well as the overstorey, destroying the stand structure that is essential in mixed-age silvicultural systems. This could become a significant problem in some western Douglas-fir forests that are attacked by the western spruce budworms. The choice in such forests may be selection forestry with defoliator control when needed versus even-aged forestry with salvage clearcutting and no defoliator control.

Western Canada does have an insect problem against which some insecticides are used: bark beetles. This problem is unique to the west, where large areas of pine forest regenerated following fires about a hundred years ago, many of them set by miners and prospectors or during railroad construction. These areas are now ideal habitat for the mountain pine beetle. Large tracts of mature spruce forest are also being killed by the spruce bark beetle. Eggs are laid by female beetles just beneath the bark, and the larvae feed on the phloem (the live inner bark). This may girdle and kill the trees, but mostly the trees are killed by a fungus introduced into them by the female beetle as a major food for some of the beetle larvae. In most cases, the bark beetle problem is dealt with by salvage logging after the trees have been killed. This has led to large clearcuts in the interior of the province. For example, large areas of mature spruce forest were killed in the Bowron River valley in central BC after an epidemic of spruce bark beetles developed in wind-thrown spruce forests. The valley was salvaged by clearcutting and is now reforested.

The large clearcuts that such salvage clearcutting produces have aggravated the public's antipathy towards clearcut harvesting. In most cases, the forester has little choice. Most of the trees are dead, and in many cases isolated surviving trees or small groups of trees would probably have been blown over had they been left. The aesthetic impact of salvage logging undoubtedly makes this practice less appealing to some than simply leaving the dead forest, but because of the considerable risk of catastrophic wildfire in extensive areas of dead forest, it is argued that salvage logging the dead trees results in less environmental impact and a much smaller social impact than leaving the dead forest unlogged. As the aesthetic and biodiversity implications of such large-scale salvage logging become more important, it is probable that greater efforts will be made to retain whatever live trees can be saved, in order to break up the very large clearcuts visually and ecologically.

Along with the salvage logging of beetle-killed pine trees, beetle-infested but still living trees are sometimes injected with an organic arsenic-based herbicide that also acts as an insecticide: mono-sodium methane arsenate, or MSMA. This kills the trees and makes them more attractive to the bark beetles. The larvae in the 'trap trees' are then killed by the insecticide properties of the chemical, or

they simply die when their host tree dies. MSMA is also sprayed on the logs from trap trees after they are cut, to kill any adult beetles that might emerge from the logs. Alternatively, trap-tree logs may be burned. Pheromones can be used to attract beetles into an area that is about to be logged, and the beetles in the logs are killed during the sawmilling process. Research is being done on the use of chemicals that confuse male beetles and prevent them from fertilizing females, thereby slowing the population growth.

One area in which insecticides and other pesticides are still commonly used in forestry is in forest nurseries. As with agriculture, raising millions of seedlings of the same species under crowded greenhouse or nursery-bed conditions can provide a veritable feast for a variety of insects or pathogens. Production of seedlings in these highly centralized, highly mechanized, and very unnatural conditions is difficult unless a variety of insect and fungal pests are controlled. If the decision is made to raise seedlings for reforestation this way, some insecticides and fungicides probably have to be used. The alternative would be to rely on natural regeneration, or to raise seedlings in smaller, decentralized nurseries. This is an important and complex question that goes far beyond the issue of using insecticides, and will not be discussed further. It should be noted, however, that the use of pesticides in forest nurseries is negligible compared to most current agricultural practices, and 'good housekeeping' practices in the nursery will nearly always greatly reduce the need for insecticides and fungicides.

Conclusions

People have used chemicals in the production of food crops for thousands of years. The use of animal and probably human manure goes back to the earliest days of agriculture, some ten thousand years ago. Over the centuries, new types of fertilizer were used, including seaweed (near the coast), composted plant wastes, litter raked from forests, and ash from the burning of wood and coal. Growing nitrogen-fixing plants as a form of 'green fertilizer' also has a long history. The history of using chemicals to control insect, weed, and microbial pests is not nearly as long because of the lack of suitable chemicals with which to do the job. However, ancient cultures are known to have ground up plants that have natural insecticidal properties – pyrethrums derived from plants are still used as insecticides today – and to have used the dust to control certain insects. Chemicals with herbicidal properties have also been used by some societies for a long time.

The use of chemicals in the growth and tending of forest crops has a much more recent history. Harvested on long rotations, most forests are able to solve their nutritional problems by themselves, or people simply accepted that forests grow poorly on nutritionally poor sites. Neither the application technologies nor the management chemicals themselves were available for forest insect and weed control, and what fertilizer resources existed were generally put into food production. Only in the past half century has there been both the need for and the possibility of using management chemicals in forestry.

The relentless growth in the human population from 1 billion around 1800 to about 5.5 billion in 1992 has resulted in massive deforestation around the world and heavy demands on the remaining areas of forest. The expected increase to between 12 and 16 billion within the next century will exert demands on the world's forest resources that probably cannot be met without the use of management chemicals. We have been incredibly wasteful of materials harvested from the forest in the past. By recycling paper and other wood fibre products, and by reusing wood where this can be done, we can somewhat reduce the pressure on the forest in the short term. However, concerns over global warming, nuclear power, and political instability in the world's major oil producing region are creating the need for greater use of renewable 'bioenergy' and leading to increases in the use of wood products in the chemical industry. There can be little doubt that the demands for forest products will go on increasing.

A reduced land base from which to obtain this increased supply will require the universal practice of site nutrient management and organic-matter conservation, and increased use of nitrogen-fixing nurse crops. However, it will probably also require the use of a variety of fertilizers. It is expected that the greatest increase in forest fertilizer use will be in the application of organic wastes, such as sewage and pulp sludges and composted plant and animal wastes, but there will undoubtedly be increased use of conventional fertilizers as well. Herbicides will probably not experience dramatically increased use in forestry, and may even decline as other ways of dealing with weed competition are developed and used. However, they should remain as an option in reforestation. Except in high-production seedling nurseries, the decline of insecticide use in forestry will probably continue. Greater reliance will be placed on biological controls or silvicultural strategies to prevent the problems from occurring in the first place.

CHAPTER 9

Are Old-Growth Forests Forever?

In older, more mature human cultures, there is a great respect for the elders of the community, for tradition, and for things that are old. Younger societies, such as those that were largely immigrant-dominated in Canada and the United States during the post-war decades, often place less value on the old and the traditional. It is therefore perhaps a measure of the coming of age of these two North American countries that there is increasing concern about the conservation of old buildings, old trees, and old landscapes. There is a growing resistance to the types of change that have been the hallmark of young, pioneer societies in the past.

The harvesting of forests creates change. It removes old trees, and can cause significant visual alterations to once-beloved landscapes. The change is not directly comparable to urban redevelopment, in which old, possibly 'heritage' buildings are torn down and replaced by modern structures of sometimes very dubious aesthetic quality, but there are parallels. Forests regrow following harvesting, and given time, a very similar forest will develop, as long as the ecosystem's mechanisms of recovery have not been damaged and the climate has not changed (see Chapter 12). However, the time required for the forest to regain the original visual qualities may be much longer than the life span of the individuals who are concerned about the logging. For them as individuals, the forest will never look the same again, just as the town or village where they grew up will never be the same again after the older sections are torn down and replaced with a modern shopping, housing, or office complex. No matter how attractive the new development is, it will be new, not old. It will lack any sense of nostalgia, and will probably not command the same respect as the history-filled structures it replaced.

There is something in the very name 'old growth' that stirs the passions. Trees that have been growing since before Canada or the United States were countries or were even known about in Europe, trees that are as tall as large buildings, and trees of a diameter that makes one feel insignificant elicit

Aesthetics and spiritual values

A

B

A Many of the forested landscapes of British Columbia are incredibly beautiful. This is an important value for both individual citizens and the tourism industry. In the past, the aesthetic impact of forestry has largely been ignored in British Columbia.

B Spiritual values of forests are important for many people. Sufficient areas of old growth and of giant trees must be set aside and managed to ensure an adequate supply of this value in the future.

feelings of awe, respect, and veneration. Forests of large trees are likened to natural cathedrals, and walking through them one can experience the sense of calm, of mystery, and of continuity that can be felt in the older cathedrals of Europe. Little surprise, therefore, that an increasing number of people around the world are responding to the harvesting of giant old-growth forests in much the same way that many Europeans would respond to the suggestion that an old cathedral be replaced by a modern office tower, or even a modern cathedral. Ancient forests have become objects of veneration.

This chapter explores what is meant by the term 'old-growth forest,' whether or not old-growth values are permanent in the absence of human interference, and whether or not these values can be managed. Can they be sustained or recreated in managed forests?

What Are Old-Growth Forests?

One of the difficulties in the current debate about old-growth forests is the lack of agreement about exactly what such forests are. People who live near, or have visited, the coast of British Columbia, Washington, and Oregon, or parts of Tasmania and southeastern Australia, for example, are fortunate enough to have experienced 'temperate rain forest' characterized by mature trees of gigantic proportions. Travellers in the tropics may have seen 'tropical rain forest' of overwhelming species and structural diversity. The impressions of what old growth is will vary between these different countries and geographical areas. The impressions about old growth will be different again among residents of northern Canada or Europe, the Brazilian savannah, or the eastern U.S. hardwood forest region. 'Ancient' forests in these different areas vary in their species composition, vertical structure, and soil conditions. All this makes it difficult to discuss the old-growth issue in a way that everyone can relate to.

Old-growth forests can have one or more of the following characteristics:

(*1*) *Very large trees.* If people could choose only

one feature by which to describe old-growth forests, they would probably choose the size of the trees. Above all else, it is the physical dimensions of giant trees that inspires people. They seem to be much more prepared to suffer the consequences of engaging in civil disobedience in order to save giant trees that may be only a few hundred years old than trees only a few metres tall that might be as old as a thousand years. In many of the forests where giant trees occur, trees can achieve gargantuan dimensions in a surprisingly short time. Under the right circumstances, trees can reach heights of 80 to 90 metres and diameters of 2 to 3 metres or more on these sites within 200 years, rather than the thousand or more years that one might expect of such trees. However, enormous tree size is not adequate as a universal definition of old growth. In cold northern or high-elevation forests, forests that have a dry climate, forests on poor soils, or forests that are disturbed periodically by fire, wind, insects, or disease, even very old trees may not be particularly large. Nevertheless, people may feel strongly about reserving areas of the largest trees that occur in these forests.

(*2*) *Very old trees.* There can be no argument that a forest of 3000-year-old bristlecone pine, of 1500-year-old western red cedar, or 1000-year-old Douglas-fir is old growth, and that to replace such trees will take a length of time equal to the tree age. But many forests of the world never reach an age in excess of 200 to 300 years, and in some fire-dominated forests, 100 to 150 years may be a ripe old age. Perhaps old-growth forests do not occur in such areas, and yet the residents of such forested regions may also feel strongly about conserving significant areas of the oldest trees and the most magnificent forests in the region. In areas of favourable climates and fertile soils, the general public has often confused 100- to 120-year-old forests of fast-growing tree species with old growth, and protested the harvesting of such forests. In cold or dry climates, or on infertile soils, forests of trees in the 500- to 1000-year age class are often harvested without public comment because the trees' small size leads the public to believe that the forests are not very old. Trembling aspen is a tree that resprouts from the root system when the above-ground parts are killed by fire. This can happen repeatedly and it is believed that many aspen stands in the Rocky Mountains that are only 20 to 80 years old developed from root systems that have undergone the fire kill-resprouting cycle for as long as 15,000 years. Are such forests 'old growth'? Clearly, there is a problem with defining 'old growth' by age alone.

(*3*) *Forest structure.* Some ecologists have defined 'old growth' in terms of the structure of the plant community. They contrast the even-aged, single-canopy layer structure that is characteristic of many younger unmanaged forests and most managed coniferous forests with the multi-layered canopy that is said to be characteristic of true old growth. Multi-layered canopies are characteristic of climax forests, in which gaps formed by the death of individual large trees are invaded by young trees, thus giving the forest a mosaic of tree age classes and canopy levels. It is also a characteristic of younger forests in which earlier seral stands are being invaded by more shade-tolerant, later-successional tree species. As these understorey trees grow up into the canopy, they give a multi-layered appearance to the forest. This structural attribute is therefore not a unique feature of very old forests. It can occur in relatively young forests, depending on the character of the past disturbance events that led to their establishment. Conversely, ancient forests can have a rather even-aged and single-canopy layer structure if after the previous disturbance the area was regenerated by shade-tolerant climax tree species and there has been little catastrophic disturbance over the life of the stand. Long-lived pioneer tree species can also develop forests of rather simple structure that can persist for many centuries and develop into cathedral-like stands that most of the public would associate with old growth.

Stand structure can thus vary enormously between different forests that satisfy the old-age or large-size

criteria. Even-aged stands of very large eucalypts in Australia and Douglas-fir in western North America may lack the multi-storeyed characteristics described above. Obviously, stand structure on its own is not the key attribute of old growth although it has been included as a key part of the definition by some ecologists.

(*4*) *Species composition.* Old-growth forest is sometimes defined as much by species composition as it is by tree age or size or stand structure alone. In some cases, old growth may simply be a forest that satisfies the habitat requirements of certain species of wildlife, such as the spotted owl of western North America or other cavity-nesting species. Alternatively, 'old growth' may refer to forests with tree species of a certain size and age. For example, the current debate about old growth in the humid parts of Tasmania refers mostly to forests of exceptionally large and awe-inspiring eucalypts of relatively modest age that will in due course be replaced by a more diverse but more diminutive temperate rain forest if the area is not catastrophically disturbed. Similarly, old-growth Douglas-fir forests in coastal areas of the Pacific Northwest of the United States and in coastal British Columbia are generally seral forests that originated following wildfire. They will eventually be replaced on most sites by more shade-tolerant species unless the forest is periodically disturbed.

(*5*) *Accumulation of dead organic matter.* Ecologists working in cool and very humid forests are naturally impressed by the enormous accumulation of large rotting logs, standing dead trees (snags), and the deep organic forest floor that characterize such forests when they have remained relatively undisturbed by fire for several centuries. As a result, the presence of large snags and of large-diameter logs on the ground have been proposed by these ecologists as an old-growth characteristic.

Deep accumulations of organic forest floor may or may not be a feature of old growth, depending on the type of soil and the type of climate. Many forests that satisfy most or all of the other criteria may have relatively thin accumulations of forest floor because of rapid litter decomposition. The presence of large-diameter snags and large-diameter logs on the ground may reflect the past history of forest growth and disturbance on the site more than the present age, structure, and tree size in the forest. Old forests in dry areas that have been subject to intense or frequent fires in the past may have very little in the way of snags and decomposing logs. Tropical forests that have rapid organic matter decompositions may also have few snags and large logs on the ground.

Old-growth forests have been defined by one, several, or all of these criteria, depending on who is making the definition and on the geographical location of the forest. Because of this variation in the meaning of the term, it has been difficult to develop policies to conserve old growth. One must agree on what old growth is before one can decide how much old growth one has, where it is located, and how its desired features can be conserved for future generations.

Are Old-Growth Values Forever?

Very often the sense of permanence is the most valued feature of old-growth forest. Many people think that by setting an old-growth forest aside as a park, a wilderness, or an ecological reserve, this value will be preserved, and sometimes this is true. But there are too many well-documented examples where attempts to 'preserve' a given environmental condition, to create 'ecological vignettes,' to treat the environment as though it were a static system with permanent features, have failed. Attempts to preserve old-growth redwood stands or old-growth, park-like pine forest in the western u.s. by giving them park status and protecting them from fire has led to a change over time in the ecological condition and visual qualities of these forests. The desirable features that led to their reservation were in part a product of periodic disturbance by fire, and it is now recognized that these forests must be burned periodically or otherwise managed if they

are to retain their original character. The recent public outrage over the fires in Yellowstone National Park reflect the same problem. The lodgepole pine forests that characterize Yellowstone were created by past wildfires, and their continued existence will depend on fire or massive insect outbreak. Ecosystems change. They cannot be framed and hung on the wall like pictures of our relatives or memories of past holidays.

Some old-growth forests are climax plant communities. The dominant trees will probably be replaced by new seedlings or existing saplings of the same species when they die. It is reasonable to expect the old-growth values of such forests to be fairly permanent, although in most forests some or all of the values may be lost periodically to wind, fire, or insect damage, only to be recreated in due course as the forest recovers from these disturbances. This will happen as long as the climate does not change. In Chapter 12, the case is made that it probably will change. Thus, even climax forests will probably not remain the same indefinitely. The comings and goings of ice ages as well as shorter-term climatic fluctuations have always led to changes in forests in the past, and there is little reason to expect that this will not continue in the future.

Where old-growth values are associated with seral forests, one might expect significant change within one's lifetime, or at least within the lifetime of one's children or grandchildren. The magnificent old-growth, wet sclerophyll eucalyptus forests of humid parts of Tasmania and southeastern Australia were established following catastrophic fire. They generally do not live much more than 350 to 400 years, after which, in the absence of catastrophic wildfire, they will be replaced by attractive and diverse but generally much more diminutive temperate rain forest species. Depending on which definitions are used, the old-growth values of these eucalyptus forests are not developed until the trees are more than 100 to 200 years old. Consequently, the 'optimum' old-growth forest condition may last only 150 to 300 years. This is certainly a long time, long enough to create reserves of such forest for future generations to enjoy. Significant areas should be reserved. However, such reservations must be made with the certain knowledge that eventually the values for which the reserves were created will be lost, to be replaced by other, different values. As this occurs, the reserves will have to be replaced by intermediate-aged forests that can provide the old-growth eucalypt values for the next one or two centuries. If society wishes to ensure that future generations can enjoy in perpetuity (whatever that means) the values provided by an old-growth reserve, conservation policy must recognize the patterns, processes, and frequency of change that result in these values. The nature and management of old-growth reserves must allow for the process of change.

Can Old-Growth Values be Sustained or Recreated in Managed Forests?

Where even-aged forests are grown for timber production on short rotations with clearcut harvesting and utilization of all the above-ground parts of the trees ('whole-tree' harvesting), the answer is clearly 'no.' None of the old-growth criteria described earlier are satisfied. But this does not mean that some, all, or various combinations of these criteria cannot be sustained or recreated in managed stands. If the forest manager is charged with the job of providing old-growth values in managed stands, silvicultural systems can be employed that can achieve this objective in many, though perhaps not all, types of forest. Climate, soil, fire, biological, and/or social constraints may limit the forester's ability to create or sustain these values in some types of managed forest.

Where large tree size is the key value to be sustained, growth of individual trees can be accelerated by reducing the competition for light, moisture, and nutrients, and increasing the supply of nutrients. Growing trees in open stands, with early weed control and with fertilization or nitrogen-fixing understorey species or 'nurse' tree species (such as lupines or alders, respectively), can result in spectacularly rapid growth in height and diameter on

moist sites with favourable climates, and even on sites that may get quite dry in the summer. Rapid tree growth can produce cathedral-like stands of trees in as little as 100 to 150 years in mild, humid climates. Growth is generally slower in drier or colder climates, and the production of large trees takes correspondingly longer in such areas. However, even in these areas, appropriate management can greatly accelerate the rate of individual tree growth.

Where stand structure is the key criterion, it may be possible in some areas to use 'two-storeyed' or even 'three-storeyed high forest' silvicultural systems. These are systems in which a significant number of trees are left uncut when the majority of the forest is harvested. As long as they do not blow over or get killed by insects, lightning, or disease, the 'leave trees' remain throughout the subsequent tree-crop rotation, and some of them may even be left for a second rotation or until they die. This can produce a multi-layered forest with trees of two or three age classes, the oldest of which can be very old. It can also provide a supply of large snags. Systems like this have rarely been used in timber management in recent decades because the larger leave trees often get blown over or badly damaged by wind, or their roots, stems, or crowns may be damaged during harvesting operations. The total yield of logs may also be reduced because some of the area is occupied by older trees whose growth rates have slowed down. It may also be more efficient to produce logs of relatively uniform size. Harvesting and sawmilling equipment work much more economically if they can be designed specifically for a rather limited range of log sizes. The production or perpetuation of large snags has been frowned on in the past by foresters because they may pose a safety problem in some types of forest. Such multi-storeyed systems can work very well in some areas, however, and if successful, can enable timber production to co-exist with the maintenance of certain old-growth values. There is growing interest in how, when, and where it might be reasonable to try such alternatives in even-aged, single-canopy forests (see Chapter 11).

Multi-storeyed stand structure is not so much a feature of old forest as of how the forest is regenerated and of the ecology of the tree species in the forest. Multi-storeyed forests can easily be created if mixtures of fast-growing shade-intolerant species and slower-growing shade-tolerant species are established. Planting of the shade-tolerant trees beneath canopies of the shade-intolerant species after the stand has been thinned can also create such structurally diverse stands. Frequently, shade-tolerant species regenerate naturally in plantations of shade-intolerant species, and all the forester has to do to create structural diversity is maintain a mixture of species and tree heights by means of the thinning regimes.

The plant species composition that characterizes old-growth forest can be recreated or sustained by implementing an appropriate planting or natural regeneration policy. However, providing the habitat conditions for old-growth animal species is much more difficult. For some old-growth-dependent species, such as cavity-nesting birds and other animals, rotting snags may be required. These can be created by killing leave trees or leaving snags standing at the time of harvest, but this may pose an unacceptable safety risk. However, if the safety risks can be rendered acceptable, there may be few technical reasons why snags and large decaying logs cannot be maintained in the forest if this is accepted as a management objective. This may make harvesting more difficult and expensive and result in a significant loss of timber volume and value. It is up to the owner of the resource (the public in the case of publicly owned land) and society in general to decide whether maintaining certain old-growth values is justified in the face of the economic and other costs involved.

Do We Need Old-Growth Forests?

For most people, the answer to this question is a definite 'yes!' There are many reasons why.

(*1*) *Old growth as an ecological reserve.* As more and more of the world's forest ecosystems are placed under some form of management, the area of forest that represents the 'natural,' unmanaged, biological potential of the site will steadily diminish. Old-growth reserves are needed as an 'ecological benchmark' against which future generations can measure the effects of forest management on the form and functioning of forested landscapes. Of course, virtually all forests on earth have been subjected to some human influence, whether this be the result of air pollution, climate change, alteration in animal populations by hunting or the accidental introduction of pests, introduction of plant diseases, alteration in the frequency and intensity of fire, and so on. However, there are large areas of forest in which significant episodic disturbance caused by humans either has not occurred or has occurred with such a low frequency that the present forest condition reflects primarily non-human influences. I believe that society needs representative examples of all the major types of forest, and all the major forest ecosystem types within each major forest type, in permanent ecological reserves. The value of such reserves for research on how forests function in the absence of frequent and intensive human disturbance (that is, management) will increase steadily as the remaining area of unmanaged forest declines.

Forested ecological reserves are not compatible with many forms of forest recreation, as these can have a significant impact on the ecosystem. However, large areas in national, provincial, or state parks receive little or no direct human impact and can fulfil the role of ecological reserves. Because such parks do not contain all types of forest ecosystem, a comprehensive network of additional reserves is needed to ensure that examples of all ecosystem types (such as the units of the biogeoclimatic ecosystem classification of British Columbia's forests) are conserved in the unmanaged condition. In some cases, relatively small areas of a few hundred hectares may satisfy the need. In other cases, it may be necessary to reserve up to several thousands of hectares in a single block to satisfy the objectives of the ecological reserve.

(2) *Old growth as a reservoir of gene variation: a gene bank.* As we increasingly select certain genetic strains of food crops, domestic livestock, and, to a much smaller extent, tree crops, there is a risk that we will lose some of the genetic variation that has been produced by evolution. Creating a network of unmanaged forest reserves to assist in the conservation of genetic variation is important if we wish to have access to this variation in the future, and it may be important for the survival of some species. An adequate system of parks and ecological reserves is an important component of any gene-conservation strategy.

(3) *Old growth as wildlife habitat.* Some species of wildlife have an absolute requirement for old-growth forest. This may be because the plants or animals they eat only live there, or because they are adapted to the microclimate or the presence of snags or large logs on the forest floor. In some environments, such as tropical rain forests, a large number of animal species may require mature or climax forest vegetation. These species will decline and may become extinct if the area of old growth is reduced to zero or if remaining patches of mature forest are smaller than some critical size. In temperate coniferous forests, the number of species that cannot exist without old growth is much lower. The spotted owl, which has received so much attention in the Pacific Northwest, requires old-growth forest because its prey require certain characteristics of such forests, and the owl needs snags with cavities in them for its nests. However, if there is a supply of nesting sites and alternative prey species, the owl will also live in younger forests, but generally at lower densities because of the lower abundance of its food in these forests. In many northern forests, very few, if any, animal species have an absolute requirement for old-growth forest; younger forests satisfy their needs. This may reflect the high frequency of wildfire in these environments and the resulting scarcity of old forests.

(4) *Old growth as a recreational environment.* The increasing pace of urban life, the increased spatial separation of people from the natural environment, and increased interest in and concern about the environment are dramatically increasing the recreational values of unmanaged forest ecosystems. They are also increasing the recreational value of managed forests.

There is a growing need for the solitude, the sense of tranquillity, and the natural beauty and splendour of mature and old-growth forests. As a species, we had our evolutionary origins as tree-dwellers, and there appears to be a growing bond between many urbanized societies and mature forest landscapes: we are returning to our roots (no pun intended!). The economic importance of 'adventure' holidays is increasing, and in some parts of the tropics this may provide a viable economic alternative to exploitive logging and destructive shifting cultivation and mining. At temperate latitudes, wilderness recreation may become an important economic force in determining how forested landscapes are managed in areas of outstanding natural beauty.

Wilderness recreation does not *require* old growth, although access to old growth as part of a wilderness trip will greatly enrich the experience. A mosaic of forests of different ages can improve landscape views, provide visual diversity, and improve various aspects of biotic diversity. However, if the mosaic lacks forests that have the visual characteristics of old growth, the diversity and quality of recreational experiences will be reduced.

(5) *Old-growth patches as migration pathways for species.* Conservation of species in the face of climate change must be proactive and will probably involve management. If the extent and rate of the predicted climate change occurs, many species may not be able to keep up with the rate of migration of climatic zones, and may face extinction. Active transfer of species may therefore be necessary. For old-growth species this will probably require a geographically extensive network of reserves, not necessarily large but providing ecological 'stepping stones' by which species can move or be moved to keep pace with

the moving climatic conditions. The concept of 'pocket wilderness' is useful in this context. One or more patches of old-growth forest should be conserved in each major valley where such forests still exist, surrounded by an area in which the forest will be managed on a long rotation. In terms of species conservation, many small reserves of this type may be much better than a few very large reserves. However, large reserves may be needed in some situations.

Clearly, there are many reasons why we should establish a comprehensive network of old-growth reserves (whatever old growth is finally decided to be). These should be developed to provide for the variety of needs for old growth, and should be geographically as well as ecologically representative. Many values may be provided by a single reserve, but in some cases more than one reserve of a given ecosystem type may be necessary. They should be large enough to ensure that the conditions they represent will be sustainable. They should also be as small as is consistent with such sustainability, to minimize land-use conflicts. In many cases, existing parks will provide the necessary reserves. Because of land-use conflicts, there may be merit in having a larger number of small reserves rather than fewer large ones, but in many cases there will be a minimum size below which the values being conserved will not be maintained.

Forestry is ultimately about people and conservation. As the needs of people change, so must forestry, and the increasing need for old-growth forest reserves is one such change. Creation of additional reserves will often cause economic hardship and some social disruption, but this may be necessary in order to achieve long-term conservation goals. However, the creation of new reserves cannot ignore the economic and social consequences of such land-use changes, and compromise may be necessary.

Summary

The pressure to feed, house, and otherwise provide for the needs and desires of the growing human population has resulted in the harvest of much of the world's previously unmanaged forests over the past two centuries. The area of land still covered by forests that resemble those of the pre-industrial period is declining rapidly, and this decline has been matched by a rapid growth in the public's awareness of the diminishing supply of old growth. As a consequence, saving old growth has joined saving whales and other marine life as a major focus of the environmental movement.

Where industrial timber management contributes only a small proportion of the employment and tax base of a region, reservation of old-growth forest that was previously dedicated to timber production may have relatively minor social consequences. It will have a negative impact on only a small proportion of the population. Where timber harvesting and silviculture make a major contribution to the economy, it is more difficult. Although proposed old-growth reserves may amount to a very small proportion of the total land base, they may constitute a much larger percentage of the more productive forest land and a major component of the economic and employment base of particular local communities. While the long-term effects of such proposed reserves on the log supply of a large geographical area like British Columbia may be almost insignificant, the loss of old-growth forest area equal to only a few per cent of the entire province may constitute a large percentage of the remaining forest that will be suitable for harvesting in a particular region or locality for several decades. Where plantations in the region are not yet ready for harvest, such reserves can result in significant social disruption in local communities.

If society places a high value on conserving old growth, it is appropriate that this be done. However, the costs must be considered as well as the benefits. These costs will not only be the loss of employment and public revenues. Future values associated with access for recreation, the abundance of wildlife species that are benefited by environmentally sound forest management, and the landscape diversity that forest management can provide will also be foregone. A common difficulty in setting aside old-growth forest that had been previously destined to be harvested is that the costs of such land-use changes are often borne by a different group of people from those who are the major beneficiaries of the change.

There can be little question that society's need and desire for old-growth, wilderness, and other values associated with unmanaged forests are going to increase. Nor is there any question that such reserves can contribute to the economy by attracting visitors from other areas, and that this may sometimes reduce to some extent the economic losses caused by the withdrawal of land from timber production. However, in satisfying these future needs and desires, there must first be an unambiguous definition of each of the values that are to be conserved. Second, there must be an inventory of the extent and geographical location of existing forests that satisfy the definitions. Plans must then be prepared that describe how these values can be sustained in various types of reserves, and the management that will be required to sustain them. Where there are unacceptable and irreconcilable conflicts between the desire to reserve old growth on dedicated timber-producing forest lands and the desire to sustain timber production, compromises can be achieved. For example, 'pocket wilderness' areas can be established to provide a core of unmanaged old growth surrounded by special management areas. By modifying rotation length, silvicultural systems, and harvesting methods, some of the desired old-growth values will be sustained over all or part of the tree-crop rotation.

The prevailing philosophy of, and overall management approach to, forest land management in British Columbia and many other parts of Canada was established at a time when there was an abundance of old growth, or it was assumed that adequate examples of such forests had already been conserved in the existing national, provincial, or regional park systems. There are many who would contend that this assumption is still true, but as the

long-planned conversion of unmanaged old-growth forest to managed forest has proceeded, the prevailing forest management approach and philosophy has been challenged. The public is increasingly concerned about the environment and its heritage of things old and precious. The 1990s will thus be a decade of change for the forestry profession. Many of the current assumptions about how forests should be managed will be critically re-examined. However, in seeking change in land use and land-use practices, a balance must be maintained between a variety of social needs, and changes must be both environmentally sound and technically achievable. Failure to develop conservation policies based on an adequate understanding of stand-level and landscape ecology, the objectives and methods of forest land management, and the diverse needs of local communities will only perpetuate the current polarization in the forestry/environment debate.

CHAPTER 10

Where Have All the Species Gone? The Question of Loss of Biological Diversity

Introduction: Concern about Loss of Species

Few of the recent conservation issues have captured the imagination of the public more than the global loss of biological diversity. The media inform us almost daily about the loss of species accompanying the clearance of tropical rain forest for agriculture, mining, and hydroelectrical projects, and the poaching of large tropical animals for their ivory, skin, and other parts. We are reminded constantly of the threat that human population growth, resource exploitation, and environmental degradation poses for many of the world's plant and animal species.

Much of the concern over loss of species diversity has focused on the tropics. Evolution has continued relatively uninterrupted at tropical latitudes for tens of millions of years, and this, in combination with the relatively predictable and unchanging physical environment of the tropics, has resulted in biotic communities of spectacular diversity. For example, as many as 700 tree species have been reported growing in just a few hectares of forest in Borneo, and several hundred species of birds and many thousands of species of butterflies, beetles, and other insects may be found in a single square kilometre of tropical rain forest in Central or South America. Although tropical rain forests cover only 7 per cent of the earth's land surface, they are reported to contain more than half the earth's known living species. In addition, it is believed that there are large numbers of tropical species, especially insects, that have not yet been identified, and most of the known species have not been adequately described. Their biology and ecology and their agricultural, medicinal, or other potentially useful properties remain unknown to the scientific world, although many of the nutritional and medicinal properties may be known by indigenous peoples where their cultures still exist and where this traditional knowledge has not been destroyed by western 'civilization.'

Compared to tropical rain forests, temperate and northern forests are relatively species-poor, especially in terms of trees and other plants and of medium and larger animals. Large areas of northern forest are dominated by a single tree species as a result of past fires – lodgepole pine or jack pine forests in Canada, larch forests in eastern Russia – and the number of dominant tree species in many other northern and temperate forests can be counted on one hand. However, some environmentalists have expressed the same concerns over the loss of biological and ecological diversity accompanying the harvesting and management of these higher-latitude forests that have been voiced about the tropical rain forest. As a result of these concerns in the United States, 'threatened and endangered' species, mostly birds, have been identified, and embargoes have been placed on harvesting of forests in the vicinity of their habitat. In order to protect the habitat of one such species, the northern spotted owl,[16] moratoria have been placed on timber harvesting in large areas of public forest in the Pacific Northwest that were originally dedicated for multiple use, including timber harvesting.

It has been suggested that the lower diversity of animals and plants in many temperate and northern forests is accompanied by greater microbial diversity, because of the greater quantity of decomposing organic matter in higher-latitude forests. Unfortunately, this cannot be confirmed at present. The microbial communities of the world's major forest types have not yet been adequately described, and the classification of living organisms into species, which works so well for most plants and animals, is much more difficult to do in the below-ground microbial world. However, research suggests that trees in temperate and northern forests form mutually beneficial relationships (mycorrhizal) with a larger number of soil fungi than do their tropical counterparts, so it may be that there is greater

microbial diversity in these higher-latitude forests. This might be a partial explanation for the greater resilience of these northern forests to disturbances in comparison to many tropical humid forests.

The loss of a species from the list of the earth's inhabitants is held by many people to be a bad thing. This concern has a number of origins.

(1) So-called 'deep ecologists' share with some of the eastern religions the idea that every species is sacred, that every species has a spirit, that every species has an equal right to exist, and that it is morally wrong for humans to cause the extinction of any other species. This philosophy appears to apply mostly to multicellular organisms: for example, one does not hear much said about the rights of various bacterial, viral, and fungal pathogens. The morality of the eradication of smallpox, poliomyelitis, or the AIDS virus, or of attempts to eradicate the tsetse fly to control sleeping sickness, does not appear to have become a part of this debate.

(2) A second reason for concern about species loss is largely nostalgic. We want our children and future generations to enjoy the species that we have enjoyed. Why do we have the right to deny them that option?

(3) All species are potentially valuable to us humans, and we do not want to squander or waste our magnificent evolutionary inheritance. We find them beautiful, fascinating, scientifically interesting, or valuable in terms of food, medicine, or some other resource value. We should conserve species on a purely selfish, self-interested basis, if for no other reason.

(4) There is a widespread concern that every species has a role to play in the complex web of life, that in many cases we do not yet fully understand that role, and that therefore it is in our best interests to keep all existing species. 'The first rule of intelligent tinkering is to keep all the parts,' as Aldo Leopold is credited with saying. Like any other species, we ultimately depend on our environment. Thus, we must keep all the parts of the environment so that it can continue to provide us with our needs.

---

16 It has been argued that the spotted owl issue is as much a reflection of the desire by some environmental groups to preserve large areas of old-growth forest as it is a real concern about the survival of the species. The Endangered Species Act has greater legal weight than other legal mechanisms by which land-use change from timber management to wilderness can be achieved in the u.s.

In spite of current public concerns, the extinction of species is a natural event that has been occurring since the earliest fossil record was laid down. Evolution has conducted many experiments over the past billion years, and most of the immense number of species that have resulted are no longer with us, having been replaced by new and more 'successful' life forms. Many other species are believed to have become extinct, not because they were 'unsuccessful' but because of catastrophic natural events such as volcanic eruptions or the impact of meteorites. Many of today's species would not exist if some long-extinct species had not suffered a timely (or untimely, depending on your point of view) demise. For example, it is likely that the human species would not have evolved if the great period of dinosaurs had not come to an end. We would probably not be here if that chapter of evolution had continued for a few million years more.

The rate of species extinction over the immensely long evolutionary period has not been constant. There were long periods of relatively minor changes in the species make-up of the planet, interrupted by times during which large numbers of species became extinct over relatively short periods. The loss of the dinosaurs about sixty million years ago is a particularly spectacular and well-known example of massive species extinctions. More recently, the evolution of *Homo sapiens* into a technological hunter about ten to thirty thousand years ago is thought to have led to the accelerated loss of animal species. It is reported that 71 per cent of the genera of large mammals in North America became extinct during this 'Pleistocene overkill,' and that many of the world's large game populations were reduced.

The runaway growth of the human population over the past two hundred years threatens to repeat the Pleistocene overkill. Over the period from 1800 to 2000, the human population will have increased from 1 billion to about 6 billion. In the two centuries before 1800, our numbers only doubled, from about half a billion in 1600. It has been a common experience that as one species becomes dominant in a landscape, other species will be lost. In the face of continuing world population growth to an anticipated maximum level of about 14 billion within the next century (estimates range from about 11 billion to 16 billion, or from two to three times the 1990 population), the concern over loss of global species diversity is fully justified. Overfishing of the oceans, overhunting of marine and terrestrial mammals, flooding of land for water storage and power generation, and clearance of forest for agriculture, cities, and highways are all human activities that pose direct threats to the abundance and species diversity of many non-human life forms. Acid rain and climate change, two consequences of human activity, pose a major threat to many species. Human-caused global climate change may pose the single greatest threat to global biodiversity in recent evolutionary history.

Global action to try to limit the impact of human activities on biological diversity can be justified on a wide variety of grounds, and it is appropriate that the impact of forest management on diversity be scrutinized to determine its contribution to the issue.

This chapter examines several topics that should be discussed when talking about the impact of forestry on biological and ecological diversity. It turns out that the question is much more complicated than it might at first appear to be. This is because there is a diversity of biological diversities.

Diversity in Forest Ecosystems

We cannot deal with the question of diversity only in terms of a list of the species in an area. Such a list is a useful and important measure of diversity, of course, but an adequate description of the biological and ecological diversity of forest ecosystems requires far more than this. There are in fact many different ways in which we can, and should, measure and evaluate biological diversity.

Species Diversity

A short walk in the forest with a group of specialized biologists can result in a list of most of the species of plants, some of the species of animals, and a few of the many species of fungi and other microbes that live there. A period of intensive study by these specialists would probably result in a much longer list that would provide a fairly complete description of the species that make up the biotic community of that small area of forest, although the below-ground microbial world may defy our attempts to catalogue species the way we can with plants and animals. This list is a measure of the *alpha species diversity* of that patch of forest. The list of plant and animal species will be relatively long if the forest is at low elevation near the equator, and relatively short if the forest is at high elevation or near the Arctic Circle. Alpha diversity is one of several measures of the biological richness or diversity of a particular local ecosystem.

If, instead of just compiling a species list for one small area, our group of biologists spent a long day hiking through the forest making lists of species as they went, one for each distinct type of ecosystem they passed through, they would produce another measure of diversity: *beta species diversity.* This is the variation in the species list as one moves across the landscape from one type of ecosystem to another. In some low-elevation tropical rain forests, there is very high alpha diversity (an enormous number of species in one hectare), but relatively little variation in the species list as you walk for considerable distances through the forest. In contrast, a walk through some temperate or northern forests would reveal relatively few species in any one small patch of forest, but a considerable variation in the species list across the local landscape. This high beta diversity may reflect a patchwork of forests of different ages that has resulted from a history of frequently repeated wildfires, wind damage, or insect attacks, or simply the mosaic of different soils, slopes, and aspects that occurs in mountainous or recently glaciated landscapes. Beta diversity is thus the outcome of both the history of development and disturbance of the living communities, *and* local variations in the physical and chemical environments in which they exist. The former is subject

to change over time and can be changed by human activities, while many aspects of the latter are essentially permanent. They are normally not changed much by forest management.

Beta diversity usually refers to variations in the biotic community across the local landscape. There is also a larger-scale *landscape diversity.* As you ascend large mountains from the foothills or valley floor, you pass through a series of climatic zones. A journey from Florida to Alaska would take you through a similar range of climatic areas. On both journeys you would pass through a wide variety of plant communities, possibly ranging from grasslands or desert through various types of deciduous and coniferous forests, to alpine meadows or arctic tundra. This landscape-level diversity is largely the result of variation in climate due to variation in elevation, latitude, and distance from the ocean or large lakes; variation between glaciated and unglaciated landscapes; and major differences in geology. It has relatively little to do with biological processes other than the long-term process of evolution and species-distribution changes associated with the change from glacial to interglacial periods.

Yet another aspect of species diversity is the change in the list of species occupying an area over a period of time: *temporal diversity.* As an ecosystem progresses through the various seral stages of its recovery from some disturbance, there will be a successive 'changing of the guard,' as plant, animal, and microbial species of earlier seral stages are replaced by those of later stages. When temperate and northern old-growth forests are disturbed by insects, disease, wind, or logging, there is usually an increase in plant species alpha diversity. Fire can either raise or lower plant diversity, depending on its severity. As trees invade the disturbed area and form a dense young forest, the diverse community of herbs and shrubs of the post-disturbance community will be greatly reduced by shading, and alpha plant species diversity will drop to low levels. The pioneer tree community is often made up of one or a few tree species. As the stand ages, however, the young forest thins itself (some of the trees die because of competition for light), thereby creating canopy gaps that permit the redevelopment of an understorey and the invasion of other, more shade-tolerant tree species; diversity rises again. If left undisturbed until old-growth conditions are re-established, plant species diversity in temperate and northern forest ecosystems may remain the same or may decline. The temporal diversity of animal species will generally reflect this changing diversity of plant species, but will also respond to stand structural diversity as described below. In some temperate forests the change in animal species numbers which accompany the plant community succession may be less than the changes in the species making up the animal community. In tropical forests, temporal patterns of change in species diversity may differ from this general temperate and northern pattern.

Structural Diversity

So far, diversity has been discussed only with respect to *species diversity*. Equally important for animal species diversity is the *structural diversity* of the plant community. Structural diversity refers to the vertical layering of the forest canopy; the presence or absence of shrub, herb, and moss layers; the presence or absence of epiphytes[17] and climbing plants; and the variation in tree canopy structure from place to place. Forests with a single canopy layer are structurally less diverse and usually support fewer species of animals than forests with many canopy layers (but see also the discussion in Chapter 11). Similarly, forests with many small gaps in the canopy caused by the death of individual large old trees are structurally more diverse than forests that have an unbroken canopy layer. The presence of standing dead trees (snags) and of decaying logs

on the ground is an important component of the structural diversity of some types of forest.

Functional Diversity

In addition to local, regional, geographical, and temporal variations in species and structural diversity, there is also *functional diversity* in our forests. Some are productive, some are not. Some cycle nutrients rapidly, some slowly. The nutrient cycles in some forests are dominated by nitrogen, while in others nutrients such as phosphorus or boron may determine ecosystem productivity. Some forests recover from disturbance rapidly while others recover slowly. Some are highly resistant to disturbance and some are easily disturbed. There is a high degree of functional diversity over quite small areas in some forests, whereas in others there may be relatively little variation in function across large areas of the landscape. In all forests there is a considerable change in function caused by disturbance, whether this is natural or human-caused, and there is a change in functional processes with time as the ecosystem recovers from disturbance.

Another aspect of functional diversity is the diversity in functional roles of the organisms in the ecosystem. A forest with four evergreen coniferous tree species all of which are shade-intolerant but tolerant of low nutrient availability would be functionally less diverse than a forest with four tree species where two species are shade-tolerant while the other two are light demanding, two species are nutrient demanding while the other two are not, and two species are deciduous broadleaved trees while the other two are evergreen, needle-leaved conifers.

Genetic Diversity

Last, but by no means least, there is *genetic diversity*. Evolution has fine-tuned individual species to be able to survive, compete, and reproduce over a range of climates and soils, and in the face of competition from a variety of other species. This ability to perform somewhat differently in different

17 Epiphytes are plants that live non-parasitically on other plants, such as mosses growing on the branches of coniferous trees, or ferns and bromeliads growing on the branches of tropical trees.

environments is a function of the genetic variation that exists in all populations of a given species: some are taller, some are smaller; some are able to tolerate drought and frost better than others; and so on. Genetically different subpopulations of a species that are adapted to different climates, soils, or biotic environments are called *ecotypes*. In forestry, a somewhat broader but analogous term is *provenance:* the area from which the seed of a particular tree species has been collected. Because of the importance of using the local provenance – the local genotype – in reforestation, only seedlings grown from seed collected locally or from areas with a similar climate (similar elevation and within a narrow range of latitude and longitude) should be planted. Obviously, this applies mainly when planting the local or native tree species. When planting species from another region or another continent, both regulations and common sense require that climate and soils be matched as closely as possible between the location of origin and the location of planting.

Frequently Asked Questions about Diversity

As in previous chapters, let us address some of the questions that people often ask about biotic diversity.

Are High Species Diversity and Structural Diversity Good?

The answer, of course, is that 'it depends.' Whether high biological or ecological diversity is better or worse than low diversity is not really a scientific question, because the question implies a value judgment. Because different people have different values, there will inevitably be a variety of answers. Whether high diversity is good or bad depends on which type of ecosystem you are talking about and the values that you want from that ecosystem. For example, if biologically diverse communities are more stable than low-diversity communities, and if some aspect of ecosystem stability is a desired ecosystem characteristic, then diversity would be considered to be good.

Are High-Diversity Forests More Stable than Low-Diversity Forests?

Regardless of whether you judge high or low diversity to be desirable or undesirable, ecosystems that vary in their diversity can differ significantly in their resistance to natural disturbance (their stability or resilience), and in their speed of recovery after disturbance (their elasticity).

As we have seen in modern agriculture, large areas planted with a single genetic strain of a single food crop species can be highly susceptible to outbreaks of insects and diseases and to competition from weed plants. This has led our food production systems to become heavily dependent on a variety of pesticides to compensate for this instability. 'Organic farming' methods, alternating crop species, limiting the area that has single-species crops, the use of species mixtures, and biological methods of pest control can produce some food crops with minimal use of chemical pesticides and fertilizers. However, the pressure to produce the quantity of food needed to feed the burgeoning human population, and food of the quality that western society is demanding at a price that is competitive, has led most farmers in industrialized countries to use low-diversity, chemically sustained agricultural systems that are undoubtedly less ecologically stable than a more natural approach to agriculture. This trend has been encouraged by the buying habits of shoppers. Most of us buy the 'specials,' or the lower-priced of two food products of equivalent quality. Most people will buy 'perfect' fruit and vegetables rather than plant products damaged by insects or fungi. As Pogo said, 'I have been out and seen the enemy, and it is us.' We, the consumers, bear much of the responsibility for what agriculture has become.

The low ecological stability (lack of resistance to disturbance) and low elasticity (slow recovery) of many agricultural ecosystems have contributed to the notion that *all* low-diversity plant communities are inherently unstable and inferior to high-diversity plant communities. However, questions of the goodness or badness or of the stability of low-

Natural diversity of forest ecosystems

A

C

B

A Tropical rain forest in Malaysia. This forest has high species and structural diversity within each stand (a few dozen hectares), but relatively low variation in this diversity across the flat landscape.

B Fire-origin forest in coastal British Columbia. The dense, even-aged, 125-year-old Douglas-fir forest in the foreground, which was established naturally after a fire in the middle of the last century, has low plant species and structural diversity. However, variation in soils, microclimate, and fire history has produced a high level of biological diversity across this land-

C A plantation of radiata pine in South Australia. This human-made forest ecosystem, using a California tree species, has a much lower species and structural diversity than the fire-degraded native eucalyptus forest it replaced, but it is very productive of timber products for house construction and chips for making paper.

diversity forest communities should be evaluated in terms of specific forest ecosystems, and not as a universal principle borrowed from agriculture. Many unmanaged forest ecosystems, such as most pine and eucalyptus forests, many Douglas-fir forests, and many deciduous hardwood forests, naturally have low-diversity plant communities in at least some of their seral stages, and both natural and planted monoculture forest crops of such species may be relatively stable, especially if they are of local genotypes and the stands are managed appropriately. Many of these low-diversity forests are very well adapted to recover rapidly from disturbance, and do so more rapidly than the more diverse forests that will replace them if they are not disturbed. Such disturbance-adapted species appear to be well suited to the disturbance regimes created by forest management.

Single-species tree crops of non-native species established to replace highly diverse native forest communities may be susceptible to severe damage should an insect or disease problem occur. However, the fact that many exotic plantations around the world have not been devastated by insects and disease suggests that such a disaster is not inevitable. Many native insects and diseases are specific to native tree species and will not attack exotic species, at least not until they have evolved the ability to do so. In other cases, these exotic plantations can be grown only if protected from native pests. For example, eucalyptus plantations in some parts of Brazil require the complete control of leaf-cutter ants if they are to be grown commercially.

The fact that a particular species is growing in a mixed-species community is commonly thought to confer on it some degree of protection from outbreaks of insect and disease pests to which it is susceptible. However, it will certainly not provide immunity. For example, elm trees in eastern Canada and the United States have been virtually eliminated by Dutch elm disease, which is spread by a species of beetle. Elms growing individually, in single-species groups, or in mixed-species stands have virtually all been found, infected, and killed by the

beetles. Similarly, chestnut blight has virtually eliminated the American chestnut from mixed-species, eastern deciduous forests, while white pine blister rust has decimated white pines in much of western North America, almost regardless of whether the pines were growing in mixtures or monocultures. On the other hand, Sitka spruce and other spruce species grown in monoculture plantations are very susceptible to serious damage from the spruce weevil in many parts of British Columbia. The weevil kills the leader (the top of the stem) and can prevent normal tree growth. Spruce grown as an understorey in a stand of other tree species often has much less weevil damage or may escape it entirely. Where the weevil is a problem, mixed stands may be essential for the successful growth of spruce.

Thus, while mixed-species forest *communities* are generally more stable than monocultures in terms of maintaining continuous forest cover, individual susceptible *species* in the mixed community may be much less protected from pests and pathogens than is sometimes thought. Although insect and disease outbreaks may develop more rapidly and spread faster through single-species forests of a susceptible tree species than in forests where this tree is mixed with less susceptible or non-susceptible trees, most of the individuals of the susceptible species may eventually be killed during an outbreak.

It is often suggested that structurally diverse climax forests with multiple tree species are more resistant to insect damage than even-aged, single-species stands. This is not necessarily the case, however. It will depend on the type of forest and the type of insect. Take the example of the western spruce budworm, an insect that eats conifer foliage and can damage or even kill conifer forests in warm, relatively dry areas of western North America. This species is reported to have done much more damage to these forests since the early 1900s than in the last century. With the reduction in wildfire since the early 1900s, there are fewer fire-origin, even-aged forests of early successional tree species such as pines and larch, which are resistant to the budworm. In their place, a mixed-species, multi-storey forest of shade-tolerant trees has developed (Douglas-fir [which is shade tolerant in these hot, dry areas], grand fir, and spruce). This provides ideal food and habitat for the insect. Interestingly, in climates where Douglas-fir is the climax species, it is generally very susceptible to the budworm, whereas in climates where grand fir is the climax conifer, Douglas-fir is much less damaged. Stand structure also plays a role. Multi-storeyed stands are reported to promote budworm outbreaks more than single-storeyed stands. This is because the young budworm larvae disperse by dropping off the branches they are feeding on. In a multi-storeyed canopy, many land on smaller trees, where they complete their feeding. In the absence of a second canopy layer, many fall to the ground and are eaten by birds, ants, and other predators. With respect to a spruce budworm attack, it is recommended that large areas of uniform late-successional or climax, multi-aged, and multi-storeyed forests be broken up into a mosaic of seral stands with an even-aged structure. Thus, within the geographical range of the budworm, simple rules about the relationship between forest diversity and budworm susceptibility do not hold true.

Are Even-Aged, Monoculture Forests Unnatural?

Many environmentalists feel that single-species forests or forests of low species diversity are less stable and are ecologically inferior to multi-species forests. A closely related idea is that single-species forests are actually unnatural. The concept that multi-aged, multi-storeyed forests are nature's way of doing things leads to the notion that even-aged forests with a single, uniform canopy level are also unnatural. Some even claim that these are not forests.

The age-class structure and the canopy structure of unmanaged forests are highly variable. They depend on the species and their light requirements, on the age of the forest since the last major disturbance, and on the temporal pattern of events that led to the re-establishment of the forest. Species

that need high light intensities for their seedlings to become established normally regenerate only after most of the overstorey has been removed. This generally occurs following fire, windthrow, or catastrophic insect and disease events. The result is generally an even-aged forest with a single-canopy layer. Such forests are often monocultures. If this low-diversity, early seral forest develops into a sub-climax or climax community before the next disturbance, a multi-age, multi-storey structure may develop. Forests in fire- or wind-prone areas rarely develop this far before the next natural disturbance, and they may exist almost in perpetuity as low-diversity, even-aged communities under the control of natural disturbance processes. Much of the boreal forest and Australia's native eucalyptus forests are like this. In areas less frequently disturbed, multi-storeyed forests of various levels of species diversity will develop.

Dense, even-aged, single-canopied, single-species stands are thus one of several different forest types that are frequently found in natural, unmanaged forest. Most of the diverse, multi-storeyed climax forests one can find have passed through an early seral stage dominated by a forest of low structural and species diversity at some time in the past following disturbance. There are species of wildlife associated with such low-diversity stages (including both common and rare species), but such forests are certainly not ideal for all wildlife species. If monoculture, low-structural-diversity forests of uniform age were to replace more diverse mature forests over large areas, as has often occurred naturally following very extensive wildfires, the temporary elimination of a variety of plant and animal species from these areas would almost certainly occur. Extensive, continuous clearcut logging will sometimes have a similar effect, especially if the harvested areas are slashburned.

How Does Forest Management Affect Species Diversity?

Again, it depends. Converting a large area of old-growth forest that has low beta diversity into a well-managed forest with many cutting cycles (see Chapter 5), will almost always increase the area's beta diversity by creating a mosaic of age classes and different stand structures. Where an original forest of high alpha diversity is replaced by a monoculture tree crop, the overstorey diversity and the diversity of associated animals will certainly be reduced, but the understorey diversity may remain essentially unaltered, depending on how the forest is managed.

The extent of understorey alteration as a result of forest management depends largely on stand density. Very dense stands managed on a short rotation may virtually eliminate understorey species, just as there is a stage in the development of most natural stands following disturbance during which the understorey becomes very sparse. The duration of this 'nudum' stage will depend on how the stand is managed. If the stand is thinned to reduce the number of trees and the density of the canopy, this stage may be short-lived, often much shorter than in unmanaged stands. By the time the stand is ready for its subsequent harvest in conventional or longer rotations, there is usually an understorey that is characteristic of the site in its unmanaged condition. Only where total weed control is practised over large areas in combination with the maintenance of high stand density, or if there is an invasion of agricultural or other non-native herb and shrub species, is the natural understorey plant community eliminated or significantly reduced over the whole rotation. Slashburning can greatly reduce plant species diversity on harvested areas, and although thinning can increase understorey species diversity, it can reduce overstorey species diversity and stand structural diversity if not planned with biodiversity in mind.

The effect of forest management on animal species diversity will depend largely on its effects on habitat diversity. This is true both at the small, local scale (alpha diversity) and at the local landscape scale (beta diversity). Where forest management reduces both the alpha and beta diversity of both plant community structure and plant species, regional animal species diversity will undoubtedly decline. However, in most cases the change in the animal community accompanying the transition from unmanaged to managed forest will be more of a change in the species composition than a change in species richness. Loss of animal species that are characteristic of mature or climax forest, such as woodland caribou or northern spotted owl, will generally be compensated for by gains in species that are benefited by access to younger forests or disturbed areas, such as deer, elk, or moose.[18] As these younger forests grow older, there will be a trend towards the pre-disturbance animal community composition. Where forest management results in the more or less permanent loss of snags or large decaying logs on the ground, there will be a loss of bird, other animal, and microbial species that depend on these ecosystem components. In some cases, these species may be able to utilize, or become adapted to use, other ecosystem components, but their abundance will probably be reduced.

In response to public and scientific concern about wildlife diversity, many studies are comparing wildlife communities in old-growth and second-growth forests and clearcuts. In one study on the Queen Charlotte Islands and the BC mainland near Vancouver, alpha species diversity of small mammals was reported to be similar in clearcuts and old-growth stands, but slightly lower in second-growth stands on the mainland. On the Queen Charlottes, the three species of small mammal captured in old-growth stands were present in equal or greater numbers in clearcuts or second-growth forests. The study was not conducted for long enough to draw firm conclusions about amphibians, but there was some indication that there may be greater abundance of tailed frogs and northwestern salamanders in the old growth. Some species were found only in

---

18 Where the decrease in abundance occurs in rare species and the increase in abundance is in common species, there will be a loss in some measures of diversity even if the total species number does not change.

clearcuts, some only in old growth. In the Queen Charlotte Islands, the number of bird species breeding was greatest in old-growth forests (about 12 versus 9 in second-growth forests and 7 or 8 in clearcuts); comparable numbers for the mainland were 13, 11, and 12, respectively. The abundance of these breeding birds in the Queen Charlottes was 265 pairs in old-growth forests, 236 pairs in second-growth forests, and 125 pairs in clearcuts; comparable numbers for the mainland were 397, 252, and 391, respectively. The preliminary conclusions from the study were that small-mammal diversity and abundance can be sustained in managed forests in these areas as long as a supply of snags and decaying logs on the ground is maintained. The data on birds were thought to be somewhat less reliable, but the study suggested some possible differences in old-growth and second-growth stands. Only one species recorded in old growth was absent from second growth, which in this study was a very young stand (D.R. Seip and J.P.L. Savard, personal communication).

A conclusion one can draw from this study is that wildlife diversity may not be greatly reduced in the first managed timber rotation, especially where logging has been 'exploitive,' the intensity of management low, and the utilization of the timber rather 'wasteful.' Under these circumstances many of the 'old-growth structures' required by old-growth dependent wildlife species are retained. However, many of these structures will not survive into a second timber rotation unless the forest is specifically managed to ensure that they are recreated. Consequently, the conclusions from this study may only be valid for the first managed rotation with the particular forest conditions and management practice that occured in the study area.

The key to predicting the effect of forest management on wildlife diversity is a knowledge of both the habitat conditions produced by management and the habitat requirements of the species. Animals that have very specific and inflexible habitat needs will be most sensitive to ecosystem change; a few

species appear to have an absolute requirement for old-growth or recently disturbed areas. Most species can be found in several different seral stages, albeit at different levels of abundance. (A good example of this can be found in Bunnell and Kremsater 1990; see references.)

What about Genetic Diversity?

In a crowd of people, some will be short and some tall. In a community of European origin, some may have blue eyes and some brown; there may be blondes and brunettes. Genetic variation is present in all populations and is important to the survival of any species. The large and visually attractive (but not necessarily delicious) fruit one buys at the market, the variety of dogs one sees on the neighbourhood street, and the docile, soft-nosed 'milk factories' one sees in a dairy farmer's field are not natural. They are all the result of deliberate selection of genetically desirable individuals from among a genetically variable population in order to satisfy human needs and desires.

The forests of northwestern North America are among the most varied in the world, and their tree species are characterized by a high degree of genetic variation: variation among different geographical areas, among different stands in any area, and among trees within any stand. This variation has ensured that many tree species are able to have extensive geographical ranges and grow on many different sites.

As a result of this variability, some trees are bigger and more resistant to diseases and produce better wood than others. Some live longer, some produce more seed, and some have smaller branches than others. However, despite its being such an ancient tradition in agriculture and horticulture, the idea of genetic improvement of forest tree crops to promote desirable tree characteristics is very new in many forest countries. Concern has been expressed that the considerable variation in the genetic makeup of a natural forest is lost when such genetic selections are made, and that this will result in a genetically uniform forest that will no longer have the genetic variability to adapt to changing climates, changing pests and diseases, and changing soil conditions.

A recent trend in forestry in some parts of the world has been 'clonal' regeneration: the development of a large number of seedlings by cuttings or by means of tissue culture from a single tree or a small group of trees. Eucalyptus forests in Brazil are often regenerated this way. This practice borrows from the field of horticulture. Many of the house plants or perennial garden plants you buy have been cloned from one or a very small number of parent plants. Where clonal forestry is done, the concerns about genetic uniformity will be far greater than where regeneration is from seedlings grown from seed collected from a population of genetically 'superior' trees. So what do the forest geneticists tell us about the risks to genetic diversity from these practices?

Some studies of the genetic make-up of coniferous tree species populations have shown that most of the genetic variability over a substantial area of coniferous forest is represented in the genes of any small group of individual trees selected from that large population. There is large within-tree and within-stand genetic diversity, but relatively little stand-to-stand genetic variation. The studies suggest that broadleaved trees present a different picture: their within-stand genetic diversity is relatively low, and their between-stand diversity is high. If this interpretation is correct, genetic improvement in broadleaved species should use a much larger population of trees gathered from a much larger area than is necessary with conifers. These conclusions were derived from a particular technique of genetic research: electrophoretic isozyme research. It remains to be seen if other research techniques in forest tree genetics will support this conclusion.

Much work remains to be done in the area of genetic diversity, and until we have a better understanding of the topic, prudence suggests that we should err on the side of caution. However, from what many forest geneticists are suggesting, it would appear that, in the case of coniferous forests at least, conventional genetic improvement programs do not threaten the genetic diversity of the tree species that are being improved. These programs require that 'genetically improved' seedlings come from wind-pollinated seed orchards that contain parent trees from up to a hundred different original parent trees in the forest. This ensures that wild pollen fertilizes the genetically-selected mother trees, and that the seed will contain genes from both selected and wild parents. Genetically engineered or clonal forests are unlikely to be a normal part of Canadian forestry. The risk of losing genetic diversity is further reduced if there is natural regeneration from the surrounding forest. Where young plantations are surrounded by forest of the same species, such enrichment of plantations is common. The risk of genetic impoverishment is also reduced by the fact that most seedlings planted today come from seeds collected from wild trees pollinated naturally by other wild trees rather from genetically-selected trees in seed orchards. This ensures that most, if not all, of the natural range of genes will be represented in the replanted forest.

In spite of these efforts at gene conservation, certain techniques in forest nurseries that produce seedlings may somewhat narrow the genetic variability of planted tree crops. Care must be taken to pass the full range of derived genetic varieties on through the entire regeneration process. If done correctly, this can result in greater genetic diversity than occurs in natural regeneration. Only a tiny fraction of all the seed produced by a forest will actively survive to become seedlings, and, according to the regeneration conditions, only a portion of the range of genetic variations in the entire population of seeds may survive.

Where there is a deliberate gene-conservation policy, future plantations may contain greater genetic diversity in the tree-crop population than in an old-growth stand of the same species. In areas where the forest is periodically disturbed by fire or other extensive disturbance events, very few trees may survive to become the parents of the subsequent forest. Such natural disturbances may periodically narrow the genetic constitution of some species, whereas clearcutting followed by planting with seedlings grown from seeds collected in many different stands will broaden the genetic base of the new forest. This would not be true for species, such as lodgepole pine and eucalypts, which have seed stored in unopened cones. Virtually all the trees killed by fire in forests of these species will contribute to the genetic make-up of the next generation.

The genetic implications of clonal forestry, where it is being done, certainly need to be considered seriously, and the present commitment to maintain the genetic diversity of our forest tree species must be maintained, no matter how they are being regenerated. Significant reductions in genetic diversity would not seem to be prudent, especially considering the anticipated change in global climate. Where clonal forestry is practised, there is usually a legal requirement to use a variety of clones in any plantation, and in some species such groups of clones can contain a similar range of genetic variation as wild seedlings.

Forest Fragmentation

In the 1950s, 1960s, and early 1970s, there was a strong trend away from 'continuous' clearcutting in Oregon and Washington. This harvesting practice was replaced by 'dispersed small clearcuts' as a result of pressure from fish and wildlife biologists and recreational interests. It was felt that having widely dispersed small patches of clearcutting was visually more attractive, that it would create a more 'natural' mosaic of stands of different age and structure, and that it would benefit many 'desirable' species of wildlife (mostly the large ungulate game species, such as deer and elk) by increasing the area of stand edge.[19]

19 Forest fragmentation is an important concern in Chapter 11 but is included here because of its implications for biological diversity.

After nearly twenty years of dispersed-patch harvesting, much of the remaining old-growth forest in areas harvested by this method is now distributed across the landscape in scattered small blocks surrounded by younger forests. Ecologists have expressed concern that this fragmented old growth cannot support wildlife species that are dependent on the old-growth condition. A parallel is drawn between the species diversity in 'islands' of old-growth forest in a 'sea' of younger forest and the species diversity on oceanic islands of various sizes. There is a strong correlation between the size of these islands and the number of species on them, and it has been suggested that this is true for old-growth reserves too. These ecologists also feel that the mosaic of younger stands of rather constant size is not natural. In nature, the combination of wind, fire, insects, and disease produces a variety of sizes of forest patches of a given age and species composition, from very small to very large. The regularity of the clearcut patch size is therefore considered to be environmentally inappropriate as well as aesthetically less pleasing than a mosaic with variable sizes of patch.

The fragmentation of the remaining mature and old-growth forests and the 'unnatural' mosaic of young stands produced by dispersed small clearcuts has led to the suggestion that the size of at least some clearcuts should be increased again so that the size of some of the patches in any particular age class is increased. The sizes of mature forest reserves should also vary from small to large. There is also the suggestion that in many cases harvesting systems other than clearcutting should be used (see the discussion of shelterwood and 'two-storeyed high forest' silvicultural systems in Chapters 5 and 11). Where clearcutting is used, there should be a diversity of clearcut sizes and shapes. Where silviculturally and environmentally appropriate, a mixture of clearcut and alternative harvesting systems would add to the landscape diversity.

The debate over forest fragmentation and its effects on forest diversity is in its early stages. Much research needs to be done to clarify the issue, and it is premature to draw any firm conclusions. However, the experience once again reminds us that all decisions in forestry have a price. 'One man's food is another man's poison.' What is good for one group of wildlife species may be bad for another group. Perhaps the best approach is to avoid all policies and regulations that require one approach to be applied everywhere. A diversity of clearcut patch sizes arranged in a pattern to achieve specific and diverse wildlife objectives in Oregon and Washington would probably have been a better overall strategy than the uniform-sized small clearcuts scattered evenly across the landscape that occurred in some areas in response to concerns about continuous clearcutting. Above all, generalizations and rigid policies should be avoided; they often seem to result in problems. Policies should be developed that are flexible, that recognize the diversity of resource values to be conserved and sustained, and that are different for different ecological conditions and different wildlife species.

'The First Rule of Intelligent Tinkering Is to Keep All the Parts': True or False?

Implicit in this frequently quoted maxim is the idea that systems are 'designed.'[20] When we take a car engine apart, we know that all of the parts are meant to be there. The engineer who designed the engine intended each component to have a specific and necessary function. Your four-cylinder car engine will not work at all if when it is reassembled you have two pistons left over, or a 'spare' timing chain or crankshaft. On the other hand, if you have a couple of washers left over, and possibly even one cylinder head nut, the engine may work fine, although the lack of more than one cylinder head nut may pose the risk of a cracked cylinder head sometime in the future. There is a small degree of redundancy built into an automobile engine, but

not much. Most of the pieces must be there if the system is to function normally, or function at all.

If one takes a religious view of ecosystems, one can reach a similar conclusion. If 'God' (whoever or whatever you consider such a deity to be, or by whatever name you call this spiritual power) created life, presumably God designed and made all the parts of our ecosystem in much the same way that a supernatural 'ecological engineer' would, so that it would function in a way that sustains life on earth. One might suppose that the deity would have been efficient in this design, so that, like the many different components in an engine, each would have its own functional role to play and there would be little built-in redundancy. On the other hand, one could argue that the deity liked diversity, and therefore provided many different organisms that perform essentially similar ecological functions, that a lot of redundancy was built into the system for the sheer pleasure of diversity. Alternatively, a wise deity might have provided diversity as insurance against the failure or loss of a critical component, in much the same way that space rocket engineers and the designers of commercial aircraft build in several computers and several control systems in case one fails.

How would a scientist interpret this maxim? That would depend on the scientist, of course: on his or her religious convictions, scientific training, and view of life. There is a great variety of opinion on such matters in the scientific world. However, from our current understanding of evolution, it is difficult to conclude that there is an exact parallel between a human-designed mechanical system and a natural, unmanaged ecosystem. Apart from the important role of periodic, catastrophic physical events (such as shifts in the earth's orbit around the sun or the tilt on its axis, major volcanic eruptions, meteor impacts, or changes in emissions of energy by the sun), evolution is believed to be the result of genetic mutations or recombinations that create new species characteristics and that can lead to new species by natural selection. Evolution works by selecting from a genetically variable population,

---

20 The reader is strongly urged to read *Discordant Harmonies* by Daniel Botkin (see Chapter 3 references).

individuals that are genetically the best suited to survive and reproduce. This evolutionary pressure to produce offspring in order to perpetuate a particular genetic type of individual has generally led to the avoidance of competition by means of specialization. One can see a parallel to this development in our economic system.

By diversifying its economy, a human community can support more people and reduce competition for economic resources. It can also be more stable in the face of changes in the economy, just as an ecosystem can support more species and its biological community may become more stable by means of ecological specialization. Contrast the general store in a small pioneer village, which sells almost everything the local people need, with the hundreds of specialized, single-product stores in a large modern shopping mall. With time, and as the population builds up, the general store seems destined to be replaced by a variety of speciality stores that avoid competition by being very good at selling just one or two things. (A few giant generalists may remain, such as Eaton's or The Bay in Canada and Sears in the States). In times of economic hardship, some of the speciality stores that flourished in good economic times may go bankrupt. This does not cause society to stop functioning, however. There is enough economic redundancy in the system so that other stores provide goods and services to the customers of stores that have closed. This is especially true when luxury stores go bankrupt. Their demise causes little or no change in the function of the community, although there may be some change in the 'quality of life' for individuals who equate luxury with quality. However, if food stores or the industries that provide heat, light, and power to your home were to go out of business, modern urban society would be in great difficulty. These economic 'species' are vital for the normal functioning of the economic community, whereas some of the highly specialized, 'luxury' economic activities are not essential. In contrast to the relative instability in a population of many different types of speciality stores, a village

general store that sells a little of most things may be relatively resistant to economic fluctuation. Thus, low diversity economic systems based an economic generalists may be much more stable than economically-diverse systems based on specialists.

Through the process of evolution, the various functions of energy capture and storage, nutrient cycling, and organic matter dynamics have been split between the many different species in a living community – like the evolution from the generalist village store to the highly specialized mall. Where evolution has continued more or less uninterrupted for a long time in a relatively predictable and physically unchanging environment, such as in a tropical rain forest or a tropical coral reef, this specialization has resulted in a myriad of different species and life forms. Frequently, the degree of specialization in these ecosystems has become extraordinarily high. For example, one species of tropical plant may be pollinated by only one or a small number of insect species. If this species or small group of pollinator species were lost, the plant species would probably become extinct.

Co-evolution, the process that has produced such intimate relationships, can produce such strong dependencies that the sudden loss of one partner in the relationship will probably result in the loss of the other partner. In many of the world's ecosystems, however, the degree of specialization is much lower – there are many more generalist species. Many insect species can pollinate many temperate flowering plants, and many temperate species are wind-pollinated. Most temperate trees are believed to form mycorrhizal relationships[21] with many (perhaps as many as several hundred) different species of fungi, the species associated with a particular root often depending on which species of fungi got there first. In physically variable, climatically

---

21 A mycorrhiza is an intimate and mutually beneficial relationship between a plant root and one or more species of soil fungus. The plant gets improved access to soil moisture and certain nutrients, and improved resistance to root pathogens, while the fungus gets a supply of carbohydrates to use for energy.

unpredictable temperate and northern environments in which there has been a much shorter period of undisturbed evolution, the ecosystem appears to have many more generalist species and to be able to function normally with or without a variety of species that are often present in the ecosystem; there appears to be a lot of functional redundancy.

If this is a correct interpretation, one can conclude that in fact many species can be lost from an ecosystem without the ecosystem 'falling apart at the hinges,' just as many specialty stores can close without a major effect on the ability of a human community to function. Natural catastrophes such as landslides, wildfire, disease, insect attack, or wind repeatedly cause the temporary loss of some species, many species, or even all species from natural, unmanaged ecosystems. Through the process of ecological succession, starting with the reinvasion of organisms from adjacent undisturbed areas, these disturbed ecosystems gradually return towards their original, pre-disturbance condition. Frequently, they can do so by a wide variety of successional pathways involving many different combinations of plant, animal, and microbial species. Several or even many different early-successional plant and animal communities can accomplish the successional change that will gradually lead back to the original community or something similar to it, under the control of the regional climate. One is left to conclude, therefore, that for most forests, the overall functioning of the ecosystem will generally continue regardless of a periodic loss of individual species because of disturbance. This is so because of the high degree of functional redundancy.

What does all this suggest about biological diversity? It suggests that, in general, ecosystem function in a given seral stage is less dependent on the maintenance of high alpha biological diversity than is sometimes suggested. The idea that the loss of a single species of bird or small mammal will result in a dramatic alteration, or even the eventual destruction, of a forest ecosystem is simply not supported by the available evidence.

It is relatively easy to think of examples that can be used to challenge this conclusion. For example, Douglas-fir trees periodically get infected by a pathogen (*Rhabdocline*) that causes them to lose many of their older leaves, thereby reducing their growth and health. However, *Rhabdocline* needle cast, as the disease is called, does not usually kill Douglas-fir because a natural parasite of the pathogen normally causes the disease to decline after a few years. The loss of this parasite could make *Rhabdocline* a fatal disease that would cause the widespread loss of Douglas-fir, in much the same way that Dutch elm disease destroyed elms, chestnut blight all but eliminated the eastern American chestnut, and white pine blister rust greatly reduced the range in which western white pine can be grown as a commercial timber species. Tree pathologists do not know of any redundancy as far as this particular natural disease control agent is concerned. So where does this leave the argument?

There certainly appears to be a lot of functional redundancy in our forests, and nature periodically eliminates many species from an area with no apparent alarming consequences. However, since we know of at least some examples (and there are probably many more) in which the loss of one species has had dramatic ecological consequences, it seems prudent to maintain nature's pattern of diversity as closely as possible. This does not mean that a given level of alpha diversity must be maintained on every hectare all the time. That is not nature's way either. Rather, we should try to duplicate nature's temporal and spatial patterns of alpha diversity, employing tree species mixtures where this is the natural condition for a particular seral stage, maintaining monocultures where nature does this, and maintaining the temporal pattern of different communities where our ecological studies suggest that this is necessary for the maintenance of overall long-term site productivity and biodiversity.

A final thought on this topic. The public, and especially environmentalists, have frequently suggested that we should maintain 'current' (or 'pre-European' in the case of North America) levels of biodiversity and species ranges. This implies that the present condition of the world's ecosystems is the way nature intended it to be, an implication that is scientifically unsupportable. Climates have always been changing and will always change. Many species have occupied their present geographical distributions for only the past few centuries or millennia, and are still changing their range in the wake of the last glacial period, or at least of the 'little ice age' in the Middle Ages. Many ecosystems owe their present condition to wind, fire, and past timber harvesting or deforestation for agriculture. Their present species diversity and structure reflect human and natural history and not what the forest would look like after another five hundred years of development in the absence of disturbance.

In most forests, biodiversity is not a fixed, God-given thing but a complex and ever-changing ecosystem and landscape characteristic. We must decide what biodiversity we want to have in our forests, and then design and implement management systems that will achieve this goal. We also have the obligation to ourselves and to future generations to maintain a 'healthy' environment, to pass on our evolutionary heritage, and not to foreclose options for future generations. Maintenance of a given pattern of diversity requires management. In the absence of management, nature will produce a continually changing mosaic of biodiversity in our forested landscapes.

We probably should endeavour to keep all the parts as we 'tinker' with forest ecosystems. This means maintaining species and species ranges wherever possible. It does not mean that the ecosystem will fail to function unless every species is present in every ecosystem all the time. A broad landscape view of biodiversity makes more sense than a very narrow local view.

Summary and Conclusions

There can be little doubt that some forest practices do result in a loss of biological diversity, be it species

diversity, structural diversity, or genetic diversity. This loss can be temporary or permanent; it can be very local or affect large areas of the landscape.

Replacement of large areas of tropical forest by monoculture pine or eucalyptus plantations represents a biological and ecological simplification that many people find unacceptable, and this practice has been widely criticized by environmentalists. Similarly, replacement of native forest by radiata pine plantations on New Zealand's North Island and in many parts of Australia was the subject of great public concern in the 1970s and 1980s. This led to the conservation of all remaining areas of native forest in New Zealand and a shift in emphasis from radiata pine to native species in Australian forestry.

Much of the plantation conifer forest on New Zealand's North Island has actually been established on areas cleared a century or more ago for agriculture, harvested by early Maori and European settlers, or deforested naturally by volcanic eruption; it did not directly replace prime native forest. These plantations have generally not, therefore, caused the loss of biological diversity that would have occurred if their establishment had been at the expense of undisturbed native subtropical or temperate forest. If managed on medium to long rotations, these plantations can result in an increase in diversity compared with agricultural pasture.

Foresters are becoming increasingly aware of the public's desire to maintain the biological diversity of our forests, and of the benefits to long-term site productivity and timber yield of doing so. There is growing interest in mixed-species plantations and in alternating crops to replicate the natural sequence of seral communities (temporal diversity). For example, the alternation or mixture of red alder (a nitrogen-fixing species) and Douglas-fir crops in coastal British Columbia, Washington, and Oregon can reduce the need for fossil fuel-based nitrogen fertilizers, maintain soil fertility, reduce fungal pathogens that cause decay in Douglas-fir, increase landscape diversity, and provide improved visual diversity.

There are indications that forestry is moving towards a system of silviculture that duplicates natural patterns in the landscape much more closely than has occurred in the past, and the trend should be encouraged. This does not imply that all managed forests should be multi-species and multi-storeyed. Many natural, unmanaged forests have low species and structural diversity. It does suggest, however, that there are many benefits to mimicking nature's temporal and spatial patterns of diversity more closely than has generally been the case.

As we tinker with forest ecosystems (hopefully with intelligence), it seems wise to sustain as many of the biological parts (at least on a local scale of a few hundred or thousand hectares) as possible because we certainly do not yet know enough about the role of all the biological components of these systems. However, we do know that nature periodically 'throws away' many ecosystem 'parts' as a result of disturbance. The resulting forests are often different to some degree from those they replace, but they generally work just fine. We also know that there are biologically simplified forests that have been managed for many centuries around the world without any recorded loss of ecosystem function (net primary production, carbon storage, and nutrient cycling), and that a number of such forests that have been degraded by inappropriate management have recovered when managed in an environmentally sensitive manner.

The prudent approach would seem to be to manage forests to maintain the diversity of conditions over the landscape found in the original unmanaged forest, and to augment this where historical events have pauperized the area. But we should also recognize that temporary reductions in various aspects of diversity in one managed area does not represent an environmental disaster. Very often, that is nature's way.

CHAPTER 11

'New Forestry': Is it Old Forestry Revisited?

What Is 'New Forestry'?

One of the latest topics in the forestry/environment debate is 'New Forestry.' Fresh from the Pacific Northwest of the United States, the New Forestry concept, also called 'New Perspectives in Forestry,' has become a rallying point for some environmental groups concerned about forestry. Terms such as 'coarse woody debris' and 'wildlife-trees,' unheard of a few years ago, are rapidly becoming part of the environmental movement's lexicon.

New Forestry is a concept developed by a group of forest ecologists[22] in Oregon and Washington as a way by which to manage forest land to conserve a range of old-growth values while at the same time allowing for the extraction of commodities such as timber. It is an attempt to move environmentalists away from their preoccupation with forest preservation, which seeks to limit the harvest of timber values, and to persuade production-oriented foresters to develop and use systems of silviculture and forest management that maintain environmental and wildlife values normally found only in unmanaged old-growth forest. New Forestry, it is suggested, offers an alternative to the conflict between preservation and intensive timber harvesting. Under New Forestry, the need for extensive old-growth reserves would be reduced, since old-growth values would be conserved in the 'working forest.' The trade-off would be reduced production of timber per hectare in the working forest.

The major concepts in New Forestry can be divided into two groups: new approaches to stand-level management and new patterns of landscape-level management. The ideas include longer rotations, partial cuts rather than clearcutting where this is ecologically appropriate, and a variety of clearcut sizes with a number of mature live trees kept to provide wildlife habitat and a future supply of snags. Other key points include: maintenance of a minimum number of snags as habitat for cavity-nesting

---

22 Major credit for the development of the New Forestry movement goes to Dr. Jerry Franklin, College of Forest Resources, University of Washington.

birds and mammals and as a source of food for birds that eat wood-boring insects, retention of a minimum level of large decomposing logs as habitat for small mammals, amphibians, and other organisms, and removal of less wood per hectare at harvest time in order to maintain site organic matter resources and carbon storage. It has been suggested that implementation of this system could lower the yield of logs from the forest by as much as 25 per cent in some cases, and that much of this volume loss would be in the more valuable large-diameter logs. In some shelterwood cuts in Oregon that are now being considered for 'green tree retention,' 30 to 35 per cent of the volume may be reserved.

What is interesting about New Forestry is that in some respects, though certainly not all, it echoes the sentiments and ideas of soil scientists and foresters of earlier in this century and the last century. To some extent, New Forestry is old forestry recycled and updated to meet the changing demands of the public with respect to forest management.

It has long been a maxim amongst forest soil scientists that the organic layer at the surface of the mineral soil in a forest (the forest floor) plays an extremely important role in soil processes, soil fertility, and long-term site productivity. Concern about the loss of forest floor was formalized in scientific studies and regulations to limit such losses in Germany nearly a century ago. The frequent collection of dead branches and tree stems for firewood, and the annual raking of needle (leaf) litter as an alternative to straw for cattle bedding, resulted in dramatic declines in tree growth in German pine forests growing on nutrient-poor soils in the first half of the last century. This attracted the attention of the German government of the day, which commissioned an eminent chemist, Ebermayer, to look into the problem. He conducted what was probably the first formal study of nutrient cycling and the relationship between nutrient dynamics and forest productivity (Chapter 4). This laid the foundation for today's branch of ecology that is concerned with the functioning and productivity of forest ecosystems.

In New Forestry, however, the concern over the magnitude and composition of the forest floor transcends nutritional considerations. It also considers the role of large dead woody material in providing habitat for animals and in maintaining forest stream diversity. This concern extends to both coarse woody debris (large decomposing logs on the ground) and snags.

The origins of New Forestry include the application of continuous (or progressive) clearcutting in Oregon and Washington in the 1950s and 1960s. In continuous clearcutting, successive clearcuts are located adjacent to the previous year's clearcut. A steadily expanding area of recently clearcut land results as the logging proceeds, until the entire valley, ridge, or forest management unit has been harvested. This method has resulted in large areas being stripped of mature forest over relatively short periods of time, with consequences for wildlife, hydrology, fish, and recreational values. Such harvesting systems result in a new forest that varies little in age over rather substantial areas, mimicking the age-class distribution produced by extensive wildfires in the past. Closely related to *progressive strip clearcutting,* a silvicultural system used successfully in Europe, continuous clearcutting in western North America has involved much larger clearcuts, which can result in very different ecological effects and silvicultural consequences than those of traditional strip clearcutting.

Another factor contributing to the development of New Forestry has been the removal of large decaying logs and snags as well as logging slash at harvest time. PUM (Piling of Unmerchantable Material) and YUM (Yarding of Unmerchantable Material), in which most of the slash and large rotting logs are removed from the site or put in piles, became popular in the Pacific Northwest in the late 1960s and early 1970s. They were instituted as a way of clearing this 'waste' material, and reducing fire hazard without slashburning – two things about which the public was expressing a growing concern. YUM and PUM were initially opposed by some forest economists as being very costly with little obvious benefit, but were promoted as an alternative to slashburning as a way of preparing a 'clean' site for planting. The economists were ignored, as was the mounting evidence that piling and burning often caused much more damage to the site than a well conducted broadcast slashburn. It was not until the ideas of New Forestry were developed by forest ecologists who were concerned about the long-term ecological implications of the removal of slash and large pieces of dead wood that YUM and PUM were re-evaluated. The loss of coarse woody debris was not the only factor that led to the development of New Forestry, but it was certainly an important contributor.

A third contributor was the development of the *small dispersed clearcut* method of harvesting. Promoted initially to reduce the visual, wildlife, and watershed impacts of continuous clearcut harvesting, this practice led to *forest fragmentation*. This term, which is discussed later in this chapter and in Chapter 10, refers to the creation of scattered small blocks of mature forest or old growth surrounded by small patches of younger forest of various ages in areas that have been harvested by the small dispersed clearcut method for several decades. Wildlife ecologists feel that such scattered small reserves cannot provide adequate habitat values for certain old-growth-dependent wildlife species.

Much of the genesis of New Forestry has thus stemmed from the loss of various old-growth wildlife values accompanying the patterns of clearcutting in U.S. Pacific Northwest old-growth forests in the 1950s and 1960s. The movement has largely come from scientists studying these old-growth forests. Unfortunately, the conviction has arisen among some environmentalists that the 'only good forest is an old-growth forest.' In contrast to the scientific study of old growth, there has developed a mystique and, in a few cases, virtually a religion about old growth that has promoted the idea that a managed second-growth forest is not a real forest. Only unmanaged old growth satisfies these people's vision of a forest. Part of the difficulty in getting some of the useful ideas of New Forestry accepted and implemented is that for some people the science has become entangled with the mysticism: the ecology has become confused with the religion.

This chapter briefly examines some of the ideas of New Forestry and the degree to which they might be applicable in British Columbia and other Canadian forests. It reviews questions of diversity and stability (also discussed in Chapter 10), the importance of coarse woody debris and snags, and the problem of forest fragmentation.

Biological Diversity and Stability at the Stand Level

A major focus of the proponents of New Forestry has been the maintenance of ecosystem resilience (the ability to resist change in the face of disturbance – one of several measures of ecosystem stability) and biological diversity. The goal of New Forestry is to manage forests in a manner that maintains various old-growth conditions and sustains the ability of forest ecosystems to withstand stress and recover from disturbance, while at the same time permitting a significant proportion of the timber values to be harvested.

The focus of those concerned with ecosystem resilience has traditionally been on the soil. Physical, chemical, and biological soil damage has repeatedly been identified as a major factor threatening the long-term productivity of a managed forest site within a particular climatic zone, as well as the potential of the forest to recover from disturbance. Without denying the importance of the soil, New Forestry advocates have advanced the idea that resilience of forest ecosystems is also a function of species diversity and diversity in the forest's vertical and horizontal structure. Sustainable forestry, it is claimed, requires more than the maintenance of soil condition. It also requires that forest managers maintain species and structural diversity in managed stands. This, it is suggested, involves the development of a multi-layered tree canopy, the retention of a minimum number of large rotting logs on the ground, and the maintenance of large standing dead tree stems in the stand. The number of snags and large rotting logs required will depend on the particular type of forest ecosystem being considered and will vary from place to place.

Forests that have a diverse vertical structure will generally support a greater variety of animal life than forests with a simple structure. It has been shown for some types of forest that the number of bird species is closely related to the structural diversity of the forest canopy, and it is frequently suggested that this is true for other animals: the greater the number and spatial variability of canopy layers and canopy tree species, the greater the diversity of all animal life.

Animals need a 'job': they need a way of 'making a living.' As a result of evolution, each animal species has become specialized in the way in which it feeds, finds shelter, and conducts various other aspects of its life cycle. By specializing, each species minimizes competition with other species. The greater the variety of physical microhabitats in the plant community, the greater the possibility for specialization in the animal community and, in theory, the greater the number of animal species. One has only to look at the diversity of economic activities in a big city to realize that humans behave in much the same way. There is generally a greater diversity of economic activities in a large city with a high degree of social and physical diversity than in a small community that is more socially and physically homogeneous.

An animal's ecological occupation, the role it plays in the ecosystem, is called its *ecological niche*. Generally speaking, the greater the diversity of plant species in the forest, the greater the structural diversity of the plant community, and the greater the diversity of sizes and species of rotting logs in a particular area, the greater the number of potential ecological niches for animals and microbes in that area, and the greater the animal and microbial alpha species diversity (see Chapter 10 for an explanation of diversity terms). Because these measures of diversity all vary during the process of ecological succession, the number of niches and the potential animal diversity will also vary from early seral, to mid-seral, to climax forest communities. The number of ecological niches and the animal diversity within each seral stage will also vary. As the community of a particular seral stage invades and replaces the plant community of the previous seral stage, there will be an increase in structural diversity, snags, and decomposing logs. This type of diversity may decrease again as seral replacement is completed. Similar increases in diversity will occur as waves of stand self-thinning occur in this new seral stage, and again as this community is replaced by plant species of the next seral stage. There is thus little evidence to support the idea of a linear increase in ecological niches and wildlife diversity accompanying the change from a young, early seral forest to a late seral or climax old-growth forest. There is significant variation in measures of diversity over time as the species composition and structural attributes of the community change through succession.

The origins of wildlife alpha species diversity are somewhat more complex than merely the structural diversity of the plant community. For example, in the low-diversity fir and spruce forests of the northeastern United States, a considerable diversity of bird species (including five species of warblers) is supported by their consumption the caterpillars of the spruce budworm, an insect whose periodic epidemics kill large areas of eastern forests. Multiple niches are created for the warblers in what initially appears to be a single niche by the division of the spruce canopy into various heights in the crown and various distances between branch tip and trunk. Each species has its own feeding territory as well as time of feeding within the canopy. This is an example of surprisingly high bird diversity in a forest with low species and structural diversity. Consider also the case of oak trees in Europe. Even-aged, single-species, structurally simple oak forests can support an amazing diversity of insect life in its canopy, but this diversity is not uniform across the geographical range of the oak. Insect species diversity has been shown to decline from south to north, and there appears to be a close relationship between the time since the glaciers retreated, which is also the time since the oaks arrived in what was previously a coniferous forest, and the diversity of canopy insects. The diversity of the insect community in the canopy of the oak woodland depends on more than the structural diversity of the forest.

Clearly, several factors determine the number of ecological niches and the diversity of animal species, not just plant species and structural diversity. This in no way negates the idea that in some types of forest higher plant species and structural diversity result in higher animal species diversity, and that in some forests this may be related to greater ecosystem stability. It does suggest, however, that once again overgeneralization and uncritical extrapolation from one type of forest to another does not help our understanding of how forest ecosystems work and how they should be managed. Some advocates of New Forestry have presented the idea that greater structural diversity in the plant community will always result in greater animal species diversity, and that the two together will always result in greater ecosystem resilience. It is unlikely that this is true. Plant and animal species that are naturally found in high-diversity forests may well be adapted to high diversity and be favoured by it. But by the same token, the many species that naturally occur in low-diversity forests are adapted to this lower diversity, which does not constitute a threat to their continued existence.

The Importance of Retaining Coarse Woody Debris

A large decaying log provides a very different microenvironment for small animals and microbes than the average forest floor that is made up of decaying branches, leaves, fine roots, and other small pieces of dead organic matter. This is especially true in forests that have a long dry summer,

whose soils are dry in the summer, and whose organic floor is very shallow. In such areas and on such soils, the forest floor and upper mineral soil may become so dry in late summer that microbial and soil animal activity ceases. Many microbes and soil animals may die or become quiescent unless they are in or can move to a moist microsite. The centre of a large rotting log may provide such a refuge, and the presence of such logs may provide a source from which microbes and soil animals can recolonize the rest of a site after the fall rains have rendered the forest floor suitable once again for their survival and growth.

If a forest with a dry summer climate or a site whose soil becomes very dry in the summer is clearcut and all large pieces of dead wood are removed, or if the area is slashburned severely, there may be a loss or reduction of soil animals and microbes. A very hot summer wildfire can have a similar effect, and unmanaged forests in dry climates that have experienced severe fires in the past often have very little coarse woody debris. If the microbial change caused by the loss of coarse woody debris and forest floor results in the loss of the fungi that form mycorrhizae with trees, it may become extremely difficult for trees to become re-established on the site. Some areas where this is reported to have happened in California and Oregon have apparently remained unforested for a long time. One would expect this to be a problem only at the limits of tree growth, such as near the treeline in subalpine forests or near the forest/grassland interface: environments where trees are already under considerable stress. Low rainfall, very dry air, and sometimes special soil conditions occur in these areas and this combination contributes to regeneration difficulties in this part of the Pacific Northwest.

It has been suggested that maintaining an adequate supply of large decomposing logs on a site is important for long-term tree nutrition and site productivity. The presence of a lot of woody slash following harvesting can, in some climates, act to immobilize nitrogen. Although this may result in nutritional

Logging debris and whole-tree harvesting

A

B

C

D

A Harvesting old-growth cedar forests results in large quantities of unusable decayed logs, broken stems, and large branches. Excessive quantities of this material may make planting or natural regeneration of a new forest impossible for many years or decades. Carefully applied slashburning is often the best way to get such sites to reforest promptly. Too much coarse woody debris can cause nutrient deficiencies and soil acidification. Too little may be bad for some wildlife species.

B Whole-tree harvesting may remove virtually all the woody material from the site. This can cause long-term loss of soil organic matter, nutrients, and site productivity. It may have negative implications for wildlife habitat.

C Whole-tree harvesting can be a problem in partially harvested forests as well as clearcut forests. This type of site, in central Sweden, can lose up to 25 per cent of its growth after mechanical whole-tree harvesting, even though it is not clearcut. Such harvesting can also cause soil acidification on nutrient-poor sites.

D Whole-tree harvesting with short rotations can cause significant nutritional problems which may require frequent fertilization. This four-year-old eucalyptus plantation grown for charcoal and oil in Brazil must be tended and fertilized much like an agricultural crop. This is literally tree farming. It replaced a scrub forest of native species which was degraded by a century of cutting for charcoal and burning for cattle grazing.

problems for the trees early in the life of a plantation, it can reduce the leaching and gaseous loss of nitrogen and release it slowly to the trees later in the life of the stand. This 'nutrient sponge' effect is largely a function of branches, small stems (logs), and roots: materials that decompose fairly quickly. Foliage litter of some species can also provide a short-term nutrient sponge. Large logs, because of their low nutrient content and slow rate of decomposition and nutrient release, play a much smaller part in this process and are generally less important nutritionally than they are in terms of wildlife habitat, and possibly in moisture retention. In summer dry areas, they may be important refuges in which small soil animals and microbes can escape the drought. It is generally thought that removal of larger woody material has much less negative impact on forest nutrition than removal of small branches and leaves, which have much higher concentrations of nutrients and often contain the majority of some key nutrients (e.g., nitrogen and phosphorous) in the entire tree. However, decaying logs may have nutritional significance on very wet or very cold soils because they provide a drier and warmer environment for roots, respectively, than the mineral soil.

Rotting logs in humid forests produce a type of humus that is very different from the humus produced from leaves, flowers, twigs, and small roots. This humus tends to be very acidic. It produces organic acids that contribute to soil weathering, soil leaching, and a soil development process called *podzolization*. A site with a lot of decaying wood can develop a rather inactive forest floor called a *mor humus form*, which is generally associated with low fertility and slow forest growth. In comparison, sites where the forest floor is dominated by leaf, small root, and branch litterfall tend to have an active humus form of the *mull* or *moder* type. These are associated with much higher soil fertility and greater forest productivity. Thus, while some decaying wood may be desirable, too much wood is not desirable if you want the soil to remain fertile and the forest productive. Excessive accumulations of

coarse woody debris in old-growth forests in humid areas can lead to extreme podzolization, very low nutrient availability, the stagnation of nutrient cycling and tree growth, and the break-up of the forest.

The humus from decayed wood may be more stable than the humus from more rapidly decomposing litter. This has implications for soil structure and long-term site fertility, but the topic has not yet been adequately researched. The absence of rotting wood in Scandinavian and European forests for many centuries because of intensive management and harvesting has not prevented these systems from functioning very well as forests. There are undoubtedly differences in soil characteristics and in the community of soil animals and microbes in these intensively managed forests compared with forests that have a natural complement of coarse woody debris. But these differences have not resulted in ecosystem breakdown unless the removal of nutrients has led to a decline in site productivity. The question of the interaction between the presence or absence of decaying wood and susceptibility to acid rain damage is discussed later.

The importance of leaving a number of large-diameter logs at harvest time to ensure a future supply of rotting logs on the site will vary greatly from one type of forest to another. Because there are so many dead, decayed, and broken trees in many old-growth forests in areas that have a humid climate, the problem following harvesting of these forests is often that there is too much large organic debris. There is little to be achieved by leaving more, and much to be said against it. However, much of the coarse woody debris already present in an old-growth forest, and the additional material created when it is harvested, will decompose over the subsequent one or two tree-crop rotations. If the second-growth stands that replace these old-growth forests are intensively managed, with all trees that would die by stand self-thinning being harvested in commercial thinnings, there will be a progressive reduction of this type of material on the site. In such forests, it may be important to re-examine the need for coarse woody debris retention in the second and third rotation even on sites where the problem is an excess of woody debris after harvesting of old growth.

Where forests are managed less intensively, trees that die from competition for light provide a steady input of logs to the forest floor. Over a long rotation of 80 to 120 years, 30 to 40 per cent of all the stemwood produced in a stand that is not commercially thinned may end up on the ground as coarse woody debris. In a cool, humid climate, these log inputs will accumulate, and it may be unnecessary to leave additional logs at harvest time. In contrast, forests in drier areas that have had a history of frequent ground fires may accumulate little or no coarse woody debris, and there may be some biological reasons for retaining logging slash on the site, unless of course this increases the risk of future site damage from fire or insects such as bark beetles. Most hot, dry forests have very low levels of organic matter in the soil and little by way of a forest floor. Coarse woody debris retention may be more important here than in cool, humid forests. Conversely, the animals and microbes of these forests are presumably adapted to this general lack of coarse woody debris, and it might be considered inappropriate to change this natural state of affairs.

The question of coarse woody debris retention must obviously be considered on a site by site, forest type by forest type basis. Policies relating to coarse woody debris should have logical and achievable biological and ecological goals (such as maintenance of wildlife habitat), should address real needs in terms of management objectives, and should reflect the current and probable future states of a forest site. They should reflect both wildlife and tree-crop management goals. There is little reason to doubt that large rotting logs play a significant ecological role in summer dry forests, and that forests lacking coarse woody debris will exhibit some biological and ecological differences from forests that have such debris. At present it is less clear just how much coarse woody debris is needed in a particular type of forest to achieve some specific objectives, and what the trade-offs are between environmental gains of coarse woody debris retention and the social values foregone by carrying out this practice.

The Importance of Snags

Several bird species of the Pacific coast forests require snags in which to nest, and some species may require snags in which to find the wood-boring insects that they eat. Some mammals may also need snags. It has been claimed that the spotted owl has an absolute requirement for old-growth forests on the basis of both the abundance of snags and the structural diversity of the old-growth forest canopy that apparently improves its hunting success. One of its major prey species, the flying squirrel, is more abundant in forests with multiple canopy layers. However, the spotted owl is apparently also found in second-growth forests if suitable snags and food species are present, albeit at lower densities.

There is little question about the desirability of having insect-feeding birds in a forest. They are known to be important in controlling insect populations when these are at relatively low densities, although it is doubtful that they can control insect numbers if changing environmental conditions trigger a major insect epidemic. Also, it is not yet clear if these 'old-growth birds' act mainly to control insect species that are found mainly in old-growth forests, or whether they are equally effective in controlling insects in younger forests. If these birds are not important in regulating the insects that may threaten immature forests, their absence because of a lack of snags in younger forests may have less significance for these younger forests than might be concluded from their role in mature forests.

There is widespread concern that if all old growth in the Pacific Northwest were to be converted to short rotation, intensively managed second-growth without providing a satisfactory substitute for snags, these cavity-nesting or snag-feeding bird species would be lost or greatly reduced in their geographical range and abundance. The spotted owl and its preference for old-growth snags has been the legal mechanism by which wilderness advocates in the Pacific Northwest have used the U.S. Endangered Species Act to set aside large areas of old-growth forest.

Recognizing the practical or social desirability of maintaining bird species diversity and accepting the reality that most of the forests in Oregon and Washington will be managed for timber production, New Forestry provides a way of producing timber without losing cavity-nesting birds and other animals. The essence of the concept is the retention of as many as possible of the 'old-growth structures,' as they are called, in managed second-growth stands. This is achieved by leaving existing snags and a minimum number of sound logs on the ground at harvest time (a practice that in the past has been vigorously criticized as wasteful logging by environmentalists and forestry unions) to provide a supply of large decayed logs for the future. In addition, a minimum number of large live trees are retained as 'wildlife trees,' to provide a future source of snags; this is referred to as *green tree retention*. Where necessary, some of the living wildlife trees will be killed by girdling to accelerate their transition to dead snags, although trees treated in this manner tend to decay from the outside in (hard snags), rather than from the inside out (soft snags), as occurs in many natural snags because it encourages decay of the centre of the stem. Blowing off the tops of the trees with dynamite has been suggested as a better way of creating future snags. Obviously, New Forestry would forego a significant economic timber value in form of these leave trees, but it is claimed that this loss would be much less than setting aside large areas entirely as old-growth or wildlife habitat reserves.

Visually, the forests harvested under the New Forestry system would look somewhat like a shelterwood (see Chapter 5), but would generally have a more 'untidy' appearance because of all the standing dead trees and the retention of a variety of intermediate-sized trees to promote future canopy diversity. In contrast to a conventional shelterwood,

the leave trees would not be harvested, even if they subsequently blew down. This could clearly be problematic where bark beetles breed in such downed logs and then attack live trees. A stand treated this way could develop into a 'two-storeyed high forest' (a forest with two distinct canopy layers, not a forest two-storeys high!) with snags. At a subsequent harvest, additional leave trees would be retained, possibly leading to a three-storeyed forest with snags, depending on how many of the original wildlife trees have survived. After several rotations of this type of management, the forest structure could approximate that of an old-growth stand, even though the majority of the trees would be even-aged and removed periodically in a final harvest.

The Problem of Forest Fragmentation

The discussion of New Forestry so far has dealt only with individual forest stands – local ecosystems. There is growing concern, however, that the focus on local ecosystems causes us to lose sight of the forest landscape. Both wildlife and visual values of our forests are affected by regional landscape-level aspects of forest management as well as by the quality of stand-level forest management. New Forestry stresses the need to consider both levels.

In the 1960s and early 1970s, concern over wildlife habitat and recreational and watershed issues in Oregon and Washington led to a forest harvesting strategy of small dispersed clearcuts. Much earlier, large-scale clearcutting was conducted in the old-growth Douglas-fir forests of this region, but with the advent of logging trucks and tractors in the early 1930s, clearcutting was largely replaced by selective harvesting: a series of successive light cuts in which the largest trees were removed. This proved to be a silvicultural disaster. The partially cut stands are reported to have suffered wind damage, insect attacks, disease problems, damage to residual trees, growth slowdown, and frequent difficulties with regeneration. The reaction to the failure of this silvicultural experiment led to large clearcuts organized as progressive clearcutting. However, the wildlife, watershed, and visual concerns about this type of harvesting resulted in the subsequent adoption of small clearcuts dispersed across the landscape.

For a couple of decades, the results of small dispersed clearcut harvesting were generally accepted by the public. Recently, concern has been expressed that the long-term result will be a forest landscape consisting of a mosaic of small patches of forest of various ages, with the remaining mature or old-growth forest distributed as small 'islands' in a 'sea' of younger managed forest. Growing interest in wildlife species that have strong affinities for old growth has led to a challenge of this harvesting strategy.

It has been pointed out that natural disturbances in forests often result in a variety of sizes and shapes of patches of forest of a given age: a lot of small and medium-sized patches, and a smaller number of large patches. The animal and plant species in these forests have presumably adapted to this range in patch size, and if we wish to sustain a 'natural' level of landscape diversity, forest harvesting should probably try to duplicate this natural pattern of disturbance sizes.

A conclusion that can be drawn from this discussion is that not all harvest areas should be the same size. There should be a variety of sizes of harvested, immature and mature forest areas from large to small. It also suggests varying intensities of harvest disturbance in the landscape, from clearcuts to shelterwood to patchcuts, according to which system satisfies the ecological requirements of desired crop trees and wildlife. In forests where periodic large-scale disturbance is the natural condition, large clearcuts may be the most appropriate pattern of harvest disturbance. Where forest replacement normally occurs in small patches, small clearcuts, patchcuts, shelterwood, or selection cutting may be a more environmentally sound, socially acceptable approach.

How Much Coarse Woody Debris and Snags Should We Retain?

The question of how many wildlife leave trees and snags to retain is mainly a question to be answered by wildlife managers and fisheries biologists. In most forests it has less to do with ecosystem function and stability. It is a problem of identifying rather precisely the various habitat needs of the species you wish to maintain in an area, and the ability of these species to adapt to new conditions. The research required to answer this question will be species-specific and forest-type-specific, and will have to be repeated in different forest types across the range of various wildlife species. Once again, relatively few useful generalizations can be made, and policies simply cannot be developed from vague concepts. A lot of research will have to be done to produce biologically rational guidelines.

The question of how many large rotting logs are needed must be answered by forest ecologists and soil biologists, with some help from wildlife ecologists. Whereas the wildlife questions with respect to snags can probably be answered in a couple of decades worth of intensive research, the question of the long-term contribution of coarse woody debris to ecosystem function is much harder to answer. It covers the areas of wildlife ecology, soil microbiology, soil zoology, soil fertility, and nutrient cycling. Some aspects of the problem (specifically the long-term contributions of rotting logs to soil humus levels and nutrient cycling) can be addressed in ecosystem simulation models such as FORTNITE and LINKAGES, and ecosystem management simulation models such as FORCYTE and FORECAST (see Chapter 15). In the absence of long-term studies, it is very difficult, if not impossible, to develop site-specific guidelines about necessary levels of coarse woody debris retention without using such ecosystem-level predictive tools.

Applicability of New Forestry Concepts outside the Pacific Northwest

Conclusions about the importance of coarse woody debris and snags based on studies in one forest type will not necessarily be valid in forests that have significantly different ecological characteristics. Undoubtedly important in many of the summer hot and dry forests of Oregon, northern California, and parts of Washington, the role of large decaying logs changes as one moves north into the cooler, wetter climates of western Canada, or into very dry forests where frequent fires in the past have prevented the accumulation of much coarse woody debris.

A major feature of unmanaged cool temperate rain forests on the west coast of British Columbia is very high accumulations of rotting wood and thick forest floors. This is the combined result of a long absence of forest fire, productive forests that produce a huge biomass of giant tree stems, periodic wind storms that blow over large numbers of trees, and slow rates of decomposition of large logs and of litterfall, in general. In some of these forests, the very large accumulation of decayed wood and the very acidic soil conditions that result are believed to lead to the stagnation of nutrient cycles and a marked decline in ecosystem productivity. If such ecosystems remain undisturbed for a long time, the break-up of the closed forest occurs. However, this probably involves more than just the accumulation of massive amounts of slowly decomposing logs (as much as many hundred tons per hectare) at the soil surface. It may also involve the accumulation of large quantities of humic organic substances in the mineral soil, which impairs soil aeration and drainage.

The periodic disturbance of cool temperate coniferous rain forests on the coast of British Columbia and Alaska by windthrow appears to be necessary to maintain the productivity of unmanaged stands. In parts of the Queen Charlotte Islands, northern Vancouver Island, and the outer coast of the central British Columbia mainland, some of the most productive unmanaged forests are those growing on the lower parts of old natural landslides, on areas that have been windthrown, or on steep slopes where gravity is continually causing minor soil slippage and churning. This physical disturbance improves drainage and aeration, which are critical to good tree growth in the cool, humid climate of these areas.

It may be that clearcutting and mechanical site disturbance during and after the removal of the logs can duplicate some of the beneficial effects of windthrow on the soils of these forests. However, it must be noted that clearcutting does not exactly duplicate windthrow. Clearcutting often causes relatively little physical disturbance to the soil and the tree stumps are not usually tipped over as they are in a windthrown forest. Although excessive amounts of decaying wood produced in a windthrow can sometimes have negative nutritional consequences for future forests, removal of *all* stemwood as harvested logs can also have negative long-term consequences. Where harvesting also removes most of the branches and foliage, the difference between the wind-disturbed and the harvest-disturbed forest is even greater. This type of harvesting has the potential to cause significant nutritional problems that could offset any physical improvement that the harvesting might cause in the soil. If timber harvesting causes soil compaction, it will have an effect on soil structure and aeration opposite to that of windthrow. Where physical disturbance of the soil is desirable, harvesting systems and post-harvesting site treatments should be designed to duplicate as closely as possible the beneficial effects of windthrow on these forests.

In cold far northern forests, the accumulation of a thick, slowly decomposing forest floor may interact with permafrost (a permanently frozen layer of soil) to produce a decline of ecosystem function and the beginning of the conversion of forest into muskeg (sphagnum bogs) unless the forest is disturbed every few centuries by fire, windthrow, or logging. The organic layer insulates the mineral soil, preventing it from warming up in the summer so that it remains cold or frozen. This prevents tree roots from growing down into mineral soil and contributes to nutritional and stability problems that cause the forest to decline. Large accumulations of decaying tree stems may accelerate this process. Obviously the role of coarse woody debris in these forests differs from that in the summer hot and dry forests of regions like southern Oregon and northern California.

Many of the world's forests have been harvested for a long time. In some forests in Japan there is evidence that forest harvesting has taken place for more than a thousand years. Although there are examples of severe site degradation in a few areas that have extremely nutrient-poor or unstable soils, most of the forests appear to be healthy and productive after this very long period of management and utilization. In Scandinavia and central Europe, forest harvesting has been occurring in some areas for five or six centuries. These forests have not had any coarse woody debris of the type seen in old, unmanaged west coast forests in North America for many centuries. Even small tree stems and branches have been continuously removed for fuel.

Although there is a widely publicized problem of 'forest decline' in Europe, recent manifestations of this phenomenon have been attributed mainly to air pollution, overloading of the soil with nitrogen from acid rain, or the toxic effects on tree roots caused directly or indirectly by sulphuric and other acids in acid rain (see Chapter 13), rather than the lack of coarse woody debris. In some cases, the problem has been greater where spruce monoculture has been grown since before the acid rain phenomenon began, and second-rotation spruce decline was reported before acid rain was a major environmental influence. Pure spruce plantations result in more acidic soil conditions than the beech/fir/spruce forests they replaced, and this is thought to have predisposed these forests to air pollution and acid rain damage.

The causes of forest decline in Europe are complex (Chapter 13) and vary in different places, but there is little evidence to suggest that the lack of rotting logs on the forest floor has been a significant disposing factor. It is possible that in cases where direct acid damage to fine feeding roots is a major part of the acid rain problem, large rotting logs might have provided these roots with some protection from the effects of the acid rain. However, it is difficult to find significant scientific support for claims that forests cannot live without coarse woody debris. Excessive amounts of decayed wood of some species can acidify the soil as much as acid rain.

Clearly, a high degree of ecological sophistication is required in deciding which of the ideas of New Forestry are appropriate for any particular forest ecosystem outside of the areas of Oregon and Washington where the ideas were developed. Although this discussion has focused on coarse woody debris retention, a similar analysis could be made for snag retention, wildlife leave trees, and various other aspects of New Forestry. Such analyses will generally lead to the conclusion that some of the ideas apply to some forest ecosystems some or all of the time, but not all of the ideas apply to all forest ecosystems all of the time.

Criticisms of New Forestry

There are some useful ideas in New Forestry that should be incorporated into forestry practice where they are consistent with the local ecology and the objectives of forest management. However, like all new ideas that challenge the status quo, New Forestry has received a lot of criticism.

There are several reasons why many experienced field foresters have found it difficult to accept New Forestry. These include an inadequate description of exactly what is to be achieved on particular sites; the lack of site-specific descriptions as to exactly how forests should be harvested and managed to meet certain environmental objectives; concerns about the safety of workers; the suggestion by some environmentalists that New Forestry means no clearcutting anywhere and that all forests should be selection harvested; the failure of some New Forestry advocates to recognize that harvesting systems should vary on different sites, with different tree species, and in different climates; and the failure to consider problems of diseases, infrequent seed production (a problem for natural regeneration in some forests), windthrow problems, and weed competition.

Some senior foresters in the Pacific Northwest

have been critical of New Forestry because they believe that some of its aspects resemble silvicultural systems that were used unsuccessfully in the Douglas-fir region in the 1930s. The partial-cut systems that were applied in many Douglas-fir forests of that time are reported to have failed to meet their timber production goals because of wind, disease, insect, and regeneration problems. These critics feel that New Forestry is too theoretical, that many of its ideas are untested, and that the 'experiment' will end in failure the way partial cutting did in the 1930s if it is applied uncritically with no consideration for the local ecology. They claim that New Forestry is reinventing an old wheel that has already been proven inappropriate and unworkable. This point of view is supported by many silviculturists in industry, research, and academia.

There are forest types in both the Pacific Northwest and western Canada where selection and shelterwood harvesting systems have been used for many years; they match the ecology of the site better than clearcutting, and they are superior in terms of regeneration, wildlife, and aesthetics. However, more than half a century of experience in this part of the world has convinced these foresters and silviculturists that there are also many forest situations in which clearcutting is the best harvesting system. They are also concerned about the loss of up to 25 per cent of the timber yield and the probability of increased harvesting and management costs without adequate documentation of the environmental benefits that this considerable investment is buying. If the alternative to practising New Forestry was to have large areas removed from the working forest, there would probably be greater acceptance. Where this alternative seems unlikely, many foresters are not ready to accept New Forestry concepts other than on a trial basis until the environmental benefits that it is supposed to confer have been demonstrated and the costs of these new systems evaluated.

Worker safety from snags, regeneration difficulties, weed problems, insects, diseases, and windthrow are all factors that may limit the application of New Forestry systems in specific instances. It is clearly inappropriate to embrace the New Forestry paradigm as the way all forests in North America should be managed until there is much more evidence about the consequences of doing so in different types of forest. Where such systems have been tried and failed, the historical evidence must be considered unless it can be demonstrated that they failed for avoidable reasons. However, some aspects of New Forestry have not yet received critical long-term field testing, and the ideas have sufficient merit that long-term trials of the proposed systems should be established in forests where they appear to be appropriate. Sometimes this will simply repeat experiences that foresters have already had, but sometimes it will probably lead to improvement in forest practices.

Much of the concerned public appears determined that New Forestry systems be tried. Some people feel that they should be applied everywhere. The most effective course of action in many cases would therefore seem to be to develop partnerships between foresters and environmental groups to establish a network of well-monitored operational trials of these systems. Such an approach has been implemented very successfully in the state of Victoria in Australia, where all parties agreed to accept the results of scientific studies of different silvicultural systems as the basis for deciding arguments about how certain types of forest should be harvested. This system of trials would be expensive to establish and monitor, and the public must be informed about their investment in this experiment. But such trials are probably less costly than continued polarization between environmentalists and foresters, and less of an economic and social threat than the risk that large areas of the working forest will be taken out of production. The proposed 'model forests' of Canada will provide for such experimentation and demonstration.

It seems premature to impose New Forestry widely until results are obtained from these trials. This in no way suggests that improvement in current forest practices should not be implemented immediately; rather it suggests that these improvements will not necessarily conform to the New Forestry paradigm, although some of them will. Because of the long period required to demonstrate the pros and cons of New Forestry, the probable consequences should be explored in the interim by using ecosystem management computer simulation models (see Chapter 15).

Summary and Conclusions

Pressure from wilderness advocacy groups for the reservation of old-growth forests and wilderness areas in the western United States and Canada has grown rapidly over the past decade. In Oregon and Washington, large areas of public forests may be removed from the working forest (the area of forest dedicated to management for multiple resource values including timber production) and assigned to wilderness or endangered-species-protection forests. The extent of these reserves and the prospect that the size of the working forest may continue to change in the future as a result of such pressure has significant implications for other social values from the forest. It is rendering the rational planning of forest management very difficult, and in some cases is reducing the willingness of forest companies to make long-term investments in forest improvement. Reserves on the same scale have not yet occurred in British Columbia, but there is growing pressure from the environmental movement to achieve them.

Faced with the prospect of substantial land withdrawals, New Forestry has been presented as a way of retaining many old-growth values while at the same time harvesting a significant proportion of the timber values. Rather than setting aside additional large areas of old growth in no-management reserves, New Forestry advocates propose that most managed forests should be managed under New Forestry regimes. It is suggested that these would conserve wildlife values that are said to be threatened, would maintain or increase biodiversity, and would protect the ecosystem's ability to withstand

stress and recover from disturbance – its resilience.

Against these potential benefits, many foresters point out that practical experience in numerous forest types suggests that New Forestry systems of stand-level management would not work. They would be impractical or unsafe, and would result in substantial yield and economic losses for little demonstrated benefit. In some cases, New Forestry systems may make the visual appearance of harvested areas even less acceptable than conventional harvesting and silvicultural systems.

Applied with intelligence and on the basis of a knowledge of local ecosystem and wildlife ecology, New Forestry systems may indeed help to overcome some of the problems of conventional forest harvesting in some types of forest, both at the stand and the regional landscape level. Many foresters appear to be increasingly willing to try to build some of these concepts into their management, especially with respect to conserving wildlife values. However, there is a great danger that the useful ideas of New Forestry will be lost if there are attempts to impose the concepts uniformly over a wide range of forest ecosystems. The ideas should be applied only to ecosystems where they are appropriate and will work.

If forests in western North America had been managed over the past two or three decades with a much greater sensitivity to local variations in site ecology, to a broad spectrum of wildlife values, and to public concerns about aesthetics, the New Forestry movement would probably not have arisen. Its development at this time reflects where we are in the evolution of forestry towards the social forestry phase. There are some useful ideas in New Forestry, and they should be applied in forests where they are relevant. However, the almost religious fervour that some environmentalists bring to their mission to have New Forestry applied universally must be tempered by the ecological reality that forest ecosystems vary enormously both geographically and over time. Attempts to force these ideas where they are not appropriate may discredit them where they are.

CHAPTER 12

Forestry and Climate Change

Introduction

Thinking about my childhood years in England evokes memories of summer vacations when it seemed to be raining all the time, and others when one repeatedly faced the risk of sunburn. Similarly, I recall some childhood Christmases as white, while others were decidedly green, gray, and wet!

The idea that weather varies from year to year is news to few teenagers. By the time they become adults they may also have noted that it varies somewhat from decade to decade. Octogenarians may hardly bother with the weather because they have seen it all: good years and bad years, good decades and bad decades (whatever good and bad mean).

Year-to-year and decade-to-decade fluctuations in weather have their origins in a variety of phenomena, from variations in sunspot activity to changes in the circulation patterns of the great oceans that cause El Niño. This climatic phenomenon, which is associated with torrential rain off the west coast of South America, drought and heat in Australia and Indonesia, and the warming of the equatorial eastern Pacific Ocean off the coast of Peru, is due to a slackening of winds in equatorial regions.

Although not precisely predictable, these climatic variations are part of the natural variability that has occurred in the past and should be expected to occur again in the future. Collectively, they define the climate of an area. They are the cause of floods and droughts, of bumper food crops and famine, and of Christmases and summer vacations that will never be forgotten.

When we talk about climate change, we are not dealing with these sometimes almost random, sometimes predictable fluctuations of weather around a relatively unchanging long-term average (the regional climate). Such averages have made places like Hawaii, the Mediterranean, and Australia into holiday meccas. These locations can have disappointing weather occasionally, but on average they are climatically safe vacation destinations. In contrast, the climate change that has been reported so frequently in the media over the past five years is a continuing directional deviation from the long-term (thirty-year) average weather conditions. It is the type of change that in the far distant past, tens of thousands of years ago, led to the onset of a new ice age (a cooling trend) or, alternatively, led to the progressive melting of ice caps, rising of the sea, shrinking of the world's forests, and expansion of deserts as an ice age gave way to a warmer interglacial period (a warming trend). Such major directional change in climate is known to have occurred periodically over the past million years, but always over very long time scales. Ice ages have come and gone in cycles of hundreds of thousands of years.

Until now, such global changes have had relatively little impact on human cultural evolution, which has occurred mainly during the past ten to twelve thousand years, after the end of the last ice age.[23] So why is there all this excitement about global climate change, and what does it have to do with forestry? That is what this chapter is all about.

Climate Change in the Past

Many factors affect the temperature of the earth's atmosphere, and thus the temperatures experienced at the earth's surface, where we live. The distance from the earth to the sun (a function of the earth's orbit), the angle of the earth to the sun (which determines the geographical distribution of solar energy received by the earth and gives rise to the different seasons), and the relative strength of the sun all affect the amount of solar energy that the earth receives. All are known to have varied over the life of our planet. However, these factors do not on their own define the earth's atmospheric temperature and global climate. Our climate is also determined by the proportion of the solar energy that is absorbed by the earth and atmosphere.

Three to four billion years ago, when our earth was very young, the sun is thought to have emitted 25 to 30 per cent less energy than today. However, climates at that time are believed to have been 10° to 15°C warmer than at present, and the evidence suggests that these temperatures persisted, give or take a little, until about a hundred million years ago (quite recently in the life of the earth), in spite of the strengthening of the sun. This maintenance of an atmospheric temperature regime in the range suitable for the evolution of life for such a long period is advanced as one of the explanations of why life evolved on earth. The stability of the atmospheric temperature in the face of changes in the intensity of the sun's energy emissions is believed to be a function of the changing chemistry of the atmosphere.

Commencing about a hundred million years ago, the earth started to cool, and this trend culminated in the onset of a series of ice ages or glacial periods interspersed with warmer periods called interglacials. The evidence suggests that initially the glacial/interglacial cycle lasted about 40,000 years, but starting about 800,000 years ago this frequency changed to about 100,000 years: about 80,000 to 90,000 years of cooling and glacial ice accumulation followed by a rapid warming and melting of the ice, and 10,000 to 20,000 years of interglacial conditions with average global temperatures about 5° warmer than at the height of the glacial period. The present interglacial period is about 10,000 years old, and this has led to the suggestion that, before the greenhouse effect that is causing so much concern, we were headed for the next ice age. However, if the past pattern is repeated, the slow cooling would have taken tens of thousands of years; glaciers and ice sheets take a long time to build up in thickness and spread out over the landscape (Figure 12.1).

There is still much debate and uncertainty about the causes of the glacial/interglacial alternation. However, there is evidence that the earth's tilt on its axis varies cyclically with a period of about 40,000

---

23 Historians and anthropologists can argue that the 'little ice age' from AD 1350 to 1870 had a major impact on the development of culture, technology, and human population growth. Ecologically, the advance and subsequent retreat of glaciers during this period certainly had dramatic effects locally. However, these were not on the same scale as a full glacial period.

years, while the earth's orbit around the sun varies with a period between 100,000 and 400,000 years. The time of year when the earth is closest to the sun varies with a period of about 20,000 years. These astronomical events are believed to be the major mechanisms that determine the timing of the glacial/interglacial events, but they are aided and abetted by 'internal' mechanisms, such as alterations in the circulation of cold and warm oceanic waters, and by variations in the chemistry of the earth's atmosphere. The details of the variations are too complex to explore here, but if you are interested, you can refer to some of the books listed in the bibliography.

Greenhouse Gases

Past climate change has clearly been related to variations in the amount of solar energy received by the earth, in the proportion of energy that is retained, and in the temperature and global circulation of

ocean water. Of particular interest at present is the variation in atmospheric chemistry over time and its relationship to the proportion of energy that is trapped, thus heating the atmosphere: the so-called *greenhouse effect.* This is of interest because human activity is changing atmospheric chemistry at an apparently unprecedented rate.

Like the glass in a greenhouse, certain gases in our atmosphere ('greenhouse gases') have the unique property of being transparent to certain wavelengths of solar radiation – they do not absorb the energy of this radiation. They are, however, opaque to other wavelengths and absorb their energy, thus heating the atmosphere. Like glass, these gases are transparent to the visible (light) wavelengths but absorb the energy of infrared (radiant heat) wavelengths.[24] In common with all objects whose temperature is above absolute zero, or -273°C, the sun emits radiant energy in the form of electromagnetic

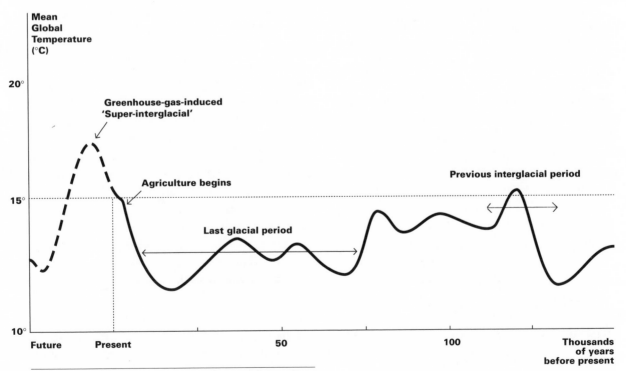

Figure 12.1 Mean global temperatures for the past 160,000 years, and predictions about what might happen in the future (based on data in Barnola et al. 1987).

waves. These vary in wavelength from very long (many metres) radio and TV waves, to infrared waves, to visible light, to very short-wavelength ultraviolet rays, x-rays, gamma rays, and cosmic rays. Visible light passes through the atmosphere almost undiminished except by clouds and aerosols, although the shorter-wavelength blue light tends to be scattered more than the longer red wavelengths, giving rise to blue skies and red sunsets.

Of the infrared-absorbing gases that are subject to significant change, carbon dioxide (CO_2) is the most important. Water vapour is the most important absorber of infrared radiation, but it is assumed that this is not increasing in the atmosphere. Methane (CH_4), a gas produced by biological decay processes under anaerobic (low-oxygen) conditions, is about twenty times more effective at trapping infrared energy than CO_2, but because it is present at much lower concentrations than CO_2, it presently accounts for only about 25 per cent as much greenhouse effect as CO_2. Chlorofluorocarbons (CFCs: synthetic chemicals used as spray can propellants, as refrigerants, and, until recently, in the manufacture of plastic and polystyrene foams), oxides of nitrogen (from automobile exhausts, industrial air pollution, agricultural activities, and natural soil processes), and very small amounts of some other gases also contribute to the greenhouse effect. In total, CO_2 is believed to account for about half of the greenhouse gas activity. Water vapour and clouds make a major contribution to the trapping of solar energy and warming of the atmosphere, although heavy, low-altitude cloud cover can cause cooling by reflecting a lot of solar radiation.

The main greenhouse effect occurs not because the atmosphere absorbs some of the energy of incoming solar radiation but because the long-wavelength radiation emitted by the earth itself is trapped. Short-wavelength visible radiation passes

through the atmosphere and warms the objects that it falls on, and is absorbed by, on the surface of the earth. Absorption of this energy raises the temperature of these objects, which then re-emit much of the energy as long-wavelength infrared. Without an atmosphere, much of this reradiation would simply go back into space, but the clouds, water vapour, and greenhouse gases of the atmosphere absorb most of it and return it to the earth's surface. This is illustrated in Figure 12.2.

How Have Greenhouse Gases Changed over the Past 160,000 Years and the Past 160 Years?

Glaciers form when snow falls in winter and does not melt completely the following summer. As the accumulating snow gets deeper, it is compressed by its own weight and eventually forms ice. The air in spaces between the snow flakes is trapped as bubbles in the ice. By drilling very deep into the thick ice sheet of Antarctica, very ancient ice cores can be obtained and the chemical content of the gas in these bubbles measured. This gives us a historical record of the chemical composition of the atmosphere at the time when the snow that turned into the ice fell. Subtle variations in snow chemistry have been shown to be a good indicator of the air temperature when the snow fell, so that these ice cores give a historical record of both atmospheric temperature and atmospheric gaseous concentrations.

Figure 12.3 shows a 160,000-year record of atmospheric CO_2 and temperature obtained from such ice cores. Clearly, there is a very close correlation between these two parameters. As atmospheric CO_2 has declined, so has atmospheric temperature. CO_2 concentrations at the height of the last interglacial period were similar to those before the start of the Industrial Revolution: about 280 parts per million. They declined over the next 100,000 years to about 190 parts per million at the peak of the last glacial period, about the same level as that recorded for the previous glacial maximum 160,000 years ago. Local temperatures in Antarctica were about 10°C lower at these glacial extremes (20,000 and 150,000 years

---

24 The absorption of ultraviolet rays by ozone in the stratosphere is not considered a greenhouse gas effect in the true sense. It heats the stratosphere while the greenhouse effect cools the stratosphere.

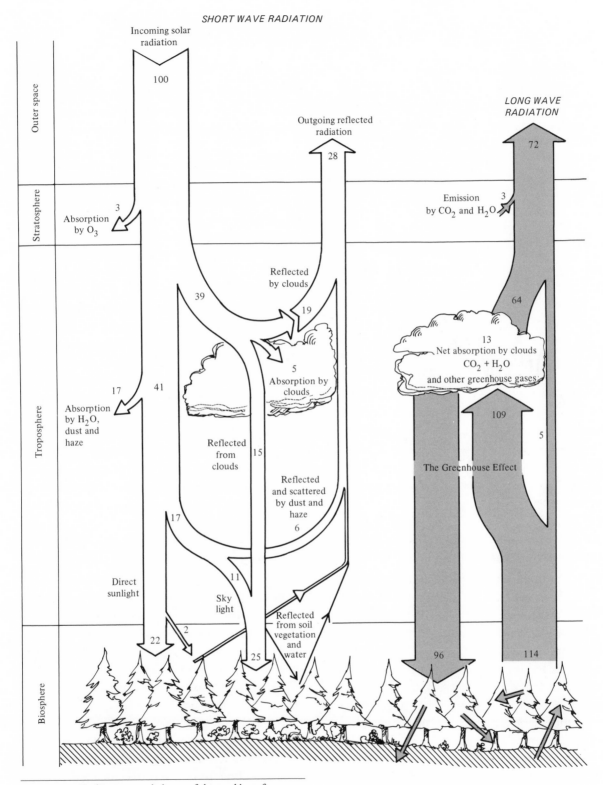

SHORT WAVE RADIATION

LONG WAVE RADIATION

Figure 12.2 Radiant energy balance of the earth's surface. The numbers show the relative magnitude of different radiant transfers, with incoming short-wave radiation equal to 100 (modified from Kimmins 1987, based on Schneider and Bennett 1975).

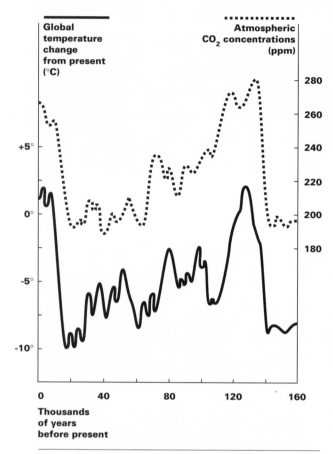

Figure 12.3 Record of CO_2 and temperature over 160,000 years. Note that in 1989, CO_2 concentrations were 350 ppm (modified from Barnola et al. 1987).

ago) than in the interglacial periods. Methane concentrations have been found to show a similar pattern of variation.

In marked contrast to this past record of slowly changing atmospheric CO_2 and methane concentrations, the Industrial Revolution, which started at the beginning of the last century, or roughly 160 years ago, initiated a period of dramatic increase in the atmospheric concentrations of greenhouse gases. Interestingly, this coincides roughly with the end of the 'little ice age.' CO_2 concentrations had increased to about 350 parts per million by 1989, an increase of about 25 per cent from pre-industrial levels. Methane has increased by almost 100 per cent. There are predictions that if current trends of CO_2 release into the atmosphere continue, CO_2

levels will double sometime in the middle of the next century. It is quite possible that the other greenhouse gases will increase even more.

Why Has the Concentration of Greenhouse Gases Increased?

It appears that the major increases in atmospheric CO_2 over the past 160 years are the result of burning fossil fuels (coal, oil, natural gas); the deforestation of a significant portion of the world's previously forested land (largely in the tropics); and the impact of agriculture on soil organic matter.

The release of carbon from the burning of fossil fuels is undoubtedly the major problem, and one that is increasing rapidly. Figure 12.4 shows the history of this release since 1950. In spite of short periods when the rate of increase in release slowed down (because of periodic economic recessions and the Arab oil embargo of the 1970s), and the temporary decline in release during the world economic recession of the early 1980s, the overall trend is a steady increase in the release of CO_2. Figure 12.5 shows recent changes in atmospheric CO_2 levels.

Deforestation caused by changing land use is thought to have contributed about 20 per cent of the CO_2 released over the past few decades. This figure, which is remarkably high considering the magnitude of the fossil fuel release, reflects the rapid rate at which tropical and subtropical forests are being stripped of trees and either deliberately converted into agricultural ecosystems or, through misuse and neglect, into unproductive grass, shrub, or 'scrub' forest vegetation types. Deforestation has also occurred extensively in northern temperate and boreal forests, especially in the last century, when there was a great clearing of forest for agricultural land. However, some of this area has reverted or is in the process of reverting to forest because the soils, the climate, or both proved to be marginal for economic agriculture, and because many of these northern ecosystems are able to recover from deforestation much faster than many of their tropical counterparts.

Exploitive forestry has also been a net contributor

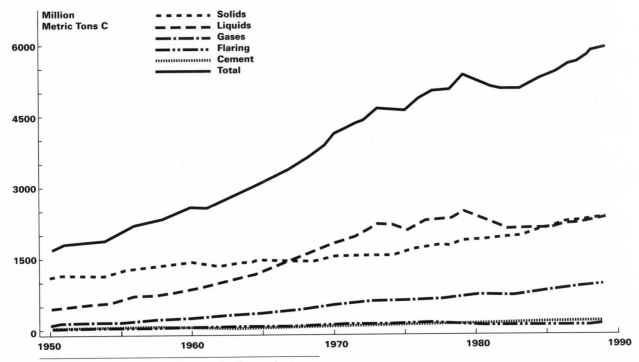

Figure 12.4 Recent patterns of release of carbon to the atmosphere caused by fossil-fuel consumption (from Marland and Boden 1991).

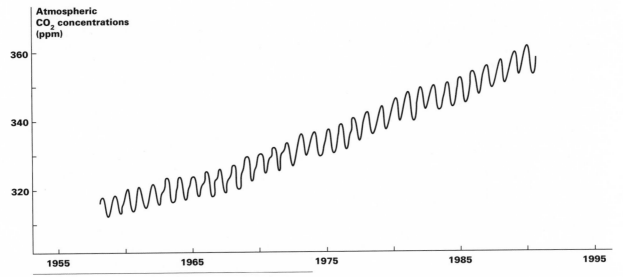

Figure 12.5 Changes in atmospheric CO_2 concentrations at the top of Mauna Loa, Hawaii, from 1958 to 1991. The annual variation results from the winter/summer variations in photosynthesis in northern hemisphere ecosystems, and seasonal variations in CO_2 release from fossil fuels. The overall upward trend is obvious (redrawn from Keeling and Wharf 1992).

of carbon to the atmosphere where soil damage or slow reforestation has resulted in very slow recovery of the biomass of trees and the organic forest floor. Throughout the tropics, the mass of carbon in unmanaged second-growth forests appears to be significantly less than in the original primary forest. However, as in temperate and boreal forests, the rate of net tree growth in well-managed tropical forests is much higher than in unmanaged tropical old-growth. When conducted on a sound ecological foundation for the production of long-lived timber products, silviculture is therefore not a net contributor to atmospheric CO_2. On the contrary, it has the potential to remove significant amounts of carbon from the atmosphere.

Much of the world's agricultural land has been managed in a way that has failed to maintain levels of soil humus. The prairie soils of Canada and the United States are reported to have lost up to 50 per cent of the carbon they contained only a century ago, and wind and water have stripped the carbon-rich surface soil from vast areas of inappropriately managed agricultural and range land around the world. Vast areas of the world's bogs and wetlands, which had been accumulating carbon in the form of peat or other types of organic deposits since the last glacial period or before, have been drained over the past two centuries. Much of the accumulated carbon has been released back into the atmosphere. The contribution of this type of soil degradation to atmospheric CO_2 has not been well documented, but it must be considerable. Deforestation, farming, and loss of peat from drained swamp areas are thought to have contributed about 36 per cent of the human-caused CO_2 release to the atmosphere since 1850.

A final but relatively much smaller source of CO_2 release is the manufacture of cement for making concrete. Cement is made with lime, an oxide of calcium (CaO). Lime is made by roasting limestone (generally using fossil fuels), which is a carbonate of calcium ($Ca(CO_3)_2$). Limestone was formed in oceans and shallow lakes where atmospheric CO_2 was dissolved in the water and combined with dissolved calcium either by simple chemical reactions or through biological action on the part of aquatic organisms that form calcium shells. The resulting calcium carbonate became deposited on the floor of the lake or ocean and ultimately became limestone. Cement production thus reverses a process that has slowly but steadily removed CO_2 from the atmosphere over millions of years, just as the burning of fossil fuels releases carbon taken out of the atmosphere by plants over millions of years. Cement production can be expected to increase as the urbanization of the world's rapidly growing population increases, as roads are paved, and as people aspire to live in buildings made of brick or concrete. If controls on other sources of greenhouse gas emissions are applied, the production of cement may become one of the significant sources of CO_2 release.

In all these cases, human activity is returning to the atmosphere the CO_2 that nature's mechanisms have removed and put into long-term storage. The earth's vegetation and major bodies of water have acted as a regulator of CO_2 concentrations in the atmosphere, increasing the rate of CO_2 removal as atmospheric CO_2 concentrations increased, and decreasing the rate as CO_2 concentrations declined. The result until the early 1800s was a remarkable century-to-century stability in atmospheric CO_2 levels. True, CO_2 concentrations have varied from 190 to 280 parts per million as glacial periods have been replaced by interglacials, but the very slow change from interglacial back to glacial is believed to have resulted in part from this stabilizing feedback mechanism. However, these global-stability mechanisms have an upper limit on their ability to maintain fairly constant levels of atmospheric CO_2. This limit is thought to be determined by the long time required for oceanic stirring.

Since the early 1800s, we have been adding CO_2 to the atmosphere faster than this feedback mechanism can remove it. It has been estimated that about 75 per cent of the fossil-fuel carbon (or 50 per cent of all the carbon released by burning fossil fuels, making cement, and land-use changes) released since 1850 is still up in the atmosphere. We have simply exceeded the earth's ability to regulate the CO_2 component of the atmosphere's greenhouse mechanism. In addition, we have increased the concentrations of synthetic and other natural greenhouse gases whose natural mechanisms of removal are even slower. Figure 12.6 summarizes the global mechanisms of atmospheric CO_2 regulation.

What Will Increased Greenhouse Gases Do to the World Climate?

If current trends in fossil fuel use, deforestation, and other contributors of CO_2 continue, the atmospheric concentration of this gas is expected to double sometime in the next century. Together with expected increases in other greenhouse gases, this may result in an average increase in world temperatures of between 1.5° and 4.5°C.[25] This may not sound like a lot, but the increases at higher latitudes are expected to be up to 10°C greater than at lower lati-

tudes, with little or no change at the equator. Some areas might become cooler because of increased cloud cover, changes in the direction of cold ocean currents, and changes in the extent and location of pack ice in polar oceans, but this is not generally considered to be likely. Some areas are expected to get wetter, because as the air gets warmer, more water will evaporate from the oceans. This will result in more clouds in some areas. Many areas are expected to get drier, in terms of either precipitation or the effectiveness of this precipitation for plant growth. The higher air temperatures will increase water loss from plants and the soil, so that plants may have reduced access to water even if rainfall goes up.

A change in average global climatic conditions is one predicted effect of the current alteration of atmospheric chemistry. Increase in climatic variability and unseasonable weather is another and perhaps

---

25 It should be noted that the global mean annual temperature has varied by less than 1.5°C over the past one thousand years.

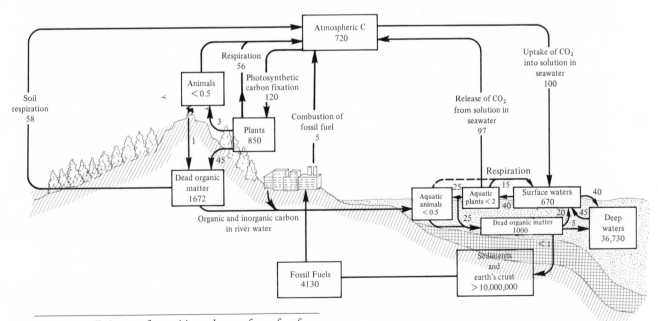

Figure 12.6 Estimates of quantities and rates of transfer of carbon in the biosphere. Units are billions (10^9) of metric tons of carbon. Transfer rates are expressed on an annual basis (modified from Bolin et al. 1979; Clark et al. 1982; from J.P. Kimmins 1987, used with the permission of Macmillan).

more ecologically significant consequence. This is not a new suggestion. In the past both climatologists and ecologists have worried that we have just come through a period of relative climatic uniformity, and that we can expect the future to be more variable, regardless of changes in average conditions. Hotter summers, it was claimed, may be followed by cooler, wetter summers. Milder winters may be interspersed with very cold periods, damaging the buds of trees and other plants. Unusually snowy winters could be followed by several years of little or no snow. Severe storms may increase in frequency. These predictions must be considered very speculative, however, because recent analyses by climatologists using global climate computer simulation models have not provided any evidence to support them. Nevertheless, their ecological significance makes it too early to dismiss them.

Present-Day Climate

Do We Have Good Evidence that the Climate Is Actually Changing?

Because of the past variability in weather, some scientists claim that we do not yet have unequivocal evidence of climate change. They point out that weather has always been changing, and claim that the recent 'abnormally' warm years are just an anomaly, to be followed soon by a cooler period and no long-term change in the average climate.

While it may be true that the available data do not yet provide statistically convincing evidence that directional climate change due to the greenhouse effect has begun, the record speaks for itself. Six of the ten warmest years in the past century were in the last decade: 1981, 1983, 1987, 1988, and 1989, with 1990 the warmest year on record. There was a gradual warming from 1900 to about 1940 (1938, 1941, and 1944 all appear in the ten hottest years), followed by a slight cooling until 1965. Since then the trend in atmospheric temperature has been strongly upward.

It is true that we will probably need another two decades of measurements before we can say with a high degree of statistical confidence that the predictions of climatic warming are correct. However, we do know that mechanisms capable of causing climatic warming – fossil-fuel consumption, deforestation, soil degradation, and cement production – are in place and increasing. There is still a lot of uncertainty about many details of the control of the world's climate, particularly concerning cloud formation, changes in ocean currents, the effect of changing ocean temperatures on the uptake or release of CO_2, and the long-term effects of elevated CO_2 levels on carbon storage in the world's forests. However, we do have enough knowledge and evidence to conclude that we are facing a potential problem of unprecedented magnitude. It is time to scrutinize all human endeavours, including forestry, to ascertain whether they are contributing to the greenhouse problem and whether they can be used as part of the solution.

How Are Future Climates Predicted?

Very large and complex computer models called Global Circulation Models (GCMs) have been developed by scientists who study the atmosphere. A major feature of the five or so GCMs currently available is the considerable agreement in their predictions about changes in global average temperature. They disagree considerably about the effects on temperature and precipitation on a smaller scale, namely, the conditions in any given locality or region. We simply still cannot make predictions that all scientists agree with about the climate of a particular area fifty years from now. Nevertheless, there is virtually unanimous agreement that there will be climatic warming (estimates range from a change of 1.5°C to nearly 5°C in mean global temperature), that the warming will be greater near the poles than near the equator, and that winters will warm up much more than summers.

The present GCMs have many shortcomings, and several new ones, or improvements to existing ones, are being developed. In spite of difficulties in using them, they provide the only available, if somewhat 'dirty,' climatic crystal balls available. And as the well-known American climatologist Stephen Schneider said, 'when do we stop polishing the dirty crystal ball and start making decisions about the images revealed inside?' GCMs are being improved, and they need to be improved before we can place great confidence in their predictions. But if what they are telling us is even half right, we have a major global problem on our hands and it requires urgent attention.

What Effects Might the Predicted Climate Change Have on the World's Forests?

Predictions from GCMs have several implications: (1) for agriculture, which would be improved in some cold northern areas but impaired at many hot, dry latitudes; (2) for sea level – a significant percentage of the world's population lives in areas that would be flooded by the anticipated rise in sea levels due to the thermal expansion of sea water as it warms. This would occur relatively quickly, whereas sea level changes due to the melting of polar ice caps would take hundreds or thousands of years; (3) for biotic diversity – many species may perish because they may not be able to adapt or move as rapidly as the changing climate alters the geographical location of their ranges; (4) for forestry; and (5) for a variety of other human and natural phenomena. The following discussion is limited to forests.

Geographic Distribution of Forests

We know that life on earth will continue in spite of climate change. The world is thought to have been 15°C warmer and atmospheric CO_2 levels much higher than at present during the Age of Dinosaurs, 65 to 200 million years ago. Life at that time was prolific and productive, and the present-day tropics are much hotter than present-day temperate and boreal latitudes. Clearly, higher temperatures per se are not a problem for forests as a vegetation type. So what is the problem? It is the *rate* of change of

temperature conditions.

Recent predictions suggest that the global temperature increase as a result of the greenhouse effect will average about 0.3°C per decade, or 3°C per century. It has been suggested that as much climate change could occur over the next century as in the past ten thousand years. In comparison, the rapid increase in temperature at the end of the last ice age was about 1°C per thousand years. At that rate of change, many plant and animal species were apparently able to keep up with the shifts in major climatic belts across the map of the world. It seems, however, that not all species were able to move at this rate. Some species are apparently still extending their range northward in the wake of the last glaciation.

A rate of temperature change thirty to a hundred times (depending on latitude) faster than the historical rate will undoubtedly threaten the survival of many species. But this is not the only problem. Where their migration pathway is now interrupted by agricultural, urban, or simply deforested areas, many animals and plants will probably not be able to move their ranges even if they can keep up with the migration of particular climatic areas. In some cases, northerly migrations of species may be prevented by major changes in topography or geology. Plant species adapted to productive low-elevation valley sites or fertile southern soils may not be able to grow, or may not be nearly so productive, when moved up onto steep, thin-soiled mountain slopes or north to areas of acidic, nutrient-poor bedrock.

The problems of the geographic shift in the distribution of species will tend to be more severe in relatively flat areas such as central Canada than in mountainous areas such as western Canada. A 5°C increase in average annual temperature could require species migrations of up to five hundred kilometres north in such flat areas, whereas in mountainous territory the species might have to move only five hundred metres up in elevation.

Species making extensive northerly shifts in location will experience different seasonal variations in daylength, which organisms use as a means of predicting the change in the seasons. Even if species are able to migrate fast enough to keep up with the migrating climatic belts, they will have to develop a new 'calendar': a new set of physiological responses to seasonal changes in environmental conditions to ensure that their metabolism, behaviour, and other aspects of their life cycle are synchronized with their environment.

Change in the Productivity of Forests

If the expected climate change moderates some factor that is limiting forest growth, such as low temperatures or soil moisture deficiencies, forests may grow better. On the other hand, if an already warm climate were to become hotter and drier, forests would generally grow more poorly and in some cases might be replaced by grassland; closed forest might become savannah forest. It is also thought that the increased concentration of CO_2 in the air may increase the rate of photosynthesis unless other factors such as soil nutrients are in short supply, which they often are. Thus, forest productivity could either increase or decrease depending on present climatic and soil conditions and on the anticipated climate change. In some cases there could be an initial decrease in forest growth followed by an increase as the present tree species are negatively affected but are then replaced by species adapted to the new climatic regime.

Significant climate change will not always imply a change in species. The considerable genetic variability within most forest plant communities will enable many species in these communities to adapt to some degree of climate change. Poorly adapted genetic types would be killed or would lose out in competition with better-adapted types. However, some long-lived tree species that do not produce seed until they are several decades old may not be able to adapt fast enough to avoid the negative aspects of climate change. While commercial species can be moved by planting, non-commercial forest species with a limited ability to adapt could

be lost. In cases where key species did not move fast enough, naturally or with human assistance, ecosystem productivity might be reduced.

Changes in Soils

As noted in Chapter 3, the character of soils reflects both the climate and the climatically determined vegetation. Soils will change as climatic belts move. Just how fast this will occur is not known, but it is known that soils can change dramatically and rapidly in response to vegetation change. Consequently, climatically driven soil change may not be a problem with respect to future ecosystem productivity as long as there is an adequate supply of soil-forming materials on the site.

The major concern with respect to soils may be the movement of a climatic belt from an area of nutritionally rich soil materials to one of nutritionally poor materials. This would occur in areas of central Canada and some parts of eastern Canada where mainly deciduous forests growing on very fertile soils derived from limestone and other sedimentary materials would be forced north by climate change onto the thin-soiled, infertile areas of the Canadian Shield.

The change in ecosystem processes, such as decomposition and nutrient cycling, that would accompany climatically driven soil change has important implications for ecosystem productivity, and the implications of climate change for soils should certainly be considered by foresters.

Changes in soil temperature will have implications for forest management independent of their effects on soil processes. Forest harvesting on wet sites in northern areas is often done in winter when the soil is frozen, in order to protect the soil and permit access to such sites by harvesting equipment. The period when such sites can be harvested would be reduced if winters in these northern areas were to become warmer, as they are expected to. Harvesting of timber from these forests would become more difficult and increase the risk of physical damage to the soil.

Change in Diseases, Insects, and Fire

Like humans, plants under stress are more susceptible to diseases and parasites. Where climate change increases stresses caused by temperature, moisture, or nutrition, it is expected that there will be increased damage to forests by these pathogenic agents. Insects are also more of a problem when trees are stressed. For example, changes in plant physiology in response to summer drought may reduce a tree's chemical defenses against insects that attack tree stems (bark beetles, for example) and may render its foliage more nutritious to leaf-eating insects.

If climate change brings hotter, drier summer conditions to temperate and boreal forest areas, forest fires will undoubtedly become more frequent and severe. In some areas, the changing risk of forest fires may be more serious than all the other risks combined. Fire can also add more CO_2 to the atmosphere than the other consequences of climate change.

Changes in Weather-Related Damage to Plants

Of all the ways in which the weather can cause damage to plants, variation in temperature conditions is probably the most important. Most people in North America are aware of how unseasonable frosts in Florida can affect the availability of oranges and other fruit. They are generally less aware of the damage that can be caused to forest trees by frosts during the growing season and by unseasonably warm periods in the winter.

Late spring or very early fall frosts can damage tree buds, but a warm snap in the middle of winter followed by a return to low temperatures can be just as damaging. If trees have already been subjected to sufficient chilling in the early winter, which 'tells' the trees that they have experienced winter and that it is time to prepare for active growth, their buds may start to lose their resistance to low-temperature damage if temperatures start to rise. The buds begin to expand, only to be caught unprepared if there is a return of low temperatures late in the winter. This may have little negative

effect on total tree growth of evergreen trees because this type of damage does not usually affect the foliage. If the uppermost buds are killed, however, the tree may fail to grow in height the year after the damage, and may produce multiple new 'leaders' (the top of the stem) the following year. This can result in forked and multiple stems, which can render the tree useless for timber or greatly reduce its economic value. They can also reduce the tree's ability to compete with individuals of other tree species that may not have been damaged.

Frost damage to buds may also prevent trees from producing seeds, making it more difficult for a forest to regenerate naturally and reducing the supply of seeds that foresters need to grow seedlings that will be used to replant harvested forests.

Another type of damage can occur if winters become warmer. As noted above, many tree species require a period of exposure to low temperatures ('winter chilling') before their buds will open in the spring. This requirement has apparently evolved to avoid the damage caused to buds by spring frosts. However, if a tree does not get enough chilling to cause it to break bud in the spring, the effect on its growth may not be much different than if the buds were killed by frost: neither new shoot elongation nor flower and seed production can occur. Obviously, the warmer winters predicted to accompany climate change pose as big a threat to plant species with strict chilling requirements as the risk of increased frost damage to buds noted above.

Change in Water Yield and Fish Habitat

Depending on how the climate changes, many rivers in northern and temperate areas could have significantly reduced summer flow rates and increased summer temperatures. If mountain snowpacks were reduced because of less snow or shorter, warmer winters, summer fish habitat and water supplies could be adversely affected. However, in some high mountain areas or polar regions snowpack might increase; even with higher global temperatures, the increased winter precipitation predicted for some areas would still fall as snow at the highest elevations, or in polar areas, resulting in deeper snowpacks.

If climate change resulted in more severe rainstorms in the late fall, when there is already snowpack in the mountains, there could be much more extensive fall flooding. Such 'rain-on-snow' hydrological events can damage fish habitats because of streambank erosion. The exceptionally heavy fall rains on top of a significant snowpack and the ensuing floods in the coastal mountains of British Columbia and Washington in November 1990 are a good example of what could happen more frequently in a future with significant climate change.

Changes in Wildlife

The major effects of the predicted climate change on wildlife would probably be a consequence of alterations in forest vegetation induced by such change. Most terrestrial animals are a lot more mobile than most plant species, and many animal species would be able to change their geographical location with the change in the spatial distribution of the vegetation on which they depend.

To the extent that the quality and availability of their habitat is improved or degraded, wildlife species would benefit or suffer from climate change. However, animals could also experience the more direct effects of climate change, such as unseasonable extremes in temperatures, changes in the length of the plant and insect growing season, changes in snowpack, freezing of rivers and lakes, and so on.

Increased summer drought would probably increase the negative effects of herbs and shrubs on the growth of trees because of increased competition for soil water. The success of reforestation on harvested areas or areas denuded by natural disturbance would be reduced, and the return of the forest would be slowed. This would benefit wildlife species that are dependent on the early seral stages of forest development.

Obviously, the effect of climate change on

wildlife will be very animal species-specific and forest type-specific, and will depend on exactly how the climate changes. We are not yet in a position to provide believable answers to many wildlife-related climate change questions.

Is Forest Management Part of the Problem or Part of the Solution?

The Carbon Balance of Forests

Forests remove CO_2 from the atmosphere and store it in roots, stems, branches, and leaves. Some of these biomass components do not live long and become litterfall, as do the trees that die. Where conditions favour decomposition processes, the carbon in the litter and dead trees is released back to the atmosphere fairly quickly. For example, maple leaves may decompose almost completely in one year, with little storage of carbon in the soil. The stem of an alder tree may last only a decade after it has fallen to the ground. In contrast, the stem of a large-diameter western red cedar on northern Vancouver Island may still be only partly decomposed a thousand years after the tree died.

Where decomposition is slow, forests can become a long-term storehouse of atmospheric carbon. However, unless the forest is growing in a swamp or in an excessively humid climate, there appears to be a maximum amount of carbon that is stored in a particular type of forest, after which a balance is established between uptake by photosynthesis and release by decomposition and periodic disturbance. Thus, in most cases there is little truth to the often-made statement that an untouched tropical rain forest or other old-growth forests constitute the 'lungs of the earth.' These forests generally do not continuously release oxygen by continuously removing atmospheric CO_2. In fact, because of rapid decomposition in most tropical rain forests, oxygen consumption by the decomposition of litter and dead trees will roughly match the photosynthetic production of oxygen. It is true that some of the carbon released by decomposition in the tropics is in the form of methane gas, whose production by termites and other soil animals does not absorb oxygen. However, this methane will eventually be oxidized in the atmosphere, so that, overall, most tropical forests are probably in carbon and oxygen balance. Also, methane is more effective as a greenhouse gas than CO_2, so methane production by forests is probably not a good thing. Some very nutrient-poor tropical forests do store carbon slowly in the development of deep peat deposits, as in eastern Sumatra and in the Rio Negro region of northwestern Brazil. This constitutes a net production of oxygen, but it occurs only in some areas, and in most cases the process is so slow that its current oxygen release and carbon storage contributions are insignificant.

Very old forests often exhibit a stagnation of nutrient cycles and reduced growth, and therefore a reduced rate of storage of additional carbon. Most forests never reach this condition because disturbance by fire, wind, insects, disease, or human activity periodically releases some or all of the stored carbon back to the atmosphere and initiates a new period of carbon storage. The release can occur rapidly (by fire) or more slowly (by decomposition of the forest floor and slash after disturbance). Whether or not a particular forest is storing or releasing carbon will depend on where it is in this disturbance/recovery cycle. Young forests almost always remove CO_2 from the air more actively than old forests, but they often have less total carbon stored because of losses during the previous disturbance. An evaluation of any forest's long-term contribution to the greenhouse problem must obviously be done over periods long enough to consider several cycles of disturbance and regrowth.

Effect of Harvesting on Carbon Storage in Forests

Because old-growth forests often have a larger total carbon store (soil + forest floor + living trees + snags + understorey) than younger managed forests, there is potentially a greater release of carbon during and after the harvesting of old-growth forests than when younger forests are harvested. If the harvested old-growth logs are used to construct long-lasting buildings, the carbon release accompanying timber harvesting will be limited to some portion of the slash, forest floor, and soil carbon, and the wood waste produced during manufacturing. But if the trees are converted to pulp and used to make disposable products such as paper and packaging material, all of the harvested carbon will be transferred back to the atmosphere as rapidly as these throw-away materials decompose. In this case, much of the carbon stored in the old-growth forest will be released to the atmosphere, where it will contribute to the greenhouse problem. However, if an old-growth forest harvested for lumber is promptly reforested with a productive young forest that is subsequently harvested for lumber, the old-growth carbon releases by decomposition and manufacturing will be recaptured over the first rotation and put back into storage. In fact, a forest managed intensively for lumber production should remove considerably more carbon from the atmosphere over the rotation than was lost from the old growth. Because of this, the development of large areas of intensively harvested saw-log plantations has been suggested as an important contribution to reducing the greenhouse problem.

As long as harvested logs are used to make long-lasting wood products rather than disposable products, managed forests are a net sink for atmospheric CO_2, despite the period of CO_2 release following harvesting. Where the end use is disposable fibre, managed forests will make little net contribution to the atmospheric CO_2 balance: the carbon is simply cycled back and forth between the trees and the atmosphere. However, if the 'waste' fibre is disposed of in landfills, it will likely produce methane during its decomposition, which is a much more potent greenhouse gas than CO_2. Thus, a 'throw-away' use of tree fibre not only returns tree carbon to the atmosphere rapidly but may do it in a way that significantly increases the greenhouse problem compared to the natural processes of decomposition. This undesirable situation can be turned into a benefit, however, if methane released from landfills is collected and used instead of natural gas or other fossil fuels. In this case, even a throw-away forest economy can contribute positively to the solution of the greenhouse problem. Obviously, there are no simple answers. It all depends on how we as a society use harvested products and deal with the disposal of waste organic matter.

Plantation Forestry as a Solution to the Greenhouse Effect

It has been estimated that if all the world's deforested lands could be immediately reforested and managed so that they grew very productively, the resulting forests would take up about five billion tons of carbon per year. This is about the same as the 1987 fossil-fuel carbon release. Thus, aggressive reforestation programs and afforestation of non-forest areas could contribute to a significant reduction in the CO_2 component of the greenhouse problem. However, unless all the resulting logs are shipped into space, sunk in a lake, buried (the latter two strategies would create coal deposits for the future), or used in permanent building structures, the benefits would occur only in the first rotation. Thereafter, the carbon would simply be recirculated. Clearly, this is not a long-term solution to the greenhouse problem even if all the world's deforested areas could instantly be reforested, which could not happen for economic, social, and practical reasons. For one thing, we simply would not have enough seedlings to plant. On the other hand, if the harvested wood is used as an energy source in place of the fossil fuels that are the major source of the greenhouse problem, such a reforestation strategy could become of major importance.

What Do Wildfire and Slashburning Contribute?

The practice of slashburning and the occurrence of wildfire are mechanisms by which carbon is returned from the forest to the atmosphere. However,

post-harvesting decomposition processes can result in about the same release of carbon from the slash and forest floor over a ten- to fifteen-year period as a light to moderate slashburn would achieve in an hour. Thus, apart from the timing of the release, light to moderate slashburns may have little long-term impact on a forest's carbon budget. Severe slashburns, which can result in the loss of most slash, forest floor, stumps, and roots, undoubtedly result in an increased release of CO_2 from the forest in the short term (up to several decades), and will often reduce recovery of CO_2 from the atmosphere by the subsequent tree crop because of the damage to the soil. Such severe slashburns should not be permitted. The trend in western North America is away from hot fall slashburns and towards light spring burns, and a general reduction in the use of slashburning. Considering all these factors, slashburning is not a significant issue in the greenhouse debate, except that it will contribute positively if it speeds reforestation and improves soil fertility.

If the incidence of wildfire were increased by climate change, there would be an increased transfer of forest carbon to the atmosphere. On the other hand, recent advances in fire detection and suppression may be changing the recent rates of carbon release by forest fire. It is difficult to assess the role of forest fires in the greenhouse effect, however, because the area of forest burned has always varied greatly from year to year.

It should be apparent from this discussion that whether or not forestry is part of the greenhouse problem or part of the solution depends on how it is carried out. Ecologically sensitive forest management that maintains healthy, rapidly growing, well-stocked forest communities and that serves a market that puts the harvested wood carbon into long-term storage or uses it as a bioenergy resource to replace fossil fuels is one of the positive things that we can do with respect to the greenhouse effect. Conversely, exploitive utilization of old-growth or younger forests that ignores the effects of harvesting and site treatment on site carbon reserves; that damages the long-term productivity of the site through soil erosion, compaction, or depletion of fertility; that fails to reforest the harvested area promptly; or that produces short-lived, disposable products is definitely a contributor to the problem. Deforestation, such as the conversion of forest to agricultural or urban areas, results in significant releases of carbon. But this is not forestry. It is a land-use change.

Summary and Conclusions

Public concerns about clearcutting, slashburning, soil erosion, and loss of biotic diversity and old growth are often valid and certainly timely. While a lot of environmentally and silviculturally sound forestry is being practised around the world, and while clearcutting and slashburning are environmentally sound practices when applied correctly in the right places at the right time, there are still far too many examples of exploitive, ecologically insensitive harvesting and of inappropriate management practices. In spite of their importance, however, most of the above local issues pale in comparison with the threat that predicted climate change poses to human comfort, health, and safety, to biotic diversity, and to the forests of the world.

In many cases, managed forests are expected to fare better than unmanaged forests in the face of climate change. In managed systems there is the possibility of deliberately altering tree species composition or the genotypes of existing species to suit new or anticipated future climates. There is also the possibility of transferring non-crop plant species and beneficial soil organisms where evidence shows that they are unable to migrate as fast as the climatic zones are expected to move. However, if management has reduced the genetic and species diversity of the forest, and has reduced soil fertility and organic matter levels, the ability of the forest to withstand climatically induced stress may be reduced.

Most of the world's ancient forests are in carbon balance. They are not the 'lungs of the earth' without which we will suffocate for lack of oxygen.

They are not continuously accumulating carbon, for if this were the case, all old forests would be sitting on exceedingly deep layers of peat or lignite. In some nutrient-poor tropical swamp forests, such as in southeastern Sumatra, and in some temperate and northern bog forests, peat accumulation does occur. Such forests appear to accumulate carbon continuously over very long periods. But most tropical and temperate forests either reach a carbon equilibrium when they have accumulated only relatively modest amounts of this element, or they are disturbed frequently enough to prevent large accumulations of carbon from developing. Most unmanaged forests that are actively accumulating carbon at present have experienced a carbon-releasing episode in the fairly recent past.

Managed forests do accumulate carbon efficiently, but in our throw-away society much of this carbon is released following the disposal of harvested wood fibre products. Where the discarded wood fibre decays in an anaerobic landfill site, the production of methane will exacerbate the greenhouse problem more than the inevitable return of the carbon to the atmosphere by fire or natural decomposition in the forest, unless the methane is collected and used as an energy source.

Although good forestry can temporarily help reduce part of the greenhouse problem, the answer to the threat of climate change lies in reducing our use of fossil fuels, in recycling carbon-containing products, in eliminating the release of synthetic greenhouse gases, in stabilizing the size of the human population, and in changing life styles to reduce per capita contributions to alterations of atmospheric chemistry. Ultimately, the greenhouse problem must be solved by us as individuals and collectively as a society. It is not primarily a forestry-related problem. However, having recognized that 'good' forestry is not the solution (although it may help through timber and bioenergy production), we must accept that 'bad' forestry that ignores carbon budgets definitely contributes to the problem.

CHAPTER 13

Acid Rain: Is It as Bad for Forests as It Is for Lakes?

Acid Rain: The Problem

There must be few people in Europe and North America who have not heard on the radio or television or read in the newspaper about *acid rain*. First publicized by aquatic ecologists and biologists concerned about declining fish populations in lakes, the concern has spread to forests over the past decade. Widespread reports of *forest decline*[26] from parts of Europe, the northeastern United States, and eastern Canada that suffer serious air pollution have intensified the concern that acid rain could destroy or substantially alter forest ecosystems in much the same way that it has killed or altered many lakes.

This is a legitimate and timely concern. It is predicted that within the next century the human population will grow to between two and three times its 1990 level. Increasing industrialization is expected in developing countries that account for 75 to 80 per cent of the world's population, and there is a considerable risk that air pollution and the acid rain it produces will increase in proportion to population growth and industrialization. Environmental concerns have often not been very high on the political agenda of developing countries. Unless present trends are reversed, the air pollution and acid rain problems that have affected Europe and eastern North America over the past two decades can be expected to occur in many other areas. Air pollution is already an acute problem in many tropical developing countries.

This brief chapter identifies the major origins and components of acid rain. It also presents a summary of the many competing theories about how acid rain is related to various cases of forest decline.

What Is Acid Rain, and Where Does It Come From?

Rain droplets generally form by the condensation of water vapour on tiny dust particles that are almost always present in the air. These particles

---

26 Forest decline is the death or loss of vigour of forest trees over large areas that is not associated with a specific insect or disease problem.

may have originated in various ways, including volcanic eruptions, wind erosion of both agricultural and unmanaged soil (such as desert areas, which are often sandy because all the fine 'dust' has been blown away), salt particles from sea spray whipped up during ocean storms, and various human-caused sources of air pollution. Some of these particles may dissolve in rain droplets to form a dilute acid.[27]

If raindrops fall through air that contains gaseous oxides of the elements sulphur and nitrogen, these gases can dissolve in the droplets and form acids. The higher the concentrations of these atmospheric pollutants, the more acidic the resulting rainfall. Similarly, snow can be very acidic. Even rain falling through 'clean' air will be slightly acidic because it will pick up carbon dioxide from the air and form a weak acid, carbonic acid. The soda water we drink is dilute carbonic acid: it is carbonated water. The acids formed by nitrogen, sulphur, and chlorine are much stronger: nitric, sulphuric, and hydrochloric acids. It is the presence of these strong acids in rainwater and snow that causes *acid rain.*

Acid rain can wreak havoc on buildings and statues. It can dissolve the mortar that holds bricks together and eat away buildings made of calcium-rich limestone. Most of the famous historical buildings and statues in Greece, Italy, and central Europe are made of these materials, and the continual washing of these cultural treasures with dilute, and sometimes not so dilute, acids in rain is steadily dissolving them.

The acid rain phenomenon in forests has turned out to involve more than just these acids. In some cases, it also involves high inputs of non-acidic

nitrogen. In others, it may involve direct toxic effects of gases, including ozone and other constituents of smog. The more the acid rain problem has been studied in connection with forest decline, the more it has been recognized that the phenomenon is highly complex. The causes vary from one area to another. The solutions to the problem must therefore vary as well, and effective solutions cannot be designed and implemented until we understand what the problem is. For example, in some parts of Germany, forest decline has been attributed mainly to inputs of sulphur with or without ozone change, while in others it appears to be due to excessive inputs of nitrogen.

What Effect Does Acid Rain Have on Forests?

In contrast to the damage acid rain causes to lakes, buildings, and statues, it has proven to be much more difficult to demonstrate negative effects on forests. Even where forests exhibit clear symptoms of distress in areas subjected to acid rain, it has been a very challenging task to link the acid rain to the forest decline. The mechanisms are complex.

Small lakes in areas with nutrient-poor granitic soils generally have very pure water. They are said to be 'chemically unbuffered.' The chemistry of these lakes is very sensitive to chemical inputs and is easily changed. In contrast, the chemistry of more nutrient-rich lakes changes more slowly in response to chemical additions. They are well buffered against such changes. In areas that receive a lot of acidity in winter snow, the rapid melt of the snowpack in the spring flushes large volumes of acidic meltwater directly into lakes over a short period of time. Where the lakes are poorly buffered, this pulse of acidity can have very deleterious effects on aquatic life in general and may prevent fish from reproducing. Such lakes can lose much or most of their living organisms. When this occurs, they are often referred to as being 'biologically dead.'

In contrast, most forests are highly chemically buffered. The presence of a lot of organic matter acts to stabilize soil chemistry, so that it takes a

---

27 Acids are chemical substances that contain free hydrogen ions (H^+). Acidity is measured in terms of pH. The lower the pH value, the greater the acidity. A pH of 7.0 is neutral; the positively charged hydrogen ions are balanced by negatively charged hydroxyl ions (OH^-). Above 7.0 there are more hydroxyl ions than hydrogen ions and conditions are alkaline. Below 7.0 there are more hydrogen ions than hydroxyl ions and conditions are acidic. The pH scale is logarithmic. This means that pH 4 is 10 times more acidic than pH 5; pH 3 is 10 times more acidic than pH 4 and 100 times more acidic than pH 5, and so on.

Damage caused by acid rain

A

B

A Damage to spruce forest in the Hartz Mountains, Germany. The combination of acid rain, summer drought, and wind-storm damage has led to the deforestation of many acid-rain affected mountain areas in central and eastern Europe. This damage is caused mainly by sulphur dioxide air pollution.

B Damage to spruce forest in the Black Forest of southern Germany. The combination of too much nitrogen in the acid rain, not enough magnesium in the soil, several severe summer droughts, insect pests, and spruce trees planted on sites to which they were unsuited has resulted in more stress than the trees could withstand.

substantial input of chemicals to alter the chemistry of the forest floor and mineral soil. The degree of buffering varies, of course. Forests growing on very acidic or nutrient-poor soils are much more subject to chemical change than forests growing on nutrient-rich sites. But even forests on infertile sites are believed to take much longer to respond to acid rain than poorly buffered lakes. As a result, it has been much harder to unravel the complexities of acid rain-related forest decline than acid rain-related lake decline.

The fact that many forests are chronically short of the nutrient nitrogen, and that nitrogen is often a major component of acid rain, has made the detection of acid rain damage to forests more difficult. In some cases, acid rain has acted as a forest fertilizer rather than as a damaging agent, at least initially. Because of the chemical buffering capacity of forests, it may take many decades or even centuries before the negative effects of acid rain on forests become apparent, or, in the case of nitrogen-rich acid rain, overwhelm the positive effects. This does not mean, however, that the acid rain is not having a progressive, chronic negative effect on the forest.

Several theories about how acid rain may damage forests have been advanced.

Direct Damage to Foliage, Resulting in Reduced Photosynthesis

The acidity, that is, the concentration of hydrogen ions, of some acid rain is not much different from that of vinegar, a naturally acidic fluid. Direct damage to foliage by exposure to acid is therefore an obvious thing to investigate in cases of suspected acid rain damage. Clouds and fog are often even more acidic than rainfall, and the condensation of acid fog on tree foliage can expose the leaves to very acidic conditions. It has been suggested that damage may occur directly to the delicate inner tissues of the leaf, and through the leaching of nutrients out of the leaves. Leaves in areas of decline are often low in calcium and magnesium, and it has been suggested that this is so because the acid has washed these nutrients out of the leaves.

Although dramatic examples of forest death caused by sulphur dioxide and ozone damage to foliage have been recorded – for example, around smelters such as that in Sudbury, Ontario, or downwind of cities, like Los Angeles and Mexico City, which produce high levels of photochemical smog – in most cases research on acid rain has not yet linked forest decline with direct damage to foliage. While foliar leaching may be increased by acid rain, and while this may be important in some cases, research results do not support the idea that this is the major mechanism of acid rain damage.

Effects on Soil Processes

If the rate of sulphur and nitrogen deposition in the forest by acid rain exceeds the uptake of these nutrients by trees, soil acidification may occur. This can lead to increased concentrations of aluminum in solution in the mineral soil water. Aluminum is a very common element in soil but is often not in a form that plant roots can take up from soil solution. When it is in a soluble form, however, it is toxic to plants and can kill fine roots. Death of fine roots reduces nutrient and water uptake by plants, leading to nutritional problems and an increased susceptibility to drought, diseases, and insects, which can then cause tree death and forest decline.

Another soil-related theory is based more on changes in soil chemistry than on actual damage to roots. Soil acidification and the presence of nitrate and sulphate ions (negatively charged subunits of the nitric acid and sulphuric acid molecules, respectively) can lead to the leaching of positively charged nutrient ions, such as calcium and magnesium, out of the soil. This can result in decreased availability of these elements to plants. Alternatively, the presence of excessive amounts of aluminum or ammonium nitrogen in the soil solution may restrict the uptake of magnesium even where adequate supplies are present in the soil. These positively charged ions compete with the positively charged magnesium at the root surface, preventing or restricting its uptake. In some cases of forest decline in Germany, the lack of magnesium in trees has been implicated in decline symptoms such as foliage yellowing.

The annual addition of large amounts of nitrogen to soils that are inherently low in magnesium may create a nitrogen/magnesium imbalance in plants independently of these soil and nutrient uptake process effects. Such imbalance can cause physiological disturbances in plants, reducing photosynthesis, growth processes, and resistance to insects, pathogens, and drought.

Changes in the chemistry of poorly buffered upper mineral soil layers caused by acid rain can cause fine feeding roots to be restricted to the relatively well-buffered forest floor on nutrient-poor sites. This can cause the death of fine roots and increase the trees' susceptibility to summer drought that dries out the forest floor. It may also render fine roots more susceptible to winter frost damage, which in turn makes it more difficult for the trees to take up nutrients.

General Stress Theories

Several theories suggest that forest decline is the combined result of different factors that collectively stress the trees, rather than the result of any single factor. Many trees that die as a result of forest decline are actually killed by insects and diseases to which they have been made susceptible by either summer drought or winter frost damage. The latter can occur where unusual midwinter warm periods melt the snowpack that usually protects the soil and fine roots from low winter temperatures. Severe freezing of the soil can kill fine roots and cause nutritional problems or increased susceptibility to drought until new roots have grown. Susceptibility to drought may also be caused by direct root damage or nutritional imbalances due to acid rain. Similarly, physiological upsets resulting from direct damage to plants by air pollution (e.g., ozone) or acidity can reduce a tree's resistance to insects, diseases, and drought. The particular combination of stress factors that collectively cause forest decline

may vary from time to time and place to place, but may have similar effects. This makes it difficult to identify a single cause of acid rain-induced forest decline; generally there is no single cause.

Natural Causes of Acidification

One of the difficulties in identifying the effects of acid rain on forests is the fact that, unlike the acidity of small lakes, the acidity of forest soils varies naturally over time regardless of whether there is any human-caused acid rain. Soil acidity is also affected by forest management.

There is often a considerable change in soil pH after a forest is naturally disturbed. By creating alkaline ash, a forest fire can neutralize soil acidity to some extent. The decomposition of leaves and branches following wind, insect, or disease damage can similarly release basic nutrients such as calcium and magnesium that can reduce soil acidity. The soil disturbance caused when forests are blown over or there is a natural landslide can mix very acidic upper soil layers with lower, less acid layers, reducing the levels of acidity in the rooting zone. As nutrients are recovered by the regrowing forest and immobilized in permanent woody tissues, and as coarse woody debris in the form of rotting logs accumulates on the ground, the pH of the forest floor declines again. In humid environments, this leads to natural soil acidification (podzolization). If this proceeds for many thousands of years without disturbance, the mineral soil may become so acidic that almost no tree roots can grow there; they are all restricted to the forest floor, which can lead to nutritional problems. This is rather similar to forest growth problems that have been attributed to acid rain by some scientists.

The pattern of soil pH change is not linear throughout ecological succession from disturbance back to mature or old-growth forest. For example, reduced acidity in clearcuts due to the 'assart' flush of nutrients may be followed by a period of intense acidification if a nitrogen-fixing species such as red alder occupies the site. Generally thought of as a soil improver because of the nitrogen it adds, alder promotes soil acidification. This can be so extreme that it reduces the availability of some other soil nutrients, such as phosphorus, to the point at which growth of the alder may be impaired. If the alder is replaced by Douglas-fir, much of the nitrogen is taken up and the soil acidity may decline again, only to increase once more when and if the Douglas-fir is replaced by an old-growth forest of western hemlock, as in British Columbia's coastal western hemlock zone. If the climax forest contains a high proportion of western red cedar, whose foliage is rich in calcium, the pH of the climax forest floor may be less acidic than in a hemlock-dominated forest.

Forest harvesting can also induce soil acidification. When logs are removed, so are quantities of calcium and other basic nutrients that would eventually be returned to the soil in an unmanaged forest. These nutrients are replaced over conventional forest rotations by precipitation inputs and by chemical weathering of mineral soil, which may be accelerated by acidification. Consequently, conventional logging on medium to long rotations will generally not pose acidification problems. However, if whole-tree harvesting is practised on short rotations, a steady depletion of basic soil nutrients, such as calcium, potassium, and magnesium, can occur, leading to acidification. In some cases, as in nutrient-poor soils over acidic bedrock, this can exceed the acidification caused by acid rain or biological nitrogen fixation.

Variations in Susceptibility to Acid Rain Damage

Because of the importance of soil chemistry in the forest decline/acid rain problem, the susceptibility of forests to acid rain problems depends greatly on the geology of the area. Forests growing on nutrient-poor soils or very slowly weathering geological materials will be less well buffered and will show symptoms of changes caused by acid rain in their soils much sooner than forests growing on nutrient-rich soils and rapidly weathering geological materials.

Most forest decline problems that have been attributed to acid rain have been associated with nutrient-poor geological materials such as granite (a rock type that weathers slowly and releases relatively few basic nutrients, such as calcium or magnesium) and/or with acidic soils in areas with humid climates. Acid rain damage to lakes is also mainly a phenomenon of areas with granitic or other nutrient-poor, slowly weathering bedrock.

The cultural history of an area may also be important. Forests that have been heavily grazed by livestock, or repeatedly burned, or in which litter has been raked and dead branches harvested annually for long periods will generally be more impoverished in soil nutrients than 'natural' areas. They will be correspondingly less chemically well buffered and more susceptible to acid rain damage. Where a native forest has been harvested and replaced by a forest of species that produce a more acidic, slowly decomposing forest floor, the new forest may also be predisposed to acid rain problems. If the new species are ecologically unsuited to a particular site, the trees will already be under stress. It will not take as much additional stress from acid rain or air pollution to produce forest decline symptoms as it would in forests of species that are well adapted to the site.

The Long-Term Threat of Acid Rain

It took many years of intense research to reach our present level of understanding of the effects of acid rain on forest ecosystems. Undoubtedly more remains to be discovered, but we now know enough to be very concerned about the threat from acid rain posed by continued population growth and unregulated industrialization. The air pollution that would probably accompany these trends constitutes a significant threat to the world's forests.

For years, forest scientists could not identify forest damage resulting from acid rain. Then, quite suddenly, symptoms of forest decline were identified in many forests affected by air pollution and acid rain. As noted earlier, it is now believed that acid rain can have a long-term chronic negative effect on forests that may withstand many years of acid rain input before their natural buffering capacity is overcome or before the negative effects of acid rain override initial positive effects. This insidious action of acid rain is related to the gradual depletion of positively charged chemicals in the soil that help buffer changes in soil acidity and regulate the uptake of nutrients by trees. Only when this process has gone on long enough to render the trees susceptible to other stress factors will the symptoms of acid rain damage be detected.

Because of this long-term effect, forests in areas with air pollution that do not exhibit acid rain symptoms today may undergo forest decline in the future unless acid rain or its effects are ameliorated. Forests affected by acid rain may also be more susceptible to climate change phenomena (including drought) and to insect and disease attack. Intensive forest harvesting can increase the risk of acid rain damage. Whole-tree harvesting and shorter rotations can reduce the buffering capacity of soils, thereby shortening the time period over which a forest must be exposed to acid rain before symptoms appear. The importance of this problem will vary from highly significant on nutrient-poor sites to insignificant on very fertile sites.

Acid rain damage to forests can sometimes be ameliorated by fertilization (adding calcium and magnesium, for example), but there is no question that the correct action is to limit the air pollution that causes acid rain in the first place.

Summary and Conclusions

There is nothing unnatural about forest soil acidification. It happens naturally when a site is occupied by nitrogen-fixing species, it is a natural process by which forest soil can degrade nutritionally, and it is one of the processes by which a forest can become 'decadent' and unproductive in cool, humid climates if the forest remains undisturbed for a long period. It is thought to be one of the causes of the stagnation of ecological processes in ancient old-growth forests in cool, humid temperate rain forests. Soil acidification in such climax forests is often associated with heavy accumulations of coarse woody debris in the form of decomposing logs, and excessive accumulation of colloidal organic matter (humic substances) in the mineral soil.

In most forests, periodic natural disturbance interrupts this acidification trend and reduces soil acidity. In acid rain-related soil acidification, there is a slow but steady acidification trend superimposed on this natural temporal pattern of soil acidity change. In managed forests in areas affected by acid rain, human-induced disturbance may mimic the natural temporal pattern of soil acidity change, but if too much biomass is removed too frequently, there may be a downward trend in soil pH over successive rotations independent of the effects of acid rain. Clearly, this is very undesirable. It could result in future forest growth problems on poorly buffered, nutrient-poor soils in areas not receiving acid rain.

Research results suggest that acid rain and the associated air pollution should be just as much a long-term concern for foresters in areas of air pollution as it is for managers of aquatic ecosystems in these areas. The risk and extent of the acid rain problem varies greatly, however, according to the fertility of the site, the underlying geology, the forest's history of natural disturbance, the way the forest has been managed in the past, and the complexity of other risk factors that act in concert with acid rain to induce symptoms of forest decline. Attempts to solve the acid rain problem must be region- and site-specific, and must be based on an understanding of the local causes of forest decline symptoms.

We can say, however, that reducing air pollution and eventually eliminating acid rain must be a very high government priority if we want to have sustainable forestry.

orth':

ry

h Columbia

orse

than Deforestation

in the Tropics?

The Causes of Tropical Deforestation

Scarcely a day goes by without some mention on radio, television, or in the newspapers of events at tropical latitudes that are leading to the loss of tropical rain forest. After more than a century of largely ignoring the tropics except for vacations in Hawaii, Mexico, or the Caribbean, the North American public has been forcibly made aware of the vast scale on which the forests at tropical and subtropical latitudes are being denuded or altered by human activity.

The history of alteration of tropical and subtropical forest ecosystems is closely related to the explosive growth of the human population in the tropics over the past century. This population growth resulted largely from improvements in medicine and agriculture that were exported from the industrialized countries. Foreign aid programs and charitable projects, such as digging wells in semi-desert areas, often contributed to the problem by providing death control without effectively providing birth control. Tropical deforestation has been increased in some areas by agricultural, forestry, mining, and hydroelectric projects financed by international aid. Some of these projects have been associated with the pressure on tropical countries to pay their international debt.

Population increase in tropical forest regions has also resulted from the migration of people from overcrowded cities to undeveloped forest areas within a single country. Large numbers of landless, unemployed peasants moved from rural areas to cities in some tropical countries following technological advances in agriculture in the absence of land reform, or simply because of overpopulation and poverty in rural areas. As agriculture became increasingly mechanized, many workers lost their jobs, and for survival they moved to urban centres hoping to find work. Governments in these countries sought to reduce the resulting problems of urban overcrowding by instituting 'transmigration' projects. Millions of people have been moved from cities or overcrowded rural areas into 'agricultural opportunities' carved out of the tropical forest, and this has become a major source of deforestation. Both Brazil and Indonesia have large programs of this type.

The reasons for what is happening to the tropical rain forest are complex and variable. So is the tropical forest environment that is being affected. The media often present the idea that there is one ecological condition called the 'tropical rain forest' that stretches monolithically throughout the tropics, and that generalizations about ecosystem fragility and sustainability derived from a specific tropical forest, usually humid areas of the Amazon basin in Brazil, apply equally to all tropical forests. This is a misconception. Although there are several characteristics common to most tropical forests, there is also enormous ecological variability in these forests.

This chapter briefly examines some of the general features and the variability of the tropical forest and the forests of British Columbia. It then examines the claim that current forest practices in British Columbia and their ecological consequences are no different from, or are worse than, the deforestation occurring in tropical rain forests, such as those in the Brazilian Amazon basin.

The ecology of the tropical forest is both fascinating and complex. Only the briefest and most superficial treatment of it can be presented here. A detailed comparison between tropical and temperate northern forests and their response to disturbance cannot be attempted in this book.

The Ecological Variability and Response to the Disturbance of Tropical Forests

Tropical forests extend from latitude 23°N to 23°S. They vary substantially in climate, from areas with a marked dry season followed by a monsoon wet season, to areas where there is relatively little variation in weather from season to season. However, even areas of tropical rain forest right on the equator experience a sufficient dry period in some years to cause significant damage to tree canopies and even the death of some trees. Accompanying the geographical variation in tropical climate is significant

variation in the forests' species composition and structure, from relatively low species and structural diversity in summer dry areas in tropical seasonal forests, to very high tree species diversity and many canopy layers in well-developed rain forests.

It is commonly thought that all tropical soils are very ancient, very weathered, and nutrient-poor, and that they all turn into brick-hard 'laterite' upon exposure to the sun. In reality there is great variation in soil age, fertility, and sensitivity to exposure. Some tropical soils, such as many of those of northern Australia and the Amazon basin, are very old and very weathered. Many tropical soils are also very nutrient-poor, such as in the bog forests of southeastern Sumatra and parts of the Amazon. However, soils in volcanic areas such as parts of Java and Central America are young and quite fertile. Recent alluvial soils in the floodplains of tropical rivers can be very fertile and support productive forests or agriculture, just as their temperate counterparts do. Deep peat deposits may be formed in the poorest tropical soils, and the water draining the forest growing on these infertile organic soils is stained dark brown just like the streams and rivers of Scottish moorland. The mighty Rio Negro River which joins the Salimoes River at Manaus, Brazil, to form the Amazon River, gets its name from this dark brown staining. In contrast, the Salimoes flows through areas with more fertile soils and has unstained water.

Tropical forests growing on extremely nutrient-poor soils generally lack the species diversity, the multi-layered canopies, the stature, and the productivity associated with tropical forests growing on more fertile sites. Where forests on nutrient-poor soils are cleared for agriculture, the soil tends to degrade very rapidly, and such areas are usually abandoned within a few years. If they are abandoned before soil fertility or soil structure has been severely damaged, an impoverished secondary forest will rapidly invade and, through the processes of ecological succession, begin to restore soil fertility and prepare the site for recolonization by the original forest. This is what lies behind the traditional practice of shifting cultivation in the tropics. If the farmers persist with their struggle for too long, however, the soil may have become so impoverished by the time the area is abandoned that no plants can grow, and the soil may remain bare for many years. Alternatively, the area may be colonized by hardy pioneer plant species such as sword grass (alang-alang) that are tolerant of the very low nutrient levels. These species may resist invasion by forest species and are not eaten by most herbivores. Burning the site may improve it briefly, but only causes a further loss of soil organic matter and nutrients. As a result, such species can dominate badly disturbed tropical landscapes for long time periods.

It is commonly thought that all, or at least most, of the nutrients in a tropical forest are in the vegetation, with very little nutrient reserve in the soil, and that these nutrients are cycled exceedingly efficiently with almost no losses from the site in the absence of disturbance. It is commonly asserted that when logged or deforested for agriculture, the tropical forest site has very little resilience and will rapidly deteriorate to a state in which it can no longer support a forest. Studies of nutrient-poor sites in the humid tropics support this concept: most of the nutrients are in the vegetation, nutrients are cycled very efficiently, the soils have very low nutrient reserves, and the ecosystems recover very slowly if they are seriously disturbed. Not all tropical forests are like this, however. Those on more fertile sites are much more resilient, and have soils with appreciable nutrient reserves. Such soils are capable of sustainable agriculture and forestry if managed in a way that conserves their organic matter, nutrient reserves, and structure, and that avoids erosion. Such sites generally revegetate and recover rapidly following disturbance.

Tropical forests are known for their remarkably high plant and animal species diversity: their alpha species diversity. Mature tropical rain forests often have very high alpha structural diversity as well. In areas of extensive low-lying floodplains, undis-turbed rain forests may have low beta (landscape) diversity: the unbroken, high alpha diversity forest may vary little over substantial areas. In mountainous areas or areas that have been subjected to human activity, such as shifting cultivation, there is often much higher beta diversity.

British Columbian Forests: Perhaps the Most Diverse in the World?

British Columbia's forests extend from just south of 49°N to 60°N; from temperate rain forest in humid, low-elevation coastal areas to arid subalpine forests and alpine tundra in continental areas in the rain shadow of high mountains; from semi-desert and savannah forest conditions to boreal and arctic tundra conditions. There are few if any political units of comparable size anywhere in the world that contain such a wide range of ecological conditions. Four out of the five major types of world climate are represented. The soils cover the entire spectrum from desert soils to humid forest soils, and from grassland soils to alpine and tundra soils. Virtually the entire area was glaciated recently and most soils are therefore young and have substantial reserves of unweathered minerals. The soils vary from glacial tills, to windblown loess and sands, and from alluvial and glacial outwash soils to marine and lake sed-iments. The materials they have developed from vary from acidic, nutrient-poor, slowly weathering (plutonic) bedrock to fast weathering and nutrient-rich volcanic and sedimentary geological substrates.

Ecologists have divided BC into fourteen distinct ecological or biogeoclimatic zones, eleven of which are forested. Most of these zones have several or even many subzones: ecologically distinct subdivisions of the biogeoclimatic zones. Each subzone has several, usually four to seven, different ecological site types. Each site type has a distinct ecological character: a distinct combination of soil, climate, animals, plants, and microbes. Each will respond differently to particular types of natural or human-caused disturbance. Each can have a different pattern and rate of recovery from disturbance.

Examples of deforestation

A

B

A Severely eroded forest landscape in southeastern China. Millions of hectares of land like this were deforested over the past eighty years by forest exploitation during the Japanese occupation, by thirty years of civil war, and by the consequences of forty years of the policies of Chairman Mao and his communist government. Much of the landscape has been replanted, frequently with inappropriate species, but the trees are generally not growing well because poor peasants cut the branches off and rake the leaves, interfering with the processes of ecosystem recovery

B Vast areas of savannah forest in Brazil have been reduced to unproductive scrub over the past hundred years by the local people cutting the forest to make charcoal for fuel, and burning the land to encourage grasses for their cattle. Vast landscapes are now barren and unproductive of trees and cattle.

The biodiversity of BC's forests varies greatly. Low-diversity, monoculture forests occur naturally in many parts of the province in response to fire, insect, or wind damage, but low diversity can also occur in climax old-growth forests. Some BC forests are quite diverse, with up to a dozen tree species in one stand and a considerable variety of herb, shrub, and moss species. In some forests, there is little change in species and structural diversity over large areas; in others, both of these measures of biodiversity change rapidly over short distances as one moves across the landscape. In many of BC's forests, there is a characteristic variation in species and structural diversity as the forest regrows following natural or human-caused disturbance. In others there is much less variation over time in some aspects of diversity.

Because of the soils and climates, many, if not most, forests in BC recover rapidly from disturbance. Other forests recover much more slowly, and there are even a very few that respond in a manner comparable to deforested areas with extremely old, acidic, and nutrient-poor soils found in some parts of the humid tropics.

Because of the enormous ecological diversity of BC, and because tropical forests also vary in their ecological characteristics, it is possible to find some local situations where limited comparisons between the ecosystem function and response to disturbance of tropical and temperate forests are useful. In most cases this is not the case, and rarely is there any value in unqualified, generalized comparisons.

Is Current Forestry Practice in British Columbia Analogous to Exploitive Logging and Deforestation in the Tropics?

Seen from an airplane a thousand metres above the ground or from a passing car, the overall initial impression of an area that has just been clearcut and slashburned in the Brazilian rain forest may not be very much different from a recently clearcut and slashburned area in humid coastal BC. The answer to the above question might seem to be yes.

Similarly, seen from a distance a paperback copy of *Hamlet* or *War and Peace* might not look much different from a cheap novel. Based on such a superficial visual examination, the conclusion that the two clearcuts are ecologically the same and will recover in the same manner would be about as profound as saying there is no difference between the content of the literary classics and the trashy paperback. Such an analysis tells us nothing about the ecological content of the two clearcut ecosystems, or about the literary content of the books.

Neither English literature, nor ecology, nor environmental impact analysis is advanced by superficial evaluations. Clearly, the question about the similarity between forest land management in BC and tropical deforestation (a land-use change) or exploitive tropical logging in Brazil or other tropical countries cannot be answered on the basis of a casual visual observation.

On the basis of a more detailed evaluation, the answer may be both 'no' and 'yes.' In terms of ecological effects, the answer to this question is clearly 'no,' for a variety of reasons:

(1) Profound ecological differences between tropical rain forests and the forests of BC render most of the former much less able to recover from management-related disturbance than most of the latter. One simply cannot make useful generalizations about such a broad range of ecological conditions. One cannot make useful generalizations that are true for all of BC's exceedingly diverse forests, just as one cannot generalize about all of the forests in a large tropical country such as Brazil. Even less can one make useful generalizations that cover both BC and a tropical country.

(2) Although the results of timber harvesting practices in BC are often visually unattractive for a few years, most of the publicly owned forests of western Canada are currently being managed according to sustained-yield timber management principles. These forests were simply exploited until about eighty years ago, and their managed use over the past half century generally lacked an adequate

Wrong choice of tree species

A

B

A Replacement of tropical rain forests in the Brazilian Amazon by a fast-growing tropical hardwood from Southeast Asia (*Gmelina arborea*) has frequently failed on upland areas with acidic, nutrient-poor soils. Such plantations have grown successfully on nutrient-rich soils in the Amazon floodplain. This plantation died when it was three years old.

B The very poor growth form of this Douglas-fir is the result of growing it in an area of the BC coast where the climate is too wet. Sitka spruce and western hemlock grew well on this site. Douglas-fir plantations grow very well when their ecological requirements are matched to the local climatic and soil conditions, but often grow poorly when planted outside of this range.

ecological foundation and concern for ecosystem sustainability. However, although there are still far too many examples of soil damage, although there is evidence that, relative to present levels of management, forests are being harvested too rapidly in some areas, and although non-timber values have often not been given adequate consideration in terms of selecting the rate, landscape pattern, and method of timber harvesting, most of BC's forests are now being managed fairly well in terms of sustained timber production. Although more remains to be done and there are still examples of unacceptable practices, maintenance of habitat for many species of wildlife and maintenance of fish and streams have improved over the past few decades. In many areas the level of habitat protection is now acceptable, notwithstanding certain notable current exceptions and past failures. There is still much to be desired in terms of visual resource management, and sometimes in terms of soil conservation, wildlife habitat, and streams. But current forestry practices in many parts of British Columbia appear to be successful in renewing and sustaining a wide variety of forest values, despite public perceptions to the contrary.

In comparison, exploitive logging (as opposed to successful plantation forestry) in the tropics is not forestry. It is exploitive logging similar to the type practised in BC in the first few decades of this century and in some areas until quite recently (phase 1 in the evolution of forestry – see Chapter 5). Unlike BC, tropical logging is frequently followed by unregulated shifting cultivation, grazing, or itinerant agriculture that prevents the reinvasion of the forest and often leads to severe soil degradation. Much of the logging in the tropics is illegal and unplanned. In contrast, the law now requires timber harvesting on public forest land in BC to be followed by site preparation, planting, or natural regeneration to ensure prompt reforestation. The young stands must be tended and protected to ensure that they grow to the stage at which they should be able to prosper with little or no further management.

Some of these requirements are very recent and in some cases have not yet been fully implemented. Sometimes, they are not very successful and more stand management is required to ensure that our future forests have desired levels of productivity and a desired species composition and structure. However, unlike the tropics, the legal framework for achieving this is in place.

(3) In BC we are dealing with geologically young landscapes and geologically young soils that in most cases are rich in reserves of weatherable minerals that contain plant nutrients. Except for nitrogen, few major nutrient deficiencies occur in BC's forests unless they are mismanaged. There are some cases of iron, sulphur, and boron deficiency, and even isolated cases of phosphorus deficiency, but nothing like the acute nutritional deficiencies that occur in many ancient Australian soils and some of the exceptionally nutrient-poor forest soils in the tropics. This difference in the nutritional status and nutrient reservoirs of many tropical and most BC soils invalidates any simplistic comparison of the environmental impact of forest harvesting in the two areas.

(4) The risk of loss of biological diversity is far higher in tropical humid forests than in BC's temperate and northern forests. Responsible forest management in BC results in increases in many measures of biological diversity (see Chapter 10) and duplicates many aspects of the temporal diversity that accompanies natural disturbance.

(5) Differences in climate result in much more rapid loss of organic matter from harvested tropical forest soils than from harvested BC sites. This difference in the dynamics of organic matter and nutrients gives the tropical forest environment a fundamentally different character and response to disturbance than BC's temperate and northern forests.

There are some parallels, however, between BC forestry and the current exploitation of tropical forests:

(1) In both regions there are unsettled native land claims, and the forest-dwelling native peoples of both areas have been displaced and often dispossessed by

European settlers or migrants from urban areas. This process started more than a century ago in both cultural environments, and has been accelerated recently in tropical areas by transmigration projects.

(2) In both areas, the forest has been disturbed by mining. In BC the greatest mining-related damage was done during the gold rush of the last century, when vast areas of forest were burned off. Most of the affected areas now have magnificent and beautiful second-growth forests that many people believe are unmanaged old-growth forests. In Brazil and other tropical areas, a present-day gold rush and the search for oil and gas are apparently wreaking havoc not unlike that which gave rise to many of the present-day mature forests in the BC interior.

(3) In both BC and tropical areas, substantial tracts of forest have been lost to water reservoirs and hydroelectricity schemes.

(4) In both areas, there has been damage to the habitat of some wildlife species, although this appears to be far more serious in the tropics than in BC. The exceedingly varied animal life of the tropics is far more threatened by tropical forest clearing for agriculture than the wildlife of BC is by the current management of the province's forests. In fact, wildlife organizations claim that many species of wildlife in BC are more abundant now than in the past. This does not mean that current forest practices in BC do not have any negative effects on wildlife, but rather that simple comparisons between tropical deforestation and forestry in BC insofar as wildlife is concerned are generally not very helpful.

These parallels notwithstanding, uncritical comparisons between BC and the tropics in terms of ecosystem resilience and the overall quality and success of the way the forest resource is being managed are simply not valid. One can only assume that those who make such statements either have not had the privilege of visiting both tropical and temperate forests and working with both tropical and temperate ecologists, or do not have the necessary scientific knowledge to comprehend the ecological aspects of what they have seen. This in no way

detracts from the importance of their concern about what is happening to the world's tropical rain forests, or from the major contribution they are making to the improvement of temperate and northern forest management. It simply means that from most points of view, the idea that Canada is 'Brazil North' does not stand up to careful scientific analysis.

Summary and Conclusions

One can always learn a lot about the ecology and environmental impact of forest management in one area by visiting and learning about the ecology and resource management of a very different area. The current experience of tropical deforestation has much to teach foresters at more northern latitudes. The basic principles of forest nutrition and nutrient cycling, the need for site nutrient and organic matter conservation, and concerns about loss of biodiversity can certainly be seen more vividly and demonstrated more rapidly in many tropical forests than in their northern counterparts. For the comparison to be useful, however, both the ecological variability within the tropics and BC and the ecological differences between these two regions of the earth must be recognized.

Many of the statements that have claimed a similarity between forest management in BC and deforestation in the tropics are not supported by our current understanding of the ecology of these two areas. They have apparently been based on a very superficial and largely visual analysis. Although such statements may have contributed usefully to the political phase of conservation (see Chapter 2), they are so lacking in a sound scientific basis as to be distracting and divisive as we move into the implementation phase. They do little to inform the public about the problems that do exist in BC and Canadian forestry, and provide little basis for developing solutions to these problems.

Future Shock in Forecasting Forest Growth and Timber Yields: How Cloudy Is Our Crystal Ball?

Sustainable Development and Overcutting

Sustainable development has become the marching cry for many if not most of today's foresters. Although there is still heated debate about exactly what sustainable development means, it appears to be little more than a reaffirmation of the principle that, in theory at least, has always defined, and in many countries has guided, forestry: maintaining the supply of a variety of resource values and ecosystem conditions in forested landscapes. In reality, forestry in much of Canada has been *implemented* by governments largely as timber management, with non-timber values viewed largely as constraints on the management of tree crops. But this does not alter the fact that in definition and origin, forestry is concerned with the conservation of a variety of resource values and the sustainable development of forests.

Sustainable development has been defined as the use of resources in a way that satisfies the needs of today without compromising the ability of future generations to satisfy their needs. The essence of sustainable development in forestry is good stewardship of forest land, and both politicians and foresters have publicly affirmed this concept. It is therefore surprising that many informed sources believe that the recent rate of timber harvesting in British Columbia exceeds the long-term sustainable capacity of the land, given present levels of forest management. For example, the 1989 timber harvest in British Columbia was about ninety million cubic metres of wood, compared to a figure of seventy-five million that is often cited as the long-term annual allowable cut (AAC) under the present management regime. Recent estimates suggest that the long-term sustainable cut might be closer to 40 million if all the land use changes and reserves that are presently under discussion were implemented without a significant intensification of forest management.

Both foresters and environmentalists have expressed growing concern about the state of Canada's forests over the past quarter century. In the early 1980s, a group of professional foresters brought to the federal government's attention the millions of hectares of Canadian forests that had been harvested in the past but not adequately reforested. This stimulated the five-year, $600 million Forest Resource Development Agreement (FRDA), a program dedicated to reforesting this enormous backlog of unregenerated forest land. The first five-year FRDA program reduced the backlog significantly. A repeated renewal of the program will help to ensure that Canada's timber resource is being managed on a sustainable basis, but it will do little in the short run to address the question of overcutting.

The question of whether Canada's forests in general, and British Columbia's forests in particular, are being harvested too rapidly is complex. The very high rates of cutting in BC in the late 1980s were the result of several factors:

(1) There was accelerated harvesting on private lands, where the rate of cutting is not regulated.

(2) Recent forest legislation that will terminate old harvesting licences on public forest lands early in the next century caused an acceleration in the harvesting of these areas before the licences expire.

(3) The recent harvesting of species previously considered to be 'weed trees' (aspen in the north, red alder on the coast, and cottonwood in many areas) has added to the volume and area harvested. Inclusion of these species in the allowable cut calculation for the first time in the 1980s resulted in a significant increase in the AAC in some parts of BC.

(4) Extensive outbreaks of the mountain pine beetle and the spruce bark beetle have resulted in the salvage harvest of large areas of forest. In some parts of the province, the rate of harvest of beetle-killed timber has exceeded the AAC. In others, the AAC was simply taken from insect-killed forest.

(5) There have been new timber-cutting commitments to support new mills (sometimes without any evidence that there was a sustainable AAC to supply them).

Forest companies in British Columbia are normally permitted to exceed their AAC in any single year by as much as 50 per cent, but must be within 10 per cent of the AAC target over a five-year period. AACs are recalculated periodically to ensure that the rate of cut is kept in balance with the resource over longer time periods. This flexibility permits the companies to respond to timber market demand, the price of lumber, and various other economic and management considerations in a way that is supposed to produce maximum economic returns for the public purse and the companies. Rates of forest harvest will always vary somewhat from year to year as a result of this built-in flexibility and the various factors that determine how much timber is actually cut, such as the market demand, strikes, weather, and damage by fire, insects, and diseases. All these factors contributed to the increased harvest rate in the late 1980s. Most people agree, however, that the annual harvest is not sustainable at the 1989 level unless there are some fundamental changes in the way our forests are managed.

Contrary to popular belief, there is no single fixed level of annual allowable cut for a particular area of forest. The volume of timber that can be harvested over time depends on many factors (see discussion in Chapter 5). These include the proportion of the biomass of the tree species harvested, called the *utilization level;* the extent to which all the tree species in the forest are utilized; the age to which the forest is grown, or the rotation length; the fertility and physical condition of the soil; and the intensity of the silviculture. The cut also depends on the rate at which young forests reach the age and condition at which they can be harvested, and the rate at which mature and old-growth forests are converted to young forests. The intensity of silviculture includes the speed of regeneration; the control of weed competition; the protection of young trees from browsing, defoliation, and other forms of animal damage; the regulation of competition between crop trees; crop fertilization; and the use of commercial thinning to salvage trees that would eventually die because of light competition. Every factor in this list can vary and every one of them can affect both the volume of timber that is harvested over the rotation and the average rate of harvest per year. The AAC thus depends on how we manage our forests, as well as on our policy concerning the rate at which we convert mature and old-growth forests into managed second-growth. The AAC also depends on estimates of the risk of timber loss due to insects, diseases, fire, and wind damage. The initially calculated AAC is reduced to reflect these risks, and may be reduced further because of anticipated or actual withdrawals of land from the working forest for parks, wilderness, ecological reserves, and various types of 'environmental protection.'

Foresters and ecologists in the Pacific Northwestern states of the U.S. have been struggling for some time to come up with a definition of the inherent productivity of forest land. A measure of this productivity is required by American legislation that states that this site productivity must not be reduced by management. Until there is some agreed-upon method of establishing what basic site productivity is, this legislation is impotent. It is also suggested by some that this measure of site productivity, once defined, should become the basis for calculating a base level of AAC.

The search for a single, fixed level of site productivity is in some ways analogous to the desire to have a single fixed annual allowable cut. Both are attractive because of the simplicity of the concept, but neither addresses the complexity and temporal variability in the mechanisms that determine production and yield in forests. The science of production ecology (see Chapter 4) tells us that the rate of net primary production, or plant growth, depends on the regional climate; the availability of site resources such as light, nutrients, and moisture; and various biological and non-biological factors, such as fire. The rate at which we can harvest this plant production depends on the level of total crop plant production, and the proportion of this that is stored in the biomass components that we harvest, such as tree stems as opposed to leaves or fine roots. Both production and the allocation of production to harvestable biomass are greatly affected by soil

fertility and the site's reserves of organic matter. Because these are so variable over time due to natural disturbance and forest management, it must be expected that both basic plant production and the proportion of that production that can be harvested will also vary over time. A given site will thus have a range of possible levels of plant production and harvestable yield. The ultimate limits of this range are set by climate and topography, while the level of growth achieved within this range depends on the current ecosystem condition (especially soil) and how we manage that condition. How much of a site's productivity can be harvested will also depend upon the allocation of this productivity between crop and non-crop species, and the proportion of the crop species biomass that we dedicate to wildlife habitat or other values.

From this discussion, I hope you can see that the question of overcutting and its implications for sustainable development can only be considered relative to the level of forest management being practised and the current condition of the forest. There is no fundamental, fixed level of AAC that constitutes sustainable development. Given the relatively low intensity of forest management in most of Canada's forests, it is probable that some of these forests are being overcut. However, if we are able to improve our forest management enough to achieve the climatically determined tree growth potential of our forests, it should be possible to significantly increase AACs in many areas. Achievement of this growth potential may be constrained by the need to maintain non-timber resource values and by the economics of timber production.

The Need for Prediction

Calculating a rate of forest harvest that will result in sustained levels of a variety of forest resource values requires prediction of both the growth of individual stands and the pattern of development of the entire managed forest. This must be done for different possible future management intensities because the sustainable rate of cut is so dependent on the way forests are managed.

As noted in Chapter 5, the single most important job of the professional forester is planning. Planning in turn requires prediction. Thus, prediction of future conditions is the cornerstone on which professional forestry is built. In the case of forest growth prediction, the first step is to classify the forest landscape into ecologically uniform units about which predictions can be made. The biogeo-climatic classification of the forests of British Columbia is a world-class example of such a system. Once we have such a classification in place, we need prediction systems with which to rank the probable outcomes of different ways of managing each ecological unit. Only when we have, and use, ecologically based forest growth and yield predictors in conjunction with an ecological site classification system can we seriously address the issue of overcutting and sustainable development.

Most activities involved in predicting the future are concerned with what will happen tomorrow (the weather), next week (the stock market), or next year (home mortgages). A few are concerned with several decades into the future (developing a ski resort or planning a national energy policy). Very few extend over time scales as long as those involved in the planning of forest resources at temperate and northern latitudes: many decades and up to several centuries. There is so much social, economic, political, and environmental uncertainty about the future that most people would be very happy if we could make tolerably accurate predictions for the next five to ten years. Foresters do not have this luxury. They must make fifty- to one hundred-year predictions of the outcomes of their decisions on an almost daily basis. Now that most foresters are committed to the concept of sustainable development, these predictions must be extended over several rotations.

The unique time scale of forestry calls for unique approaches to predicting the future. The next two sections of this chapter examine the types of prediction that must be made in long-term forest plan-

ning, and the types of long-term prediction systems that have been traditionally used. They pose the following question: Are these systems adequate for the future or are we facing a case of 'future shock'[28] in forestry forecasting? Are our methods of predicting the future able to adjust fast enough to changing forest management, social, and environmental conditions to produce believable visions of the future over one or more rotations?

The Types of Predictions Needed in Forestry

Foresters need to have at least 'ball-park' estimates of a wide variety of future conditions if they are to be able to select management strategies that are logical and effective in terms of present-day objectives (including sustainable development) but also flexible enough to adjust to changing economic and public pressures on the resource.

In terms of timber management, the major prediction needs can be summarized as prediction of the future demand for timber products and the global supply of timber to meet these needs; prediction of the future area of Canadian forests where timber will be produced, that is, future land-use conflicts and their resolution; prediction of timber losses due to fires, insects, and disease; and prediction of how forests will grow in the future. These growth predictions include the growth of individual stands, the future size-class and age-class structure of the whole forest, and the geographic distribution of different types and ages of forest.

In terms of non-timber resource values, forest managers need to predict the effects of their management on wildlife habitat; on the risk of fire, insects, and disease; on landscape aesthetics and recreation values; and on employment and

---

28 Alvin Toffler's book *Future Shock* pointed out that the rate of change in social, political, economic, and other conditions is increasing relentlessly. In the past, our social institutions were able to adjust fast enough to keep up with such changes, but as the rate of change has accelerated, our organizations and institutions have become unable to adapt fast enough, resulting in 'future shock.'

community stability. Foresters also require something that is currently not available: predictions of future climate and future air pollution/acid rain conditions.

Predicting the future *global demand* for forest products is closely related to predicting growth in the human population, future changes in standard of living and per capita consumption of forest resources, and future technological developments in terms of substitutes for wood products or fuel wood. There is great uncertainty attached to all these questions, but there is little doubt that the population will at least double, and it may triple. It is also likely that when the population eventually stabilizes, per capita consumption of forest resources will rise. Considering the concern over the greenhouse effect, predictions of a massive replacement of wood products and fuel wood by fossil fuel-based resources are increasingly questionable.

Predicting the future *global supply* of forest products involves knowing the present area of productive forest in each timber-producing country, and predicting probable trends in the establishment of new forests and the deforestation of existing ones. This involves predicting climate change as well as land-use changes. Estimates must also be made about the ability of forest management programs in various countries to sustain or increase growth and yield in forests managed for timber.

The balance between these estimates of global demand and global supply is the basis for predicting the international market in which Canadian forest products will be traded. Trade and tariff barriers, present and future wars, and other unpredictable events, such as the rapidly changing political, economic, and resource situations in the former USSR. obviously have to be considered. The difficulty of predicting such social and political events is a major problem for those whose job is to predict the future of our forests.

Predicting the risk of losses in Canada's forests to fires, insects, and diseases is exceedingly difficult –

it is probably about as difficult as predicting long-term global demand and supply. Estimates of future losses are largely based on a forward projection of historical rates of loss modified by knowledge of the forest's current condition and the relationship between that condition and the risk of loss. If climate change occurs, it will greatly affect these risks.

Predicting the future characteristics of our forests, such as the total volume, age-class structure, and geographic distribution of stands with various characteristics is accomplished through the use of whole-forest computer models. These take current information about these characteristics (the current inventory of our forests) and calculate the future values for these characteristics that can be expected given different forest management strategies. A comparison of the probable whole-forest outcomes of these different scenarios permits one to select the strategy that would most closely satisfy the long-term management objectives.

The accuracy of predictions from whole-forest models depends heavily on the accuracy of the current inventory of the forest. This often leaves a lot to be desired. We generally do not have an adequate knowledge of the volume, age, and size-class distributions of our forests. We often lack a complete knowledge of their species composition, stand structure, health, and rate of growth. It also depends on our predictions of the growth of the individual stands that make up the forest, but our ability to accurately predict future stand growth is also questionable, as discussed in the next section. In addition, the accuracy of the rotation-length predictions of the whole-forest models also depends on the accuracy of assumptions about losses of forest land to other land uses, and losses of timber to insects, diseases, and fire.

It should be apparent from this discussion that there is considerable uncertainty about the rotation-length consequences of different ways of managing our forests. There are several ways to reduce this uncertainty. The following section describes some of them.

Methods of Predicting Future Growth and Yields of Individual Forest Stands

Experience-Based Prediction in Forestry: The Historical Bioassay

The time scale of prediction in forest planning is very long. Until very recently, we have lacked the knowledge needed to make knowledge-based predictions over such long periods. Consequently, the traditional approach of foresters has been to base their predictions on experience.

No one 'knows' better than a tree how well a tree can grow on a particular site over a hundred-year rotation. An accurate record of how forests have grown in the past still provides the best basis for projecting how forests will grow in the future under similar conditions. This constitutes a *historical bioassay*[29] of a site's growth potential, and is undoubtedly the most believable basis for predicting future growth as long as one important condition is met: that the future growth conditions are essentially the same as those that prevailed in the past.

Many scientists believe that the greenhouse effect is going to alter the global climate significantly. Long-term forecasts suggest that global timber demand will exceed the global supply within 25 to 30 years, implying changes in the way timber-producing forests will be managed. This has implications for the soil characteristics that influence forest growth. Consequently, it is most unlikely that future growing conditions will be sufficiently similar to those of the past to allow us to continue using historical bioassay growth and yield predictors without modification. Their predictions may be satisfactory for short-term (5 to 20 years) evaluations, but they cannot provide the basis for evaluating

sustainability over multiple rotations. This raises important questions about the accuracy of the existing experience-based methods of predicting forest growth and yield, and suggests the need to develop new experience-based predictors that are valid for the new conditions. However, we cannot afford to wait the 50 to 100 years that it would take to develop a bioassay of the forest growth potential under the new conditions. How would we manage our forests in the meantime? Also, by the time we had the new historical bioassay, conditions would probably have changed again: a case of future shock in the forecasting of forest yield.

Knowledge-Based Prediction as an Alternative

The need to make a decision about situations for which we lack prior experience is not an uncommon experience in life. That we are able to do so reasonably successfully is a reflection of the development of the human brain, and its ability to synthesize knowledge gained through experience and education and use it to make predictions about the future. Knowledge-based as opposed to experience-based prediction and decision making is one of the things that is thought to separate the human species from most of the other animal species.

Over the past century, science has generated an impressive body of knowledge about forest ecosystems and their components. Though this knowledge is unquestionably superficial relative to the full complexity of ecosystems, our knowledge is now enough for us to begin making knowledge-based predictions about some of the long-term responses of forest ecosystems to various types of disturbance. Such predictions certainly cannot be completely accurate, but we do know enough to build computer simulation models of sufficient complexity that their predictions can be considered our best educated guess about the future in the absence of the appropriate experience. Such models can certainly be used to rank the probable outcomes of different ways of managing forest ecosystems, even though the absolute predictions should

---

29 Bioassay is the use of a living organism as a method of measuring some environmental condition. Canaries were used in mines as a bioassay of poisonous gases before analytical instruments were available to do the job. Plant growth is still the most sensitive measure of the plant growth potential of a soil. The growth of a forest over the past rotation is the best available measure of the rotation-length growth potential under the conditions that prevailed over this period.

be treated with considerable caution.

If knowledge-based methods of prediction are so good, are they replacing experience-based prediction methods in forestry? The answer is no. Although we know how to develop such predictive tools, the task is both complex and expensive. Given a budget equivalent to NASA's man-on-the-moon project, we could develop such predictors for many of the world's forests. But considering the very modest resources available to the developers of such models, the task is still too complex and expensive for all but a few scientific research institutes. The highly complex computer models that are involved are still well beyond the reach of the average forester, and are likely to remain so for some time to come.

Compromise in Yield Forecasting: The Use of Hybrid Predictors

Historical bioassay predictors have all the reliability and believability that comes with experience, but we generally lack experience of the future conditions about which we wish to make predictions. Knowledge-based prediction offers all the flexibility we need to account for changing future conditions, but in most cases the appropriate predictors have not yet been developed for lack of resources. Sometimes their development has been prevented by lack of knowledge, but this restriction is steadily being reduced.

Both the experience-based and the knowledge-based approaches to predicting forest growth and yield have advantages and drawbacks. Interestingly, the strength of one is the weakness of the other. By combining the two, we can develop prediction models that are firmly based on our experience of the past, but are flexible enough to deal with changing future conditions because they incorporate knowledge-based predictions of the consequences of anticipated changes. This 'hybrid simulation' prediction approach offers the best solution to our stand-growth prediction needs, either until we have gained experience of forest growth under the future

conditions or until we have the knowledge and resources to develop and use purely knowledge-based prediction systems.

Several of the available ecosystem management models are of the hybrid simulation type. These include the American LINKAGES, FORTNITE, and ZELIG models and the Canadian FORCYTE and FORECAST models. The bibliography lists references that can give you more information about these.

Prediction of Timber Yields and Other Resource Values at the Whole-Forest or Landscape Level

Ultimately, the believability of forecasts about future wood supply depends upon the accuracy of predictions about the growth of the individual stands that make up the forest. However, many important questions related to both the timber resource and several non-timber values cannot be answered by stand-level prediction models. They relate to the whole forest – to the entire forested landscape. Questions about water yields, water flow regimes, fish habitat, wildlife, and aesthetics cannot be addressed by stand-level models on their own because these models do not represent the spatial pattern of forest conditions across the landscape and over the whole-forest management unit.

Traditionally, future timber supplies from large forested areas have been predicted by using whole-forest models. These describe the age-class structure of all the stands in the forest, and the stemwood volume in stands of different ages. The change in stemwood volume of each stand over time is estimated by using a stand-level model, usually of the historical bioassay type. In the past, whole-forest models generally lacked any spatial representation, and therefore shared many of the limitations of stand-level models. They could not deal adequately with the implications for wildlife, recreation, and so on upon the spatial pattern of stands of different ages across the landscape.

Foresters have usually overcome this limitation by using maps – the average forest planning office is a veritable library of maps – but the traditional map format also has its limitations. Maps are simply a statement of the spatial pattern of certain forest characteristics at one point in time. In the past, maps took a long time to prepare and quickly became unusable if too much information was added to a single map. Development of folios, or collections, of maps representing all the different values of the forest was a way of overcoming this problem, but storing information for a large forest area in this format becomes problematical. Much of the information on a map of a managed forest becomes obsolete as time passes, requiring periodic updating of the map.

To overcome these difficulties, a new approach has been developed: the *Geographical Information System,* or GIS. This is a computer-based information storage and retrieval system. At the press of a button, new multicoloured maps can be produced representing any desired combination of forest characteristics described by the stored data. GIS technology offers a way to quickly and accurately analyze the spatial relationships in forest management. It represents a great step forward in the ability of foresters to plan the orderly management of the landscape.

Of course, GIS on its own is not the answer. It is merely a quick and convenient way of presenting and analyzing information about the spatial distribution of different existing resource values across the landscape. Successful long-term forest planning requires a marriage between GIS and whole-forest models that are used to predict future values of the conditions described in the GIS. These whole-forest models must, in turn, be married to hybrid simulation stand-growth and yield models that give the best estimate of the future growth of individual stands under various hypothetical stand management regimes. The linking of technology does not stop there. As remote sensing by satellite becomes ever more sophisticated, data on current forest conditions obtained by satellite will be fed into GIS systems to update the inventory of such conditions.

All of these technologies are still in their early stages of development, but, used with intelligence, they offer a great advance in the area of forest planning and prediction.

Conclusions

The urgent need to achieve sustainable development and to halt the steady deterioration of the global environment requires that there be a substantial upgrading of our ability to predict the future and to incorporate such predictions in the planning of resource management. This is as true for forestry as it is for any other renewable resource.

Significant advances have been made in the technology of forest ecosystem monitoring and prediction over the past decade, but most of these have yet to be adopted in the mainstream of forest management. It is time to commit the resources needed to ensure that these new planning tools become suitable for general use and are implemented in the day-to-day management of our forests. They will not solve all our problems, but they will help, especially if they are soundly based in a knowledge of ecosystem function, production ecology, and ecosystem dynamics. The prediction systems must address whole ecosystems and landscapes if they are to provide an adequate basis for planning sustainable multi-resource management.

CHAPTER 16

Sustainable Development and Forestry: Can We Use *and* Sustain Our Forests?

In contrast to exploitive logging, forestry, as defined in Chapter 5, is founded on the concept of sustainability. Much of the forestry of the past, and some of the forestry of today, has failed to achieve its objective of sustaining various social and environmental values. But this is a reflection of the various stages that forestry evolves through, and not the lack of this fundamental objective. The need to sustain both timber and non-timber values in our forests has been mentioned throughout the book, but the importance of the topic requires that we revisit the subject in this, the final chapter.

Sustainable development of forests dedicated for human use is a global imperative. It must be achieved. But the design of methods to do so requires that we understand what is meant by sustainable forestry. We must know how to recognize when forestry is or is not being practised in a sustainable manner, and how to differentiate between change that does not threaten resource sustainability and change that does.

The Time Dimension of Sustainability: Ecological Rotations

On the time scale of ice ages, very few things are sustainable. Almost everything changes. But most of us are not concerned with such long periods of time. We want forest values to be either maintained or renewed over much shorter periods. The problem is, what is a reasonable time scale over which to assess sustainability?

If next year turns out to be much hotter than this year, we cannot conclude that the climate is getting warmer. Weather varies considerably from year to year, and time periods of twenty to thirty years are usually required to define the average climate of a region. Because of this variability, assessment of change in climatic conditions may take fifty years or longer.

Many insect, bird, and mammal species exhibit considerable fluctuation in numbers from year to year. Take, for example, the famous ten-year cycle of the snowshoe hare in the North American boreal forest, and of predators such as the lynx that feed on the hare. These species are known to have exhibited a remarkably regular and dramatic fluctuation in abundance over a cycle of about ten years for at least the past three centuries, and possibly for a millennium. The lemmings of the Arctic do the same, but on a shorter cycle of four to five years. Assessing the sustainability of populations of these species requires that measurements be taken over many cycles. Simply noting that the abundance of lynx, hare, or lemmings is low in any particular year tells us little or nothing about whether the species is threatened or under abnormal stress. To draw such a conclusion requires knowledge of the expected cyclical variation in animal abundance in that particular ecosystem. Many species of salmon also exhibit a regular cycle in the numbers of fish returning from the ocean to spawn in forest streams.

In contrast to natural systems, such as large rivers or lakes that, in the absence of human impact, show little directional change over periods of one or two centuries, forests are always undergoing change. All forests are disturbed periodically. This may be small-scale disturbance caused by the death of individual large trees, or the result of large areas being killed by insects, fire, or wind. Sometimes the disturbance is frequent. Sometimes it is infrequent. But regardless of the temporal or spatial scale of disturbance, if you monitor forests over several decades or centuries, you will observe patterns of forest change that are not connected to human activity and those that are human-caused. Assessing whether human activity has reduced the sustainability of the forest ecosystem thus involves a comparison between the observed pattern of ecosystem change (the 'temporal fingerprint' of the ecosystem in question) and the pattern of change expected for a 'healthy ecosystem.'[30] As in the case of lemmings and lynx, the comparison must be made over a long enough period to characterize the disturbance/recovery cycle, and the question of long-term sustainability may require observations over several cycles.

Predicting the long-term sustainability of various values in a managed forest requires an understanding of the concept of *ecological rotation* (Chapter 4). Observations about the change in forest conditions immediately following natural or human-caused disturbance may be an accurate measure of the change at that moment, but are often not a suitable measure of whether or not the long-term sustainability of those conditions has been threatened. This is because if sufficient time passes before an ecosystem is disturbed again, and if the processes of recovery remain intact, the ecosystem will recover to the pre-disturbance conditions or something very similar. Sustainability in the face of disturbance is therefore the combined result of three factors: the degree to which the ecosystem has been changed, the rate at which it recovers from the disturbance, and the length of time before it is disturbed again. Ecosystems that recover rapidly are sustainable in the face of frequent low- to medium-intensity disturbances or occasional severe disturbances. Ecosystems that recover slowly will sustain a particular set of conditions over the long term if disturbed only infrequently. (Figure 16.1)

As noted above, assessing the sustainability of productivity, biodiversity, and other aspects of forest ecosystems may sometimes require observations over several cycles of disturbance and recovery. Because of the long time scale of most disturbance/recovery cycles in forests, this is generally a long-term proposition. That is why there is an urgent need to develop and use modern ecosystem-level computer prediction tools (Chapter 15) to evaluate the sustainability of our forests and to estimate ecological rotations. We cannot afford to wait the several centuries over which the question can be assessed by simply looking at the forest.

The question of long-term sustainability involving variation of ecosystem conditions around an

---

30 A 'healthy ecosystem' is one in which the physical, chemical, and biological mechanisms of ecosystem recovery are operating at rates that are characteristic of that ecosystem.

unchanging long-term average is different from the question of short-term sustainability. Many people think of sustainability in terms of a lack of change in conditions over short time periods. Maintenance of unchanging water quality, beauty of a landscape, or numbers of particular species of birds or mammals in a certain area is what is expected. In some types of forest, these values can remain largely unchanged for long enough to give the impression of permanence. But change is occurring even in these forests. Water quality varies from year to year, and can decline dramatically during heavy rainstorms because of either natural or human-caused landslides, stream bank erosion, or other sediment-producing events. Animal populations fluctuate because of weather, disease, predation, and other natural risks. The number of salmon returning from the ocean each year to lay their eggs in a forest stream varies greatly in unlogged, undisturbed watersheds as well as in managed watersheds. And the visual quality of a landscape may be altered by fire, insect outbreak, disease, or wind damage in the absence of human interference. If such disturbance events do not occur in our lifetime, we may think that landscapes are permanent, but the historical record suggests that, for most forests, long-term stability is the exception and change is the rule.

Assessing sustainability is thus very much a question of time scales. If change occurs over very short time periods, such as the annual ploughing of a farmer's field, we hardly notice the cycle of change because the system repeatedly recovers to a similar condition within our lifetime. At this rate of disturbance and recovery, it is usually easy to assess within a few years whether or not average conditions are being sustained. If change occurs over very long time scales, everything will have an air of permanence much of the time. Nothing will appear to be changing. At intermediate time scales, we will notice the change, but it may be difficult to tell if average ecosystem conditions will be maintained in the long term because the return to original conditions is slow. Forest harvesting generally occurs on

such intermediate scales. It can cause dramatic changes in ecosystems, changes that generate great concern among the public. The recovery is often slow enough so that people may not notice it for several years. Unlike in agriculture, the cycle of ecosystem disturbance and recovery is not fast enough for people to experience the restoration of the lost conditions.

Spatial Dimensions of Sustainability

If you observed a thousand-hectare tract of mature, undisturbed tropical rain forest from a distance, you might conclude that it was unchanging over many years. An annual inventory of the entire area over this period would probably support this conclusion. However, within this thousand-hectare patch, great changes would be occurring. Individual large trees or small groups of large trees would be dying or be blown over during wind storms, flattening the forest over areas varying in size from a fraction of a hectare up to a few hectares. There would be continual change in the many thousands or tens of thousands of such small patches over the area. Thus, what appears to be unchanging over the large area is really a mosaic of significant changes at a smaller scale. Similarly, when viewed from space, the boreal forest of Canada appears to be a vast, relatively unchanging tract of dark green forest. But when viewed from the ground, there are huge areas of fire-killed, logged, windthrown, and insect-killed forest, all of which are in the process of recovery. Our perception of permanence is thus largely determined by the scale at which we judge it.

There are many examples in forestry – such as the effects of forest harvesting on streams and on timber supply – in which changing the spatial scale over which you assess sustainability will change your conclusions about whether or not good stewardship is being practised.

Timber harvesting generally results in significant short-term changes to small, first-order streams. It can also cause measurable and sometimes significant changes in second- and even third-order streams; these changes are usually temporary but can sometimes be unacceptably persistent. But unless there is unrestricted exploitive logging, or deliberate and permanent large-scale deforestation, changes to larger streams and rivers caused by timber harvesting are usually unmeasurable. Any changes are within the natural range of variation in these larger bodies of water.

Continuous clearcut logging of a large valley may remove all the timber over a couple of decades and eliminate any further timber harvesting in that valley for a half century or more. At a local level, this is clearly unsustainable timber harvesting. However, the rate of harvest may in fact be sustainable if considered at a regional level. On the other hand, distribution of the same rate of clearcut harvest over a much larger area, or harvesting by non-clearcut methods, can result in a small timber harvest being taken from that valley every few years. However, this apparently sustainable local harvest may be part of a regional rate of timber harvest that is too high: it may not be sustainable at the regional level.

In some cases, sustainability *should* be judged at the local level: a particularly beautiful view, an old-growth stand of giant trees, a critical wildlife habitat, or the supply of harvestable timber to sustain a local sawmill and human community, for example. In other cases, it may be appropriate to consider sustainability over larger spatial scales.

Sustaining Ecosystem Potential versus Achieving the Potential

Ensuring that sustainable forestry is being practised requires performance standards. We must know when we have it and when we do not. Planning forestry activities so that they sustain long-term site productivity requires a definition of what site productivity is. Such a definition has two major components: the *potential* site productivity and the *achievement* of that potential.

The potential productivity of a site is largely determined by the local climatic and soil conditions. The temperature, precipitation, atmospheric

humidity, wind, and length of frost or snow-free growing season, together with the moisture, aeration, and fertility of the soil, determine which organisms can occupy an area, and their rate of growth. Soil conditions vary considerably within a climatic area, and therefore the potential productivity of the forest varies at different locations in the local landscape. But some aspects of soil conditions also vary over time, causing a variation in potential productivity over time. Thus, there is no such thing as a fixed, unchanging productivity potential for any particular site. It depends on site conditions.

The growth of trees established after a mature forest has just been logged will be very different from their growth on the same site after a century of unsustainable agricultural activity, even if the climate were to remain the same. The altered levels of soil organic matter and nutrients and the changed physical and chemical conditions of the mineral soil will be reflected in very different tree growth rates. The growth of successive rotations of tree crops will also be different if the soil conditions change between rotations. Examples of both declining growth where soils have been impoverished and increasing growth where soils have been improved can be found in the forestry literature.

Because of the change in the potential productivity of the site as soil conditions change, it may be difficult to establish a fixed productivity performance standard for a particular site. Do we take the growth of the first managed tree-crop rotation after an unmanaged old-growth forest has been logged as our measure of the long-term site potential? The growth of this first managed crop may reflect the organic matter and nutrients it inherited from the old-growth as much or more than the true long-term potential of the site. Or do we use tree growth in the second or third rotation, when much of the biological legacy from the past has been used up and tree growth reflects the current ecological balance of the site? Do we take tree growth in an unmanaged forest as the standard of potential productivity, or should our standard be the growth we can achieve under intensive management?

Everyone should be concerned about conserving forest soils and thereby maintaining potential ecosystem productivity. But conservation of soils will not, on its own, guarantee that timber, wildlife, and other values are sustained. It will ensure only that the *potential* to sustain these values is maintained. *Attainment* of productive stands of trees, of diverse and abundant wildlife, and of various other values depends on the rate and pattern of ecosystem recovery from disturbance, and the subsequent disturbance by insects, fire, wind, and so on. There are many cases where forest harvesting has not damaged the soil and forest ecosystem potential, but because the successional processes of ecosystem change have been altered, neither timber values, aesthetic values, nor wildlife habitat values have been renewed at an acceptable rate. Similarly, failure to protect forests from fire or other risks may prevent the ecosystem from developing to its full potential and may threaten the sustainability of a variety of values even if the site potential has not been damaged.

Large areas of forest around the world have been degraded, not because of soil damage or loss of microclimate (although this has also occurred on much too large a scale) but because of the loss of appropriate plant, animal, or microbial species, or the loss of locally adapted populations thereof. Alternatively, exploitive use of the forest may have created relatively stable early seral communities, such as grass or shrub communities, that are highly resistant to invasion by trees. Fire or grazing has often maintained these areas in a non-forest condition indefinitely, even though the soil and climatic potential for forests to redevelop continue to exist. Many of the world's grasslands were once forests.

Sustainability of fish and wildlife populations also involves sustaining the quality, quantity, and diversity of fish and wildlife habitat (the potential) and the populations of animals to utilize this potential. Overfishing, unregulated hunting, or some other human-caused or natural event that reduces fish or wildlife abundance can threaten their sustainability even if their habitat remains intact.

Major Threats to Sustainability

Population
There can be little doubt that the single greatest threat to the sustainability of the world's forests is too many people. It makes little difference whether we are talking about the decline in fishing success in our favourite lake because of overfishing, about the loss of wilderness values in a remote valley that is now overrun with visitors, or simply about the total number of people in the world. A population of 5.5 billion people heading for between twice and three times this number lies behind all our other environmental problems.

Many people believe that the world already has more people than can be supported indefinitely. Few believe that we can sustain the numbers of humans that are expected to occupy this planet by the end of the next century. Although some countries, such as China, are trying to limit their population growth, others, such as Malaysia, are deliberately encouraging growth in order to develop their economies and international influence. It seems likely that many of the world's forests, especially those at tropical latitudes, are destined to be either converted for food production or degraded because of unregulated exploitation or management practices that are insensitive to local ecological and social conditions.

Atmospheric and Climate Change
Climate sets the potential for biological activity. It defines the type of forest in an area and its potential productivity. Climates have always been changing, but in the past this change was relatively slow. Forests were able to adapt and change their geographical location as the major climatic zones moved across the face of the earth. Human activity over the past half century has been altering the

chemistry of the atmosphere at an unprecedented rate, and the alteration in world climate that many believe will accompany this chemical change must be considered one of the greatest threats to the sustainability of our forests.

The impact that climate change could have on our forests is potentially far greater than the impact of clearcutting, the use of herbicides, the managed use of fire, or other practices that cause public concern. Changes in the intensity and extent of wildfires, insect outbreaks, and forest tree diseases; changes in precipitation patterns, snow accumulation, and streamflow; and changes in the tree species composition of many of our forests that could accompany human-induced climate change constitute one of the greatest, but least predictable, challenges to forest sustainability.

Damage to Soil

Appropriate soil conditions constitute one of the major factors that determine whether the climatically defined biological potential of an area can be achieved. There is a long history of abuse to forest soils around the world. This is especially common in cases of illegal and exploitive logging, but it also occurs sometimes in what is declared to be sustainable forestry. There is still far too little understanding by many loggers and some foresters about forest soils and the impact that timber harvesting and other forest practices have on them. In many cases, damage to soils is associated with poor road construction and inadequate road maintenance on steep slopes in areas with high rainfall. But damage has also been done to soil by the use of inappropriate harvesting equipment, by the removal from nutrient-poor sites of too much organic matter and nutrients (by whole-tree harvesting, for example), or by the use of inappropriate post-logging site preparation practices.

It is unlikely that we will sustain a variety of forest values if we do not sustain appropriate soil conditions. This must become a basic tenet of sustainable forestry.

Loss of Genetic and Species Diversity

Achievement of the biological potential set by climate and soil will occur only if populations of appropriate species with appropriate levels of genetic diversity are available. There are examples around the world of the replacement of native forest or the reforestation of degraded landscapes by non-native species or native species that normally grow on different sites. In many cases this has resulted in sustainable timber crops, but not always. There have been examples in which the wrong choice of tree species has led to plantation failure. (see page 210). Where forestry is based on a sound ecological foundation, it is unlikely that this type of mistake will occur: species will be matched to the site. Where forestry lacks such a foundation, the problem will undoubtedly recur in the future.

The genetic diversity of the plants and animals in forests is important. It is nature's insurance policy. A species that has a lot of genetic variation will be much better equipped to survive damage from wind, fire, insects, diseases, or unseasonable weather (such as summer frost), and will be able to grow over a wider range of sites than a species with a narrow range of genetic variation.

The seed collection and reforestation policies of most modern forestry programs are specifically designed to sustain or increase local genetic variability. Although some of these programs may also produce 'genetically improved' seedlings – trees with straighter stems, smaller branches, and above-average disease resistance – care is normally taken to retain a broad genetic base. However, if seedlings are reproduced vegetatively (that is, they are *cloned),* the entire population of trees in a plantation may be derived from a small number of parent trees. Such a strategy may render plantations more susceptible to damage caused by climate change or natural enemies. In areas where there is a significant risk of this type of damage, clonal regeneration may not be a sustainable strategy unless there are strictly applied regulations to ensure that enough clones are represented in the new forest to include most of the genetic variations in the original forest.

'Natural' Risks

Although fire, insect, disease, and wind are natural disturbance factors that have played an important role in the ecology of many forests, they may threaten the sustainability of timber harvesting, employment, wildlife habitat, and other values in managed forests. The historical frequency and intensity of these types of disturbance have contributed to the forest ecosystem conditions we have inherited, but with the additional disturbance created by forest management and the harvesting of timber, wildlife, and fish, the historical pattern of natural disturbance is often incompatible with the concept of sustainability.

If we wish to change the historical intensity and frequency of disturbance processes, we must understand the effects they have had on forest ecosystems and how these ecosystems will develop in their absence. In cases where natural disturbance has been responsible for sustaining desirable ecosystem conditions, management-caused disturbance must be designed to duplicate these effects.

Poor-Quality Resource Management

Excessive rates of timber harvesting; inadequate forest regeneration; lack of consideration for soils, watershed, and wildlife values; insensitivity to the aesthetics of timber harvesting; and poor road construction and maintenance are among the many problems that may occur if forestry is not planned and implemented on the basis of sustainable management principles and performance standards.

The major resource-use threat to many of the world's forests is deforestation accompanying planned changes in land use, or unplanned and illegal exploitative logging followed by unregulated agricultural activities. However, there are also many examples in which resource values have been lost and their long-term sustainability reduced by poor-quality forest management in forests that have been dedicated to the sustained production of these values.

Forestry must be guided by a set of principles of sustainable forest management, and site-specific, ecology-based codes of practice that are consistent with these principles. Management that fails to conform to these principles and codes of practice should not be tolerated.

Inadequate Investment and Inappropriate Tenure Systems

Sustainable forestry generally requires a significant investment of time, effort, and money. Global poverty has been identified as one of the most significant and fundamental threats to the environment; similarly a lack of economic health among the government agencies and private organizations that manage and harvest forests is often one of the reasons why forestry is not practised at an acceptable level.

Planning is an indispensable part of sustainable forestry, but it is expensive. Where funds are short, or where the organization conducting forestry is too small to pay the considerable costs involved, there may not be enough planning to avoid conflict between timber harvesting and other resource values. Ideally, the planning team should include resource specialists in hydrology, soils, wildlife, road building, and so on. Normally, only large organizations are able to afford such planning teams.

Site-specific management generally requires the use of different timber harvesting equipment on different sites. Unless a logging company or private landowner has a bank balance large enough to own several different types of logging equipment, a single type of equipment may be used in many different types of forest, and this will almost certainly result in negative effects on some of the harvested ecosystems.

The willingness of individuals, companies, or government agencies to make long-term investments in planning, equipment purchase, and forest management appears to be closely related to the probability that they will receive the benefits of such investments. Few of us would be willing to pay out of our own pocket to repaint a house that we were only renting for one month. If we intended to live there for five years, we probably would be willing to make this personal investment. If we were sure that we would occupy the house for twenty years, we might even pay for structural modifications: we might remodel an old kitchen or bathroom. In general, though certainly not always, a forestry organization that has a secure long-term tenure – they own the land or they have a dependable long-term contract to manage an area of public forest – will be more willing to make long-term investments in better forestry than those whose tenures are short-term or insecure.

Are Large Timber Companies a Threat to the Sustainability of Our Forests?

Recently there has been a lot of public antagonism in Canada towards large timber companies operating under licence to the government on public forest lands. There appears to be a public preference for small, local forestry organizations over large national or international corporations. 'Small is beautiful' and 'large is bad' appears to be a popular philosophy. However, the relationship between size of organization and quality of resource management should be judged on the basis of performance, not on the basis of a theory about this relationship.

Based on visits to forests in many different countries, I have concluded that the quality of forest management has more to do with the knowledge and commitment of the people involved to sustainable management, and with how long they have been and will be involved with a particular forest, than with the size of the organization. One can observe both good and bad forest management on private forest land and in public forests. The quality of forest management varies considerably between different small landowners as well as between different large landowners. Different small logging companies and different large logging companies may have either a good or a bad reputation with respect to

their impact on the environment. Similarly, there are both small and large forest management organizations that manage the forests under their control in a sustainable manner, and there are those that do not. The key to good forest management includes adequate knowledge and training by forest planners, managers, and workers; adequate planning and supervision of their work; a sufficiently long tenure to encourage long-term investment and stewardship; an economic climate that encourages investment in good management; and a commitment to sustaining the resource. The question of length and security of tenure features strongly in this list.

If a large timber company is committed to practising sustainable forestry; if it has a long-term secure tenure, an experienced and committed staff of technical and professional foresters and timber harvesters who respect the land and understand the relationship between their activities and the goals of sustainable management; and if the company is conducting profitable forestry, I would expect the quality of resource management to be higher than in a much smaller operation that does not have the human, equipment, and financial resources to respond flexibly to the ever-changing demands of forest management. Small companies can sometimes have greater local knowledge, a greater commitment to sustaining local communities, and a greater ability to respond rapidly to small-scale market opportunities, but if they do not have the financial and human resources to conduct the type of multiple resource management that the public is demanding, they will not necessarily practise sustainable forestry. They may not be better, or even as good, as a larger company with greater resources. A well-balanced economy will have a mixture of both large and small companies. The public support for, or criticism of, any company should be based on its performance and not on its size.

Essentials for Sustainable Forestry

It is difficult to come up with a single list of conditions and activities that will ensure sustainable use and development of all forests. The critical issues vary significantly between different forest areas. However, the following are probably fundamental to most forests.

An Adequate Ecological Foundation

The historical record suggests that an adequate understanding of the ecology of the trees, wildlife, and other species that one wishes to sustain, and an understanding of how ecosystems function, is essential if forests are to be managed sustainably. An important component of this ecological foundation is an ecological site classification, such as the biogeoclimatic classification of British Columbia, accompanied by interpretations of the management significance of the different ecological units. All forestry activities should be conducted within the context of this classification: forest inventory, choice of species for reforestation, choice of site-preparation and stand-tending techniques, rotation length, and so on. Such a classification will not guarantee that forests are managed sustainably, of course. The issue of sustainability is much more complex than simply whether or not forestry is soundly based on the science of ecology. But without an ecological site classification and the accompanying ecological knowledge, it will be much more difficult to achieve sustainability.

An Accurate Inventory of the Values to Be Sustained

It is almost impossible to plan sustainable management for various values if you lack information about the extent and location of these values. Lack of adequate inventories of wildlife habitat and populations has been a major problem in designing forest management strategies that will sustain wildlife values. Similarly, the lack of an adequate definition of what old-growth forests are, and the lack of an inventory of old-growth values has proven to be a major problem in developing a policy to ensure that adequate areas of old growth are reserved.

Ecosystem-Level Prediction Tools

In the absence of experience of the consequences of forest management over several rotations in many parts of North America, we are forced to predict these consequences. This is a difficult task. To help foresters rank the possible consequences of alternative ways of managing particular forests, we must develop and use ecology-based prediction tools. These must incorporate our latest understanding of how ecosystems work and how they respond to management. They must be updated regularly as our knowledge improves.

Economic Viability

Sustainable forest management requires investment, and unless the public is prepared to subsidize uneconomic forestry, it must show a profit. One of the major objectives of management in most public forests is the creation of economic capital that can be used to fund social services such as hospitals, schools, roads, water and sewage services, policing, and fire protection.

Where timber management is undertaken as an economic activity, timber will not be harvested if a profit cannot be made, unless there is some other economic justification for the activity. Where the profit margin is very small, or where the costs of timber management and harvesting exceed the selling price of the wood, shortcuts may be taken to reduce costs. Such shortcuts may have negative environmental consequences or impair non-timber values. Sustaining the supply of logs to mills, avoiding the environmental damage that results from sloppy forestry, and reducing the conflicts between different resource values requires that there be a favourable economic climate for forestry.

Stable Land-Use Strategy, Management Objectives, and Tenure

Because of the long time scale involved in forestry, it is important that society decide on a strategy for the use of its public land, and decide what it wants from public forests that are to be managed. The economic and management uncertainty that exists in the absence of a comprehensive and stable land-use strategy does not encourage sustainable forestry. And what might be sustainable forestry under one land-use strategy and management objective may be unsustainable under a different strategy and objective. Stable, long-term tenures with clearly defined and stable management objectives are as important to sustainable forestry as an ecological foundation is.

Of course, both management objectives and land use will probably change on public forests from time to time as the human population increases and as values and technology change. However, changes in objectives and land use should be made only after careful consideration of the consequences of such changes for the quality of forest management. Such changes will inevitably be made from time to time, but must not be made in a manner that causes an unacceptable reduction in the sustainability of various values.

Integrated Planning for Multiple Values

Forestry in many of the world's forests has focused on timber management. Sustaining (or attempts to sustain) other values in these timber-production forests has been achieved by constraining timber management. Sometimes this has worked well, but sometimes it has not.

There are many ideas about how forests should be managed to protect multiple values: multiple use, best use, integrated use, and so on. Some people advocate managing forests to sustain all values in all forests all the time. Others recommend the stratification of the forest into a mosaic of single-use areas according to the balance of values that each area can provide: timber production areas, wildlife corridors and reserves, stream protection forests, wilderness areas, and so on. Secondary uses and values would exist in these single-use areas only if they did not interfere with the main value. Another approach is to identify some areas as single-use – such as plantations near mills; wilderness

areas – and to achieve a mixture of uses and values in the rest of the forest, the balance of uses varying according to the potential of the ecosystem to sustain the values, and the social demand for them.

It is probable that no single approach is ideal for all forests. However, a primary focus on timber managed by one agency, with other values managed by different agencies in the form of constraints on timber management, is a recipe for conflict. Systems of more integrated management with a single agency responsible for, and benefiting from, multiple resource values, may be a better approach. However, there are often many impediments to the development of such a system, even where it offers significant benefits.

Accountable, Informal Public Involvement

Concerned members of the public have the right and the responsibility to be involved in deciding how public forests should be managed. However, to be effective this involvement must be accountable and based on an adequate understanding of the issues. People cannot make decisions that will affect the safety, health, and employment of other people or the integrity of forest ecosystems without being responsible to some degree for the consequences of these decisions. And unless the decisions are based on an adequate understanding of the ecological and sociological aspects of their consequences, they may not contribute to sustaining various values; they may even be counterproductive.

Many people living in rural areas desire to become involved in forestry on public lands through the creation, where they do not already exist, of community forests. This is an excellent idea. But for this involvement to be effective and accountable, the community should become economically dependent to some degree on the community forest. This could be achieved by reducing transfer payments to the community from senior governments in proportion to the reduced revenue that the senior governments would get from the area of public forest that has been transferred to the community. It would then be up to the community to decide how its forest should be managed (subject to all the existing regulations, of course) and how much revenue should be generated from the community forest to pay for social services.

A Commitment to Sustainable Development

All the planning and the management techniques will be in vain if there is no commitment to sustaining the many different values provided by our forests. There must be a stewardship ethic among government policymakers, the corporate levels of forest industry, and those who plan and manage forest resources on the ground. This stewardship ethic should cover the environmental, social, and economic values of our forests. These different and sometimes conflicting issues cannot be separated if we are to achieve sustainable use and development of our forests.

Many forests take a long time to grow, and the benefits or losses that result from our decisions and actions are the forest legacy we leave to our children and grandchildren, and their children and grandchildren. We must consider the balance between short-term benefits for today's generation and the long-term benefits for future generations: a balance that is referred to as *intergenerational equity*. Unless we as a society make the commitment to sustain values for the future, the quality of that future will become increasingly questionable.

Conclusion

We can use and sustain a wide variety of values in our forests. We can 'have our cake and eat it.' But this will be true only if we manage forests with both a biophysical and a sociological/economic perspective, and with a commitment to sustainable management.

Sustainable forestry is not just about maintaining the supply of raw materials and jobs. It is also about maintaining the functioning of the global ecosystem and global biodiversity. But sustainable forestry must be concerned about people and their needs. It cannot focus only on environmental issues such as wilderness, biodiversity, and old growth.

The greatest threat to the world's forests is people, and one of the major threats to the world's people is the loss or degradation of the world's forests. People and forests are thus inextricably linked. It has been this way throughout most of the evolution of our species. If we are to continue to live on this planet, we must learn to exist in harmony with our forests. This does not imply that there will be no change in any of the world's forests, but that the cycles of ecosystem disturbance and recovery should be such that desired ecosystem conditions and values are sustained at acceptable levels and that the long-term trends in ecosystem development conform to society's goals.

Thanks to public concern about the environment, the issue of sustainability is now high on the agenda of many of the world's politicians. It is almost unimaginable that there could ever be a return to the old attitudes towards the environment. Although we face a long and uncertain path to the ultimate achievement of sustainable management of the world's forests, public pressure has moved us a significant distance.

Forestry began as an organized human activity to sustain a variety of desired environmental conditions and a supply of desired products from our forested landscapes. 'Sustained yield' has been the maxim under which most foresters have operated: some successfully, some unsuccessfully. A significant number of non-foresters are now equally concerned about sustainability, though the values they wish to sustain are often different from those that have been the traditional focus of foresters. This difference has been the cause of much of the present conflict between forestry and the environmental movement. It is time to resolve the conflict and recognize that both forestry and conservation have the same origin: sustainability. The energies and talents of both sides of the debate are urgently needed to design and implement systems that will sustain *all* the values we want from our forests.

Reality, Pictures, and Words

Reality

The major threat to the global forest environment is people: about 5.5 billion of them in 1992, with double or even triple this number expected by the time young forests established in various parts of British Columbia in the summer of 1992 are ready for final harvest. The resource use, air and water pollution, soil damage, global climate change, and loss of species diversity that are expected to accompany this population increase constitute a reality that conservation and sustainable development must face in the 1990s and beyond.

War, famine, disease, and political upheaval are expected to continue to divert resources that are so urgently needed to help stabilize the world population. As a result, it is probable that the most fundamental environmental threat, global poverty, will continue for the foreseeable future. If this pessimistic scenario is accurate, the developed countries must make a far greater commitment to helping the developing countries stabilize their population. These countries must be assisted in reaching a stage of social and political evolution in which much less of their national resources are spent on military activities and national security. Only then will environmental protection become a major focus of their government policy. It was the conclusion of the World Commission on Environment and Development that, among other things, this will require sustainable development of resources to create the wealth necessary to achieve these goals.

There is still no agreement about exactly what sustainable development means, and even less on how to achieve it. Yet we must achieve it if we as a species hope to be more than the merest blip on the evolutionary record. Our efforts to achieve sustainable production of renewable food and fibre crops without ever-increasing reliance on fossil fuel-based mechanical and chemical technologies have been limited by lack of public and political will, and by the externalization of the environmental costs of production – assuming that environmental degradation is free: it does not have to be paid for. If and when society makes the commitment to sustainable development, the question will undoubtedly remain in the minds of many people as to whether resources can be used sustainably and whether we understand enough about ecosystems to manage them in a sustainable manner.

Pictures

Some environmentalists repeatedly promote the idea that once disturbed by timber harvesting, a forest ecosystem can *never* return to its original condition. They illustrate their contention with pictures of freshly logged old-growth forests. Some of these pictures tell a very important story of failed and unacceptable harvesting or other management practices. The environmental movement is to be commended for forcing foresters to confront these examples of mismanagement. However, many of the pictures, though visually distasteful, do not portray the permanent loss of ecosystem condition that is often alleged. Many are a frozen-in-time image of what is a rapidly changing condition. They are like looking at a single frame from a movie. They often tell us very little about the medium-term and long-term consequences of the conditions they depict.

The two-dimensional pictures and the verbal images that are widely used to depict the environmental consequences of forest management generally lack that critical ecosystem dimension: time. Ecosystems are constantly changing, the way a movie does when a number of frames are flashed on the screen in succession. If a photograph of a harvested forest were taken every year for a century and the images spliced and run through a movie projector, one would have a film of one hundred years of ecosystem development following disturbance. No single frame in this movie would accurately describe the entire sequence. Only when one considers how ecosystem conditions will change over an entire rotation or more can one begin to decide whether a particular management strategy satisfies one's management objectives or not.

It is frequently said that we do not know enough about ecosystems to be able to manage them. It is doubtful that we will ever learn everything about any particular ecosystem, just as a medical doctor will probably never know everything about a particular patient. However, great medical advances in the past forty years have permitted medical triumphs over diseases and ailments that maimed or killed on a regular basis until very recently. Similarly, great strides have been made in our scientific understanding of forest ecosystems over this same period. Even though it is not always used by foresters, the knowledge now exists to avoid the failures that have damaged the reputation of forestry and foresters in the past. For the foreseeable future, we must continue to extend, refine, and improve our understanding of forest ecosystems, but the most urgent need today is for political, economic, and management mechanisms that can translate what we already know into sustainable management systems that are used to improve on the management of the past.

It is time to change the image of the ecosystem as a static entity that, once disturbed, cannot recover. It is time to change the idea that we do not know enough to be able to improve the way we manage most of our forests, or to manage them sustainably. However, it is also time to require that all forestry, private, public, and industrial, be required to use a current knowledge about forests to improve their management. If we approach sustainable development of forest resources with an understanding of ecosystem functioning and dynamics based on available scientific knowledge, it should be possible to achieve society's demands for sustainable management. Forest management problems often have more to do with a failure to apply what we know than with an absolute lack of knowledge. Such problems have more to do with the unwillingness or inability of government and industry to invest sufficient human and financial resources in forest management than with a lack of desire by most foresters to manage forests sustainably for a variety of resource values.

Words

Both environmentalists and experienced field foresters should be members of the multi-disciplinary team that contributes to the development of policies to guide the sustainable use and development of forests. For such a partnership to be effective, there must be agreement at the outset concerning the meaning of words that are used in discussions. Loaded terms like 'never' and 'forever' would be best 'checked at the door.' Phrases like 'ecologically sound' and 'ecologically rational' should be replaced by 'environmentally sound' and environmentally rational.' Words must be used in a manner that conforms to society's commonly accepted definitions of these words, and not some current, popular redefinition of their meaning by any of the parties at the table. Without agreement on the information content of specific words, communication becomes virtually impossible – we are speaking different languages. Only with such agreement will the appropriate contributions of the science of ecology and the value-based judgments of society to the development of policy be recognized and used as a basis for designing sustainable development policies and practices.

Closing Comment

Forestry originated as a conservation activity, although sometimes the way it has been practised in various places around the world has been closer to exploitation than conservation. Such examples do not constitute what forestry is intended to be.

In its early phases, forestry often fails to achieve its objectives, in part because of the lack of an appropriate ecological foundation. When based securely on such a foundation, it is generally possible to achieve sustainable silviculture, but this does not necessarily satisfy all of society's needs or desires. Only when forestry is developed to be both ecology-based and responsive to the diverse local and regional needs of people will it reach the goal for which it was originally developed: the management of forested landscapes to assure a sustained supply of a variety of goods and services desired by society.

Sustainable development of forests for the extraction of commodities and the maintenance of non-commodity values is possible. It is also essential, but not everywhere. Some forests will be dedicated as wilderness, ecological reserves, wildlife reserves, riparian stream-protection forests, slope-protection forests, and so on. The management these forests receive will be consistent with their land-use designation. However, the majority of the world's forests will be managed to provide the resources to satisfy the needs of today's human population, while ensuring that future generations will be able to satisfy their needs.

The environment is too important for us to go on arguing about it. All sides in the forestry/environment debate must enter a partnership to ensure sustainable development. We must base this partnership on social and environmental realities and our current scientific knowledge. We must use pictures and images that accurately portray the problems we face, and ensure that in our verbal and written communication we use our language in a way that accurately communicates our knowledge and goals.

Chapter 2: The Peter Pan Principle in Renewable-Resource Conflicts

Blackie, J.R., E.D. Ford, J.E.M. Horne, D.J. Kinsman, F.T. Last, and P. Moorhouse. 1980. *Environmental Effects of Deforestation: An Annotated Bibliography.* Occasional Paper No. 10. Freshwater Biological Association. Ambleside, Cumberland, UK. 173 pp.

Clark, W.C. and R.E. Munn. 1986. *Sustainable Development of the Biosphere.* Cambridge, UK: Cambridge University Press. 491 pp.

Rees, W.E. 1989. *Planning for Sustainable Development: A Resource Book.* Vancouver, BC: UBC Centre for Human Settlements. 145 pp.

World Commission on Environment and Development (WCED). 1987. *Our Common Future.* Oxford: Oxford University Press. 400 pp.

Chapter 3: Causes and Time Scales of Environmental Change

Botkin, D.B. 1990. *Discordant Harmonies: A New Ecology for the Twenty-First Century.* New York: Oxford University Press. 241 pp.

Botkin, D.B., M.F. Caswell, J.E. Estes, and A.A. Orio (eds.). 1989. *Changing the Global Environment: Perspectives on Human Involvement.* New York: Academic Press. 459 pp.

Pielou, E.C. 1991. *After the Ice Age: The Return of Life to Glaciated North America.* Chicago: University of Chicago Press. 366 pp.

Thirgood, J.V. 1981. *Man and the Mediterranean Forest: A History of Resource Depletion.* New York: Academic Press. 194 pp.

Chapter 4: A Brief Primer on Ecology and Forest Ecosystems

Edmonds, R.L. (ed.). 1982. *Analysis of Coniferous Forest Ecosystems in the Western United States.* Stroudsburg, PA: Hutchinson Ross. 419 pp.

Kimmins, J.P. 1990. Modelling the sustainability of forest production and yield for a changing and uncertain future. *Forestry Chronicle* 66:271-80

——. 1972. The ecology of forestry: The ecological role of man, the forester, in forest ecosystems. *Forestry Chronicle* 48:301-7

——. 1987. *Forest Ecology.* New York: Macmillan. 531 pp.

Meidinger, D.V. and J. Pojar. 1991. *Ecosystems of British Columbia.* Victoria, BC: BC Ministry of Forests. 330 pp.

Reichle, D.E. (ed.). 1981. *Dynamic Properties of Forest Ecosystems.* Cambridge, UK: Cambridge University Press. 683 pp.

Spurr, S.H. and B.V. Barnes. 1980. *Forest Ecology* (3d ed.). New York: J. Wiley & Sons. 687 pp.

Waring, R.H. and W.H. Schlesinger. 1985. *Forest Ecosystems: Concepts and Management.* New York: Academic Press. 340 pp.

Chapter 5: A Brief Primer on Forestry

Fernow, B.E. 1911. *History of Forestry.* Toronto, ON: University of Toronto Press. 506 pp.

Heske, F. 1938. *German Forestry.* New Haven, CT: Yale University Press. 395 pp.

Kimmins, J.P. and Dorli M. Duffy. 1991. Sustainable forestry in the Fraser River Basin. In A.H. J. Dorcey (ed.), *Perspectives on Sustainable Development in Water Management: Towards Agreement in the Fraser River Basin.* Westwater Research Centre, Fac. of Graduate Studies, Univ. of BC, Vancouver. 217-40

Klinka, K., R.E. Carter, and M.C. Feller. 1990. Cutting old-growth forests in British Columbia: Ecological considerations for forest regeneration. *Northwest Environmental Journal* 6:221-42

Lavender, D.P., R. Parish, C.M. Johnson, G. Montgomery, A. Vyse, R. Willis, and D. Winston (eds.). 1990. *Regenerating British Columbia's Forests.* Vancouver, BC: UBC Press. 372 pp.

Mustian, A.P. 1978. History and philosophy of silviculture and management systems in use today. In *Uneven-Aged Silviculture and Management in the United States.* USDA For. Serv., Timber Management Research, Washington, DC, Gen. Tech. Rept., WO-24. 1-17

Smith, D.M. 1962. *The Practice of Silviculture* (7th ed.). New York: Wiley & Sons. 565 pp.

Thirgood, J.V. 1981. *Man and the Mediterranean Forest: A History of Resource Depletion.* New York: Academic Press. 194 pp.

Troup, R.S. 1952. *Silviculture Systems* (2d ed.). (E.W. Jones, ed.) Oxford: Oxford University Press. 216 pp.

Winters, R.K. 1974. *The Forest and Man.* New York: Vantage Press. 393 pp.

Chapter 6: Clearcutting: Ecosystem Destruction or Environmentally Sound Timber Harvesting?

Anderson, H.W., M.D. Hoover, and K.G. Reinhart. 1976. *Forests and Water: Effects of Forest Management on Floods, Sedimentation, and Water Supply.* Berkeley, CA: USDA For. Serv., PSW For. Range Exp. Sta., Gen. Tech. Rept. PSW-18. 115 pp.

Anon. 1974. Research into problems of clearfelling and clear-felled areas at the Royal College of Forestry. *Special Number Sveriges Skogs vårdsförbunds Tidskrift* 72(1):1-246

Ballard, R. and S.P. Gessel (eds.). 1983. *IUFRO Symposium on Forest Site and Continuous Productivity.* Portland, OR: USDA For. Serv., PNW For. Range Exp. Sta., Gen. Tech. Rept. PNW-163. 406 pp.

Bell, M.A.M., J.M. Beckett, and W.F. Hubbard. 1974. *Impact of Harvesting on Forest Environments and Resources: A Review of the Literature and Evaluation of Research Needs.* Contract Report to Canadian Forestry Service, Pacific Forest Research Centre, Victoria. 141 pp.

Bell, M.A.M., J.M. Brown, and W.F. Hubbard. 1974. *Impact of Harvesting on Forest Environments and Resources.*

Ottawa: Canadian Forestry Service. Forestry Technical Report 3. 237 pp.

Blackie, J.R., E.D. Ford, J.E.M. Horne, D.J. Kinsman, F.T. Last, and P. Moorhouse. 1980. *Environmental Effects of Deforestation: An Annotated Bibliography.* Occasional Paper No. 10. Freshwater Biological Association, Ambleside, Cumberland, UK. 173 pp.

Bosch, J.M. and J.D. Hewlett. 1982. A review of catchment experiments to determine the effect of vegetation changes on water yield and evapotranspiration. *Journal of Hydrology* 55:3-23

Dyck, W.J. and C.A. Mees. 1989. *Research Strategies for Long-Term Site Productivity.* FRI Bulletin No. 152. IEA/BE A3 Report No. 8. Min. of Forestry, Forest Research Institute, Rotorua, NZ. 257 pp.

EPA. 1975. *Logging Roads and Protection of Water Quality.* U.S. Environmental Protection Agency, Region X, Water Division, Seattle. 312 pp.

Freedman, B. 1981. *Intensive Forest Harvest: A Review of Nutrient Budget Considerations.* Canadian Forestry Service, Maritimes Forest Research Centre, Fredericton, NB Info. Rept. M-X-121. 78 pp.

Gessel, S.P., D.S. Lacate, G.F. Weetman, and R.F. Powers. 1990. *Sustained Productivity of Forest Soils.* Proc. 7th North American Forest Soils Conf. Univ. of British Columbia, Faculty of Forestry, Vancouver, BC. 525 pp.

Gimbarzevsky, P. 1988. *Mass Wasting on the Queen Charlotte Islands: A Regional Inventory.* BC Ministry of Forests, Land Management Report 29. 96 pp.

Herman, R.K. and D.P. Lavender (eds.). 1973. *Even-Age Management.* Proc. Symposium. School of Forestry, Oregon State Univ., Corvallis, OR. 250 pp.

Horowitz, E.C.J. 1974. *Clearcutting: A View from the Top.* Washington, DC: Acropolis Books. 179 pp.

Johnson, H.J., H.F. Cerezke, F. Endean, G.R. Hillman, A.D. Kiil, J.C. Lees, A.A. Loman, and I.M. Powell. 1971. *Some Implications of Large-Scale Clearcutting in Alberta: A Literature Review.* Northern Forest Research Centre, Canadian Forestry Service, Edmonton, AB. Info. Rept. NOR-X-6. 114 pp.

Klinka, K. and R.E. Carter. 1991. *A Stand-Level Guide to the Selection of Reproduction Methods for Regenerating Forest Stands in the Vancouver Forest Region.* Report to BC Ministry of Forests, Victoria, BC. 19 pp. + App.

Klinka, K., R.E. Carter, and M.C. Feller. 1990. Cutting old-growth forests in British Columbia: Ecological considerations for forest regeneration. *Northwest Environmental Journal* 6:221-42

Loomis, R. and M. Wilkinson. 1990. *Wildwood: A Forest for the Future.* Gabriola, BC: Reflections. 55 pp.

Lousier, J.D. and G.W. Still. 1988. *Degradation of Forested Land: Forest Soil at Risk.* Proc. 10th BC Soil Science Workshop, Feb. 1986. Land Management Report No. 56. BC Ministry of Forests, Victoria, BC. 331 pp.

Montgomery, J.M. 1976. *Forest Harvest, Residue Treatment,*

Reforestation and Protection of Water Quality. U.S. Environmental Protection Agency, Region X, Seattle. EPA 910/9-76-020. 273 pp.

Perry, D.A., R. Meurisse, B. Thomas, R. Miller, J. Boyle, J. Means, C.R. Perry, and R.F. Powers (eds.). 1989. *Maintaining the Long-Term Productivity of Pacific Northwest Forest Ecosystems.* Portland, OR: Timber Press. 256 pp.

Smith, D.M. 1973. Maintaining timber supply in a sound environment. In *Report of the President's Advisory Panel on Timber and the Environment.* Arlington, VA. 369-428

Stone, E. 1973. The impact of timber harvesting on soils and water. In *Report of the President's Advisory Panel on Timber and the Environment.* Arlington, VA. 428-67

USDA. 1980. *Environmental Consequences of Timber Harvesting in Rocky Mountain Coniferous Forests.* USDA For. Serv., Intermountain For. Range Exp. Sta., Ogden, UT. Gen. Tech. Rept. IWT-90. 526 pp.

Weetman, G.F. 1983. Forestry practices and stress on Canadian forestry land. *In* W. Simpson-Lewis, R. McKechnie, and V. Neimanis (eds.), *Stress on Land in Canada.* Environment Canada, Lands Directorate, Ottawa. Folio No. 6. 259-301

Chapter 7: Slashburning: Responsible Land Management or Playing with Fire?

Cramer, O.P. (ed.). 1974. *Environmental Effects of Forest Residues Management in the Pacific Northwest: A State-of-Knowledge Compendium.* USDA For. Serv., PNW For. Range Exp. Sta., Portland, OR. Gen. Tech. Rept. PNW-24. 19 chapters + App.

Hanley, D.P., J.J. Kammenga, and C.D. Oliver (eds.). 1989. *The Burning Decision: Regional Perspectives on Slash.* College of Forest Resources, Univ. of Washington, Seattle. Institute of Forest Resources Contribution No. 66. 374 pp.

Intermountain Fire Research Council. 1970. *The Role of Fire in the Intermountain West.* Proc. Symp. School of Forestry, Univ. of Montana, Missoula, MT. 229 pp.

Kozlowski, T.T. and C.E. Ahlgren (eds.). 1974. *Fire and Ecosystems.* New York: Academic Press. 542 pp.

Mooney, H.A., T.M. Bonnicksen, N.L. Christensen, J.E. Lotan, and W.A. Reiners (eds.). 1981. *Fire Regimes and Ecosystem Properties.* USDA For. Serv., Gen. Tech. Rept. WO-26. 593 pp.

Slaughter, C.W., R.J. Barney, and G.M. Hansen. 1971. *Fire in the Northern Environment: A Symposium.* USDA For. Serv., PNW For. Range Exp. Sta., Portland, OR. 275 pp.

Walstad, J.D., S.R. Radosevich, and D.V. Sandberg (eds.) 1990. *Natural and Prescribed Fire in Pacific Northwest Forests.* Corvallis, OR: Oregon State University Press. 317 pp.

Wein, R.W. and D.A. Maclean (eds.). *The Role of Fire in North Circumpolar Ecosystems.* SCOPE Rept. 18. New York: J. Wiley & Sons. 322 pp.

Chapter 8: Chemicals in Forest Management

Ames, B.N. 1983. Dietary carcinogens and anticarcinogens: Oxygen radicals and degenerative diseases. *Science* 221:1256-64

Balfour, D.M. 1989. *Effects of Forest Herbicides on Some Important Wildlife Forage Species.* BC Ministry of Forests and Forestry Canada, Victoria. FRDA Report 20. 58 pp.

Bohmont, B.L. 1990. *The Standard Pesticide User's Guide* (rev. ed.). Englewood Cliffs, NJ: Prentice Hall. 498 pp.

Brent, K.J. and R.K. Atkin. 1987. *Rational Pesticide Use.* Proc. Ninth Long Ashton Symposium. Cambridge, UK: Cambridge University Press. 348 pp.

Dodge, A.D. 1989. *Herbicides and Plant Metabolism.* Cambridge, UK: Cambridge University Press. 277 pp.

Edwards, C.A. 1973. *Persistent Pesticides in the Environment* (2d ed.). Boca Raton, FL: CRC Press. 170 pp.

Gips, T. 1987. *Breaking the Pesticide Habit: Alternatives to Twelve Hazardous Pesticides.* International Alliance for Sustainable Agriculture, Univ. of Minnesota, Minneapolis. 372 pp.

Grover, R. (ed.). 1988. *Environmental Chemistry of Herbicides* (vol. 1). Boca Raton, FL: CRC Press. 207 pp.

Haeussler, S. and D. Coates. 1986. *Autecological Characteristics of Selected Species that Compete with Conifers in British Columbia: A Literature Review.* BC Ministry of Forests and Forestry Canada, Victoria, BC. FRDA Report 1. 180 pp.

Hamilton E. 1990. *Vegetation Management: An Integrated Approach.* Proc. 4th Annual Vegetation Management Workshop. BC Ministry of Forests and Forestry Canada, Victoria. FRDA Report 109. 127 pp.

Hedin, P.A. (ed.). 1985. *Bioregulators for Pest Control.* ACS Symposium Series 276. American Chemical Society, Washington, DC. 540 pp.

Kimmins, J.P. 1975. *Review of the Ecological Effects of Herbicide Usage in Forestry.* Forestry Canada, Pacific Forest Research Centre, Victoria, BC. Info. Rept. BC-X-139. 44 pp.

Kimmins, J.P. and P.G. Comeau. 1989. *Forest Vegetation Management Research Strategy for the Southern Interior, British Columbia.* Report to Research Branch, BC Ministry of Forests, Victoria, BC. 101 pp. + App.

Kimmins, J.P. and P.N. Fraker. 1973. *Bibliography of Herbicides in Forest Ecosystems.* Forestry Canada, Pacific Forest Research Centre, Victoria, BC. Info. Rept. BC-X-81. 261 pp., 1614 refs.

Lavender, D.P. and M. Newton. 1984. Forest regeneration and forest health. In *Impacts de l'Homme sur la Forêt.* IUFRO Symposium, Strasbourg, France. INRA, Paris. 215-36

Mandava, N.B. (ed.). 1985. *CRC Handbook of Natural Pesticides: Methods.* Vol. 1, *Theory, Practice and Detection.* Boca Raton, FL: CRC Press. 534 pp.

National Academy of Sciences. 1974. *The Effects of Herbicides in South Vietnam.* Washington, DC: National Academy of Sciences

Örlander, G., P. Gemmel, and J. Hunt. 1990. *Site Preparation: A Swedish Overview.* BC Ministry of Forests and Forestry Canada, Victoria. FRDA Report 105. 61 pp.

Racke, K.D. and J.R. Coats (eds.). 1990. *Enhanced Biodegradation of Pesticides in the Environment.* ACS Symposium Series 426. Washington, DC: American Chemical Society. 302 pp.

Radosevich, S.R. and J.S. Holt. 1984. *Weed Ecology: Implications for Vegetation Management.* New York: Wiley-Interscience. 265 pp.

Ragsdale, N.N. and R.J. Kuhr (eds.). 1987. *Pesticides: Minimizing the Risks.* ACS Symposium Series 336. American Chemical Society, Washington, DC. 183 pp.

Reynolds, P.E. (ed.). 1989. *Proceedings of the Carnation Creek Herbicide Workshop.* 7-10 Dec. 1987. Forestry Canada/BC Ministry of Forests, Victoria. FRDA Report No. 063. 349 pp.

Scrivener, B.A. and J.A. Mackinnon. 1989. *Learning from the Past: Looking to the Future.* Proc. Northern Silviculture Committee 1988 Winter Workshop, Prince George. BC Ministry of Forests and Forestry Canada, Victoria. FRDA Report 30. 140 pp.

Sullivan, T.P. and D.S. Sullivan. 1981. Response of a deer mouse population to a forest herbicide application: Reproduction, growth and survival. *Canadian Journal of Zoology* 59:1148-54

——. 1988. Demographic response of small mammal populations to a herbicide application in coastal coniferous forests: Population density and resilience. *Canadian Journal of Zoology* 68:874-83

Sutton, R.F. 1985. *Vegetation Management in Canadian Forests.* Info. Rept., Great Lakes Forest Research Centre, Canadian Forestry Service, Sault St. Marie. No. O-X-369. 35 pp.

Walstad, J.D. and F.N. Dost. 1984. *The Health Risks of Herbicides in Forestry: A Review of the Scientific Record.* College of Forestry, Forest Research Lab., Oregon State Univ. Corvallis, OR. Special Publication #10. 60 pp.

Walstad, J.D. and P.J. Kuch (eds.). 1987. *Forest Vegetation Management for Conifer Production.* New York: Wiley-Interscience. 523 pp.

Williamson, D.R. and P.B. Lane. 1989. *The Use of Herbicides in the Forest* (3d ed.). London: HMSO

Chapter 9: Are Old-Growth Forests Forever?

Cadrin, Carmen. 1991. *A Bibliography on Old-Growth Forests in British Columbia.* Ministry of Forests, Prov. of BC, Victoria, BC. 261 pp.

Faculty of Forestry and School of Continuing Education, Univ. of Toronto (eds.). 1990. *Old Growth Forests ... What Are They? How Do They Work?* Proc. Conference on Old Growth Forests. 20 Jan. 1990. Univ. of Toronto and Ontario Ministry of Natural Resources. Toronto: Canadian Scholars' Press. 197 pp.

Franklin, J.F., K. Cromack, Jr., W. Denison, A. McKee, C. Maser, J. Sedell, F. Swanson, and G. Judau. 1981. *Ecological Characteristics of Old-Growth Douglas-Fir*

Forests. USDA For. Serv., PNW For. Range Exp. St., Portland, OR. Gen. Tech. Rept. PNW-118

Harmon, M.E., W.K. Fewell and J.F. Franklin. 1990. Effects on carbon storage of conversion of old-growth forests to young forests. *Science* 247:699-702

Kimmins, J.P. 1990. Forests and forestry [article on old-growth forests]. In *McGraw-Hill Yearbook Science and Technology.* New York: McGraw-Hill. 154-7

Klinka, K., R.E. Carter, and M.C. Feller. 1990. Old-growth forests. *Northwest Environmental Journal* 6(2):221-32

Maser, C. 1989. *Forest Primeval: The Natural History of an Ancient Forest.* San Francisco: Sierra Club Books. 282 pp.

Norse, E.A. 1990. *Ancient Forests of the Pacific Northwest.* Washington, DC: Island Press. 327 pp.

Pearson, A.F. and D.A. Challenger (eds.). 1990. *Forests – Wild and Managed: Differences and Consequences.* Proc. Symposium to Discuss the Ecology of Wild Forests and Plantations. Students for Forestry Awareness and Forestry Undergraduate Society, Faculty of Forestry, UBC, Vancouver. 196 pp.

Spies, T.A. and J.F. Franklin. 1988. Old-growth and forest dynamics in the Douglas-fir region of western Oregon and Washington. *Natural Areas Journal* 8:190-201

Chapter 10: Where Have All the Species Gone?

Brown, E.R. (tech. ed.). 1985. *Management of Wildlife and Fish Habitat in Forests of Western Oregon and Washington.* USDA For. Serv., PNW For. Range Expt. Sta., Portland, OR. Publication No. R6-F&WL-192-1985. 332 pp.

Bunnell, F.L. and D.S. Eastman. 1976. *Effects of Forest Management Practices on Wildlife in the Forests of British Columbia.* Proc. Div. I, IUFRO World Congress, Oslo, Norway. 631-89

Bunnell, F.L. and L.L. Kremsater. 1990. Sustaining wildlife in managed forests. *Northwest Environmental Journal* 6(2):243-70

Carlson, C.E. and N.W. Wulf. 1989. *Silvicultural Strategies to Reduce Stand and Forest Susceptibility to the Western Spruce Budworm.* USDA For. Serv., Agric. Handbook No. 676. 31 pp.

Carlson, M. and A. Yanchuk. 1990. Maintaining Genetic Diversity in Future Man-Made Forests: What Are We Doing Today. Unpublished manuscript, BC Ministry of Forests, Research Branch, Victoria. 31 pp.

De Graaf, R.M. and W.M. Healy. 1990. *Is Forest Fragmentation a Management Issue in the Northwest?* USDA For. Serv., NE For. Exp. Sta. Gen. Tech. Rept. NE-140. 32 pp.

Devall, B. and G. Sessions. 1985. *Deep Ecology.* Salt Lake City: Peregrine Smith Books. 267 pp.

Franklin, J.F. 1990. 'New forestry' and the old-growth forests of northwestern North America. *Northwest Environmental Journal* 6:445-61

Franklin, J.F., D.A. Perry, T.D. Schowalter, M.E. Harmon, A. McKee, and T.A. Spies. 1989. Importance of ecological diversity in maintaining long-term site productivity. In D.A. Perry et al. (eds.), *Maintaining the Long-Term Productivity of Pacific Northwest Forest Ecosystems.* Portland, OR: Timber Press, 82-97

Harris, L.D. 1984. *The Fragmented Forest.* Chicago: University of Chicago Press. 211 pp.

Hunter, M.L. 1990. *Wildlife, Forests and Forestry: Principles of Managing Forests for Biological Diversity.* Englewood Cliffs, NJ: Prentice Hall. 370 pp.

Kimmins, J.P. 1991. *Biodiversity: An Environmental Imperative.* Proc. 72d Annual Meeting, Woodlands Section, Canadian Pulp and Paper Association, Montreal, PQ. E233-231.

Ledig, F.T. 1988. The conservation of diversity in forest trees. *BioScience* 38:471-9

Ledig, F.T., C.I. Millar, and L.A. Riggs. 1990. Conservation of diversity in forest ecosystems. Proc. Symp., USDA Forest Service and Western Forest Genetics Association. *Forest Ecology and Management* (Special Issue) 35:1-197

Perry, D.A., M.P. Awaranthus, J.G. Borchers, S.L. Borchers, and R.E. Brainérd. 1989. Boot-strapping in ecosystems. *BioScience* 39:230-7

Seip, D.R. and J-P. L. Savard. 1990. Maintaining Wildlife Diversity in Managed Coastal Forests. Unpublished Annual Report. Ministry of Forests and Canadian Wildlife Service, Victoria, BC

Thomas, J.W. (ed.). 1979. *Wildlife Habitats in Managed Forests.* USDA For. Serv., Agric. Handbook No. 533. Washington, DC. 512 pp.

Wilson, E.O. and F.M. Peter (eds.). 1988. *Biodiversity.* Washington, DC: National Academy Press. 521 pp.

Chapter 11: 'New Forestry'

Atkinson, W.A. 1990. *Another View of New Forestry.* Paper presented at Annual Meeting, Oregon Society of American Foresters, Eugene, OR

Behan, R.W. 1990. Multi-resource forest management: A pardigmatic challenge to professional foresters. *Journal of Forestry* 88(6):12-18

DeBell, Dean S. 1990. *Silvicultural Practices and 'New Forestry.'* Paper presented at 'New Forestry in the 90s' Workshop. Coos Chapter, Society of American Foresters and Southwestern Oregon Community College, Coos Bay, OR. 5 pp.

Fiedler, C. 1992. New forestry: Concepts and applications. *Western Wildlands* 17(4):2-7

Franklin, J.F. 1990. Old growth forests and the new forestry. In A.F. Pearson and D.A. Challenger (eds.), Proc. Symp. on *Forests – Wild and Managed: Differences and Consequences.* Students for Forestry Awareness and Forestry Undergraduate Society, Faculty of Forestry, UBC, Vancouver. 1-20

——. 1990. 'New forestry' and the old-growth forests of northwestern North America. *Northwest Environmental Journal* 6:445-61

——. 1990. Thoughts or applications of silvicultural systems under new forestry. *Forest Watch* 10 (7):8-11

Gillis, A.M. 1990. The new forestry: An ecosystem approach to land management. *BioScience* 40:558-62

Gregg, N.T. 1991. Will 'new forestry' save old forests. *American Forestry* 97:49-53, 70

Hopwood, D. 1991. *Principles and Practices of New Forestry: A Guide for British Columbians.* BC Ministry of Forests, Victoria. Land Management Report 71. 95 pp.

Isaac, L.A. 1956. *Place of Partial Cutting in Old-Growth Stands of the Douglas-Fir Region.* USDA For. Serv., PNW For. Range Exp. Sta., Portland, OR. Res. Pap. No. 16. 48 pp.

Long, J.N. and S.D. Roberts. 1992. Growth and yield implications of a 'new forestry' silvicultural system. *Western Journal of Forestry* 7 (1):6-9

Mann, J.W. 1990. *Proposals for Alternative Silvicultural Practices and 'New Forestry': Are We on the Right Track?* Proc. of 1990 Soc. Amer. For., Nat. Convention, Washington, DC, 29-31 July. 313-15

Martin, C.W., C.T. Smith, and L.M. Trilton (eds.). 1988. New perspectives on silvicultural management of northern hardwoods. In Proc. of the 1988 Symposium on the Conflicting Consequences of Practising Northern Hardwood Silviculture. USDA For. Serv., NE For. Exp. Sta., Durham, NH. Gen. Tech. Rept. NE-124. 107 pp.

Maser, C., R.F. Tarrant, J.M. Trappe, and J.F. Franklin. 1988. *From the Forest to the Sea: A Story of Fallen Trees.* USDA For. Serv., PNW Res. Sta., Portland, OR. Gen. Tech. Rept. PNW-GTR-229. 153 pp.

O'Keefe, T. 1990. Holistic (new) forestry: Significant difference or just another gimmick? *Journal of Forestry* (April 1990):23-24

Pearson, A.F. and D.A. Challenger (eds.). 1990. *Forests – Wild and Managed: Differences and Consequences.* Proc. Symposium to Discuss the Ecology of Wild Forests and Plantations. Students for Forestry Awareness and Forestry Undergraduate Society, Faculty of Forestry, UBC Vancouver. 196 pp.

Smith, D.M. 1962. *The Practice of Silviculture* (7th ed.). New York: Wiley & Sons. 565 pp.

——. 1970. *Applied Ecology and the New Forest.* Western Reforestation Proc. Western Forestry and Conservation Association Meeting, Vancouver, BC. 3-7

USDA. 1978. *Uneven-Aged Silviculture and Management in the United States.* USDA For. Serv., Timber Management Research, Washington, DC. Gen. Tech. Rept. WO-24. 234 pp.

Weetman, G.F., E. Panozzo, M. Jull, and K. Marek. 1990. *An Assessment of Opportunities for Alternative Silvicultural Systems in the SBS, ICH and ESSF Biogeoclimatic Zones of the Prince Rupert Forest Region.* Report to BC Ministry of Forests, Smithers, BC. 154 pp.

Chapter 12: Forestry and Climate Change

Abrahamson, D.E. (ed.). 1989. *The Challenge of Global Warming.* Washington, DC: Island Press. 358 pp.

Ausubel, J.H. 1991. A second look at the impacts of climate change. *American Scientist* 79:210-21

Barnola, J.M., D. Raymond, Y.S. Korotkevich, and C. Lorius. 1987. Vostok ice core provides 160,000-year record of atmospheric CO_2. *Nature* 329:408-14

Boden, T.A., P. Kanciruk, and M.P. Farrell. 1990. *Trends '90: A Compendium of Data on Global Change.* Carbon Dioxide Information Analysis Centre, Environmental Sciences Division, Oak Ridge National Laboratory, Oak Ridge, TN. 257 pp.

Bolin, B., B.R. Doos, J. Jager, and R.A. Warrick (eds.). 1986. *The Greenhouse Effect, Climate Change and Ecosystems.* SCOPE Report 29. New York: Wiley & Sons. 541 pp.

Harmon, M.E., W.K. Ferrell, and J.F. Franklin. 1990. Effects on carbon storage of conversion of old-growth forests to young forests. *Science* 247:699-702

Houghton, J.P., G.J. Jenkins, and J.J. Ephraums (eds.). 1990. *Climate Change: The IPCC Scientific Assessment.* Cambridge, UK: Cambridge University Press. 364 pp.

Houghton, R.A. and G.M Woodwell. 1989. Global climate change. *Scientific American* 260(4):36-44

Idso, S.B. 1989. *Carbon Dioxide and Global Change: Earth in Transition.* Tempe, AZ: IBR Press. 292 pp.

IGBP/ICSU. 1990. *The International Geosphere–Biosphere Programme: A Study of Global Change.* Report No. 12. The Initial Core Projects. IGBP/ICSU, Stockholm. 12 chapters + App.

Johnson, D.W. 1992. *Effects of Forest Management on Soil Carbon Storage.* Technical Bulletin No. 628, NCASI, New York. 61 pp.

Keeling, C.D. and T.P. Whorg. 1992. Mauna Loa: Atmospheric CO_2 – modern record. In T.A. Boden, R.J. Sepanski, and F.W. Stoss (eds.), *Trends '91: A Compendium of Data on Global Change.* Carbon Dioxide Information Analysis Centre, Environmental Sciences Division, ORNL/CDIAC-49, Oak Ridge National Laboratory, Oak Ridge, TN. ESD Publ. No. 3797. 14-17.

Kimmins, J.P. 1987. *Forest Ecology.* New York: Macmillan. 531 pp.

Marland, G. and T.A. Boden. 1991. CO_2 emissions – global. In T.A. Boden, R.J. Sepanski, and F.W. Stoss (eds.), *Trends '91: A Compendium of Data on Global Change.* Carbon Dioxide Information Analysis Centre, Environmental Sciences Division, ORNL/CDIAC-49, Oak Ridge National Laboratory, Oak Ridge, TN. 386-9.

Perry, D.A. and J.G. Borchers. 1990. Climate change and ecosystems. *Northwest Environmental Journal* 6(2):293-314

Peters, R.L. 1988. The effect of global climatic change on natural communities. In E.O. Wilson (ed.), *Biodiversity.* Washington, DC: National Academy Press, 450-61

——. 1990. Effects of global warming on forests. *Forest Ecology and Management* 35:13-33

Peterson, E.B., M.M. Peterson, and R.D. Kabzems. 1983. *Impact of Climatic Variation on Biomass Accumulation in the Boreal Forest Zone: Selected References.* Canadian Forestry Service, Northern Forest Research Centre, Info. Rept. NOR-X-254. 355 pp.

Pielou, E.C. 1991. *After the Ice Age: The Return of Life to Glaciated North America.* Chicago: University of Chicago Press. 366 pp.

Schneider, S.H. 1989. *Global Warming: Are We Entering the Greenhouse Century?* San Francisco: Sierra Club Books. 317 pp.

Schneider, S.H. and R.D. Bennett. 1975. Climatic barriers to long-term energy growth. *Ambio* 4:66-74

Shands, W.E. and J.S. Hoffman (eds.). 1987. *The Greenhouse Effect, Climate Change and U.S. Forests.* The Conservation Foundation, Washington, DC. 204 pp.

Shukla. J., C. Nobre, and P. Sellers. 1990. Amazon deforestation and climate change. *Science* 247:1322-5

Topping, J.C., Jr. (ed.). 1989. *Proceedings: Second North American Conference on Preparing for Climate Change.* The Climate Institute, Washington, DC. 696 pp.

UNEP. 1989. *Environmental Data Report* (2d ed.). GEMS Monitoring and Assessment Research Centre, London, UK / World Resources Institute, Washington, DC / UK Dept. of Environment, London. Oxford, UK: Blackwell. 547 pp.

Wall, G. and M. Sanderson (eds.). 1990. *Climate Change: Implications for Water and Ecological Resources.* Proceedings of an International Workshop. Dept. of Geography, Univ. of Waterloo, Kitchener, ON. 342 pp.

White, J.C., W. Wagner, and C.N. Beale (eds.). 1989. *Global Climate Change Linkages: Acid Rain, Air Quality, and Stratospheric Ozone.* New York: Elsevier. 262 pp.

Winjum, J.K., P.E. Schroeder, and M.J. Kennedy (eds.). 1991. *International Workshop on Large-Scale Reforestation.* Global Change Research Program, Environmental Research Lab., EPA, Corvallis, OR. 148 pp. + App.

World Meteorological Organization. 1988. *Conference Proceedings: The Changing Atmosphere.* Secretariat of the World Meteorological Organization, Geneva. 483 pp.

Chapter 13: Acid Rain: Is It as Bad for Forests as It Is for Lakes?

Binkley, D., C.T. Driscoll, H.L. Allen, D. Schoeneberger, and D. McAvoy. 1988. *Acidic Deposition and Forest Soils: Context and Case Studies in the Southeastern United States.* New York: Springer-Verlag. 149 pp.

Fraser, G.A., W.E. Phillips, G.W. Lamble, G.D. Hogan, and A.G. Teskey. 1985. *The Potential Impact of the Long Range Transport of Air Pollutants on Canadian Forests.* Canadian Forestry Service, Economics Branch, Hull, PQ. Info. Rept. E-X-36. 43 pp.

Freedman, B. 1989. *Environmental Ecology: The Impacts of Pollution and Other Stresses on Ecosystem Structure and Function.* San Diego: Academic Press. 424 pp.

Klimo, E. and J. Materna (eds.). 1990. *Verification of Hypotheses on the Mechanisms of Damage and Possibilities of Recovery*

of Forest Ecosystems. Proc. of the Workshop. Institute of Forest Ecology, Faculty of Forestry, Univ. of Agriculture, Brno, Czechoslovakia. 356 pp.

Likens, G.E. 1989. Some aspects of air pollution effects on terrestrial ecosystems and prospects for the future. *Ambio* 18(3):172-8

Linzon, S.N. 1985. *Forest Damage and Acidic Precipitation.* E.B. Eddy Distinguished Lecture Series. Faculty of Forestry, Univ. of Toronto, Toronto, ON. 30 pp.

Morrison, I.K. 1983. Acid rain, forests and forestry. In E.L. Stone (ed.), *Forest Soils and Treatment Impacts.* Proc. 6th North American Forest Soils Conference, Univ. of Tennessee, Knoxville, TN, 209-19

Schulze, E-D., O.L. Lange, and R. Oren. 1989. *Forest Decline and Air Pollution: A Study of Spruce (*Picea abies*) on Acid Soils.* Ecological Studies 77. New York: Springer-Verlag. 475 pp.

USDA/EPA. 1988. *Proceedings of the US/FRG Research Symposium: Effects of Atmospheric Pollutants on the Spruce-Fire Forests of the Eastern United States and the Federal Republic of Germany.* USDA For. Serv., Northeastern Forest Exp. Sta., Broomall, PA. 543 pp.

Zöttle, H.W. and R.F. Huttl (eds.). 1991. *Management of Nutrition in Forests under Stress.* Dortrecht: Kluwer Academic Publishers. 666 pp.

Chapter 14: 'Brazil North'

Blackie, J.R., E.D. Ford, J.E.M. Horne, D.J. Kinsman, F.T. Last, and P. Moorhouse. 1980. *Environmental Effects of Deforestation: An Annotated Bibliography.* Occasional Paper No. 10. Freshwater Biological Association, Ambleside, UK. 173 pp.

Detwiler, R.P. and C.A.S. Hall. 1988. Tropical forests and the global carbon cycle. *Science* 239:42-7

Grainger, A. 1988. Estimating areas of degraded tropical lands requiring replenishment of forest cover. *International Tree Crops Journal* 5:31-61

Jordan, C.F. 1985. *Nutrient Cycling in Tropical Forest Ecosystems.* Chichester, UK: J. Wiley & Sons. 190 pp.

Mergen, F. (ed.). 1981. *Tropical Forests: Utilization and Conservation. Ecological, Sociopolitical and Economic Problems and Potentials.* Yale University, School of Forestry and Environmental Studies, New Haven, CT. 199 pp.

Myers, N. 1982. Depletion of tropical moist forests: A comparative review of rates and causes in the three main regions. *Acta Amazonica* 12:745-58

Palo, M. and G. Mery (eds.). 1990. *Deforestation or Development in the Third World* (vol. 3). Finnish Forest Research Institute, Division of Social Economics of Forestry, Helsinki. Bulletin 349. 189 pp.

Repetto, R. and M. Gillis. 1988. *Public Policies and the Misuse of Forest Resources.* New York: Cambridge University Press. 432 pp.

Schneider, A. (ed.). 1989. *Deforestation and 'Development' in*

Canada and the Tropics: The Impact on People and the Environment. Centre for International Studies. Univ. Coll. of Cape Breton, Sydney, NS. 251 pp.

Chapter 15: Future Shock in Forecasting Forest Growth and Timber Yields

Clark, W.C. and R.E. Munn. 1986. *Sustainable Development of the Biosphere.* Cambridge, UK: Cambridge University Press. 491 pp.

Dixon, R.K., R.S. Medahl, G.A. Ruark, and W.G. Warren (eds.). 1990. *Process Modelling of Forest Growth Responses to Environmental Stress.* Portland, OR: Timber Press. 441 pp.

Ek, A.R., S.R. Shifley, and T.E. Burk (eds.). 1988. *Forest Growth Modelling and Prediction* (vols. 1 and 2). Proc. IUFRO Conference, 23-27 Aug. 1987, Minneapolis, MN. USDA For. Serv., North Central For. Exp. Sta. Minneapolis

Kimmins, J.P. 1988. Community organization: Methods of study and prediction of the productivity and yield of forest ecosystems. *Canadian Journal of Botany* 66:2654-72

—— . 1990. Modelling the sustainability of forest production and yield for a changing and uncertain future. *Forestry Chronicle* 66:271-80

Meadows, D.H., D.L. Meadows, J. Randes, and W.W. Behrens III. 1972. *The Limits to Growth: A Report to the Club of Rome's Project on the Predicament of Mankind.* London: Pan Books. 205 pp.

Perry, D.A., R. Meurisse, B. Thomas, R. Miller, J. Boyle, J. Means, C.R. Perry, and R.F. Powers (eds.). 1989. *Maintaining the Long-Term Productivity of Pacific Northwest Forest Ecosystems.* Portland, OR: Timber Press. 265 pp.

Wensel, L.C. and G.S. Biging (eds.). 1990. *Forest Simulation Systems.* Proc. of IUFRO Conference 2-5 Nov. 1988, Berkeley, CA. Univ. of California, Division of Agriculture and Natural Resources, Bulletin 1927. 420 pp.

World Commission on Environmental and Development (WCED). 1987. *Our Common Future.* Oxford: Oxford University Press. 400 pp.

Chapter 16: Sustainable Development and Forestry

Baskerville, G.L. 1990. Canadian sustained yield management – expectations and realities. *Forestry Chronicle* 66:171-5

Bormann, F.H. and G.E. Likens. 1979. *Pattern and Process in a Forested Ecosystem.* Berlin & New York: Springer-Verlag

Keith, Lloyd B. 1963. *Wildlife's Ten-Year Cycle.* Madison: University of Wisconsin Press. 201 pp.

Kimmins, J.P. 1974. Sustained yield, timber mining, and the concept of ecological rotation: A British Columbian view. *Forestry Chronicle* 50:27-31

—— . 1990. Monitoring the condition of the Canadian forest environment: The relevance of the concept of 'ecological indicators.' *Environ. Monitoring and Assessment*

15:231-40

—— . 1991. The future of the forested landscapes of Canada. *Forestry Chronicle* 67:14-18

—— and Dorli M. Duffy. 1991. Sustainable forestry in the Fraser River Basin. In A.H. J. Dorcey (ed.), *Perspectives on Sustainable Development in Water Management: Towards Agreement in the Fraser River Basin.* Westwater Research Centre, Fac. of Graduate Studies, Univ. of BC, Vancouver. 217-40

Louks, O.L. 1970. Evolution of diversity, efficiency and community stability. *American Zoologist* 10:17-25

Meidinger, Del and J. Pojar (eds). 1991. *Ecosystems of British Columbia.* BC Ministry of Forests, Victoria, BC. Special Report Series #6. 330 pp.

Methven, I.R. 1991. Sustainable use of forests: The new Holy Grail? In K. Sanderson (ed.), *Sustainable Use of Canada's Forests: Are We on the Right Path?* Proc. Symposium, Canadian Society of Environmental Biologists, Toronto. 39-46

Oliver, C.D. and B.C. Larson. 1990. *Forest Stand Dynamics.* San Francisco: McGraw-Hill. 467 pp.

Sanderson, K. (ed.). 1991. *Sustainable Use of Canada's Forests: Are We on the Right Path?* Proc. Symposium, Canadian Society of Environmental Biologists, Toronto. 158 pp.

Squire, R.O. 1983. Review of second rotation silviculture of *P. radiata* plantations in Southern Australia: Establishment practices and expectations. In R. Ballard and S.P. Gessel (eds.), IUFRO Symposium on *Forest Site and Continuous Productivity.* USDA For. Serv., PNW For. Range Exp. Sta., Portland, OR. Gen. Tech. Rept. PNW-163. 130-7

Index

Printed on acid-free paper ∞

Set in Adobe Garamond and Univers

Printed and bound in Canada by
D.W. Friesen & Sons Ltd.

Copy-editor: Frank Chow

Proofreader: Stacy Belden

Designer: George Vaitkunas

DATE DUE